2

TO

HELEN AND MAURICE,

THROUGH WHOSE FRIENDSHIP
HAS BEEN OPENED UP SO MUCH
" CONCERNING HIMSELF "

CONCERNING HIMSELF

BY

MAISIE SPENS

LONDON
HODDER & STOUGHTON LTD

FIRST PUBLISHED . . . FEBRUARY 1937
SECOND IMPRESSION . . . DECEMBER 1949

Made and Printed in Great Britain for Hodder and Stoughton Limited,
by Butler & Tanner Ltd., Frome and London

FOREWORD

NOW in our day is being most literally fulfilled " upon the earth distress of nations, with perplexity . . . men's hearts failing them for fear, and for looking after those things which are coming on the earth ". The chaos permeating alike our international, national, industrial, economic, social, and individual life is humanly insoluble. It admits of only one true comment—one passed centuries ago by Jesus Christ : " Apart from Me ye can do nothing ". Politicians, economists, financiers, social reformers, and even the Church in its present human functioning, are alike impotent to salvage our world, either by their most earnest or most disinterested efforts.

Jesus Christ alone can save us from ourselves ; but only when we can, out of our own personal experience, endorse St. Paul's " I *know* Whom I have believed, and am persuaded that He is able . . . " ; and the tragedy is that, although many know *about* Him, know Him *from the outside* from the incidents of the Incarnate Life, so few of us even begin to know HIM as He was in the inner man.

None of us can apprehend Him Himself except—as for the disciples on the road to Emmaus and for the disciples before the Ascension—He becomes His own interpreter, and opens our minds and spirits to understand Him. The prime obligation for every professing Christian to-day is so to yield to the Holy Spirit that He can enable us to know our Lord in His full redemptive nature.

All too many of us do not really expect to grow to know Him deeply ; but we have no right to be unexpectant, since He came precisely to give us that knowledge of Himself in His oneness with the Father, which is itself eternal life. We ought to expect an answer to His own prayer " that they may behold My Glory ", and each one of us echo it with

v

heart-hungry " Lord, that I may receive my sight ", believing that by His Spirit we shall be led out into all the truth of His Beauty and Being in His own way and time.   .

There is, however, a far more compelling necessity than our own personal, or even corporate, salvation which makes it incumbent upon us that we should come to *know* Him— the satisfaction of the Father's desire for worshippers (lovers) in spirit and in truth.   Intimate knowledge—deepening into all-embracing reverence and passionate adoration—of the Son, Who is the express image of His glory, is the *sine qua non* enabling the Holy Spirit to offer through us, in union with the Pre-existent, Incarnate, Crucified, Risen, Ascended, and Glorified Jesus, *worship* which shall be acceptable to the Father, and the fulfilment of that for which alone we were created.

Exhaustiveness being a total impossibility, this book can only—as its uttermost aspiration—hope to be faintly suggestive in such a way as to kindle in some soul, or souls, a fresh yearning to *seek* to *know* more of HIM.   It goes forth in prayer for response to His :

" Come unto Me . . ."

His love-invitation to You.

Thanks are offered to the Rev. R. O. P. Taylor, and to the many whose prayer alone has enabled the completion of this book.

To the kindness of the Dean of Exeter is owed permission here to incorporate articles on " The Mystery of Jesus Walking on the Sea ", and " Elijah with Moses in the Transfiguration ", published in *Theology* in May 1934 and August 1935.

CONTENTS

HIGH PRIEST

THE MYSTICAL BODY: AND COMMUNION OF SAINTS

INTRODUCTION

" LET this Mind be in you which was also in Christ Jesus "—gripping and magnetic words. During a prolonged attempt to try to learn, under the illumination of the Holy Spirit, something of the Mind of Christ, there came from a Cairo missionary's wife a letter containing these words :

> " I think our Lord's teaching was so effectual because it was always taken off the background of His own experience. The whole of the Gospels were lit up for me by going through each of the Great Sayings, and trying to see off which of His experiences it was taken ".

At once new vistas opened. There flashed the thought of a number of strips of coloured paper—blue, green, yellow, and so on—each cut in half : experience and saying of the same colour to be pieced together. Time was put aside for this. The outstanding experiences—Baptism, Temptation, Transfiguration, Agony, Passion—leapt to mind ; and then —pause. It was unthinkable that Jesus Christ, the most sensitive man Who ever lived, could have had, in comparison with even the most humdrum of us, such a sparsity of experience. Slowly there dawned the realisation that His experiences in all their necessary fulness remained as yet essentially unknown. Immediately there followed a vivid remembrance of the story of Jesus on the way to Jairus' house, read so often as though from within the very skin of Jairus in agony at the delay over the healing of the woman in the crowd ; the woman in her flare of faith, her awe and joy ; the disciples in their utter bewilderment at His " Who touched My garments ? " ; and the crowd themselves, some sceptical, some longing and yet not daring to launch out similarly in faith for their own healing ; all keyed up in expectancy or curiosity. But Jesus, the doer of the miracle, the comforter of Jairus and the woman, *as Himself,* what it all meant *to Him,* what it cost Him, what place it took in His life and experience—that had never before been taken into account. The Gospels had been read more for what they meant to those for whom Jesus wrought and taught, and for what they could mean to us, than for what they would yield of HIMSELF.

Nakedly was laid bare the need to get really to know Him in the Gospels ; and for this there was an aid which has been indispensable—*The Life of our Lord,* by Reginald G. Ponsonby (G. Bell & Sons, 3s. 6d.), whose " main idea and purpose . . . is to present a clear and complete consecutive life of Jesus Christ arranged chronologically as an historical Life, and compiled entirely from the New Testament in the very words of the four Gospels, and by combining the narratives giving the fullest possible account of each incident . . . the text used is that of the Revised Version ".

Out of this came a revolutionary steeping in the Gospels simply and solely from His point of view ; beginning, not with His outer life as key to the inner, but with His inner life and essential Personality as revealed by the Incarnation as the necessary key to the outer. Through this Divine Treasury the Holy Spirit opens a new world with the progressive unfolding of the adorable Mind and Person of Jesus, which unfolding will fill all Eternity.

It is in the light of ' Higher Criticism ', with full and grateful recognition of the positive, illuminating, and interpretative value of its findings, and not from any tenet of ' verbal inspiration ', that this book deliberately assumes the historical validity of the Gospels—Johannine no less than Synoptic—to be such as makes it not merely justifiable, but inevitable, to build upon their recorded sayings of our Lord as an expression of His Mind, interior dispositions, and teaching, none the less *essentially true* for not being His *ipsissima verba.*

Note : Quotations from the Bible have been taken from the A.V. or from the R.V. as seemed best in each individual instance.

THE MIND OF CHRIST

"THE BOY JESUS"

" JESUS advanced in wisdom and stature, and in favour with God and man." Here St. Luke, writing of " the boy Jesus ", by inspiration furnishes us with the key to the whole Incarnate Personality. The Greek verb προέκοπτεν, translated ' advanced ', was used originally of the pioneer cutting his way through brushwood. What a *living* Jesus emerges ! Gone at once is all thought—or possibility—of a life more ' plain-sailing ', more easy of solution than the average ; or of a route so mapped out in detail as to render following it automatic. Here is one Who had to requisition every faculty and power ; and vigorously forge through to fulness of truth and purpose along a virgin track. Here is the thrill of life, of effort, of struggle, of masterly progress from the beginning right on to the end. Life, striving, and the ordered pursuit of a deliberate quest are basic characteristics of the Incarnate Christ.

It was through His wrestling with the personal problems with which He found Himself confronted ; and through His handling of His experiences, both interior and exterior, that the Mind (i.e. whole spiritual nature, quality of thought and feeling) of Jesus matured to its perfection. His experiences were never passed through as desultory happenings, but by prayerful reflection were interpreted and wrought into a synthesis whose significance lay in its correspondence to the Will of the Father.

His mother Mary, ever pondering, ever praying for Him, could not fail to observe how " the child grew, and waxed strong, filled with wisdom : and the grace of God was upon Him." As the customary time approached for Him to accompany her and Joseph to Jerusalem for His first Passover, the sword must have pierced her as she realised that the time had also come when she *must* impart to Him—even

3

although it meant shadowing Him with aweing problems beyond even her love and power to solve for Him—the knowledge which was His birthright.

The boy Jesus—as gradually He heard His mother unfold the mysteries of His Incarnation—was by the age of twelve put in possession of facts about Himself unique in the whole history of the world. Human imagination cannot really picture what it must have meant to Him to receive these tidings ; because no such *could* ever come to any other save He. But the content of these tidings has been told us.

It was a supernatural panorama that was unfolded before Him. First the Annunciation of His birth by the Angel Gabriel—told by Mary with all the awe with which she received it—only enhanced by years of pondering. " And the angel said . . . Fear not, Mary . . . thou shalt bring forth a son, and shalt call His name Jesus. He shall be great, and shall be called the Son of the Most High : and the Lord God shall give unto Him the throne of His father David : and He shall reign over the house of Jacob for ever ; and of His kingdom there shall be no end. . . . The Holy Ghost shall come upon thee, and the power of the Most High shall overshadow thee : wherefore also that which is to be born shall be called holy, the Son of God." Then the story of the Visitation to Elizabeth. The appearance of the angel to Joseph in a dream, with his prophecy—the like of which had never been uttered of any before—". . . thou shalt call His name Jesus ; for it is He that shall save His people from their sins." The Nativity in the stable : followed by the coming of the shepherds with their tale of " keeping watch by night over their flock. And an angel of the Lord stood by them, and . . . said . . . Be not afraid ; for behold, I bring you good tidings of great joy which shall be to all the people ; for there is born to you this day in the city of David a Saviour, which is Christ the Lord . . . And suddenly there was with the angel a multitude of the heavenly host praising God, and saying, Glory to God in the

highest, and on earth peace among men in whom He is well
pleased."

His Presentation in the Temple, with the righteous
Simeon's recognition of Him the Babe as "the Lord's
Christ" and God's "salvation, which Thou hast prepared
before the face of all peoples ; a light for revelation to the
Gentiles, and the glory of Thy people Israel" ; and his
prophecy : "Behold, this Child is set for the falling and
rising up of many in Israel : and for a sign which is spoken
against [the Greek means literally 'debated about']
. . . that thoughts out of many hearts may be revealed."
(Mary, for love of her Child, would surely have suppressed
Simeon's "Yea and a sword shall pierce through thine own
soul.") And Simeon's recognition of Him there, followed
by that of Anna, the aged prophetess, who "gave thanks
unto God, and spoke of Him to all that were looking for the
redemption of Jerusalem." The later coming of the star-
led Magi to Bethlehem with their offerings to the Infant
Jesus of gold, frankincense, and myrrh.

So far, only awe and glory : because we may be sure that
Mary also suppressed for Him the immediate cost of her self-
abandoning "Fiat". But suffering was early to break
across the glory, with King Herod's Massacre of the Innocents in and around Bethlehem, in a vain attempt to kill
Him, after Joseph had had angelic warning in a dream to
"take the young Child and His mother and flee into Egypt."
The whole culminating in the divine recall from Egypt to
Nazareth. What an inundation of mystery for a boy : aweing burden of mingled exhilaration and loneliness. The
knowledge of His preservation in the Massacre of the
Innocents must have deepened the almost overwhelming
sense of obligation upon His life. How inevitable His boyish "I *must* be about My Father's business" ; and the so
much later, "*Behoved* it not the Christ to suffer these things,
and to enter into His glory ? "

Mary's revelations to Him, taken in conjunction with His
own interior pressures, must have taxed His incarnate

powers of mind and spirit to the uttermost in regard to His vocation. The angel-prophecy, " He shall save His people from their sins ", must have remained with Him as an ever-present, inescapable enigma—an enigma intensified by His realisation of the complete disparity between His own attitude and that of all others to sin ; by His abhorrence of it and His perception of its intrinsic enormity and significance.

The problems raised by this unique birthright of Jesus must directly have emerged clear-cut to the exceptional clarity of perception with which, even as a boy, He was already endowed. At the age of twelve, therefore, He knew Himself consciously confronted with the necessity for solving —sooner or later—the mysteries of :

(1) His own Personality :
  (a) In relation to God.
  (b) In relation to Man.

(2) The interior essence, and outward expression and fulfilment, of His vocation.

(3) The reconciliation of the human and Divine, limitlessness and limitation :
  (a) In His own Nature.
  (b) In His external circumstances.

By the time the Man Jesus delivered His Sermon on the Mount, He could—out of His own developing spiritual knowledge and experience tallying with the Scriptures—say : " Think not that I came to destroy the law or the prophets : I came not to destroy, but to fulfil " (Matt. v. 17). But this knowledge was not instantaneously nor effortlessly come by. His " the wind bloweth where it listeth, and thou hearest the voice thereof, but knowest not whence it cometh, and whither it goeth ; so is every one that is born of the Spirit " was voiced out of His own vocational experience. The end was not even for Him humanly seen in the beginning.

He embarked upon His divinely engendered redemptive mission for mankind in uttermost humility ; altogether divested of self-choosing, and even initially of human self-consciousness. His whole Nature and Personality had to find, and expand in, a totally new medium of God-dependent expression. He became, at His Nativity, as it were, a stranger to God in His own human consciousness, that in Him might be revealed the process of progressive falling in love with the Father. So His growth in understanding the purpose of the Incarnation was perforce a gradual one ; and long after His boyhood He had need to work it through, not only in terms of the universally inescapable " Whence, why, and whither ? ", but also in the light of His uniquely experiential " Before Abraham was I am." The boy Jesus had to prepare Himself to meet problems which *could* only receive complete enlightenment in maturity ; but He was not without singularly potent resources for His approach to them.

" The grace of God was upon Him." The whole initiative lay with God the Father ; and His Wisdom and Love furnished the Child with all the requisite interior equipment for His spiritual quest. The thought-life of Jesus was from His earliest years orientated towards God : it was enquiring, receptive, studious, expectant. All His thought-desires trended in the direction of knowledge of God and of His truths and Will, and of unbroken communion with Him.

Faced with truly unique problems, He had in a very real sense to work them out as between Himself and the Father alone ; but in an equally real sense, it was no isolated development with the Father alone, but a development within the Communion of Saints and Angels. His sole dependence was upon the Father ; but the Father chose to send much of His message and enlightenment to Him as the fruits—and through the medium—of others' prayer and life and work for God. Jesus, at the time decreed of God's Wisdom, was born into a spiritually rich heritage : a heritage comprising all the divine energy infused into, and released by, the prayer of Mary, Joseph, Elizabeth and Zacharias, Simeon and Anna : " All them that were looking for the redemption of Jerusalem " ; Moses, Elijah, and the whole line of prophets ; the doctors in the Temple, and of all Angels.

2

Through the example and infectiousness of Mary's self-abandonment as a slave of the Lord, through her self-effacing humility and silent recollection, through her prayer and spiritual teaching, and through her sacrificial love of Him, the boy Jesus must have received such incalculable inspiration as lastingly permeated His whole subsequent life. The deeply simple revelations that the pondering Spouse of the Holy Spirit could unfold to Him were His initiation into conscious human understanding of life. What loving wisdom of the Father that so it should be!

Through Joseph also came similarly incalculable inspiration, as is at once evidenced by Jesus' earliest conception of God in terms of Fatherhood. Joseph's filling of the rôle of human 'father' being so beautiful, that it inevitably pointed beyond himself to a God, Who was experienced supremely by the Child Jesus as loving and lovable when thought of as 'Father' in the dawning light of the content of 'father' implicit in the character of Joseph. The mental and spiritual cost of the birth of Jesus was certainly not less for Joseph than for Mary. A man who had risen to such costly heights of faith and obedience to God, and a man who had had faith and obedience so supernaturally vindicated, he had very much to impart of the wonder of the ways of God—and of the peace of abandonment to them, be the cost what it might—to the boy Jesus, Whose faith and obedience were later to receive a testing even more agonising than his own.

The boyish incident—recorded by St. Luke—of His remaining behind in Jerusalem after His first Passover feast, when His parents and the rest of their company had set out on their homeward journey, is an illuminating one. Already at the age of twelve His relationship with His Heavenly Father stands exposed as the dominant reality of His life and being. There is an interior impulsion—" I *must* be about My Father's business "—to correspond to, and co-operate with, the grace that was upon Him, drawing Him into ever-deepening union with the Divine disposition for the saving of the world. His listening and questioning with the doctors in the Temple—the expert exponents of the Scriptures—showed how He valued all the living spiritual deposit contained in recorded Jewish history and prophecy ; and how His study must have been given to the Scriptures from the earliest age for Him already to have attained an inner understanding of them so amazing to others.

" Ask . . . seek . . . knock : for every one that asketh receiveth ; and he that seeketh findeth ; and to him that knocketh it shall be opened " : in maturity He was to counsel this His childhood's active questing way as *the* spiritual way for all to truth, and life, and fulfilment. His " Verily I say unto you, Except ye turn, and become as little children, ye shall in no wise enter into the Kingdom of Heaven " was spoken out of His own experience in entering as a child into this Kingdom.

UNDERSTANDING OF HIS VOCATION

TO Jesus life was vocation : vocation life. The whole and sole significance of His Incarnate Personality and experience lay for Him in its relatedness to His vocation ; and the significance of His vocation in its being not self-fulfilment, but the fulfilment of the Will of His Father, so beloved and implicitly trusted. All human experience served Him as the raw material and vehicle of His vocation, throwing light upon it and providing one of the mediums of its expression. All His experiences of every kind whatsoever were vocationally integrated in prayer—prayer the very essence of His Being. Vocation, experience, prayer : these were inextricably one in His life—though here inevitably they needs must be treated in some measure separately.

From a child He knew Himself to be humanly existing solely for this vocation : a vocation none the less constraining because His whole Being went out into it in active, ardent, volitional response even before He consciously understood its specific essence. During His public ministry He enunciated His vocation with a clarity and fulness, whose quintessential simplicity is apt to veil the intensity of spiritual travail and prayer underlying this transparency. Understanding was infused in no one completed flash, but gradually over years of cumulative enlightenment was vouchsafed in many different ways.

The given starting-point for His understanding penetration to the heart of His vocation was the pre-natal angelic revelation and prophecy—

" He shall be called the *Son of the Most High* . . . and of *His Kingdom* there shall be no end " ; and

" Thou shalt call His name Jesus ; for it is *He that shall save his people from their sins* "—

which defined it for Him in terms of Divine Sonship,

Kingship, and Saviourhood ; but He had to learn in prayer, and through developing relationship with God and with men, precisely what these involved.

Illumination came partly through the discovery of His effect on others ; and through His realisation of His essential dissimilarity from them.   The recognition of Him as " the Lord's Christ ", " the redemption of Jerusalem ", by Simeon and Anna at His Presentation, when disclosed to Him by His Mother, must potently have objectified His vocation in the human sphere, and provided an outward seal upon the supernatural and subjective elements in it.   He could not but discover early in life—and increasingly as He grew older —the fundamental difference between His own relationship to God and that of all others, even his Mother and St. Joseph. How often He found indifference to God, ignorance or guilty fear of Him, conceptions of Him travestying His Love and Holiness ; fluctuations in desire for Him even in those professing His worship—always a barrier of separation through sin and self-imprisonment.   Yet He, Who was cognisant of the intrinsic nature of sin as none other, maintained unbroken, fearlessly free union with God, Whom He *knew* as Father all-loving, infinitely desirable, between Whom and Himself was never even a momentary disharmony or abatement of mutual delight in perfection of response One to Other.

Similarly He could not but discover the fundamental difference between His own relationship, and that of all others, to men :   His own indissoluble identification of selfless, sacrificial, faith-full love with each and all regardless of rank, temperament, or deserts—as contrasted with the general permeation of selfishness and distrust between one and another.   He could not fail to see and to sense, on all hands, men's misconceptions, not only of one another, but also of God and of themselves.   Hence it followed inevitably that *interpretation* must be one of the primary functions comprised in His vocation :   He must reveal God to Man and Man to himself—Man as he was designed to be.   But since after the Fall Man could not of himself in any way revert to his original destiny, He must also provide the possibility—and enkindle the desire—for his so. doing.

Divine Sonship, Kingship, Saviourhood, all bespeak privilege and power. But Jesus the Carpenter of Nazareth was humanly devoid of these. He knew no exemption from the daily exactions of poor artisan life ; humanly circumscribed by poverty, lowly rank, and the necessity for unremitting labour in a limited environment. How *could* He reconcile these with the privilege and power necessarily inherent in that to which He was called ? Only, He found, by a complete reversal of the human norm of privilege and power. Privilege and power, He perceived, must lie, not in receiving and exacting, but in giving and forbearing. His privilege—and power—was that of unique, sacrificial self-donation to the Father and on behalf of men.

Never has any one so clearly and profoundly understood the full purport of life, as gradually through prayer did He, Who in His public ministry enunciated with such lucidity the purposes of His Incarnation. In a few sentences—brief and simply worded—He summed up designs pregnant in all Eternity :

" I am come in My Father's name."

" I am the Way, the Truth, and the Life."

" I am the Light of the World."

" I am the door : by Me if any man enter in, he shall be saved. . . ."

" To this end was I born, and for this cause came I into the world, that I should bear witness unto the truth."

" I am come that they might have life, and that they might have it more abundantly."

" I am the Resurrection and the Life : he that believeth in Me—though he were dead, yet shall he live : and whosoever liveth and believeth in Me shall never die."

" Other sheep I have, which are not of this fold : them also I must bring, and they shall hear My voice, and there shall be one flock and one shepherd."

Having ·early in this ministry appropriated to Himself :

" The Spirit of the Lord is upon Me,
Because He anointed Me to preach good tidings to
the poor :
He hath sent Me to proclaim release to the captives,
And recovering of sight to the blind,
To set at liberty them that are bruised,
To proclaim the acceptable year of the Lord " ;

and later on, the Messianic Psalm (Ps. cx.)—with which He challengingly confronted the Pharisees on the Tuesday in Holy Week—with its :

" The Lord hath sworn, and will not repent,
Thou art a priest for ever
After the order of Melchizedek."

His taxing penetration to clear and exhaustive vision of the exact content of His vocation—to be one with the Father in Divine Sonship and Kingship ; to reveal Him to men and men to themselves, and by His High-Priestly ministry to restore Man's sin-forfeited relationship to God —was, however, no end in itself ; but merely the prelude to the still more perplexing task of penetrating to the discernment of how this vocation was to find its concrete expression and fulfilment.

TEMPTATION

SONSHIP, Kingship, and Saviourhood were not dis-joined relationships or functions comprised within His vocation, but interpenetrating and interdependent : His Kingship and His Saviourhood only subsisting in His Divine Sonship. No single temptation ever experienced by our Lord but originated wholly and solely within the essence, expression, or fulfilment of His vocation. Temptation pierced each domain of Sonship, Kingship, and Saviourhood.

The Person of our Lord is fraught with mystery for us : the depths and heights of His Majesty, Beauty, Wonder, Holiness, Wisdom, and Power must ever remain humanly impenetrable—only the veriest fringe of inexhaustible Truth being comprehensible to us in Time. The author of the Epistle to the Hebrews—that unique and glowing portrait of Jesus the High Priest—plunges deep into this mystery with its : " For we have not an high priest which cannot be touched with the feeling of our infirmities but was in all points tempted like as we are [Weymouth translates : " . . . One Who was tempted in every respect, just as we are tempted "], yet without sin " (Heb. iv. 15). None could ever have dared postulate this of Jesus Christ : it could only—in His infinite generosity and compassion—have been deliberately divulged by our Lord Himself within the apostolic circle to be passed down as a comfort to all souls throughout time.

By the intrinsic holiness of His Nature, and by His unique receptivity to all spiritual influences, our Lord was open to fiercer and more subtle temptation than any sinner could ever be. (Cf. Holmes : " Only he has felt the full forces of temptation who has never yielded to it.") The range of His temptation was beyond anything we could ever understand, let alone undergo ; but it also included every temptation to

which any and all human souls could ever be susceptible.
Whole reaches of temptation most acute to our egotism and
innate sinfulness could never, from entire lack of interior
inclination—" The prince of this world cometh and hath
nothing in Me "—have afforded Him any direct personal
temptation. But in His love-identification with men for
their salvation He must during the course of His life
psychically have experienced *as His own every type* of
temptation by which any, the holiest or most sinful, could
ever be assailed—simply that in Him each and all could be
assured of experiential understanding, and " grace to help in
time of need ", precisely because the identical temptation
had been victoriously triumphed over by Him, and so
potentially finally conquered for all who choose to unite
with Him in His resistance to it.

The Gospels—extremely reticent as for the most part they
are concerning the inner feelings of our Lord—allow to be
very clearly seen the scalding costliness of this gamut of
temptation, which He condescended to endure in its full
tempest in His human nature even while His Divine Nature
unperturbedly rested in peace-union with His Father.
During the Last Supper His generous love offers its thanksgiving to His disciples for that " Ye are they which have
continued [Gk. lit. remained or stood by, persevered]
with Me in My *temptations* ", not ' failures ' nor ' sufferings '.
When calmly free of temptation He *knew* Himself sinless—
" Which of you convicteth Me of sin ? "—but temptations
to Him, the sinless, must have been a fiery agony while they
lasted, so interiorly isolating that He was actually grateful
not to have been humanly abandoned during them.   Later
that very night, in the Garden of Gethsemane, He was to
crave the companionate prayer and vigil of His most beloved
disciples during His supreme temptation.   His experiential
recognition of the extreme perilousness of temptation is
evidenced by the fact that while fearlessly acquiescing in
future persecution, ostracism, and suffering of every kind
even to a violent death, for His disciples, His prayerful

yearning that they should not be brought into temptation ranks alone with, and second only to, that for their deliverance from evil itself.

St. Luke expressly records the fact—knowledge of which must and could only have been originally disclosed by Jesus Himself—that after the Temptation in the Wilderness it was only a temporary respite from temptation which our Lord experienced. " When the devil had completed [Gk. lit. exhausted] every temptation he departed from Him for a season." The Gospels only specifically instance *as temptation* a few of the outstanding crises of temptation to which He was subjected, but none the less they abundantly reveal how persistently temptation recurred for Him—sometimes straightforwardly, but more often as a subtle undercurrent percolating through the whole atmosphere of the " adulterous and sinful generation " of His day, and inherent in His unremitting suffering for Man's redemption.

Temptation for our Lord was not only in the permissive, but also in the designed, Will of God. Immediately after His Baptism, as St. Matthew records, " Jesus was led up of the Spirit into the wilderness to be tempted of the devil " : the outcome being a gainful and creative one—" And Jesus returned in the power of the Spirit into Galilee " (Lk. iv. 14). The Temptation in the Wilderness was immediately recognised, and subsequently disclosed, by our Lord to be definitely diabolic. Much of His later temptation, though apparently purely in the human sphere (i.e. arising out of the actions, words, and thoughts of human beings around Him), when taken cumulatively, and not episodically, reveals a studied progression of such malevolent *genius* as to prove personalised diabolic direction behind the human agents. This our Lord Himself clearly perceived at Cæsarea Philippi, when He repulsed Peter's desire to have Him escape suffering with that harsh : " Get thee behind Me, Satan : thou art a stumbling-block unto Me . . ." (Matt. xvi. 23).

There was a brilliant, though infinitely cruel, pitting of temptation against our Lord in a way supremely calculated to wear down resistance : exhaustive and varied temptations of body, mind, and spirit ; temptation within temptation ; certain temptations recurring again and again in identical essence, only in different settings and through different media, right through from the Temptation in the Wilderness to the very Cross itself. The devil attacked Him from the heights of spiritual vision and exaltation, and from the depths of physical pain, exhaustion, and spiritual stress ; and also through those human beings whom of all others He had most entrenched in His love, or whose religious profession entitled Him to expect understanding and allegiance.

In the Wilderness our Lord was subjected to a diabolic onslaught of concentrated and concurrent temptation in regard to each element of His vocation. The Synoptists appear only to record three distinct temptations ; but each is multiple, even if taken separately, let alone in conjunction.

" And when He had fasted forty days and forty nights, He afterward hungered. And the tempter came and said unto Him, If thou art the Son of God, command that these stones become bread " (Matt. iv. 2–3). Upon His exalting baptismal experience, sealed by the Father's confirmatory " This is My beloved Son, in Whom I am well pleased ", there follows a fierce assault on His unique vocation to Divine Sonship : temptation humanly to wonder whether it is really true, or merely self-desired or self-imagined ; temptation to seek proof of its genuineness. In this temptation is implicit the whole question of the extent of His miraculous power and its legitimate exercise ; and the crude temptation to experiment with it for self-advantage. Then beyond that there was the further subtle temptation to experiment with it on a vaster scale for the sake of others ; involving also the question of the whole relation of material and spiritual ministry. Acute realisation of widespread material and physical suffering involved temptation—directed against His Saviourhood—to absorption in endeavour primarily to meet the temporal, rather than the eternal, needs of men ; and also the temptation to see in this method an easy way of winning their allegiance to His Kingship by working miracles of economic, social, and political amelioration. In short, the temptation to save men from poverty and suffering as such, rather than from sin—their root cause—simply as an outrage against the holiness of God and His design for men.

" And he [the devil] led Him to Jerusalem, and set Him on the pinnacle of the temple, and said unto Him, If Thou art the Son of God, cast Thyself down from hence : for it is written,

> " He shall give His angels charge concerning Thee, to guard Thee :

and,

> On their hands they shall bear Thee up, lest haply Thou dash Thy foot against a stone " (Lk. iv. 9–11).

Here is renewal of temptation—even after previous victory against it—to doubt and try to prove to Himself His Divine Sonship ; and that by *presuming* upon it to defy the natural laws of the Father simply for the purpose of mental and spiritual self-gratification. In short, the temptation to disobedience and irreverence. Both times temptation is by miraculous power to prove His Divine Sonship not only to Himself, but also to others ; firstly, by a purely utilitarian, and secondly, by a sheerly spectacular use of it. In each case the temptation is to win men by a short cut—almost, it might be said, by bribery or compulsion—instead of by the gradual love-wooing of their free-will to choose Him for Himself, gifts and feats altogether apart, simply for His oneness with the supremely loving and lovable Father. The fierceness of the temptation is enhanced by the plausibility of such an end as the welfare and salvation of the whole of mankind justifying the seemingly quickest and most effectual means to ensure it.

" And the devil taking Him up into an high mountain, shewed unto Him all the kingdoms of the world in a moment of time. And the devil said unto Him, All this power will I give Thee, and the glory of them : for that is delivered unto me ; and to whomsoever I will I give it. If Thou therefore wilt worship me, all shall be Thine " (Lk. iv. 5–7).

This temptation, directed against His Kingship, involved temptation both as to the nature of His Kingdom, and the method whereby He was to become possessed of it. There was implicit, too, temptation so to concentrate upon, and regard fulfilment of, personal vocation and the furthering of men's good as supreme ends in themselves, rather than mere components in *the* sole end—undivided worshipful allegiance to the Father in the fulfilment of His Will. Thus, if blinded by such well-intentioned underlying motives, self-aggrandisement, possessiveness, spiritual compromise, and self-appropriation of power and glory might have remained unrecognised as such, and utterly polluted all worship of the Father in spirit and truth.

The totality of the Temptation in the Wilderness far exceeded the sum of the particularised temptations in it. This Temptation cannot be separated from His Baptism. The coming of the sinless Jesus to John's baptism of repentance was in no sense—*could* not have been—a personal act, i.e. an act relating to His own private concerns. He came to it as the vicarious penitent on behalf of each and every single soul created by the Father throughout time. Out of His sinlessness, He offered to the Father through His Baptism the *perfect* contrition which it is impossible for any sinner ever to offer, simply by reason of inability perfectly to abhor sin after even one fall into it. He offered vicarious penitence for sinfulness and for all specific sins. His recognition of being *driven* by the Spirit into the Wilderness after this vicarious penitential offering could not but be instantly connected—by One so steeped in the Scriptures as He—with the ancient Jewish annual sacrifice of atonement, detailed in Lev. xvi. Vivid would be His remembrance of the high priest's sin-offering first for himself and his house, and then his making sin-offering for the people with two goats—one goat to be *killed*, and the other to " be presented *alive* . . . for a scapegoat." " . . . he shall present the live goat : and . . . lay both his hands upon the head of the live goat, and confess over him all the iniquities of the children of Israel, and all their transgressions, even all their sins ; and he shall put them upon the head of the goat, and shall send him away by the hand of a man that is in readiness into the wilderness : and the goat shall bear upon him all their iniquities unto a solitary land : and he shall let go the goat in the wilderness."

By His baptismal offering as vicarious penitent our Lord became veritably the ' scapegoat ' for the sins of the whole world. His long-conscious suffering over men's engulfedness in physical and material needs ; spiritual blindness and scepticism ; and false values and worldliness was all brought to a head by His great baptismal vision of the opened heavens, contrasting supreme Reality with the transient and counterfeit. The *essence* of the Temptation in the Wilderness—a recurrent temptation with climax in Gethsemane and on Calvary—was precisely His willingness to bear upon Him to extinction the sin of the world in all its dread weight. Our Lord's Temptation was a sharing in the *suffering* resultant upon the world's sin.

Temptation as to His Divine Sonship assaulted our Lord many times after He emerged from the Wilderness. The general non-recognition of this Divine Sonship by the professedly religious was in itself a temptation to doubt ; and a temptation which was enhanced by His frequent acclamation as Son of God by those possessed of devils. Human reason and human circumstances all combined seemingly to favour as truth the common attitude adopted towards Him : " Is not this Joseph's son ? " ; " Is not this Jesus, the son of Joseph, whose father and mother we know ? how doth He now say, I am come down out of heaven ? ", rather than the Divine Sonship directly proclaimed by the Father at His Baptism and Transfiguration, and revealed to Peter at Cæsarea Philippi.

His Divine Sonship was the supreme stumbling-block for the Jews ; and His claim to it the basic ' charge ' held

against Him by the high priests and Sanhedrin : " We have
a law, and by that law He ought to die, because He made
Himself the Son of God." All the wilful hostility against,
and resistance to, His Divine Sonship was in itself diffusive
of temptation—as is all sin to others brought into any kind
of contact with it.

The Wilderness Temptation to prove to Himself beyond
doubt His Divine Sonship was renewed with fiery cruelty
upon the Cross, when body, mind, and spirit were spent
with cumulative suffering ; and when every human circumstance appeared to give the lie irrefutable to all He *knew* in
His innermost being. The agony of enduring such assault
upon this, the anchorage of His whole life, is beyond human
imagining to plumb : it can only be recorded in a spirit of
innermost penitence for our having laid Him open to it :

" And they that passed by railed on Him, wagging their
heads, and saying . . . if thou art the Son of God, come
down from the cross " (Matt. xxvii. 39–40). The diabolic
force of this temptation lay in His *ability* to meet their
challenge, and seemingly continue and further His ministry
by so doing. It was intrinsically a repetition of the Wilderness Temptation to resort to the spectacular to impress
Himself upon men.

" In like manner also the chief priests mocking Him, with
the scribes and elders, said . . . He trusteth on God ; let
Him deliver Him now, if He desireth Him : for He said I am
the Son of God " (Matt. xxvii. 41–43). The diabolic force of
this temptation lay in its being scaldingly reminiscent of the
Scriptural " He that is hanged is accursed of God " (Deut.
xxi. 23), with all the horror implicit in such a state.

After the Wilderness Temptation He was likewise, at
many different times and in varying ways, assailed by
temptation on the score of His Kingship. A village carpenter turned poor itinerating teacher and healer, ever in
conflict with the authorities ; a man possessed of undeniable
gifts and powers, who nevertheless consistently refused ever
to assert them to conciliate or dominate His fellow-men ;

His whole earthly career—with one temporary and critical exception—was, from obscure start to disgraced finish, the absolute antithesis of potential human kingship.

The crisis-temptation directed against His Kingship followed immediately upon the feeding of the five thousand, " when Jesus therefore perceived that they would come and take Him by force to make Him a king . . ." (Jn. vi. 15) ; " Straightway He constrained His disciples to enter into the boat and to go before Him unto the other side to Bethsaida, while He Himself sendeth the multitude away. And after He had taken leave of them, He departed into the mountain to pray " (Mk. vi. 45–46).

His action makes it abundantly clear that the people had raised for Him an issue which so taxed Him mentally, morally, and spiritually, that He could not delay an instant getting away from all human influence to ascertain the Will of His Father. The urgency with which He had to fling Himself isolatedly upon the Father shows that the issue was not a mere variant, or repetition, of the kingly temptation in the Wilderness, but an altogether fresh issue. There it was question of obtaining the " kingdoms of the world " by compromise with the devil ; and there that temptation was finally rejected. But here was something altogether different. *The people desire* to make Him king : and has not the establishment of His Kingship—the Divine sovereignty of Love—been the goal of all His ministry ? Is this now the threshold of consummation ? Have the people recognised *Him* in His selfless love as Lord of all ; or are they merely desirous for material benefits to be expected under His rule ? And supposing it is only this lower motive, could He not, by yielding to their desire of kingship, more quickly lead them on to true vision ? Here was an absolute crisis in His ministry : to accept or reject the will of the people now would stamp the whole remainder of His ministry irrevocably—either way the ministry could not remain what it was before. The tide of popular acclaim had risen ; and henceforward it must be a definite swimming either with it or against it. To baulk the people of their desire would certainly be to forfeit public support. On the one hand there beckoned apparent assured success, and on the other equally assured failure threatened ; between them He had to make deliberate choice, a choice to which resultant events would hold Him. In this choice was involved in acute degree the temptation implicit in every choice.

On Palm Sunday the popular desire for His kingship expressed itself in open acclamation : "A great multitude that had come to the feast, when they heard that Jesus was coming to Jerusalem, took the branches of the palm trees, and went forth to meet Him, and cried out, Hosanna : Blessed is He that cometh in the name of the Lord, even the King of Israel" (Jn. xii. 12–13). "And as He was now drawing nigh, even at the descent of the mount of Olives, the whole multitude of the disciples began to rejoice and praise God with a loud voice . . . saying, Blessed is the King that cometh in the name of the Lord . . ." (Lk. xix. 37–38). Our Lord did not silence or refuse their homage, but completely abstained from turning it to any personal or political use. This could only have been because the earlier temptation involved in the popular desire for His kingship had had to be met by a final, and irrevocable, rejection of Jewish kingship. The clue to the necessity for this rejection He articulated to Pilate at His trial : "My Kingdom is not of this world . . .". National, earthly, temporal kingship had had to be rejected as incompatible with the Father's revelation of His kingship in terms of the Eternal and Universal.

Good Friday brought fresh temptation in connection with His kingship. His claim to kingship was hypocritically plied by the Jews as a lever to force Pilate's hand to the Crucifixion of Jesus : "If thou release this man, thou art not Cæsar's friend : every one that maketh himself a king speaketh against Cæsar. . . . Pilate saith unto them, Shall I crucify your King ? The chief priests answered, We have no king but Cæsar" (Jn. xix. 12). Diabolically clever cornering of Pilate, it was—in the open knowledge of the Jewish detesta-

3

tion of the Roman domination—nothing less than brazen, shameless mockery.

But His kingship was scurrilously insulted in yet other ways on that morning of cruelty run riot : " The soldiers of the governor took Jesus into the palace, and gathered unto Him the whole band.   And they stripped Him, and put on Him a scarlet robe.   And they plaited a crown of thorns and put it upon His head, and a reed in His right hand ; and they kneeled down before Him, and mocked Him, saying, Hail, King of the Jews !   And they spat upon Him, and took the reed and smote Him on the head " (Matt. xxvii. 27–30). Evil always generates temptation for those who are its victims, and presented with choice of reaction to its per- petrators :   and these calculatedly vile outrages humanly invited *loathing* of all concerned in them.   But not even yet was the assault upon His kingship concluded.   It pursued Him to the very Cross itself, where " the soldiers also mocked Him, coming to Him, offering Him vinegar, and saying, If Thou art the King of the Jews, save Thyself " (Lk. xxiii. 36–37).   Echo of the temptation in the Wilderness to win His people by spectacular employment of His miraculous powers ! But now, as then, His rejection of it was unwavering.

It was, however, our Lord's Saviourhood which was provocative of the most persistent and exhaustive tempta- tion.   Ἴδε ὁ Ἀμνὸς τοῦ Θεοῦ ὁ αἴρων τὴν ἁμαρτίαν τοῦ κόσμου —" Behold the Lamb of God which taketh away the sin of the world "—was said of Him by John the Baptist very soon after He emerged from the Wilderness.   The Greek plainly shows His taking away the sin of the world as *a continuous process*.   The laying down of His life *in death* on Calvary is not, for sacrificial and redemptive efficacy, to be divorced from that daily laying down of His life *in life* from the stable in Bethlehem to the Via Dolorosa.   This Saviour- hood of His exercised so unremittingly was fraught through- out with temptation both from without and within.

Only very gradually —and at literally heart-breaking cost —did our Lord learn what Saviourhood involved.   The very

nature of the temptations in the Wilderness show that there
had not, as yet, begun to dawn upon Him any idea of the
Cross as the ultimate expression *on earth* of His vocation as
Saviour. Then, in the Wilderness, the winning of men to
their salvation was not in doubt—only the right method of
winning them ; but later temptation shifted from the
method to the winning itself.

Temptation of His Saviourhood from without took many
guises, and sprang from countless sources. It welled up
from what increasingly He perceived to be in men : their
deliberate choice of darkness rather than light—so that
finally they chose as against Him, Who came " that they
may have life, and may have it abundantly ", a man who
was a robber and a murderer—and their widespread *lack of
desire* for the life and truth as well as light He offered them.
It welled up not only from the obstacles presented by the
mental and spiritual attitudes of men ; but also in the
bindingness and enormity of that from which they needed
saving. *Could* men, either perversely or in unwitting
blindness, rejecting all that was offered them in the way of
salvation—" How often would I have gathered thee . . .
but thou *wouldest* not "—be saved from such universally
corrosive sin ?   Sin hydra-headed even in the individual, let
alone in the mass.   Deliberate and repeated rejection of the
salvation He proffered, and sought by every means to make
men desire ; rejection so flagrant that even the Twelve were
asked by Him, " Would ye also go away ? " must—together
with the ever-recurrent disappointingness of the Twelve on
whom had been lavished so much love and faith and teaching
—have given rise to temptation to doubt if men could ever
be brought to abiding holiness.

Love coming to woo men from Self to God, by the gift
of His all, was baulked at every turn. The excuses with
which, in His parable of the Great Supper, He furnished the
invited guests are transparently representative of some of
the experiential excuses with which He was met in His
own ministry : " A certain man made a great supper ; and

he bade many : and he sent forth his servant at supper time to say to them that were bidden, Come ; for all things are now ready. And they all with one consent began to make excuse. The first said unto him, I have bought a field, and I must needs go out and see it : I pray thee have me excused. And another said, I have bought five yoke of oxen, and I go to prove them : I pray thee have me excused. And another said, I have married a wife, and therefore I cannot come " (Lk. xiv. 16–20). Possessions, work, human relationships, substituted for His gift of Eternal Life, and giving rise to temptation to despair of Man in his selfishness and folly, and also to temptation to believe Love's offering of its very all was failing. *What* bitterness, when originally it seemed as though Love must—could not but—speedily win unreserved response.

There was temptation in all the deliberate antagonism against His Person and His mission. His death was no accidental outcome of momentary, lost-headed excitement, but was only the successful *one* of a *series* of attempts upon His life. The tenacity, virulence, and continuity of Jewish determination to kill Him is apt to be overlooked, but it runs right throughout the public ministry—and realisation of it cannot but evoke fresh worship of Him Who undeviatingly endured so much for us.

The first recorded attempt upon His life occurred very soon after the opening of His ministry ; and carried with it all the most intensified bitterness of " He came unto His own and His own received Him not ". It was at His native Nazareth, when in the synagogue He read and appropriated to Himself Isaiah's :

" The Spirit of the Lord is upon Me,
     Because He anointed Me to preach good tidings to the
          poor :
     He hath sent Me to proclaim release to the captives,
     And recovering of sight to the blind,
     To set at liberty them that are bruised,
     To proclaim the acceptable year of the Lord."

" And they were all filled with wrath in the synagogue, as they heard these things ; and they rose up, and cast Him forth out of the city, and led Him unto the brow of the hill whereon their city was built, that they might throw Him down headlong " [Gk. lit. " throw down a precipice "] (Lk. iv. 16–30).

Later, after the healing of the man at the Pool of Bethesda, " for this cause did the Jews persecute Jesus, because He did these things on the sabbath. But Jesus answered them, My Father worketh even until now, and I work. For this cause therefore the Jews sought the more to kill Him, because He not only brake the sabbath, but also called God His own Father, making Himself equal with God " (Jn. v. 16–18). After His so pregnant " I am the living bread which came down from heaven : if any man eat of this bread, he shall live for ever : yea and the bread which I will give is My flesh, for the life of the world " . . . " Jesus walked in Galilee : He would not walk in Judæa, because the Jews sought to kill Him " (Jn. vi. 51 ; vii. 1). The more He gave to men the more their antagonism increased.

Almost immediately after this, following upon His sabbath healing of the man with the withered hand in the synagogue, " the Pharisees went out, and straightway with the Herodians took counsel against Him, how they might destroy Him " (Mk. iii. 6). Later still, after His unfathomable " Verily, verily, I say unto you, Before Abraham was, I am ", the Jews " took up stones therefore to cast at Him ; but Jesus hid Himself, and went out of the temple " (Jn. viii. 58–59). Again, when at the feast of the dedication at Jerusalem, He declared " I and the Father are one ", " the Jews took up stones again to stone Him ", and after further words of His culminating in " the Father is in Me, and I in the Father ", " they sought again to take Him : and He went forth out of their hand " (Jn. x. 30–39).

Shortly before our Lord set forth upon His final journey to Jerusalem, the chief priests and Pharisees said : " This man doeth many signs. If we let Him thus alone, all men will believe on Him : and the Romans will come and take away both our place and our nation. . . . So from that day forth they took counsel that they might put Him to death " (Jn. xi. 47–53). For His Palm Sunday cleansing of the Temple the chief priests and scribes again " sought how they might destroy Him : for they feared Him ; for all the multitude was astonished at His teaching " (Mk. xi. 18). This determination to have Him destroyed intensified steadily' during Holy Week : the chief priests and the elders of the people " took counsel together that they might take Jesus by subtilty, and kill Him " (Matt. xxvi. 4.)—and finally they were aided and abetted by one of the inner circle of His most intimate disciples. All this unflagging plotting for His destruction must inevitably have afforded recurrent temptation of many kinds.

There was temptation for Him in all His saving relationship with "sinners and publicans", which brought down upon Him continual rebuke and opposition from the Pharisees and self-righteous. None of them really wanted sinners to be given the chance of conversion and salvation. There was the temptation to the expediency of withdrawing from company which compromised Him in His ministry : and the far fiercer temptation to fail in love those who were themselves so unloving.

His Saviourhood was externally tempted not only in the spiritual and moral, the physical, the material, and economic spheres ; but also in the purely political sphere as well. The temptation when He perceived, after the feeding of the five thousand, " that the people were about to come and take Him by force to make Him king " was a *political* tempting of His Saviourhood as well as His kingship— temptation to become a national saviour of His people against their overlords the Romans. And yet again was His Saviourhood politically tempted from this point of view when the Pharisees and Herodians, on Holy Week Tuesday, with design to entrap Him asked : " Is it lawful to give tribute unto Cæsar or not ? Shall we give, or shall we not give ? " (Mk. xii. 14–15).

The cost, subtilty, and danger of the temptation which assaulted Him from without was, however, almost as nothing compared with that which assailed Him interiorly.

He was tempted in His *power*—His power to save at every level : tempted in ways impossible to any ungifted with His miraculous powers.   There must have been many occasions after—as well as during—the Temptation in the Wilderness, when to forgo His saving power on a lower level in order to exercise it more hiddenly, more surely, and in keeping with the Father's Will, on a higher level, must have involved indescribably fierce temptation.   Two such instances stand out particularly in the Gospels.   The first was occasioned by the murder of John the Baptist.   St. Matthew (xiv. 13) tells us simply : " Now when Jesus heard it, He withdrew from thence " [i.e. " the other side of the sea of Galilee, which is the sea of Tiberias "] " in a boat to a desert place apart "—obviously for prayer.   It is easy to overlook what this news must have meant to Jesus, both in itself and coming when it did.   It meant the loss, not only of a close relative, but of a human medium of much spiritual blessing to Him. John the Baptist was probably *the* human being who came nearest to understanding Christ's mission.   He was a great spiritual force :   Jesus Himself had called him " more than a prophet ", and said of him, " among them that are born of women there hath not risen a greater ".   John had been His foreteller, and the first to recognise Him as the Lamb of God :   and his death meant a blank in human moral support.

The loss was spiritual rather than emotional.   The news of John's death must inevitably have raised *whys* for the human Jesus.   Why should John—having been faithful and obedient—have been permitted to come to *such* an end ? Why could not he have been allowed to live and co-operate spiritually with Him in the founding of the Kingdom ? There was the temptation—never for an instant yielded to— to question God's way of working ; to lose heart over the mission upon which John had been His human launcher ; to fear to what similar or even worse end obedience might

bring Him Himself. But the fiercest temptation arose
from the following of John's death so comparatively soon
upon His raising of Jairus' daughter. Implicit in the
experiential knowledge that He *could* recover death's
victims must inevitably have been temptation to raise John
—entirely with good motives and for spiritual ends.

The second instance occurred on Calvary. " And one of
the malefactors which were hanged railed on Him, saying,
Art not thou the Christ ?   Save Thyself *and us* " (Lk. xxiii.
39).   To know He *could* even then have released both the
robbers from their crosses !   What temptation before He
could forgo doing so, in order that the universal and eternally redemptive efficacy of the Passion might not be frus-
trated by the temporal intrusion of the miraculous *qua*
miraculous.

He was tempted in His virtues.   Especially was He
tempted in His *humility*.   There was no human cocksure-
ness of His kingship and Saviourhood.   All the scorn, unbelief, and shocking invectives so often hurled against Him
—" Thou hast a devil " ; " He hath a devil and is mad "—
all the continual questioning of His authority so shaking to
self-confidence, had as their victim One humanly *emptied*
of self-conceit and self-dependence to the point of knowing
as an ever-present reality : " I can of Myself do nothing ".
The incarnate humility must often have pulled most strongly
in temptation against His Divinity with its unshaken and
unshakable knowledge of truth.

The incessant interior temptation of His life must have
been to fix a limit to His willingness for self-sacrifice : the
temptation to go the first sacrificial mile, but to withhold
the second.   The supreme temptation on the Cross to
" save thyself " was the temptation to revoke His lifelong
practice of " deny thyself ".   The exhaustiveness of temptation of His willingness for sacrifice He Himself has laid bare
for us : " . . . whosoever he be of you that renounceth not
all that he hath " [the Gk. covers ' property ; all that is at
one's command ;   present advantages ;   natural parts ;

talents '] " he cannot be My disciple ". The cost also of this temptation, merely in one direction alone, He has also let us glimpse : " The disciples say unto Him, If the case of the man is so with his wife, it is not expedient to marry. But He said unto them, All men cannot receive this saying, but they to whom it is given. For there are eunuchs, which were so born from their mother's womb : and there are eunuchs, which were made eunuchs by men : and there are eunuchs, which made themselves eunuchs for the kingdom of heaven's sake. He that is able to receive it, let him receive it " (Matt. xix. 10–12).

We cannot know all He had to endure of temptation ; but enough can be known—even if only superficially understood—to melt to contrition the hardest heart. Different souls will find Him most adorable, most near as companion, in different temptations according to their own experience and need.

Many, probably, will find their hearts most wrung by that one of the temptations in the Agony, in which—having lived at such cost to fulfil the vocation He recognised as the *raison d'être* of His whole incarnate life—there comes in the Garden, alone in cold and dark and identification with the sin of the world, the dread fear that because this vocation obviously cannot now be consummated *on earth*, it means it must for ever remain unfulfilled. *What* agony, even had this been the sole content of the Agony in Gethsemane.

Truly all temptation was ' exhausted ' against Him.

HIS OVERCOMING OF TEMPTATION

AFTER the Last Supper, on the eve of His death, our Lord gave utterance to His exultant : " I have overcome the world "—the world in the sense of " the world as apart from God its Creator, the world as self-sufficient, consequently running counter to its Creator and thus evil in its tendency ". He had overcome temptation for Himself : glorious achievement in itself ! But it was far more than that. The particular tense used in the Greek " denotes that the action of the verb is to be regarded as brought to its appropriate conclusion at the time of speaking in such a way that its results *still remain in action*." He had, therefore, overcome in such a way that others could—if they chose—enter into His victory, which was a conquest in perpetuity over temptation.

His resistance to temptation was not a thing of chance mood, nor tempered according to circumstances ; but a *habit* of will resulting from an inner state harmonised under the dominance of two dovetailing motives—" Father, glorify Thy name " : " For their sakes I sanctify Myself, that they themselves also may be sanctified in truth". His conquest of temptation was never a merely negative refraining from wrongdoing, but always an active love-offering towards the furtherance of the Father's glory and the sanctifying of sinners. St. Paul's, " Be not overcome of evil, but overcome evil with good " is directly traceable to our Lord's principle and practice.

" Thou, Father, art in Me, and I in Thee " : here He Himself has furnished us with the key to that which alone made possible a life-time of undefeated resistance to temptation. It was this interior union with the Father which was a living centre of peace and holiness which no temptation had power to penetrate. This union from the side of the human

Jesus was not, however, achieved effortlessly, but only sacrificially. Daily there had to be the laying down of any incipient self-life in order to suffer no mental nor emotional human reaction to break in upon His union with the Father. All the human plots, the exhibitions—open or covert—of feeling against Him, could not but evoke reaction from a man as sensitive to love, and lack of love, as He. But always it was the God-reaction that was simultaneously yielded to and not self-reaction : the offering of penitence to the Father—and intercession—on behalf of those withstanding Him. Only by this holocaust of self to God could He have been victoriously enabled to withstand as He did all the temptation by which He was ever assailed.

He did not objectify His temptations into additional strength and reality by setting Himself to fight them for what they were ; but rather He dropped them off behind as—maintaining His oneness with the Father—He soared to their antipodal good.

He deliberately equipped Himself to forestall—or where this was not possible to meet—temptation : and this by a variety of methods.

The advice He gave to Peter, James, and John, in the Garden of Gethsemane on the eve of *their*, as well as of His own, supreme testing-time—" Watch and pray, that ye enter not into temptation "—was born of His own experience as how best to arm against it. The alertness which never allowed Him to be caught off His guard : and prayer—as the Greek shows—with the content primarily of worship and of consecration, rather than of petition, though this too He counselled. Other words of His that same night—" the prince of the world cometh : and He hath nothing in Me "— show the completeness of that consecration : not a single unconsecrated entrance left the devil to gain interior foothold within Him.

Our Lord had always His own means of determining the right and wrong course of action : means unlike those all too usually adopted by us. He withdrew from human

advice, and ruled out every consideration of human expediency.   Instead, He betook Himself to the Father, to seek
afresh in contemplative prayer the further revelation of His
All-Holy and All-Loving Will.   He dropped the human
problem at the Father's feet, and concerned Himself with
the Father Himself :   and through His worship and self-
oblation the Father poured back illumination and light.

His meeting of the temptations in the Wilderness abundantly shows what was one of the strongest of all the weapons
in His armoury—the Scriptures.   He was so steeped in
prayer and meditation upon them that there was an assimi-
lation of their essential truths and underlying spiritual life
as a practicable basis of daily living.   He had so absorbed
these truths and life into His innermost being, until they
became a part of Himself, that they overflowed spontaneously
as occasion arose.   The Scriptures were for Him a potent
light and defence.

Tempted in the Wilderness to turn stones into bread, He
rebuts it by a quotation from Deuteronomy (viii. 3) : " Man
shall not live by bread alone, but by every word that proceedeth out of the mouth of God."   No isolated ' text ' to
Him ;   but remembered in its rich context of Moses' creative
interpretation of the corporate experience of the Exodus :
" And He humbled thee, and suffered thee to hunger, and
fed thee with manna, which thou knewest not, neither did
thy fathers know ;   that He might make thee know that man
doth not live by bread only, but by every word that proceedeth out of the mouth of the Lord doth man live."
Dwelt upon often in earlier days of quietness, what an incentive to faith in the boundlessness beyond human imagining of God's resources :   what an incentive to humble trust
and obedience in the face of any strait or obstacle that
might ever arise.   Now, that faith, trust, and obedience
take the decisive lead, and become a path of action to
triumphant resistance.   Again in the Wilderness, from
Deuteronomy (vi. 16)—" Thou shalt not tempt the Lord
thy God "—He rebuts the temptation to throw Himself

down from the pinnacle of the temple.   And yet again there
from Deuteronomy (vi. 13)—in which spiritual saga He
must have found a close and illuminating foreshadowing of
His own—He rebuts the temptation to worship the devil.
Thus it was He carried into victorious effect the ' reso-
lutions ' of His meditations.

The Scriptures time and again during the public ministry
were the instrument by which He met and conquered temptation both without and within.   The tempting criticism of
the Pharisees over the disciples' plucking of the ears of
corn on the Sabbath He met by reference to 1 Sam. xxi. 6
(in Mk. ii. 25–26) ;   and Num. xxviii. 9 and Hos. vi. 6
(in Matt. xii. 5–7).   Both Scriptural *history* and *prophecy*
were impressed by Him into His warfare against temptation.
The tempting criticism of Scribes and Pharisees as to the
disciples' eating of bread with unwashed hands He meets
by reference to Is. xxix. 13, and follows it up by drawing
upon Ex. (xx. 12 ; xxi. 17).

When tempted to that which was not in the Father's
scope for Him, He refused in a way strongly reminiscent of
Ex. xviii. 13–23—where Jethro advises Moses in the matter
of judging between the people :   " The thing that thou
doest is not good... . . . Be thou for the people to Godward
that thou mayest bring the causes unto God "—" And one
of the multitude said unto Him, Master, bid my brother
divide the inheritance with me.   But He said unto him,
Man, who made Me a judge or a divider over you ? "
(Lk. xii. 13–14).   When " a certain lawyer stood up and
tempted Him, saying, Master, what shall I do to inherit
eternal life ? " (Lk. x. 25), He met it by referring him to the
Law.   When the Pharisees deliberately tempt Him on the
question of divorce (Mk. x. 2), He refers them directly to
Moses, and then in His own treatment of the subject takes
them back to Genesis.   In like fashion He referred the
Sadducees who tempted Him over the Resurrection of the
dead to Ex. iii. 6.

Prophecy lighted Him through the darkness of mental

and spiritual temptation inextricably involved in the progressive trend of the public ministry toward human failure and defeat : prophecy prayed through until it became established as His own inner vision and conviction. " Behold, we go up to Jerusalem, and *all things* that are *written by the prophets* concerning the Son of Man shall be accomplished. For He shall be delivered unto the Gentiles, and shall be mocked, and spitefully entreated, and spitted on : and they shall scourge Him and put Him to death : and the third day He shall rise again."

It is clearly seen how He drew from the whole range of the Scriptures, and was able to *apply* them to temptation as occasion necessitated. His, " O foolish men, and slow of heart to believe in all that the prophets have spoken ! Behoved it not the Christ to suffer these things, and to enter into His glory ? And beginning from Moses and from all the prophets He interpreted to them in all the Scriptures the things concerning Himself ", spoken after His Resurrection to the two disciples on the road to Emmaus, show how entirely He had assimilated the personal message of the Scriptures for Himself. He drew light from all sources. Different prophets differed in their detailed perception of His Messianic vocation : but He took *all* lights without particularising exclusively, and so came through to the harmony of perfection, i.e. completeness.

The temptations of His betrayal and Passion were largely met by His anchorage in Scriptural prophecy—the Father's purposes revealed to His chosen ' forth-tellers ' of it. What bitterness there must have been in reconciling Himself to His betrayal by one of the innermost circle of those upon whom He had showered the heart of His love and teaching, and for whom He never ceased to intercede. But all temptation to loss of peace was dispelled by the motive and quality of His acceptance of it—" that the Scripture may be fulfilled, He that eateth My bread lifted up his heel against Me " (Ps. xli. 9 in Jn. xiii. 18). His capture is likewise accepted beforehand, as after the Last Supper He says to His disciples : " For I say unto you, that this which is written must be fulfilled in Me, and He was reckoned with transgressors " (Is. liii. 12) " for that which concerneth Me hath fulfilment " (Lk. xxii. 37). To Peter in the Garden of Gethsemane, forbidding him to use his sword again against His would-be captors, He says : " Or thinkest thou that I cannot beseech My Father, and He shall even now send Me more than twelve legions of angels ? How then should the Scriptures be fulfilled, that thus it must be ? " (Matt. xxvi. 53–54)—thus He defeated temptation to self-defence and human escape.

In time of temptation on the Cross, too, the Scriptures served Him as a medium of offering obedience and loving trust to God in place of yielding to self-concern. He triumphed over temptation all through His life by His worship of—and self-oblation to—the Eternal purposes of the Father as revealed and made known to Him in the Scriptures.

His turning at Cæsarea Philippi to Peter, anxious to save Him from suffering and ignominy, with His : " Get thee behind Me, Satan : thou art an offence unto Me ; for thou savourest not the things that be of God, but those that be of men " (Matt. xvi. 23), illustrates another of His methods of dealing with temptation—namely, that of putting it immediately and steadfastly from Him ; refusing to compromise with the purely human element in any situation, but instead retaining undeflected the Divine viewpoint. He never permitted Himself, even momentarily, to pander to any natural human weakness or shrinking from suffering in Himself—compassionate as He was towards the weakness and suffering of others—but drew consistently upon supernatural strength to overrule it.

At His physically weakest, after lack of sleep, and after mental and emotional and spiritual stress the like of which none other in the world has ever had to endure, on the Cross His habitual triumph over temptation reached its apex.

He overcame there temptation to pride : and was content
to appear as though He *could* not save Himself, and was
undesired by God. He conquered completely the manifold
temptations implicit in physical pain and—far more wonderful still—in *exhaustion*. There was no yielding to complaint,
self-pity, or escape : which last He knew was potentially
open to Him throughout—" I lay down My life . . . No one
taketh it away from Me, but I lay it down of Myself. I have
power to lay it down, and I have power to take it again."
He refused the merciful drugged drink—apparently so
justifiable—in order to remain maximumly clear in mind and
spirit. He let no stress of body or mind sap Him to indifference to spiritual things. He conquered the temptations
implicit in a hostile external atmosphere : He let none of the
clamour, the hatred, the unbelief, the mockery, the sordidness, impinge on His union with the Father. He conquered
the temptation to false sentiment ; and accepted suffering
for others as for Himself—so infinitely much harder—for His
nearest and dearest, and for the robbers whom He could have
delivered had He chosen ; so as not to hinder God's ultimate
all-embracing purposes of redemptive love.

" The Father hath not left Me alone " ; " I am not alone,
because the Father is with Me "—thus it was He prevailed
over temptation : God the All-Holy in Him—because He
welcomed Him at all times and desired His indwelling above
all things, and paid the price of death to self to secure it—
overcoming temptation for and within Him. He overcame
temptation by virtue of His love for the Father ; by His
practice of constant and instantaneous obedience to His
wishes—" I do always those things that are pleasing to
Him " ; " My meat is to do the Will of Him that sent Me,
and to accomplish His work "—and by His utter self-
renunciation. His eye was single to the Father's glory.
He was in love with the Father in His Holiness : and so
His whole Being was full of light—the light of holiness
which refuses entrance to sin, or to anything less than
perfection.

Adored and thanked be He for His unwavering, ever-undefeated resistance to temptation: His victory our victory—if we choose to draw upon and unite with Him in it—against our temptations, whensoever or howsoever they may assail us.

ALL the recorded instances of the expression of our Lord's prayer are only representative—and the outcome —of His interior dispositions and practice of a life-time.

The Gospels reveal to us something of our Lord's prayer-life :

(a) Exteriorly ;

(b) Interiorly ;

(c) Through His teaching on prayer : both direct and parabolic ; and all of it derived from His own personal experience of praying ;

and in them we are shown, too, something of His penetration to the essentials of prayer.

His words to the Samaritan woman very early in the public ministry : " . . . the hour cometh, when neither in this mountain, nor in Jerusalem shall ye worship the Father . . . but the hour cometh and now is, when the true worshippers shall worship the Father in spirit and truth : for such doth the Father seek to be His worshippers " (Jn. iv. 21 ff.), were voiced out of His own complete spiritual liberty in prayer, freed from bondage to external atmosphere at a deep interior—and fruit-bearing—cost of discipline and self-giving to the uttermost. But He Who Himself in spiritual freedom and spontaneity incarnated the worship of the Father in spirit and truth was the very same Who said of the Law—so predominantly concerned with worship and its methods : " Whosoever therefore shall break one of these least commandments, and shall teach men so, shall be called least in the Kingdom of Heaven : but whosoever shall do and teach them, he shall be called great in the Kingdom of Heaven " (Matt. v. 19). He realised that the Kingdom could be attained without conformity to externals ; but He also realised that on earth the ' better part ' is to worship

in spirit and in truth neither because, nor in spite of, but
through them. Our Lord, Who never mistook a means for
an end, was definitely in favour of the retention of a whole-
hearted subscription to recognised laws of worship. This
can only have been because He Himself found conformity
to the Law a medium of life in worship. In His prayer
He penetrated to the freedom not to be confounded with
lawlessness, the freedom of Reality ; which Reality is the
finding—and abandoning self to union with—God at the
heart of everything, the Spirit behind every bare vehicle
of form.

The Gospels reveal to us something of our Lord's *earthly*
prayer-ministry ; and foreshadow His *heavenly* prayer-
ministry, which is revealed to us—in part at any rate—in the
Epistle to the Hebrews. All through both prayer-ministries
it is evident that there are two concurrent levels : the
temporal and the Eternal. Incarnate in time, much—indeed most—of His prayer was in the Eternal and not in the
temporal sphere at all ; and in His heavenly prayer-ministry,
Himself free from all limitations of time and space, eternally
worshipping and glorifying the Father, He yet ceaselessly
intercedes for those still enmeshed in the temporal.

The FULNESS of His prayer : this primarily it is which the
Gospels and the Epistle to the Hebrews lay bare for us in
connection with the prayer-life of our Lord. He embraced
all the richness of prayer from every aspect, and through a
variety of methods : but none the less His prayer was never
scattered nor discursive (i.e. desultory) ; it remained always
a unity—this unity " the expression of a right relationship
with God " (Bishop Geoffrey Gordon's definition of true
prayer).

The ways of prayer, commonly known as the purgative,
illuminative, and unitive, are easily traceable in the Gospel
revelation of our Lord's prayer-life ; but as concurrent, and
not successive stages. The pattern of His prayer-life disclosed by the Gospels can, however, be traced in another
way, namely, by methods external and interior.

External Methods :

(*a*) *Vocal prayer.*—His regular participation in the corporate worship in synagogues and Temple ; and His devotional use of the Psalms, in which He steeped till they became His own.

(*b*) *The Out-of-doors element in His prayer.*

The out-of-doors is essentially God's atmosphere : the indoors primarily Man's. Our Lord's love of, and immersion in, the out-of-doors gave a spaciousness to His spiritual life, and anchored it in objective reality rather than in subjective sensibility.

The out-of-doors was the background of all His deepest spiritual experiences recorded by the Evangelists—with the one exception of the Last Supper in the Upper Room. A river was the setting for His Baptism when the heavens opened to Him as He was praying ; the Wilderness for His Temptation ; a mountain overlooking the sea for His contemplative vision of His Kingdom not of this world ; a mountain for His Transfiguration ; a Garden for His Agony ; a hill for His Crucifixion ; a mount for His Ascension. Much of His teaching was given, many of His miracles worked, and the majority of His Resurrection appearances took place, out-of-doors. As though by special choice, and often when in particular need of fresh illumination as to the Father's Will, He frequented hills and Garden for prayer— by day and night : at dawn and in starlight, as well as in noon-day sun or cloud.

Much of His perception of the Divine Personality and purpose came through Nature as revealer : and constant fresh realisation of the Father as Creator, and the Spirit of God always brooding over all Creation. He perceives in the wind the creative and re-creative Spirit of God. " The wind bloweth where it listeth, and thou hearest the voice thereof, but knowest not whence it cometh, and whither it goeth : so is every one that is born of the Spirit " (Jn. iii. 8) : these words of His to Nicodemus are no mere apt simile, but the outcome of His own personal exhilarating experience of a specific wind, or winds, interpreting to Him in their baptismal infilling the functioning and vocational inspiration of the Holy Spirit.

He perceives in sun and rain God's character of universal Love. " Your Father which is in heaven . . . maketh His sun to rise on the evil and on the good, and sendeth rain on the just and on the unjust " (Matt. v. 45) ; God's bountifulness, and generous and sustaining care, irrespective of the worthiness or unworthiness of the recipients of His love. He perceives in the bird creation God's never-failing care for *all* His creatures, we humans pre-eminently included. " Behold the birds of the heaven, that they sow not, neither do they reap nor gather into barns ; and your heavenly Father feedeth them. Are ye not of much more value than they ? " (Matt. vi. 26 ; cf. Lk. xii. 24). " Are not two sparrows sold for a farthing ? and one of them shall not fall on the ground without your Father . . . Fear ye not therefore, ye are of more value than many sparrows " (Matt. x. 29 ; cf. Lk. xii. 6, where the Greek means literally ' left disregarded, or neglected ') ; through pondering on a fallen sparrow He penetrated to certainty of God's protection and purpose and knowledgable care for each and all His creatures, from least to greatest.

He perceived in the *Beauty* of lilies gem-studding the short-lived grass the property of God ever to provide necessities for all. " Consider the lilies of the field how they grow ; they toil not, neither do they spin : yet I say unto you that even Solomon in all his glory was not arrayed like one of these. But if God doth so clothe the grass of the field, which to-day is, and to-morrow is cast into the oven, shall He not much more clothe you, O ye of little faith ? Be not therefore anxious, saying, What shall we eat ? or, What shall we drink ? or, Wherewithal shall we be clothed ? . . . your heavenly Father knoweth that ye have need of all these things. But seek ye first His kingdom and His righteousness ; and all these things shall be added unto you "

(Matt. vi. 28 ff.).   Through Beauty—the overflowing of the
Being and lavishness of God—He realised God's sufficiency
for everything, however mundane or practical ; and the
Eternal sufficingness of God's love and generosity to satisfy
all needs whatsoever, spiritual or material.

Created Beauty evoked from Him worship and thanksgiving ; not primarily—although partly—for its own intrinsic wonder and delightsomeness, but as the reflection of
the Mind of the Creator ; and more than that, as the *open
sesame* to the timeless and universal, and to conscious
absorption of humanity in Divinity.   Always the heart of
Beauty was for Him the instinctive prayer of ever fresh
union with the innermost Being of the Father.

All the agricultural life, and country sights and activities
about Him (a hen and her chicks ; a man ploughing ; a
sower scattering seed), and growth in Nature (seed cast on
the earth ; a grain of mustard seed ; wheat and tares ; a fig
tree), equally with the Scriptures, provided Him with
material for prayerful meditation :   and far from being
merely " of the earth earthy " for Him were always parabolic of the spiritual and Eternal.   His unfailing perception
of the spiritual analogy in Nature was so deeply ingrained
in Him, that on the threshold of Holy Week—on Palm
Sunday—He instinctively summed up the crucial experience
just about to come upon Him in a metaphor drawn from
Nature :   " The hour is come that the Son of Man should be
glorified.   Verily, verily, I say unto you, Except a grain of
wheat fall into the earth and die, it abideth by itself alone ;
but if it die, it beareth much fruit " (Jn. xii. 23–24).

The out-of-doors was for Him the sacred and beloved
Presence-Chamber of the Father ; and there ' prayer
of recollection ' ever flowed ceaselessly and unself-consciously.

Interior Methods (some of which necessarily overlapped) :

Prayer of unbroken Union with the Essential Being and
dispositions of the Father.

The Glory-Motif prayer.

Prayer of Worship of the Father's Will.
  (*a*) Designed.
  (*b*) Permissive.
Prayer of Correspondence to Grace.
Prayer of Faith.
Prayer of Self-Oblation, and Surrendered Will.
Meditation.
Contemplation and Adoration.
Prayer in the Communion of Saints and Angels.
Worship through Beauty.
Thanksgiving.
Prayer of Joy.
Prayer of Humility.
Prayer of Self-denial ; Self-discipline ; Endurance and Perseverance.
Intercession.
Prayer of Penitence and Reparation.
Prayer of Silence.
Prayer of the Body.
Prayer of Active Service.
Prayer of the Drinking of the Cup.
Prayer of Rejected Offering.
Prayer of Peace and Serenity.
Prayer of Compassion ; Patience and Understanding.
Prayer of Sanctity.
Prayer of His Blood.
Prayer of TRUTH.
Prayer of LIFE.
Prayer of SIMPLICITY.
Prayer of CHANGELESSNESS.
All gathered up in the—
Prayer of LOVE to the UTTERMOST : the Seven Words from the Cross the crystallised expression of His prayer-life ; His life-time of prayer.

(For His *heavenly* prayer-ministry, see pp. 312 ; 315 f.)

All these interior methods taken in the aggregate, in the light of Père de Grandmaison's definition of a mystic " . . .

a human life in which the soul is normally and habitually more acted upon than acting, in which the purification of the powers of the soul is effected and especially is completed by a divine operation which the person undergoes rather than accomplishes under the inspiration of grace ; in which there is substituted in large measure for our ordinary knowledge of divine things one of a higher order, which is general and full of relish, unformulated and affective, at times giving the impression of being immediate . . .", reveal Jesus as the mystic *par excellence.* " The grace of God " was upon Him from a child up : progressive spiritual growth—the initial operation ever on the Father's side. From His earliest years He had a sense of being apprehended by the Father for His own purposes : a sense of Divine seizure for Divine purposes. Indeed before His Incarnation even : " God so loved the world that He gave His only begotten Son . . ."—the Father's desire to give the Son had been operating reflexively in the soul of the Pre-existent Jesus. He was *driven* of the Spirit of God into the Wilderness to be tempted of the devil. Always He was conscious of His ' hour ', whether it was come or not yet come : the undergoing of experience according to the Father's plan, and not His own—even inspired—initiative.

His Prayer of Union with the Father : and Glory-Motif

Nowhere, perhaps, in our Lord's earthly prayer are the two levels—Eternal and temporal—more clearly seen than in His whole relationship with the Father. There is His adoration of, resting in, and love-outpouring to, the Father simply in His (the Father's) own Being altogether apart from Creation, time and space : partly flowing through the spiritual, as opposed to the merely intellectual, knowledge and the deep unquenchable remembrance Jesus had of His pre-existent union with the Father—" Before Abraham was, I am " (Jn. viii. 58) : " . . . the glory which I had with Thee before the world was " (Jn. xvii. 5)—the reciprocal Love of Father and Son generating the Holy Spirit, Who *is*

the reciprocal and indissoluble Love between Father and
Son. Father, Son, and Holy Spirit a Trinity of such *inexhaustible* livingness, holiness, and satisfyingness as to be
absolutely complete in Itself without ever any Creation,
which was but the prodigal overflowing of a Love without
reproductive bound. Jesus incarnate never ceased His
eternal prayer of interchange of Love with the Father *at its
source*, and *for its own sake*, altogether apart from the
existence of Creation, let alone its need of redemption. His
earthly union with the Father was rooted in the love-secret :
" No one knoweth Who the Son is, save the Father, and Who
the Father is, save the Son . . ." (Lk. x. 22). Con-
currently, however, with this eternal love-prayer was the
temporal prayer of the co-operation of Jesus in spirit, mind,
and body, with the Father's Will for Creation under temporal conditions.

" Verily I say unto you, Whosoever shall not receive
[Gk. welcome, take or accept what is offered] the Kingdom
of God as a little child, he shall in no wise enter therein "
(Mk. x. 15) : these words of our Lord's to His disciples
disclose a principle and practice basically enshrined in His
own prayer-life with the Father. A very large part of His
prayer consisted simply and solely in *receiving from the
Father* : a continuous laying Himself open—in mingled
activity and passivity—to receive welcomingly the Father's
Self, graces, thoughts, and power within Himself. The
perfection of His earthly union with the Father was made
possible by His unreserved willingness to be consistently
dependent upon the Father for literally everything ; and
not that only, but ever so to keep that dependence avowed
both to Himself and to others as to annihilate any self of His
own separate from God. " The Son can do nothing of
Himself, but what He seeth the Father doing : for what
things soever He doeth, these the Son also doeth in like
manner." " I can of Myself do nothing . . . I seek not
Mine own will, but the will of Him that sent Me." " I am
come in My Father's name " (i.e. character, personality).

" My teaching is not Mine but His that sent Me."   " I speak
the things which I have seen with My Father."   " The
words that I say unto you I speak not from Myself : but the
Father abiding in Me doeth His works."

" And in the morning, a great while before day, He rose up
and went out, and departed into a desert place, and there
prayed " (Mk. i. 35).   Here St. Mark, recording in few words
an early episode of the public ministry, affords us an insight
into something of the nature and quality of our Lord's
prayer.   It was a daily aloneness with the Father that He
owed to the Father and *needed* for Himself : a mutual desire
for an ever fresh interchange of love between Them.   On this
particular morning after the Capernaum Sabbath of miracles
—the man with the unclean spirit in the synagogue ; Simon's
wife's mother holden of a fever ; and all the numerous sunset
healings of sicknesses of every sort and kind—His heart
must have been overflowing to the Father ; and there must
have been even more Jesus wanted to hear from Him than
to tell Him.   What a sweep of adoring gratitude there must
have been for the almightiness of the Father's power and the
glorious compassion with which He let it be drawn upon for
those in need.

Our Lord's own needs at such a time—temporarily drained
vitality ? mental perplexity ?—would have a place in His
prayer, but only a subordinate place.   He knew that, far
from tiring Him more to break into His night to pray, it was
His one chance of being able to continue right with, and of
effective use to, God and Man.   He took pains to try to
ensure Himself against interruption in His prayer : and He
deliberately sought the God-atmosphere of out-of-doors.
He rested in the Father : drinking in physical, mental, and
spiritual refreshment, renewing spent energy and receiving
fresh strength as a *trust*.   It was the intercourse of perfect
understanding between Father and Son : mutual joy and
deepest satisfaction.

What thanksgiving Jesus must have offered up for the
previous day : what upholding in faith of those who had been

healed. How, quietly, He must have sought the Father's
will for the new day about to dawn. How He must have
taken to the Father for His enlightenment problems beginning to press more urgently. How to combine physical
healing with all else in His ministry of reconciliation of Man
to God ? Was this physical healing an integral part of His
ministry ; and if so, with so much sickness and physical
limitation on every hand, where would it stop ? Or was it
only a side-issue, and as such, distracting ? Humanly far too
complex a question to settle : it threw Him back more than
ever upon God in conscious dependence and trust. He
clarified everything through the Father's vision of redeeming
the world in His (the Father's) own way. In the stillness—
interior as well as external—He cemented His oneness with
the Father ; and bulwarked Himself for the tasks, difficulties, and infinite self-giving of the coming day. He
steeped Himself in God ; and claimed with assurance *all* the
enablement, spiritual, mental, and physical, He needed for
the Father's work.

St. Luke (vi. 12) records an instance of our Lord's praying
all night. This will be referred to more fully under His contemplative prayer : suffice it here to realise the absorbing,
necessitous quality of communion with the Father underlying it.

In His prayer of self-abandonment to the Father, He knew
His whole Being to be plumbed and quickened by the
Father's perfect understanding ; and simultaneously He
knew that He Himself was plumbing the whole Being of the
Father. There was nothing left in Either hid from Other :
self-donation was mutually—continuingly—complete. " As
the Father knoweth Me, even so know I the Father " (Jn. x.
15) ; in reciprocal, indissoluble, and inexhaustible Love (that
is, in the Holy Spirit) ; in identity of nature and purposive
desire ; and in absolute mutual affiance. Jesus humanly
knew the Father in obedience, humility, joy, faith, suffering,
and thanksgiving.

He was always so transcendently aware of the Father that

the *inevitability* and nature of His relationship to the Father
seemed to Him as though it must be self-evident to others.
As a child of twelve He asked His mother : " How is it that
ye sought Me ?   Wist ye not that I must be about My
Father's business ? " (Lk. ii. 49) ; and on the eve of His
death He asked one of His closest disciples : " How sayest
thou, Shew us the Father ?   Believest thou not that I am
in the Father, and the Father in Me ? " (Jn. xiv. 9–10).   His
awareness of the living Father was such that He could think
of the Temple only as " My Father's house " : a place not
of ceremonial, nor even primarily of corporate worship, but
just one where the Beloved Father especially dwelt.

The nature of the intercommunion between Father and
Son was publicly disclosed with beautiful simplicity by our
Lord Himself just before the raising of Lazarus : " And
Jesus lifted up His eyes, and said, Father, I thank Thee that
Thou hast heard Me, and I knew [ἤδειν : denoting *con-
tinuous* action in past time] that Thou hearest Me always "
(Jn. xi. 41–42).   Prayer for Him was never a solo to the
Father ; but always a love-duet with Him : the Father never
failing freshly to respond to His every fresh overture of
love and faith.   Experientially over years He had so proved
the immutability of the Father's responsiveness to His
prayer that He anchored in it as infallible.

The Gospels—the Holy Spirit's selective revelation of the
incarnate life and Personality of our Lord, and of the life and
Nature of the Persons of the Trinity—unfold the Glory-
motif running throughout time and Eternity.   This Glory-
motif is there apparent as an active and unifying principle
in the Trinity :

> The Father glorifying the Son
> The Son glorifying the Father
> The Holy Spirit glorifying the Son.

All through the incarnate life of our Lord it is also to be
found : in the angelic announcement of His birth ; in the
praise of the shepherds after seeing Him in the manger at
Bethlehem ; in Simeon's prophecy at His Presentation ; in

His own prophecies of His second coming ; in His signs and
works of mercy ; in His teaching ; in His Transfiguration ;
in His Holy Week entry into Jerusalem, and in the seeking
of " certain Greeks "—who had come up to the Passover—
to see Him ; in the departure of Judas from the Last Supper
to betray Him ; in the grounds of promise He gave for
prayer in His name to be answered ; in His Holy Week
' high-priestly ' prayer (Jn. xvii) ; in His Passion-entry
into His glory. Not only is it revealed as the basis of His
' high-priestly ' prayer, but also of His whole temporal and
eternal prayer-life which may all be said to be comprehended
in His " Father, glorify Thy name."

' Glory ' and ' glorify ' are words which have tended—
like all elemental words defying satisfactory definition—
to remain essentially unweighed by many people. ' Glory '
(δόξα) as used in the Gospels would seem to represent the
intrinsic and plenary perfection of the galaxy of Divine
attributes so invincible and inexhaustible as to be an entity
in itself. ' Glorify ' is there used in connection with this
entity in the diverse senses of :

(1) Divine revelation of it. " Father, glorify Thy name "
(Jn. xii. 28).

(2) Human perception *and acknowledgment* of it. " And
one of them [the ten lepers cleansed by our Lord], when he
knew that he was healed, turned back, with a loud voice
glorifying God " (Lk. xvii. 15).

(3) Communication of it. " And now, O Father, glorify
Thou Me with Thine own Self with the glory which I had
with Thee before the world was " (Jn. xvii. 5).

(4) The voluntary human offering it back in thanksgiving
and sacrificial obedience and self-oblation to its Divine Source

(*a*) as its only possible abiding-place ;

(*b*) in order to have it yet more widely reflected and
perceived, so as to inspire fresh adoration of God
as He is simply in His own Being.

" I glorified Thee on the earth, having accomplished the
work which Thou hast given Me to do " (Jn. xvii. 4).

" Herein is My Father glorified, that ye bear much fruit
. . ." (Jn. xv. 8).

" Now this He spake, signifying by what manner of
death he [Peter] should glorify God " (Jn. xxi. 19).

The whole end and aim of human personality as taught
by our Lord in His Sermon on the Mount was summed up
in His : " Even so let your light shine before men, that they
may see your good works, and *glorify your Father* which is
in heaven " (Matt. v. 16).   The glorification of the Father :
this was the whole *raison d'être* of life for Him.   The desire
for God's glory was ever dominant with Him : and His
entire being was consistently directed towards it.   This
ceaseless desire was an unbroken prayer of aspiration.   He
continuously disclaimed everything from Himself to the
Father : both in word, and in the *manner* of performing
His deeds of wonder—this was part of His perpetual incarnate prayer of humility and self-denial.

Jesus said to the Samaritan leper, who alone after his
cleansing turned back and glorified God : " Arise, and go
thy way : thy faith hath made thee whole " (Lk. xvii. 19)—
whole, as distinct from and additional to, *cleansed*.   This was
pronounced out of our Lord's own experiential knowledge
of the unifying of the whole personality in the prayer of
glorifying God.

Towards the end of the incarnate life the glory-motif
became increasingly sublime.   On Palm Sunday, " certain
Greeks among those that went up to worship at the feast
. . . came to Philip . . . saying, Sir, we would see Jesus.
Philip cometh and telleth Andrew : Andrew cometh, and
Philip, and they tell Jesus.   And Jesus answereth them,
saying, The hour "—the ' hour ' of His uttermost human
suffering and dereliction—" is come, that the Son of Man
should be glorified " (Jn. xii. 20 ff.).   A short passage,
which can all too easily be read over without realising all
that it meant for Jesus, Whose answer was given in the light
of His meditative insight into the personal application to
Himself of Isaiah's prophecy : " Thou art My servant . . .

in whom I will be glorified. . . . It is too light a thing that thou shouldest be My servant to raise up the tribes of Jacob, and to restore the preserved of Israel : I will also give thee for a light to the Gentiles, that thou mayest be My salvation unto the end of the earth " (Is. xlix. 3 ff.).   From Him Who had so often and so deeply pondered the prophecies of Isaiah in prayer, the ensuing analogy—of the grain of wheat having to fall into the earth and die in order to bear fruit— came spontaneously in the knowledge that He too it was Who would be " as a lamb that is led to the slaughter " (Is. liii. 7).   Yet at this very moment He is able clearly to proclaim : " He that loveth his life loseth it : and he that hateth his life in this world shall keep it unto life eternal."

But none the less, despite His transparent perception of the truth and His assent to it, He cried out : " Now is My soul troubled ; and what shall I say ? Father, save Me from this hour.   But for this cause came I unto this hour, Father, glorify Thy name " (Jn. xii. 27 f.).   In this foretaste of His still more terrible Agony in the Garden His humanity was shaken, and craved rescue and escape.   He had faced His ' hour ' in anticipation ; but now it had to be faced in inexorable present reality.   Only prayer could save retreat. At the supreme moment of interior struggle between human shrinking and spiritual willingness to fulfil His vocation, be the cost what it might, not even His wondrous would-be redemptive love for humanity—love such as none other has ever had—could upstay Him.   Nothing less than the God-motive could suffice.   That ceaseless prayer of aspiration— " Father, glorify Thy name "—alone was capable of proving the sticking-point for victory.   And this fresh utterance of His life's prayer immediately evoked from the Father that fresh response on which He could always *count* : " There came therefore a voice out of heaven, saying, I have both glorified it, and will glorify it again."

At the Last Supper, at the precise moment when He knew that Judas had gone out to betray Him, He exulted that :

" Now is the Son of Man glorified, and God is glorified in
Him "—in His own human extremity His innermost prayer
was still for the Father's glory, and His perception directed
away from His own personal suffering toward it—" and
God shall glorify Him in Himself, and straightway shall He
glorify Him " (Jn. xiii. 31 f.).   The relationship between
Father and Son was one in which mutual glorification was
inevitable : inherent in the very nature of the love-union
between Them.

His prayer of glorifying God largely found its expression
simply in His continuous and unfolding revelation of the true
Nature of the Father.   " No man hath seen God at any time,
the only begotten Son which is in the bosom of the Father,
He hath declared Him " (Jn. i. 18).   His revelation of the
Father was offered to all in His teaching, but pre-eminently
was it unveiled in Himself—" He that hath seen Me hath
seen the Father " (Jn. xiv. 9)—in His whole incarnate life,
that divine revelation culminating on the Cross, so that His
very Being was one unbroken prayer of glory.

Jesus' Worship of the Father's Will

To Jesus the Will of God was never an impersonal thing
with a probable connotation of suffering, hardship, un-
pleasantness, or negation ; but the personal Love and
Wisdom of the Father in tangible design.   To Him the Will
of God was the very Heart and Mind of the Father Who is
All-Love and All-Holiness : and as such He reverenced and
adored it, and abandoned Himself to it not in inevitable
resignation, but in active quest to penetrate further and
further into it.   " I seek not Mine own will, but the Will of
Him that sent Me " (Jn. v. 30).   His Father's Will He
recognised as the life of His life, the *reality* making His
incarnate life purposeful and unified, and gloriously ' worth-
while '.   " My meat is to do the Will of Him that sent Me,
and to accomplish His work " (Jn. iv. 34) : He literally
hungered for the Will of God, and found in it His life's
sustenance.   He was in love with the Father's Will—as

essentially one with the Father's very Self—and never in fear of it. It was His life's anchor.

He *trusted* in the desirability and wisdom of the Father's Will even when it seemed to run dead counter to all the cumulative sense-perception, feeling, and reasoning of his whole human nature. The *sole* sanctuary left Him in the Gethsemane Agony of mind and spirit was to make a holocaust of His entire incarnate nature to the Will of the Father, which He had learned so to know that His whole Being unassailably assented to it as the supreme Perfection, Beauty, and Harmony infinitely to be desired be the human cost what it might. Faced with what even for Him—indomitable in courage—was well-nigh unfaceable, by a culminating act of love and faith and worship He left unfettered the Will of the Father : " Abba, Father, all things are possible unto Thee ; remove this cup from Me : howbeit not what I will but what Thou wilt " (Mk. xiv. 36). Deeper than all human thought and feeling there was a spirit-unity of will between Him and the Father, to safeguard which literally *nothing* was too great a self-sacrifice for Him to offer.

His worship of the Father's Will issued in an ever-practical outcome : " I do always the things that are pleasing to Him " (Jn. viii. 29). " Thy Will be done " was not merely enshrined as a petition in the prayer which He gave as a model to His disciples at their request : it was enshrined in His Being—both Pre-existent, and Risen, Glorified, and Ascended, in Eternity ; and incarnate in time. He was able Himself to pray this very petition in the extremity of the Agony because His whole Existence was a ceaseless pleading of desire for it.

The unity of will between Father and Son rested in an identity of Nature and purpose, i.e. Love living to love and be loved : and as such began not in time but in Eternity—having its perfect diverse expression proper to each state. The Pre-existent Son one with the Father in Creation—and in seeing that it " was very good " (Gen. i. 31)—shared

5

with joy the Will of Love for love's extension. Then with
Man's falling away from God's perfect creation, He shared
the Father's Will of Love for his redemption. Unity of
will flowed unbrokenly through every wish of the Father
unreservedly corresponded to by the Son. The Father
desired to give His Son : the Pre-existent Son desired to be
given—to save the world. Incarnate, Jesus clearly perceived and enunciated this universally redemptive Will of
the Father : " I am come down from heaven, not to do
Mine own will, but the Will of Him that sent Me "—what
perfection of unity between this ' come ' and ' sent ' ; what
perfection of worship of the Father's Will in this glad,
voluntary obedience of the Son—" And this is the Will of
Him that sent Me, that of all that which He hath given Me
I should lose [Gk. metaphorically ' fail to save ', Abbott-
Smith] nothing, but should raise it up at the last day. For
this is the Will of My Father, that every one that beholdeth
the Son, and believeth on Him, should have eternal life . . ."
(Jn. vi. 39–40).

Pre-existent, His correspondence to the Will of the
Father, His co-operation with it—in other words, His loving
—was exercised without limitation of any sort, other than
the infinite bound of Holiness implicit in the very Nature of
God. Incarnate, it ceased to be exercised in the freedom of
the pre-existent glory, and on an equality with the Father,
but had through the constraints of human nature and circumstances to find and mature a fresh expression : which
expression took the form of utter self-surrender in humility
and faith to minute obedience to the exact *how* of the
Father's redemptive plan for the world. Jesus had to be
constant in prayer to receive the detailed unfolding of the
Father's Will ; and to receive the Father's empowerment to
fulfil it. This was acquired through the intense and progressive quality of His communion with the Father, which
stamped upon His human mind and nature not so much
detailed instructions as to conduct and action, as identity of
interior disposition with the Father. Thus His reaction to—

and initiative in—changing circumstances developed *instinctively* in union with the Nature and purposes of the Father.

Jesus worshipped the Father's designed Will by His love of
Love and Holiness, and by His sacrificial self-oblation in order
to enable the Father to reconcile fallen Man to Himself. Over
and above this, He saw in all events—however humanly
awry—the *permissive* Will of God, identical with His designed Will in that it too was redemptive, transmuting evil
into good. This simple and unanalytical viewing of *all*
happenings as part of the permissive Will of the Father entrenched Him in peace ; and was the key to the imperturbable serenity with which He received what to anyone else
would have come as interruptions—intrusions upon His
privacy and all too scant leisure ; overlappings of demand
for His help and services. For Him there was no such thing
as an interruption. Whatever presented itself outside His
choice He accepted as part of the work given Him by the
Father, and carried it through smoothly and harmoniously
with the rest.

His ever-conscious realisation of the all-embracingness of
this permissive Will of the Father's brought Him majestic
serenity, courage, and freedom in the face of the most appalling circumstances that evil could ever array against any
man. In the Garden, where Man at his vilest and most full
of self was out to capture and kill Him regardless of justice,
when all human malice was concentrated against Him, all
diabolic powers arrayed against Him, He looked through
Man's sin and devil's venom, and saw the whole situation
only as the permissive Will of the Father : " the Cup which
the Father "—not Man, nor devil—" hath given ".

So, too, this reverence for, and unbroken recognition of,
the Father's permissive Will freed Him completely from all
false " respect of persons ". When on trial for His life,
" Pilate therefore saith unto Him, Speakest Thou not unto
me ? knowest Thou not that I have power to release Thee,
and have power to crucify Thee ? Jesus answered him,
Thou wouldest have no power against Me, except it were

given thee from above " (Jn. xix. 10 f.).   How intrinsically
free the peasant prisoner at once appeared ; how fettered
the imperial judge !   He received everything as direct from
the hand of God, and never perplexed Himself with human
intermediaries, and the whys and wherefores, motives,
blameworthiness, or otherwise of their actions.

His constant attributing of all things to the permissive
Will of the Father was part of His acknowledgment and
worship of the Father as All-Love, All-Wisdom, and
redemptively Almighty for Holiness.

Correspondence to Grace

The Father's promise of empowerment and support antici-
pated the whole incarnate life of Jesus ; and through angels
was pronounced God's authoritative proclamation of His
Son's Coming and Mission.   The Father's omnipotent support was behind Him from the very start and throughout ;
and His protection for just so long as it was needed—
especially as a Child—and His unbroken enablement.   The
initiative lay always with the Father : the Son corresponded
in the identity of the aim of His love.   The grace of God
which was upon Him as a Child but increased with His
progressive response to it.

Jesus, through the Father's fresh gift of the Holy Spirit
and His expressed love and approval at His Baptism, received special grace for His public ministry.   At His Transfiguration another outpouring of special grace was given
Him by the Father for His ' exodus ' (i.e. Passion and
Crucifixion) ; and in His Agony yet further strengthening
special grace was given Him by the Father through the
ministry of an angel.   On each occasion the grace was
appropriated, and the Father's appointed work accomplished
to His Glory.

His correspondence to grace was unself-conscious and
habitual, instantaneous and unreserved.   It stands incidentally revealed from time to time in teaching of His
based on His own personal experience.

" And He said, So is the Kingdom of God [cf. His " The Kingdom of God is within you "] as if a man should cast seed upon the earth ; and should sleep, and rise night and day, and the seed should spring up and grow he knoweth [Gk. lit. perceiveth] not how " (Mk. iv. 26 f.). His spiritual life was a day-to-day process, for the most part almost imperceptible to Himself—objective rather than subjective. He let divine growth take place unhindered, co-operating with it simply, perseveringly, and disciplinedly.

" For every one shall be salted [Gk. = sprinkled with salt (of sacrifices or of those who offer sacrifice) ; kept fresh and sound and so acceptable to God] with fire " (Mk. ix. 49). This was said by " Him, Whom the Father sanctified " (Jn. x. 36), out of His own experiential knowledge of *grace* as a hallowing *fire* to which He yielded His whole Being.

"And when they lead you to judgment, and deliver you up, be not anxious beforehand what ye shall speak : but whatsoever shall be given you in that hour, that speak ye : for it is not ye that speak, but the Holy Ghost " (Mk. xiii. 11) [cf. Lk. xxi. 14: " Settle it therefore in your hearts not to meditate beforehand how to answer . . ."]. This command He gave to His disciples out of His life-experience of the Holy Spirit's never-failing operation of grace within and through Him to meet each need or situation *as it arose* according to the Will of the Father. His human reason and will were ever attendant upon grace : and they never tried either to forestall or to check it.

Prayer of Faith

The Gospels record several instances of our Lord's wonder at lack of faith. " And He marvelled because of their unbelief " (Mk. vi. 6) ; because, and only because, by experience He knew faith to be the rational, bedrock basis of life ; the practicable, creative basis.

It was by faith He apprehended His vocation.

It was by faith He harmonised His Divinity with His humanity and so integrated His incarnate Personality. It

was by faith He reconciled the temporal with the Eternal ;
and human appearance with divine reality in spite of every
seeming contradiction of human sense and reason.   Late in
the public ministry He could affirm : " Father . . . I knew
that Thou heardest Me always " (Jn. xi. 42) ; and this in spite
of prayer for His disciples and ministry which might humanly
all too often have seemed unanswered in human failure.

  ' Faith ' is another of the words which defy satisfactory
definition, and so has gathered to itself a number of different
—sometimes vague, and sometimes faulty—associations.
Faith as the Gospels show it to have been exercised by our
Lord reveals a very rich content indeed.   He Himself
summed it all up for His disciples in His : " Have faith *in
God* . . ." (Mk. xi. 22).   Fundamentally His faith was an
anchorage in the Father as He is in His Own Being apart
from aught else ; and subsequently a relating all else to the
known character of the Father, and an interpreting of it only
and solely in that light.   He gave free play to the divinely
implanted intuition of Truth infused into His innermost
spirit—that region beyond intellect and sense impressions—
by the Father.   His faith was a perception of intrinsic
Reality and Perfection as embraced in the Father All-Holy
and All-Loving ; and that Reality and Perfection was the
sole power which He acknowledged and co-operated with as
ultimately and enduringly potent.   He Himself declared :
" The lamp of the body is the eye : if therefore thine eye be
single, thy whole body shall be full of light " (Matt. v. 22) :
His prayer of faith was this singleness towards God.   It was
His habitual and unbroken concern with and for God rather
than self, this trust in the Father's omnipotent Love and
Wisdom, which rendered Him absolutely fearless throughout
the whole of His life ; and enabled Him from experience to
show His disciples, in the storm on the lake, real faith as the
antithesis of personal fear and preclusive of it.

  Although " He knew all men, and . . . needed not that
any one should bear witness concerning man ; for He Himself knew what was in man " (Jn. ii. 24–25)—knew all his

sin and selfishness as no sinner could ever know it—yet He had a faith in the potentialities of human personality which would literally stagger us could we come to consider it as though for the first time, and *realise* it. " Thou art Simon the son of John : thou shalt be called Cephas (which is by interpretation, Peter) " (Jn. i. 42). He could see clear through present sinfulness and instability to the sanctified character which would ultimately emerge. He Who said " Give not that which is holy unto the dogs, neither cast your pearls before the swine, lest haply they trample them under their feet . . ." (Matt. vii. 6), entrusted His sublimest teaching on worship to a woman whom He knew to be even then ' living in sin '—simply because in spite of this He believed her to be capable of assimilating it (Jn. iv. 5 ff.).

He had faith that sinful, selfish men could grow in the supernatural spirit of the Sermon on the Mount to be perfect even as their Father in heaven. He had faith in the dense, proud, self-seeking, cowardly, hot-tempered, and retaliatory disciples becoming so revolutionised in character as to become to the world the interpreter of Him Who was the interpreter of the Father. He had faith in men becoming finally established in holiness even after innumerable falls ; and in the possibility of publicans and harlots entering the Kingdom of God. He had faith that individualistic and separative men would become one even as He and the Father are one.

His faith in human personality was so unquenchable simply because it was basically faith, not in Man as such, but in God and His ultimate working out of His design for him. His incarnate faith was a creative channel for the Divine redemption and transfiguration of personalities of every type. Through His faith a woman with seven devils became a saint ; and a man who had desired to call down fire from heaven on those who refused to receive our Lord became the apostle and evangelist of Love. Our Lord's faith was a receptivity to the good beyond human imagining designed by the Father.

He had faith for human miracle even in a spiritually hostile atmosphere, as is shown by the healing of the man sick of the palsy, and of the man with the withered hand. In the cases of the Centurion's servant, the nobleman's son, the Syrophœnician woman's daughter, His faith enabled Him to give *assurance* of the accomplished healing in answer to His prayer, without His humanly seeing the result at all.

His whole Being *believed* that " with God all things are possible ". He knew He had but to ask to be heard and receive the Father's granting of His request. This involved deliberate choice—in His exercise of faith—of what He should ask. The most momentous instance of such a choice took place in the Garden of Gethsemane. There, in the presence of the multitude of His would-be captors, He asked Peter " thinkest thou that I cannot beseech My Father, and He shall even now send Me more than twelve legions of angels ? " (Matt. xxvi. 53). He knew God could have delivered Him, but He deliberately refrained from exercising His faith in God's love on His own behalf in order that He might exercise it on behalf of all mankind. By His refusal to seek deliverance for Himself, and by His " drinking of the cup " of suffering and death proffered to Him by the Father as Love's supreme opportunity, He actively freed Love's redemptive energy in a *universal* instead of merely *individual* application. His whole exercise of faith was an unbroken prayer of homage, trust, and sacrificial love offered to the Father in such a way as to release the redemptive flow of His Holiness and Love into each and every circumstance as it arose.

His ' prayer of faith '—as every other element in His prayer—attained its zenith on the Cross, where Jesus offered the superlative act of faith of all time. There, out of a *dereliction* incomprehensible to sinful minds, He cried : " My God, My God, why hast Thou forsaken Me ? " (Mk. xv. 34). Later came His " I thirst " (Jn. xix. 28). This ' word ' is commonly taken to apply to—

(*a*) physical thirst ;˙
(*b*) spiritual thirst for the souls of men.

But following upon the cry of dereliction—couched in words from the psalms He had used so deeply and constantly all His life—was not that " I thirst " surely His expression of thirst for GOD : in His heart the words of the psalmist : " My soul thirsteth for God, for the living God, when shall I come to appear before God ? " (Ps. xlii. 2) ? Finally came His " Father, into Thy hands I commend My spirit " (Lk. xxiii. 46) : as offered by One dying a death held to be accursed of God, His cause apparently both humanly and divinely repudiated and annihilated, surely an unparalleled act of faith. But to make it even more sublime, there is nothing to prove—nor even suggest—that when this act of faith was offered the spiritual dereliction had passed (His " It is finished " (Jn. xix. 30) in all probability indicating *only* the completion of the ' work ' which the Father had given Him to do). There is, on the other hand, almost a moral *necessity* that Love offering its *all* would *have* to offer its supreme and final act of faith in a humanly impenetrable night of sense and soul. So in death He offered it : His innermost spirit cleaving despite all to the Father by Whom and in Whom and with Whom He had lived in faith.

Prayer of Self-Oblation and Surrendered Will

This prayer was offered in simplicity, without introspection, and without strain. It was offered once for all as an initial act flowing on in unbroken continuity, rather than as a series of separate and repeated acts—the offering being a unity which embraced all details, and not a diversity of details designed to compose a whole. " Wherefore when He cometh into the world, He saith, Sacrifice and offering Thou wouldest not, but a body hast Thou prepared Me : In burnt offerings and sacrifices for sin Thou hast had no pleasure. Then said I, Lo, I come (in the volume of the book it is written of Me,) to do Thy will, O God " (Heb. x. 5–7). The prayer of His surrendered will was but the negative aspect of His positive worship of the Father's Will.   He annihilated self-will, not as an end in itself, but simply as the means of giving limitless free play to the Will of the Father within and through Him.   So did He empty Himself (Phil. ii. 7, R.V.) that He might be filled with all the fulness of God.

There was nothing of self-initiated spiritual activity—with its consequent drain of vitality—in His self-oblation and ' surrender ' ; rather was it a still life, an interior hiddenness, in the Father *infused* by the Holy Spirit and received—in that passivity which is supreme activity—by Him in the depths of His human soul.

Meditation

How early, how continuingly, how deeply our Lord studied the Scriptures ; and something of what they meant to Him practically in daily living has inevitably emerged already in the sections on " The Boy Jesus " and " His Overcoming of Temptation ".

Jesus all His life steeped in the Scriptures which the Holy Spirit made to be light to His mind and spirit ; food for His soul ; part-interpreter of His vocation ; a ready weapon against temptation ; and a ground-work for both His devotional and ethical life.

' Meditation ' for Jesus was never mere reading and thinking, or ideas as ideas or stimulus to sensible devotion ; it was self-abandonment to communing with the Spirit of God Who reveals the Being, Will, and operations of the Father ; a communing *for the sake of* union with God, primarily simply as union with Himself, and secondarily for the furtherance and fulfilment of His designs.

The Scriptures were one medium through which our Lord received—by meditation—the Holy Spirit's revelation of the Father's agelong preparation for His Incarnation ; the fulness of equipment to be given Him by the Father for His vocation ; and the illimitable suffering divinely foreseen to be implicit in the Messianic office.

It was the heart of the Holy Spirit's content of the Scriptures which our Lord assimilated. In vocal prayer He drew richly upon the psalms : and in His Passion these afforded Him ' darts '—' aspirations '—which expressed and carried to the Father the cry of His whole Being. The historical events recorded in the Scriptures were never to Him mere historical happenings of the past : each yielded to Him an eternal and abiding truth and significance upon which He drew in the present circumstances and difficulties of His own life. His knowledge of the Scriptures was so intimate and profound that He was always able, at will, to interconnect from quite different contexts passages of like matter and spirit. By meditation He penetrated the Scriptures as a *unity* rather than as a compilation. He pierced through the apparent surface meaning of the Law to the utmost limit of the Holy Spirit's revelation of the Father's Will implicit in it : and this provided the practical basis of His own ethical life and teaching.

Jesus' own words to the Sadducees : " Is it not for this cause that ye err, that ye know not the scriptures, nor the power of God ? " (Mk. xii. 24) ; and the way in which, after His Resurrection, He interpreted to the disciples on the walk to Emmaus "in all the scriptures the things concerning Himself " (Lk. xxiv. 27) divulge, more than anything else could do, the potency of light and life which He received from the Holy Spirit in meditation.

Contemplation and Adoration

He Himself declared : " The Son can do nothing of Himself but what He seeth [βλέπη = to perceive, look at ; therefore here equivalent to ' watch '] the Father doing : for what things soever He doeth, these the Son also doeth in like manner " (Jn. v. 19). His was the prayer of SIMPLE REGARD issuing in action unitive with the Father's eternal generation of Love. His prayer was selfless God-regarding prayer. Every event He always first viewed in its Godward relation, and then in its relation to His fellow-men, before ever taking it into consideration in its personal relation to Himself. His concentration was upon the Father to the exclusion of self-independence and self-initiative.

Like a still, incalculably deep Scottish loch mirroring the mountains overshadowing it ; so the still, fathomless pool of His human soul received the impress of the 'express image' of the Father, and unself-consciously reflected the peaks of His Beauty, Holiness, and Love. (Cf. St. John of the Cross : "Contemplation is to receive.") His human contribution to enable God to communicate Himself to Him, and to infuse into Him His gifts, was simply self-emptying and obedience unremittingly accompanying a perpetual, single lover-gaze towards the Father.

St. Luke (vi. 12, A.V.) tells us of one occasion—undoubtedly typical of many—when Jesus ". . . went out into a mountain to pray, and continued all night in prayer *to* God." (R.V. likewise ". . . prayer *to* God." Weymouth : " He remained all night in prayer to God." Moffatt : " He spent the whole night in prayer to God.") The Greek is literally " passed the night in the prayer *of* God." This substitution of " prayer *to* God " for " prayer *of* God " disastrously loses the whole inner reality enshrined in this passage, which in the original unveils for us the essence of Jesus' contemplative prayer—so far as it is possible for us to apprehend it. This prayer was not initiated from Jesus' side. It was no mere human outstretching towards God. It was initiated by the Father : Jesus only responding by deliberately yielding Himself in still silence—interior as well as exterior—to the Holy Spirit's drawing of Him to the Father. It was the invasion of the human Jesus by Divine Love in such a way as to evoke in return the whole love both of His human and divine natures, inextricably one in the Incarnation. This prayer was nothing other than Jesus' yielding to the Father's catching of Him up whilst still in the flesh into the eternal flux and reflux of Love within the Trinity.

Jesus as contemplative is revealed subjectively by St.

John and objectively by the Synoptists. In St. John we glimpse something of the inner processes of His prayer : in the Synoptists we receive—through His recorded sayings— some of the fruits of this prayer. The portraits of Jesus as drawn by St. John and by the Synoptists are often so sharply contrasted as to make them appear contradictory, if not almost irreconcilable with one another. Study of Jesus as contemplative dispels this completely. Underlying many of the sayings of Jesus recorded by the Synoptists are implicit, and *absolutely requisite*, precisely the inner prayer-processes of the Johannine Christ. In St. John's Gospel we see Jesus from within to the without ; in the Synoptists we see Jesus from without to the within : but the more deeply we penetrate both, the more inescapably are we confronted with identity of personality. The Johannine Christ and the Christ of the Synoptists—it is the same Jesus : Jesus as He Himself was ; even though the angle of delineation, in the wisdom of the Holy Spirit, is different.

The contemplation of Jesus was primarily and essentially union with God. But contemplative vision was the fruit of this union, and this vision in its turn was the source of ever fresh unitive adoration of God the Fount of all Truth and Light. His contemplative vision was a penetration of Truth eternal, spaceless, and timeless. The supernatural realities which He voiced *could* only have been unveiled to Him through contemplation. Union with the Father admitted Him within the Mind, Will, and purposes of the Father, and interpreted for Him all things according to their significance with the Father.

The Gospel narratives of Holy Week, taken in conjunction with one another, lay bare for us as much as sinners can ever understand or realise upon earth of His pure, contemplative life and its fruits. In Holy Week, Jesus—in face of the earthly end He knew to be so near—was confronted by many pressing human problems. What was to become of the disciples—and how was the work to be carried on—without Him ? How could the disciples be best equipped against

His departure, and how enabled to spread the Gospel throughout the world and found the Christian Church ? Jesus knew with His whole being that in the last resort all fundamental human problems can only receive illumination in relation to their eternal Other-World setting, and not to their partial and incomplete earthly time-setting. In the Holy Week nights and silent Holy Wednesday of prayer these problems and many more—without any mental concentration upon *them*, but simply in contemplative adoration of the Father in His Wisdom and Omnipotent Love—were offered to the Father for His resolving. They were offered in an ecstasy of faith and rejoicing in the Father simply as being what He is. Through this Holy Week contemplation, which cannot be divorced from all the life-time of contemplation preceding it, was vouchsafed to our Lord the full vision of Pentecost and of the Mission of the Holy Spirit, and of the perennial Life-givingness for all time of that most Blessed Sacrament of His Own Body and Blood, whose Institution—together with His Holy Thursday discourses—was brought to birth through His contemplative abandonment in the Holy Spirit to union with the Father.

His contemplative penetration of Truth embraced :

(*a*) The Person of the Father ;

(*b*) His own Person and Vocation ;

(*c*) The Person and Mission of the Holy Spirit ;

(*d*) The Other Side ; and the Kingdom of Consummated Love.

Jesus Himself said : " Not that any man hath seen [ἑώρακεν, perfect tense of ὁράω, a verb used in ' durative ' sense] the Father, save He which is from God, [Gk. here indicates ' source or origin '] He hath seen [ἑώρακεν] the Father " (Jn. vi. 46). This statement clearly affirms nothing less than our Lord's absolutely unique fontal union with the Father, and His equally unique vision of the Father resulting from that union. The Greek perfect tense has " as much to do with present as with past time, since it describes the present result of a past action. The perfect tense does not occur very frequently in the New Testament. Its use denotes that the action of the verb is to be regarded as brought to its appropriate conclusion at the time of speaking in such a way that its results still remain in action."

Since this is so, the fact underlying these words of our Lord's is a fontal-union vision of the Father : a vision complete and perfect at His very origination—' past ' so far as time is concerned because before time, and equally ' present ' in time because eternally ' durative '. Yet this vision, though complete and perfect, was not static, being the vision of the Source of Life, i.e. Love ever newly fresh. This vision was an established fact, but also an eternal and progressive continuity. Received by our Lord in His Godhead glory with the Father before the world was, it was an inherent part of Himself which could not be lost—nor lapse— in His Incarnate Personality being the Eternal Word made flesh. The source and culmination of all His contemplation was simply and solely this : " I and the Father are one " (Jn. x. 30). The Will of the Father was to Jesus—as He waited upon Him—an open book.

All this is as explicit in the Synoptists as in the Fourth Gospel, although they forgo the Johannine attempt to penetrate the interior processes of our Lord's mind and spirit whereby He was enabled to receive, and then declare, the truths which they are content merely to give in His words— and accept as facts—without systematically investigating the inner life and foundation from which they have sprung, the growth whereby they have come to light. It is the *Synoptists* who record these words of His : " All things are delivered unto Me of My Father ; and no man knoweth the Son, but the Father ; neither knoweth any man the Father, save the Son, and he to whomsoever the Son will reveal Him " (Matt. xi. 27 ; cf. Lk. x. 22) ; and also : " Even so it is not the will of your Father which is in heaven, that one of these little ones should perish " (Matt. xviii. 14). They are as unmistakably pronounceable only by a contemplative as any of the most ' mystical ' of the Johannine sayings.

Inundated by Love, a holocaust to Love—Love the Be-getter of His Person, the Initiator of His vocation—crystal clear understanding of Himself and a supernatural vision of His vocation progressively emerged for Him from His contemplative union with the Father of Love, Light, and Truth. Gradually there unfolded within His soul that *knowledge*—altogether independent of physical, or even of intellectual, ' seeing '—which is the ' seeing ' of the inner-most spirit. Contemplative vision (i.e. apprehension of truth) made known to Him that " the Father had given all things into His hands, and that He came forth from God, and goeth unto God " (Jn. xiii. 3).

St. John (vii. 37 f.) records for us one of the incidents of our Lord's public ministry whose SUPERLATIVENESS is easy to miss in the utter restraint of his language.   " Now on the last day, the great day of the feast "—Jerusalem seething with myriads of pilgrims : a spectacle to bring inescapably to mind, as does every great crowd, the infinitesimalness of the individual over against the multitudinousness of countless mankind—" Jesus stood and cried, saying, If any man thirst, let him come unto Me, and drink. He that believeth on Me, as the scripture hath said, out of his belly shall flow rivers of living waters." A single man, not dwarfed by a host, but stimulated by it to a prodigality of proffered sharing of the upsurging, almost it would seem superfluous, life within Him. No sane human daring could have asserted anything so palpably humanly impossible. Such an offer of inexhaustible and universally satisfying life could never have been prompted by anything less than interior recogni-tion of Himself as both unique Son of God, God Who is Life, and unique Son of Man, Man created by God to be the recipient of eternal Life ; and such a recognition could never have taken root and flowered within Him save in the soil of His contemplative union with the Father.

His contemplative vision was a supernatural revelation against all standards of human expectancy, as He himself bore witness : " For verily the Son of Man came not to be ministered unto, but to minister, and to give His life a ransom for many " (Mk. x. 45). In two other supreme utterances He voiced the almost humanly incredible supernatural revelation of the fruits of His fulfilled vocation as learned by Him from the Father :

" And I, if I be lifted up from the earth, will draw all men unto Myself " (Jn. xii. 32) : His contemplative vision of the eternal magnetism of the Cross ; and

" He that believeth on Me the works that I do shall he do also ; and greater works than these shall he do ; because I go unto the Father " (Jn. xiv. 12) : His contemplative fore-vision of the ultimate development of His High-Priestly vocation at its most limitless as exercised ' from above ' after the Ascension.

Our Lord's incarnate abandonment in the Holy Spirit to contemplative union with the Father issued in such an interpenetration of Being between Father, Son, and Holy Spirit, as to reveal to Him the Holy Spirit as His own *Alter Ego*, the Father's Vindicator, Fructifier, and Continuator of His own earthly life, ministry, and death, in His Body, the Church.

On the eve of His death our Lord told His disciples : " In My Father's house are many mansions " (Jn. xiv. 2). This—like every other truth He ever declared—was spoken out of experiential knowledge. He knew of these mansions by personal penetration into them during His homing to the Father in contemplative union, which temporarily freed Him from time into Eternity and took Him even before death Across to the Other Side. His knowledge of the *many* mansions presupposes not merely one such taking Across, but a number ; since the spirit's ' showings ' and ' hearings ' are most apt to come as *single* illuminations with only one newly unveiled truth upsoaring at a time, so as to impress itself indelibly for time and eternity. Glimpses of these penetrations are recorded equally in the Synoptists as in St. John.

Jesus' insight into the life on the Other Side was so intense

that He was able to—and on a number of occasions did—
share it with His disciples. Not only had He insight into
this life on the Other Side, but He had the closest affinity
and intercourse with it whilst still on earth. God's way in
human extremity being always to send help in the precise
personal way in which it can most readily be appropriated,
His sending angels to minister to Jesus in the Wilderness, and
in the Garden of His Agony, points to His previous fellowship
of creative spiritual union with them in His Father's
mansions.

Jesus had, as a child, heard from His Mother how the
Angel Gabriel had before His birth prophesied of Him that
" . . . the Lord God shall give unto Him the throne of His
father David : and He shall reign over the house of Jacob
for ever ; and of His kingdom there shall be no end." After
His miraculous feeding of the five thousand the people were
desirous of taking Him by force to make Him their king.
We dare not, and cannot, try to reconstruct the way in
which on that night, alone in prayer, He received from His
Father the illumination He was so urgently forced to seek as
to the exact nature of His promised kingdom.

But that there was given Him an interior vision of it is
shown us by St. John (xviii. 36) : a vision so transcendent
that even at the end of His life He could do no more in
human words than veil the inner core of it behind a negative
hint—" My Kingdom is not of this world : if My kingdom
were of this world, then would My servants fight, that I
should not be delivered to the Jews : but now is My kingdom
not from hence." This hint to Pilate was in the negative,
but the vision as received by Him was essentially creative ;
and to receive it He needs must have been taken through
contemplative prayer right out to the Other Side, His body
remaining on the mountain-side, His spirit freed from space
and time into Eternity, i.e. the Ocean of Love imperishable
and immortal. Thus rapt in communion with the Father,
He was caught up into the vision of His promised kingdom
as the Kingdom of consummate Love Invincible.

One of the most striking things about His contemplative vision was its utter and consistent unshakableness in face of all human-seeming calamity and contradiction. The secret of His conscious poise lay in His *knowledge* of His real Nature and Personality—and the purposes of the Incarnation—having their source, continuance, and goal in the Being and Glory of the Father. In the dawn hours of Good Friday He declared to the chief priests and scribes in council : " Hereafter [Gk. = henceforth] shall the Son of Man sit on the right hand of the power of God " (Lk. xxii. 69). *What* a vision of this He must needs have had to give Him the titanic interior assurance necessary to enable Him to pronounce these words that cold dawn ! Humanly everything was against Him : cold and dawn ever demoralising to physical and mental energy and the confidence born of them ; inveterate and undisguised hostility determinedly set on His destruction and having all predominance of human power on its side ; all the literally terrific cumulative emotional strain of the Last Supper, the Agony, the desertion of the disciples and His denial by Peter ; His whole human energies being well-nigh drained to the dregs. Yet unassailable both from without and from within, He maintained His Eternity vision in time against all the machinations of earth and hell, senses and appearances.

Equally as striking as the unshakableness of His contemplative vision was the absolute human LONELINESS in which He had both to enjoy and to travail in obedience to it. During His earthly life-time before the Pentecostal coming of the Holy Spirit as Illuminator, never was there one—not even His Mother nor the Beloved Disciple—who was able to enter at all fully into understanding of the truths to Him so inescapably and manifestly all-in-all in Reality and Life-givingness. This complete lack of human sharing in any real understanding of the depth and height of His vision must, in human loneliness, for Him—so uniquely sensitive to, and understanding of, the innermost thoughts, aspirations, and visions of others—have entailed one long-drawn series of sword-pierces beyond our power to conceive. The measure of His continuing unwaveringly to hold fast to this vision, in the absence of *any* eye-to-eye, soul-to-soul human companionship in it, is proof of the precise measure of His contemplative identification with the intense unity and livingness of the inextinguishable Life of the Holy Trinity, ever reproductive of Love—Love that was the source and fulfilment of His whole Being.

His contemplative prayer was an immersing of Himself through the Holy Spirit in the Father ; the most intensely *personal* mingled activity and passivity conceivable ; but the fruit of it—far from being merely individual as between Himself and the Father—was universally penetrative and all-embracing. The supreme " apostolate by contemplation " was that of Jesus : " No man hath seen God at any time ; the only begotten Son, which is in the bosom of the Father, He hath declared [Gk. = interpret, unfold] Him " (Jn. i. 18). The contemplative union of Jesus with His Father has *given* the Father to all mankind—' given ' in the sense of making available. It reflected the Father's Very Self in such a way as potentially to enable men to apprehend Him as He is in truth—which after the Fall they could never of themselves have done—and to stimulate their desire to be made one with Him, the All-Lovable as well as All-Loving, through progressive union with His Son ever indissolubly united to Him in the Holy Spirit.

Prayer in the Communion of Saints and Angels

The Transfiguration is a mystery magnetic and mysteriously glorious indeed, like the mysteries of the Crucifixion, Resurrection, and Ascension : and so, " many have taken in hand " to try in some measure to interpret it. But for all that has been written about it, it would seem that one aspect throwing much—perhaps most—light upon the inner life of Jesus has but been somewhat superficially taken for granted, and its real inwardness overlooked, or at least insufficiently explored. This aspect is the presence and part in the mystery of Moses and Elijah, who are usually regarded simply as " representatives of the Law and the Prophets ".

Representative of Law and Prophecy, Moses and Elijah certainly are ; but it is incidental to the mystery of the Transfiguration, and cannot be dismissed as the sum significance, even purely as regards their own share in it. Mere ' representativeness ' is too abstract to be the core of such a unique mystery. At the bed-rock heart of every spiritual experience there must always be the intensely personal element, because of the love-flaming Personality of God its source. Moses and Elijah participated in the Transfiguration as their own *individual* selves, in virtue of their personal relation, not to the body of the Law, nor to the school of the Prophets, but to Jesus Himself. Their appearing in glory and conversing with Him was not a mere external episodic expression, in spiritual crisis, of " witness to Jesus as the Messiah " ; but the unitive outcome of a life-affinity which—in the vocation of revelation of God to Man, and the reconciliation of Man to God—our Lord sensed with Moses and Elijah.

This affinity between our Lord and Moses, and Elijah, must first have been kindled to consciousness for Him through His study of the Scriptures, whence it emerged for Him experientially as so strikingly close as to be a creative and revealing factor for His own inner life. The vocations of Moses and Elijah as they unfolded in meditation before Him, in their striking analogies to His own, must have come to Him as a mine of comfort and illumination, as pointing direct from the Father upon the path that He Himself must follow. Not only *before* He embarked upon His public ministry were Moses and Elijah instructive and inspiring to Him ; but often afterwards, events in their lives must gradually have mediated fresh comfort in the light of developing events in His own.

The vocation of Moses—as His own, too, proved to be— taken as a whole, was an ever-swaying alternation between the glory of God's unfolding Self-revelation and Will, and

ceaseless human travail and suffering on behalf of, and
at the hands of, the people to whom God sent him.   Jesus
must have found both ample encouragement and warning
in Moses' fulfilment of his vocation, as in prayer He steeped
Himself in it so that it became to Him as present, living
reality.   No mere historical record can the life of Moses
have been to our Lord ; but a soul-drama which—in deeply
intensified and transcended measure—was being re-enacted
in His own Person.

Much in prayer was deeply common to our Lord and
Moses.   The revelation of God given to Moses in the mount ;
and our Lord often seeking to the hills in His God-revealing
prayer.   All the vision that Moses received of worship, in
connection with the Tabernacle and the Ark, was the stirring
to birth of the vision of consummated worship apprehended
by our Lord : ". . . the hour cometh when neither in this
mountain, nor in Jerusalem, shall ye worship the Father.
. . . But the hour cometh, and now is, when the true worshippers shall worship the Father in spirit and truth . . ."
(Jn. iv. 21–23).

But in *intercession* was the deepest bond.   Surely
through the unfolding of Moses' intercessory ministry (e.g.
Ex. xxxii 30–32 ; Deut. ix. 18 ff.) the Father gradually
bespoke to the young Jesus—with the gamut of prayer still
to learn in all its fulness—the inner meaning and conditions
of intercession.   Through Moses' achievement God must
have pointed Him a far-transcending ideal of vicarious
penitence, sacrificial self-oblation and pleading of righteousness, which was eventually to culminate in nothing less than
an Eternal High-Priestly intercession, ceaselessly pleading
before the Father the one and only " full, perfect and
sufficient sacrifice, oblation and satisfaction for the sins of
the whole world".   Jesus' faith in the potency of such
intercessory prayer must have been kindled by the repeated
efficacy of Moses' prayer-intervention for the sinful and
rebellious (e.g. Num. xi. 1–2 ; xii. 13–14).

Through meditation on the record of the life of Elijah,

and its spiritual extension in that of Elisha, the Father
must have opened up altogether new vistas to the boy
Jesus : bringing the supernatural into practical relationship
and harmony with the natural for the effecting of God's
purposes, and giving Him an inexhaustible vision of the limitless Divine resources of spiritual law transcending, but not
contradicting, natural law.

Our Lord must have felt an innate oneness with Elijah,
the " solitary prophet" belonging to no prophetic settlement
nor company, whose office was grounded simply and solely
in his personal relationship and response to God—" As the
Lord God of Israel liveth, before Whom I stand "—a
relationship of vital communion with God : a ministry of
obedience ever in His Presence.

The story of Elijah's raising from the dead the widow's
son by prayer was provocative witness to Jesus of the power
of prayer to achieve the humanly impossible in life-giving
renewal and comfort to others : and much meditation on
this must have preceded His own miracles of raising the
dead.

Elijah's moral courage in bringing to a head, on Mount
Carmel, the spiritual issue between the worship of Jehovah
and of Baal, with all the human odds against him and in
spiritual loneliness, must have been to our Lord an inspiring
prefiguration of His own setting His face toward Jerusalem,
deliberately to force the spiritual issue of all time—" Now is
the judgment of this world", through the inescapable choice
to be made between Him and " the prince of this world".

The taking up of Elijah by the whirlwind into heaven,
and the bestowal of a double portion of his spirit upon
Elisha, must have given our Lord infinite food for meditation, and thrown light upon the final training-goal for His
disciples ; and it would extend His affinity with Elijah to
Elisha also—an inextricable spiritual unity.

The story of the deadly pottage, rendered harmless by
Elisha's casting meal into the pot, must have been used by
the Father to open up to the boy Jesus the whole vision of

transmutation of death into life, of sin into holiness—which became the substance of His ministry in time and in Eternity.

But Moses and Elijah were not mere historical prototypes to our Lord : not even analogous experiences of spirit and ministry exhaust the link. The link was a conscious living personal relationship in the Communion of Saints : for Him humanly an *attrait* given by the Father for Kingdom purposes. Having passed through death, the eyes of Moses and Elijah must have been opened to the vision of the Messiah, Who should crown their labours by saving His people and perfecting the worship of God. *How*, and with what *understanding*, must Moses, who suffered so oppressively at the hands of those whom he was called to lead out of Egypt (Num. xi. 11), have prayed for Him Who should bear the sins of the whole world, and give His own flesh to be the life of Man. Inevitably the prayer of Moses and Elijah ' from above ' must have drawn Him into a vital spiritual relationship with them ; and often must He have been conscious not only of inspiration from their earthly ministry, but mediation from their heavenly ministry also. Their appearing and conversing with Him at the Transfiguration was, though supernatural, yet a natural consummation of a lifelong communing of spirit. It is an enrichment to realise our Incarnate Lord's prayer anchorage in the Communion of Saints, as well as in individual union with the Father.

It is at least deeply thought-provoking—for those to whom the ministry of Angels is not a consciously, or at any rate easily, recognised reality—to realise how vital was the bond between our Lord and Angels. As a child He must have been drawn to them in reverent wonder and awed thanksgiving, when told by His Mother of the part played by them in connection with His birth and infancy ; in pre-natal prophecy which revealed Him as Son of God, Eternal King, and Saviour of the world ; in worship ; and in warning, preservation, and guidance for His young life.

Was not the dominant desire of His whole life—simply to glorify the Father at all times, in all places, and in everything—in all probability consciously kindled by the unutterable thrill with which He first heard His Mother continue her account of the appearance of the Angel of the Lord to the shepherds on the night of His birth : " And suddenly there was with the Angel a multitude of the heavenly host, praising God, and saying, Glory to God in the highest . . ." ? How often throughout His earthly life He must have passed through individual and corporate worship in time into the worship of Eternity, as freshly and deliberately He identified Himself with the multitude of the heavenly host ceaselessly praising God for Himself and for Love's redemption of the world.

In His contemplative vision of His consummated Kingdom He knew the Angels—whom alternatively He described as " the Angels of God " and as Angels of the Son of Man— to be actively associated with Him in bringing that Kingdom to perfection for the Father : ". . . so shall it be in the end of the world. The Son of Man shall send forth His angels, and they shall gather out of His Kingdom all things that cause stumbling . . ." (Matt. xiii. 40–41 ; cf. xxiv. 31 : " He shall send forth His angels . . . and they shall gather together His elect from the four winds, from one end of heaven to the other ").

As contemplatively He foreknew the Angels to be fellow-workers with Him in His heavenly prayer-ministry, so experientially He knew them to be such also in His earthly prayer-ministry : both in personal spiritual refreshing and strengthening to Himself in His offering in the Wilderness the prayer of resistance to temptation, and in the Garden the prayer of desire perfectly to drain the Father's Cup ; and in common contemplative intercession for others. He told His disciples (Matt. xviii. 10), " See that ye despise not one of these little ones ; for I say unto you, that in heaven their angels do always behold [βλέπουσι = *look at*, see] the face of My Father which is in heaven "—the Angels beholding always, not the little ones, but God ; guarding and ministering to them by their worship of God, and by worshipping Him on behalf of the little ones as well as on their own, and not by vigilance over the little ones on the purely personal human plane.

He knew the Angels' worship and obedience to be a constituent part of the Glory of the Father, and as such must often have flung His whole Being into uniting with them in it.

Worship through Beauty (already touched on in " The Out-of-doors element in His prayer ", see pp. 42 ff)

There was always awe and wonder, as well as joy, in our Lord's innate response to Beauty ; because unfailingly He pierced through all perceptible Beauty to the immanent— and yet at the same time transcendent—Loveliness of its Divine Artist-Creator, Whose partial Self-expression He recognised it to be.

No Beauty ever escaped Him.   Fleeting or prolonged, on miniature or panoramic scale, mattered not ; it drew His whole Being to the Father in a fresh surge of *reverence* as well as of love.   Each new discernment of Beauty so swept soul, heart, and mind as a fresh baptism of Love and Holiness that He was impelled to offer to the Father in adoration not Himself only, but also the whole earth with each and all of its myriad inhabitants.

Beauty was for Him ever a sacrament of unity.   He beheld in it the all-embracing mantle of God's universal Love enfolding all creatures, whether they were conscious— or desirous—of it as His or not.   He experienced in the heart of Beauty, expulsive of all consciousness of self and time, that nest of Eternity where Man truly finds and is found of God : God as Life and Peace, and Man as He created him to be—incorporated in Himself through worship.

Beauty was for Him the great Stiller.   Beauty, evanescent in time, was yet Eternity's antidote to the sin and human

tumult ever clamant around Him on earth.   Perceptible
Beauty was for Him the Spirit's earnest that Light can never
be finally engulfed by Darkness : that Holiness alone has
enduring reality.

In His utter purity—by His ' single ' eye—He was able
to enter through the veil of perceptible Beauty to that which
constitutes it, i.e. the Very Self of God Who Himself is
Beauty.   Time and again, trees, hills, sea, sky, stars, flowers,
colour, even a single leaf, must have *thrust* upon Him their
transparent theophany of their Creator.   Worshipping
through them He could only exult experientially : " Blessed
are the pure in heart : for they shall see God "—be thrill-
ingly one with Him, spellbound in a reverence that dare not
approach, let alone touch, the almost humanly unbearable
sacredness of the material Beauty enwrapping Him.

In all the processes of Nature, the ways of bird and beast,
which Jesus watched with such deep, assimilative appreciation and delight, He perceived the rhythmic Beauty of purposive design ; and worshipped the Wisdom of God in it all.

His response to Beauty was never self-indulgence in a
barren emotion, as is shown by the light which He Himself
threw on His whole æsthetic experience : " Consider the
lilies, how they grow: they toil not, neither do they spin ;
yet I say unto you, Even Solomon in all his glory was not
arrayed like one of these.   But if God doth so clothe the
grass in the field, which to-day is, and to-morrow is cast into
the oven ; how much more shall He clothe you, O ye of
little faith ? " (Lk. xii. 27–28 ; cf. Matt. vi. 28–29).   His
was disciplined meditation upon perceptible Beauty, until
He passed beyond mere initial " contour in feeling " to
apprehend *and express* the further depths of Beauty hidden
beneath external Loveliness.

Every faculty of His spirit, mind, and heart combined by
true appreciation to appropriate all God-created Beauty, so
that He could offer it back as a gift to the Father in worship.
But not only was He *receptive* to every particle of Beauty
created by the Father ; He was also stimulated by it to a

counterpart creation of His own of Beauty of thought, word, and deed to be offered as homage to God, the *Lover* as well as creator of Beauty. The innermost core of His worship through Beauty was His never letting Himself—in the power of the Holy Spirit—be or do anything that was less than perfectly beautiful, i.e. " full of grace ". So in Beauty His incarnate life was moulded and offered as a consistent, responsive, and progressive harmony with the Eternal Beauty of the Father ; the *simplicity* that is Beauty's heart being His too.

Prayer of Thanksgiving

The Gospels record a few instances of our Lord's verbal thanksgiving : these are simply the overflowing of an interior thankfulness habitually permeating every fibre of His Being. His thankfulness never fluctuated, because it was based, not upon temporal circumstances, but upon the Eternal Being of God and all pertaining to His omnipotent Will, all-holy, all-loving, and all-wise, the *sole* ultimately unassailable ground for thankfulness existent. This ground of thankfulness was to our Lord all-satisfying to the extent of outweighing anything and everything humanly adverse. Hence His thanksgiving often overflowed at the precise times when all on the human plane was most discouraging, simply because it welled up from His boundless confidence in the Father for Whom He knew no obstacle could ever possess any enduring reality, let alone insuperability.

To Jesus human odds were—in proportion to their intensity—*exhilarating* rather than depressing, because He recognised them as a touchstone evoking and proving the invincibleness of the Father's love and power and, as such, a vital contributory factor towards the glorifying of God which was His fundamental concern. The root thankfulness which He unbrokenly reposed in the Being of the Father overflowed into thankfulness for the share given to Himself in that Being, and in the Mind and Operations of the Father. His very disposition of thankfulness was in itself

a prayer : a prayer of worship and joyous laudation of the
All-in-Allness of the Father.

Jesus Himself, in one of His precepts, throws upon His
prayer of thanksgiving a flood of light which is so intensely
practical and creative an inspiration for all who try to pray
—however diverse the medium of their prayer—that it is
essential here to penetrate it as far and as fully as may be,
even although it necessarily involves forestalling something
of what rightfully belongs to the later section dealing with
our Lord as teacher.

All that Jesus taught on prayer came out of His own experience ; and therefore His, " When thou prayest, enter
into thine inner chamber, and having shut thy door, pray to
thy Father which is in secret . . ." (Matt. vi. 6), illustrates
one of the principles of His own prayer-practice.   The Greek
word ταμεῖον (tameion), translated ' inner chamber ', means
literally a storehouse or treasury ; and taken in this light
the fact that *treasure* is one of the foremost running-thread
ideas unifying all our Lord's teaching is surely very pregnant.
Again and again He returns with such emphasis to the idea
of ' treasure '—and always infusing into it such practical
and eternal import—that it is well to assemble His diffused
' treasure ' teaching, in order more easily to realise in visual
juxtaposition its *cumulative* significance :

" Lay not up for yourselves treasures upon the earth,
where moth and rust doth consume, and where thieves
break through and steal : but lay up for yourselves treasures
in heaven, where neither moth nor rust doth consume, and
where thieves do not break through nor steal : for where thy
treasure is, there will thy heart be also " (Matt. vi. 19–21 ;
cf. Lk. xii. 33–34 : " . . . make for yourselves purses which
wax not old, a treasure in the heavens that faileth not . . .").

" The good man out of the treasure of his heart bringeth
forth that which is good, and the evil man out of the evil
treasure bringeth forth that which is evil : for out of the
abundance of the heart his mouth speaketh " (Lk. vi. 45 ;
cf. Matt. xii. 35).

" The kingdom of heaven is like unto a treasure hidden in the field [in His immediately preceding parable our Lord Himself interpreted " the field is the world "] which a man found, and hid ; and in his joy he goeth and selleth all that he hath, and buyeth that field " (Matt. xiii. 44).

" . . . Therefore every scribe who hath been made a disciple to the kingdom of heaven is like unto a man that is a householder, which bringeth forth out of his treasure things new and old " (Matt. xiii. 52).

" So is he that layeth up treasure for himself and is not rich toward God "' (Lk. xii. 21) was His summing up of His parable of the rich fool suddenly cut off in the midst of his worldly possessions.

[To the rich young man He said :] " One thing thou lackest : go, sell whatsoever thou hast, and give to the poor, and thou shalt have treasure in heaven : and come, follow Me " (Mk. x. 21).

In this connection the parable of the " man that sowed good seed in his field " (Matt. xiii. 24–30) is illuminating in the original.   The evangelist introduces it by : " Another parable set He before them. . . ".   The Greek verb translated ' set before ' means also a ' storing up ; a storing of provision'.   Our Lord was therefore designedly adding to the disciples' spiritual *equipment* in this parable, which He concluded by putting on to the lips of the owner of the field these words : " . . . and in the time of harvest I will say to the reapers, Gather up first the tares and bind them in bundles to burn them : but gather the wheat into my barn " [Gk. = storehouse].

It is abundantly evident that the ' treasure ' idea occupied a prominent place in our Lord's spiritual economy ; and with His unique meditative powers of penetrating the heart of the Scriptures He must, with joy, have made His own Malachi's rarely beautiful verse (iii. 10) : " Bring ye all the tithes into the storehouse, that there may be meat in mine house, and prove me now herewith, saith the Lord of Hosts, if I will not open you the windows of heaven, and pour you out a blessing, that there shall not be room enough to receive it."

"When thou prayest, [Gk. here emphasises worship rather than petition] enter into thine inner chamber . . ." ; for Him prayer was never something which had in cold-blooded travail to be created almost as though for the first time at each fresh 'turning to prayer'. It was rather a *continuity* : a withdrawal into something already created and therefore enduring—a withdrawal into already accumulated and imperishable spiritual treasure—to reach out farther from thence to God. All past prayer and spiritual experience was the single springboard from whence in the present His thankful soul—in surety of the eternal continuity of Love—took jubilant flight in the Holy Spirit to the Father.

Our Lord allowed no special value nor interest to His thoughts and experiences solely on the ground that they were *His*. He never indulged in introspection for its own sake. His spiritual experiences were never analysed by self for its own ends ; but because they were part of an abiding treasure to be utilised for the glory of God, and in trust for others, He deliberately extracted exhaustive individual and cumulative value out of them by methodical meditation.

All life's diverse experiences, emotions, and thoughts— which for so many continue to remain chaotically and insensately disconnected—He integrated within His prayer of unifying thanksgiving. In imperturbable thanksgiving for the Being and Will of God He attained to the coherence and significance in all things, both interior and exterior. He could not help being in love with life *altogether irrespective of human circumstances and feelings* because He perceived it— life itself—as a treasure, as a pearl of great price ; because originating and flowing from the Father Uncreate it is none other, both in time and eternity, than the Adorable Father willing, and progressively enabling, all creatures, all creation, to become a living unity in His inexhaustibly Glorious Self.

Our Lord's prayer of thanksgiving is illuminated by the conclusion of the Sermon on the Mount. "Every one there-

fore which heareth these words of Mine, and doeth them,
shall be likened unto a wise [Gk. = understanding, thought-
ful, practically—in contradistinction to theoretically—wise]
man, which built his house upon the rock : and the rain
descended, and the floods came, and the winds blew, and
beat upon that house ; and it fell not : for it was founded
upon the rock " (Matt. vii. 24–25) : the spiritual life a house
to be *built*—this, too, was experiential to our incarnate Lord
Himself.   On the rock of the Father—Whose Will and Self
He ' declared ' in the Sermon on the Mount—He raised *in
thankfulness* His own spiritual edifice, gradually consolidat-
ing it, harmonising it, unifying it by progressive interpretation of His experiences, and building new truths into the
whole.

At any given moment He knew precisely what He had
available in His storehouse to glorify God—or to meet the
needs of Man—according to that moment's circumstances.
His storehouse was carefully kept in order.   As a ' householder ' He could at any time, by force of habitual self-
discipline in regard to the material with which life furnished
Him, instinctively bring forth out of His *treasure*—His storehouse—things both new and old.   Neither the serving of
their initial purpose, nor personal benefit to Himself, exhausted for our Lord the potential value of any of the
Father's gifts : He held the *essence* of each as a perpetual
trust—to be used again whensoever, for whomsoever, the
Father might require it.

A rough inventory of our Lord's *tameion*—His storehouse,
His treasury—would include treasure both ' natural ' and
' supernatural'.   Seeing how often and how deeply He Himself must have dwelt upon it, it is good for us to set it before
our own eyes also :

Our Lord's Tameion
' Natural '

His Mother : all it meant as a child and through life to have
such a Mother, and to be brought up from His earliest

conscious memory in the knowledge of God. The ideal
of womanhood personified for Him in His Mother.

Joseph : all that lay behind his ability—after abandonment
to God in his spiritual furnace—to reflect so purely
the Fatherhood of God.

The Scriptures : their power to reveal God ; to quell
temptation ; and to interpret His vocation.

Corporate worship in synagogue and Temple.

His innate sense of Vocation.

Human friendships.

The Beauty of Nature.

His powers and life of labour.

Soundness of body, mind, and spirit : a balanced temperament.

' Supernatural '

All the facts in connection with :

  His Birth.

  His Presentation.

  The Visit of the Wise Men.

  The Massacre of the Innocents.

  The Flight into Egypt.

  The Return to Nazareth.

His Prayer-Union with the Father.

John the Baptist's Recognition of Him as " the Lamb of
God".

His Baptism : the opening of the heavens, the descent of
the Spirit of God upon Him ; the Father's seal upon His
Divine Sonship.

His Eternal Vocation.

Fellowship in the Communion of Saints and Angels.

The Angelic Ministry after His Temptation in the Wilderness.

His Miraculous Powers.

His Power to Forgive Sins.

" All things are delivered unto Me of My Father."

" The Father loveth the Son, and sheweth Him all things
that Himself doeth."

7

His Kingdom " not of this world".

Peter's Cæsarea Philippi Confession of Him infused by the
Father : " Thou art the Christ, the Son of the living God."

The Transfiguration.

" I am not alone, but I and the Father that sent Me."

" Ye are from beneath ; *I am from above* : ye are of this
world ; *I am not of this world.*"

His Stainless Conscience of Utter Sinlessness : " I do
always the things that are pleasing to Him."

" . . . the truth, which I heard from God."

" Before Abraham was, I am."

" Father, glorify Thy name. Then came a voice from
heaven, saying, I have both glorified it, and will glorify
it again."

His foreknowledge of His Resurrection.

" Father . . . I knew that Thou hearest Me always."

The Last Supper.

His foreknowledge of His power to send the Holy Spirit to
His disciples after His death.

" The Cup which the Father hath given . . ." ; Bethlehem
to Calvary in time ; glory to glory in Eternity before and
after time.

" Though He were a Son [impassible Pre-existent Son of
God] yet learned He obedience by the things which
[incarnate] He suffered."

" . . . the glory which I had with Thee before the world
was . . . for Thou lovedst Me before the foundation of
the world."

The Angelic strengthening in the Garden of the Agony.

On one of the numerous occasions of the disciples' misunderstanding of His teaching, our Lord said to them : " Do
ye not yet perceive, neither understand ? have ye your
heart hardened ? Having eyes, see ye not ? and having
ears, hear ye not ? and do ye not remember ? When I brake
the five loaves among the five thousand, how many baskets
full of broken pieces took ye up ? They say unto Him,

Twelve. And when the seven among the four thousand, how many basketfuls of broken pieces took ye up ? And they say unto Him, Seven. And He said unto them, Do ye not yet understand ? " (Mk. viii. 17–21.) He clearly wished them, like the " wise man " building on rock, meditatively to take intelligent stock of past spiritual experience *from the objective side* so as in its light—light always of the Love and Power of God—to interpret aright the present. Surely He would have us too each take grateful stock of our own individual *tameion*—the storehouse of treasure—entrusted to us. To attempt this is more creative and sustaining for the entire prayer-life than could ever be imagined until it is seriously, thoughtfully, and prayerfully undertaken at leisure

Our Lord's prayer of thanksgiving was a seeing *everything* as potential ' treasure ' within the one central, all-embracing TREASURE of the Father's Self.

Prayer of Joy

On the Return of the Seventy from their successful Mission, Jesus " rejoiced [Gk. = rejoice *exceedingly*, and has the connotation of great joy, exultation, transport of joy] in the Holy Spirit, and said, I thank Thee, O Father, . . . for so it was well-pleasing in Thy sight " (Lk. x. 21). Here is disclosed for us the essence of our Lord's prayer of joy in time and in eternity : His selfless delight in the satisfaction of the Father. His incarnate joy was the flower of the Holy Spirit's interpretation of all temporal things in eternal terms of the Being, Mind, and purposes of the Father. His prayer of joy, so variously evoked and expressed, was fundamentally the realisation and ecstatic acknowledgment—offered to God as worship—that all things *save sin alone* express God and serve for His satisfaction ; and that even sin must of necessity be finally annihilated by His Love and Holiness, and in its very annihilation glorify Him.

Sensibility to joy and sensibility to pain are in direct ratio to one another ; and so consequently just as He, the most sensitive human being who ever lived, plumbed uniquely and exhaustively the depths of suffering, so too He scaled uniquely and exhaustively the pinnacles of joy.

He was singularly responsive to all joy—both natural and supernatural—wherever and however it presented itself. This responsiveness was the outcome of the simplicity of a single nature which, free from self, intuitively divined loveliness or potential loveliness everywhere, and in everyone, and in everything.

He found great and ever-fresh joy in all natural Beauty ; and instinctively passed sheer through the human delight in it to deepened knowledge of—and union with—the Father, supremely satisfying and to be desired, Whose inexhaustibly lovely Mind Creation in some faint measure reflects.

He found unfailing joy in the natural zest and interest, as well as in the extreme SACREDNESS of life : life which He recognised as so purposeful, and infinite in promise in the Wisdom and Love of the Father.

He found untold joy in human friendship, and in all beauty of character, however diverse. He divined and appreciated every spark of human goodness, loveliness or lovableness, however hidden beneath other traits less worthy or attractive. His faith in the ultimate potentialities of holiness for each and every soul afforded Him joy so ceaseless and so vivid, that their present imperfections or vices—however ingrained or longstanding they might be—could never appear to Him irretrievable. His joy in men and women was a prayer of rejoicing *by faith* in the invincibleness of holiness and love : a prayer of denial of ultimate power or durability to sin and self and ugliness.

All His communion with the Father, and every aspect of His prayer-life, was irradiated by joy : joy altogether irrespective of the ceaseless momentary fluctuation between adverse and propitious human circumstances in which that prayer had to be initiated. Deeper even than any travail, agony, or storm of His spirit was its unquenchable joy—a joy not, however, by any means always *sensed* emotionally or even mentally. This indestructible joy was a perpetual prayer of CONFIDENCE : confidence in the Father's Self, and *certainty* in the face of all human appearances to the contrary that despite the Fall the end—as the beginning—of His Creation must, and will, be " very good " (Gen. i. 31. Gk. = exceedingly beautiful), i.e. exquisitely perfect and eternally satisfying. God's *re-perfecting* of His Creation was that " joy that was set before Him " for which He " endured the Cross, despising the shame " (Heb. xii. 2) : this joy which could only be consummated in Eternity, He made in time a prayer of faith unbrokenly glorifying God All-Potent and All-Merciful.

In our Lord's parable of the Talents, delivered towards the very end of His life, He gives as the climax of blessedness for all servants : " Enter thou into the joy of thy Lord " (Matt. xxv. 21) ; this was because He, " the Suffering Servant ", through perfect faithfulness in the work entrusted to Him, had Himself experienced this entry into the joy of His Father. What an experience ! Ponder it. To enter into the joy of the Father : the joy of Love utterly holy, utterly faithful, utterly selfless, absolutely *given* unreservedly, exhaustively to Love for the perpetual generation of more Love and fresh Beauty.

Our Lord said to His disciples : " If ye keep My commandments, ye shall abide in My love ; even as I have kept My Father's commandments, and abide in His love. These things have I spoken unto you, that My joy [i.e. joy founded upon obedience] may be in you, and that your joy may be fulfilled " (Jn. xv. 10–11). And again, in talking with them of His going to the Father : " . . . ye shall be sorrowful, but your sorrow shall be turned into joy . . . and your joy no one taketh from you " (Jn. xvi. 20–22). And incorporated in His supreme prayer—' the high-priestly prayer '—was the design for which admittedly He had striven : " that they may have My joy fulfilled in themselves " (Jn. xvii. 13). He could only have laid such stress on the desirability of joy, not as pleasure or mere antithesis of pain, but because

He recognised it as an intrinsic element in the Eternal
Being of the Father.   Our Lord's incarnate prayer of joy,
one with the essential joy of the Father, was Love's delight
in Love, Love's knowledge of Love's invincibility.

Prayer of Humility

St. Luke (ii. 51) records that after Mary and Joseph found
the twelve-year-old Jesus in the Temple with the doctors,
" He went down with them, and came to Nazareth ; and He
was subject unto them ".   What plenary humility is here
implicit.   He had just asked them in genuine amazement—
born of His irresistible sense of divine union and call—" How
is it that ye sought Me ?   Wist ye not that I must be about
My Father's business ? "   Yet, possessed not only of a
deeper spiritual insight than theirs, but also of a dominant
consciousness of His sonship to *God* rather than to Man,
which might plausibly have been thought to exempt Him
from lesser human obligations, He voluntarily and deliberately set Himself under a continuing obedience precisely
to those whose vision—high though it was—fell short of His
own.   His immediate, unquestioning turning with Mary and
Joseph for a life of obedience to them in Nazareth was a
sublime act of humility, whose spontaneity could only have
sprung from a vein of humility already become habitual and
instinctive.

Humility was already ingrained in our Lord as a child
because it went back beyond time into Eternity : back to
that initial and supreme act of humility, source of sempi-
ternal humility in Him, wherein with the free and deliberate
assent of His whole Being He gave His " FIAT "—" So let it
be "—to the Father's Will for His Incarnation.   (Our every
breathing of " Thy Will be done " should be in union with—
and the echo of—this perfect " Fiat " of His.)   It was a profundity of humility that no mortal can ever begin to fathom
that He, the Only-Begotten Son of God, Light of Light, Very
God of Very God, should have been willing to be ' sent '
from the glory which *in perfect equality with the Father* He

had shared with Him since before the foundation of the world to become Man ; that He should have been willing to exercise His divine freedom to assume the veil and limitations of flesh, and as a babe forgo—and only gradually *grow* back into—consciousness of that knowledge of God which through all Eternity He had already possessed.

What humility that He should have been willing to remain incarnate when " He was in the world, and the world was made by Him, and the world knew Him not " ; and have been content to keep veiled all that could have forced men to recognise the uniqueness of His glory and Person : that He should have chosen to dwell among men as distinct from them in no other way than in the excess of His love—finding its supreme voluntary expression in precisely those acts so lowly that no one else would perform them if able to avoid doing so—and in that habitual putting last and least of Self, in thought and word as well as deed, so alien to the innate pride of fallen Man. What humility, too, in His incarnate forgoing of all the unique advantages which were His divine prerogative, and in His choosing less rather than more of the ' natural ' advantages open to the average man, so as to live human life at its *hardest* and not at its most privileged and sheltered.

Humility was the subsoil of His entire incarnate life from Bethlehem to Calvary. His humility was at bottom a prayer of abandonment—begotten of sheer love of God—to the Will of " My Father . . . greater than I " ; and it was exercised concretely in countless different ways, e.g. : in submitting *sinless* to John's baptism of repentance—Love's vicarious offering to God for Man ; in His submitting Himself to temptation throughout His life, and so allowing the prince of this world to measure his forces with Him in Whom by right he " hath nothing " ; in submitting, sinless, to death the wages only of sin ; in His restraint in the use of His miraculous powers, never exploited even for the advancement of His cause, let alone for personal benefit ; in His public and reiterated emphasis on His own nothingness

apart from the Father ; in the deliberate *hiddenness* from
man of the heart of His prayer and fasting ; in His " Blessed
are the poor [Gk. = beggars] in spirit : for theirs is the
Kingdom of Heaven " (Matt. v. 3)—the experiential
acknowledgment of His incarnate spiritual poverty entirely
dependent on the liberality of the Father ; in His thinking
no one—be they notorious ' sinner ' or outcast—unworthy
of His closest friendship if they desired it ; in His willingness
to incur the odium of the ' religious ' and the ' respectable '
for His championing and companioning of those whom they
had ostracised ; in His unconcern with human opinion of
Him ; in His refusal to defend His human nature or justify
His incarnate actions by His divinity ; in His lifelong " I
am in the midst of you as He that serveth " (Lk. xxii. 27) ;
in His offering of His Resurrection Body to the self-chosen
testing of Thomas.

Nevertheless, His humility was *a continuous interior
disposition* rather than a series of ' acts ' of humility
expressed—however beautifully and incessantly—in deed
and word and aspiration.   " I am meek and lowly in heart "
became instinctive ' second nature ' to Him, and so in-
wrought was it by Him into the essence of His incarnate
personality that it was utterly unself-conscious.

Our Lord's humility issued, not from His relationship to
men : it was not a *human* offering to humanity ; but issued
as prayer from the consciousness of His relationship with
God, and was the expression of the Divine necessity of Love
ever to GIVE itself regardless of the human merits or status
of those to whom it gives.   A crowning instance of this was
the sublime prelude to the Institution of Love's Gift of Very
Body and Blood : " Jesus, knowing that the Father had
given all things into His hands ; and that He came forth
from God, and goeth unto God, riseth from supper, and
layeth aside His garments ; and He took a towel, and girded
Himself.   Then He poureth water into the bason, and began
to wash the disciples' feet, and to wipe them with the towel
wherewith He was girded " (Jn. xiii. 3 ff.).

Jesus' prayer of humility was a perpetual adoration of the Majesty of God ; it was also a perpetual self-oblation at the disposal of Man—" What wilt thou that I should do unto thee ? "—for the purposes of his redemption.

Prayer of Self-Denial ; Self-Discipline ; Endurance and Perseverance

Jesus never explicitly drew attention to His self-denial or self-discipline, and certainly never paraded it ; indeed, the reverse, since His enemies were able to charge Him—albeit falsely—with laxity. But in His recorded teaching and actions the Holy Spirit has laid bare the self-denial and self-discipline of Jesus as a reality so inexorable, so uncompromising and unremitting that none who really ponder it can—for the selfishness that is in them—help blenching before it, until of its everlasting Beauty and Power penitence and the desire to die to self are born.

In saying after saying in the teaching of Jesus, war to the death is relentlessly waged against self from one angle after another, until finally there is left simply no sanctuary for self at all. Since these sayings are not mere sayings nor theoretical precepts, but the white-hot, practical outcome of His own personal experience of warfare against self, they unfold—as nothing else could—His prayer of self-denial, self-discipline, endurance, and perseverance ; and for this reason it is good to have them set forth in their entirety as concentratedly as possible :

" And if thy right eye causeth thee to stumble [σκανδαλίζει. In N.T. this verb " always metaph. of that which hinders right conduct or thought "] pluck it out, and cast it from thee : for it is profitable for thee that one of thy members should perish, and not thy whole body be cast into hell. And if thy right hand causeth thee to stumble, cut it off, and cast it from thee : for it is profitable for thee that one of thy members should perish, and not thy whole body go into hell " (Matt. v. 29–30). Unintermittently at death-grips with self as none other has ever been, He was never once defeated and therefore blinded or deadened by it. Hence He alone measured to the full the force of its insidious and virulently destructive power, and realised that to yield any quarter whatsoever to self must always be virtual suicide.

" Take heed that ye do not your righteousness before men, to be seen of them . . . When therefore thou doest alms, sound not a trumpet before thee. . . . But when thou doest alms, let not thy left hand know what thy right hand doeth : that thine alms may be in secret. . . . And when ye pray, ye shall not be as the hypocrites : for they love to stand and pray in the synagogues and in the corners of the streets, that they may be seen of men . . . Moreover when ye fast, be not, as the hypocrites, of a sad countenance ; for they disfigure their faces, that they may be seen of men to fast. . . . But thou, when thou fastest, anoint thy head, and wash thy face ; that thou be not seen of men to fast, but of thy Father which is in secret " (Matt. vi. I ff.). This is voiced out of His own denial of any self-gratification in His religion : the consistent refusal to allow self to seek or to bask in any spiritual notice or credit from others, or *even to substitute for this its own.*

" Enter ye in by the narrow gate : for wide is the gate, and broad is the way, that leadeth to destruction . . . narrow is the gate, and straitened the way, that leadeth unto life " (Matt. vii. 13–14) : this reflects the deliberate renunciatory choices He had had to make, not episodically, but perpetually as His *modus vivendi.*

" The foxes have holes, and the birds of the heaven have nests, but the Son of Man hath not where to lay His head " (Matt. viii. 20) : security and comfort sacrificed in obedience to the Father's Will for the spreading of the Kingdom. ' Security ', ' comfort ', easy to skip over verbally ; but what fettering idols they all too often are in daily life and thought.

" No man having put his hand to the plough, and looking back, is fit for the kingdom of God " (Lk. ix. 62) : refusal to give place to discouragement, to faltering motive, to fluctuating moods or circumstances : to permit self any

respite from costly obedience, or the false ease of succumbing
to defeat.

". . . he that endureth [Gk. = stand one's ground ;
stand firm] to the end, the same shall be saved " (Matt. x.
22) : the maintenance of His own spiritual life only achieved
at the cost of the unflagging resoluteness of His whole Being.

". . . be not afraid of them which kill the body [Gk. =
the physical nature] but are not able to kill the soul [Gk. =
the real self] . . ." (Matt. x. 28) : literally everything—to
physical life itself—of the lower self must be fearlessly
sacrificed for the ' real self ' created and willed by God.

" Take heed, and keep yourselves from all covetousness
[Gk. = grasping selfishness] : for a man's life consisteth not
in the abundance of the things which he possesseth " (Lk.
xii. 15) : our Lord even whilst able to enjoy the Father's
material gifts to the full " sat loose " to them all. His life
passed beyond the Father's gifts to centre solely in the
Father Himself.

" Be not anxious for your life, what ye shall eat ; nor yet
for your body, what ye shall put on " (Lk. xii. 22) : refusing
to self undue concern even with regard to necessities, let
alone superfluities.

" If any man would come after Me, let him deny [Gk. =
say ' no ' to himself, disown] himself, and take up his cross
daily " (Lk. ix. 23) : His self-denial was not the forgoing of
mere *things*, e.g. comfort, ease, luxury, belongings, wealth ;
but the forgoing of very possession of a ' self ' at all apart
from that abandoned to, and entirely subsisting in, God—the
natural immolated to the supernatural.

[After the questioning of the disciples as to their failure
with the " dumb spirit " which our Lord cast out from the
child at the foot of the Mount of Transfiguration, Jesus
replied :] " This kind can come out by nothing, save by
prayer [some MSS. add : and fasting] " (R.V., Mk. ix. 29).
The Greek connotes continuance in a state of inner worship
of God and abnegation of self, as the *sine qua non* for effectual
redemptive action.

" If any man would be first, he shall be the last of all, and minister of all " (Mk. ix. 35) : to self no advancement ; but a waiting upon the pleasure and need of others, be they who or what they may, congenial or uncongenial.

" If any man cometh unto Me, and hateth [Gk. = despise relatively to something else] not his own father, and mother, and wife and children, and brethren and sisters, yea and his own life also, he cannot be My disciple. Whosoever doth not bear his own cross, and come after Me, cannot be My disciple . . . whosoever he be of you that renounceth [Gk. = set apart, assign specially, bid adieu to] not all that he hath [Gk. here covers property and all at one's command ; present advantages ; natural parts ; talents] he cannot be My disciple " (Lk. xiv. 26 f.) : the immolation to God of *everything*—all natural affections for those given and chosen to be specially beloved humanly ; every circumstance of life, be it good or bad, and every desire ; all that which constitutes the personality as a separate entity—simply nothing kept in reserve for self.

" No servant can serve two masters : for either he will hate the one, and love the other ; or else he will hold to one, and despise [Gk. = think little of] the other " (Lk. xvi. 13) : any self-attention absolutely incompatible with the true service of God.

" Whosoever shall seek to gain [Gk. = acquire for oneself] his life shall lose it : but whosoever shall lose his life shall preserve [Gk. = preserve alive, bring to birth] it " (Lk. xvii. 33) ; cf. " He that loveth his life loseth it : and he that hateth his life in this world shall keep it unto life eternal " (Jn. xii. 25)—self-absorption and self-gratification are destructive ; self-oblivion is creative.

[" The disciples say unto Him, If the case of the man is so with his wife, it is not expedient to marry. But He said unto them], " All men cannot receive this saying, but they to whom it is given. For there are eunuchs, which were so born from their mother's womb : and there are eunuchs, which were made eunuchs by men : and there are eunuchs.

which made themselves eunuchs for the kingdom of heaven's sake. He that is able to receive it, let him receive it " (Matt. xix. 10–12). This was said from the experiential knowledge of His own vocational gift, and of the cost to self of fulfilling it. Beneath that " He that is able to receive it . . ." is veiled a profundity of dearly practised self-denial, before which our reverence can only—and cannot but —dumbly adore. To none has the cost of self-denial ever been as great as to Him, the most intensely alive and sensitively responsive being who has ever had to regulate reaction to life and people.

" In your patience [Gk. = holding out ; steadfast endurance of the quality shown by martyrs] ye shall win [Gk. = acquire] your souls " (Lk. xxi. 19) : His was heroic endurance of spirit, mind, and body, which stopped not short even at literal martyrdom.

Every word uttered by our Lord in connection with the annihilation of self He had either already put into practical effect in His own life, or else—open-eyed to the cost—was deliberately prepared to do as soon as ever occasion demanded it. Many are the recorded actions of Jesus which are representative proofs of the living, experiential basis of all His teaching in regard to self-denial.

Very early in His public ministry, at the wedding at Cana in Galilee, when virtually urged to action by His Mother, our Lord replied : " Mine hour is not yet come " (Jn. ii. 4). Considerably later in the ministry, when expressly challenged to action by His brethren before the feast of tabernacles, He again replied : " My time is not yet come " (Jn. vii. 6). An enduring disposition this : denying Himself any and all scope for acting on natural human impulse. With His passion for souls, with His inexpressible yearning—the Father's own measureless yearning infused into Him—for the redemption of the world, with His craving to consummate the offering of His *all* to God and for Man, what incalculable denial of all the impulses and desires of self in His waiting in obscurity until He was " about thirty

years of age " even to begin His public ministry, and until
He was thirty-three before He laid down His life and " gave
up His spirit". Once at least—the day after His Transfiguration—He Himself let fall words which hint at something of what this cost Him : " O faithless generation, how
long shall I be with you : how long shall I bear with [Gk. =
endure] you ? " (Mk. ix. 19).

   To our Lord, with His exceptionally keen sensitiveness to
Beauty, beauty of holiness and beauty of form, there must
have been infinite self-denial on the æsthetic plane alone
in His mixing with—and allowing Himself so often to be
approached by—sinners and sufferers of every kind, including hypocrites, idiots, epileptics, and lepers. He
never shrank from any in moral, mental, or physical need,
no matter how humanly repulsive might be the sheer ugliness of their condition : " insomuch that as many as had
plagues pressed upon Him that they might touch Him.
And the unclean spirits, whensoever they beheld Him, fell
down before Him . . ." (Mk. iii. 10–11). He allowed self
no protection against this ugliness which was a crying hurt
to every human nerve and sense and taste ; but in compassion, love, and self-oblivion He offered His whole Being,
body, mind, and spirit to the Father, to mediate to the
afflicted, the perverted, and depraved, as intimately as need
required.

   He never denied Himself to any who came to Him—
whether singly or in a crowd—irrespective of what they
sought of Him. One aspect of the cost of this complete
denial of self that He might be at the disposal of each and
all is naïvely recorded for us by St. Mark (iii. 20) : " And
the multitude cometh again together, so that they could not
so much as eat bread " ; and again ((Mk. vi. 31) : " For
there were many coming and going, and they had no leisure
so much as to eat "—and these, doubtless, were but two such
of many similar instances of this.

   St. Mark (vii. 24) also records another aspect of this cost
—lack of privacy, a truly costly self-denial indeed : " He

. . . went into the borders of Tyre and Sidon. And He
entered into a house, and would have no man know it :
and He could not be hid " ; and again : " And the apostles
gather themselves together unto Jesus ; and they told Him
all things, whatsoever they had done, and whatsoever they
had taught. And He saith unto them, Come ye yourselves
apart into a desert place, and rest awhile. . . . And they
went away in the boat. . . . And the people saw them
going, and many knew them, and they ran there together
on foot from all the cities and outwent them. And He came
forth and saw a great multitude, and He had compassion on
them . . ." (Mk. vi. 30 ff.). The disposition expressed by
" I am in the midst of you as He that serveth " (Lk. xxii. 27)
laid Him open to demands upon His self-giving from any
one at any moment they—not He—might choose ; and
from this ever-ready accessibility to the needy in body,
mind, or spirit, He never withdrew.

He gave prodigally at all times to whosoever sought, or
would receive it, of the life which incessantly He drew from
the Father : even at those times when His own human
need was most acute. In His going up to Jerusalem with
the foreknowledge of His Passion there, the superhuman
task ahead of Him never for a moment made Him miss the
opportunities *en route*. There was no present saving of
Himself in order that He might have greater reserve of
strength to meet his future ordeal more easily. He gave
light to another—blind Bartimæus—as He approached His
own Calvary darkness. He gave moral and spiritual life
to another—Zacchæus—as He approached His own supreme
moral and spiritual agony in Gethsemane. His Passion is
one unbroken record of specific giving in personal detail
to each and every participant in it within the giving of
His all for all souls living, departed, and then as yet unborn.
His instantaneously sending away the multitude when He
perceived that they wanted to " come and take Him by
force to make Him king "—and also sending on ahead of
Him His disciples whom He knew would be sure to side with

the popular desire, since it exalted Him—that He might *alone* in prayer ascertain the will of the Father, witnesses forcibly to the unreservedness of His denial of self in every domain. Even when human advancement was thrust upon Him He would not accept it without knowing whether or no it came within the compass of the Father's Will. Self was allowed no say in reaction to external circumstances even as affecting His *cause*, dearer to Him by far—because the Father's—than His own person.

Time and again the Gospels record instances of hurtful things said or done to Him to which He allowed no reaction at all, either of anger, fear, resentment, or pity for Himself. So detached from self was He by perpetual denial of any self-life or self-love at all that He remained spiritually invulnerable to all personal attacks made upon Him mentally, morally, or physically. Even the most humanly crushing blow ever dealt to our Lord—His betrayal by Judas—He saw and received *impersonally*, not in relation to Himself, but in relation to the whole plan of the Kingdom : " Judas, betrayest thou *the Son of Man* . . ? " not " Betrayest thou Me, Who have done so much for you ? "

Our Lord's hours on the Cross were His supreme prayer of self-denial : there self was refused any consideration at all by Him ; in order that His *all* might be offered to the Father and on behalf of mankind. He even abstained from the drugged drink customarily offered to those being crucified—a seemingly legitimate occasion for recourse to a drug if ever there was one—that He might offer to the full all that was possible to offer, and offer it in maximum mental and spiritual clarity.

Our Lord's self-discipline was a fragrant and fruitful prayer, because it was simply—in every tiniest detail of it— a love-offering to procure the fulfilment of the Father's Will.

He consistently met life in a spirit of discipline. He never resented adverse circumstances, nor chafed over limitations. Earthly life for Him was simply so much raw material for glorifying God ; and all that it brought, within the permissive Will of the Father. Hence nothing was trivial ; and nothing overpowering. There was significance and opportunity in all things. His reaction to life was serene, because He based it, not upon fluctuating natural emotions, but upon a disciplined anchorage of living faith in the Father Uncreate, in Love and Holiness eternally omnipotent.

All the discipline externally imposed upon Him by home life ; legitimate human authority ; poverty ; labour ; the requirements of His craft ; the conditions of His day and environment ; obscurity, and subsequently public life ; the temperament of those with whom He had to associate— particularly the diverse temperaments of the Twelve ; and all the suffering of spirit, mind, and body which fell to His lot in His vicarious identification with sinful Man, the begetter by his sin of all suffering ; He accepted, not in passive resignation, but in an active embrace of love which was a perpetual act of worship.

He was not content merely to acquiesce in such discipline as was necessarily entailed by daily life and circumstances, but simply and unostentatiously imposed upon Himself additional discipline in a number of different ways and directions :

In His obedience to the Father : ceaseless and instantaneous obedience without a hairbreadth's deviation—" Mine hour is not yet come " ; " I am not sent but to the lost sheep of the house of Israel " ; " I speak nothing of Myself " ; " I have finished the work which Thou hast given Me to do."

In His prayer : rising up before dawn to pray ; keeping night-long vigils with the Father ; deliberately going to trouble to seek out immunity from interruption in His prayer ; letting no excuses of tiredness or overwork—however humanly plausible or legitimate—short circuit time or energy devoted to prayer ; in His meditation, and in developing *fulness* of prayer in rich variety of love-offering— including the ascetic element of prayer (as witnessed by His own words : " This kind can come out by nothing save by prayer and fasting " (A.V. Mk. ix. 29).

8

In the matter of religious observances : He was regularly to be found in the synagogue " as His custom was ", although with His transcendent spiritual enlightenment it could not *give* Him a tithe of what He already possessed interiorly. He joined in corporate worship, though knowing only too well the hypocrisy and formalism of many taking part in it. He disciplined Himself always to regard all religious observances from their Godward and not their human side : in terms of pure worship to God, never of gratification for Himself.

In His dealings with people : taking them at their level and helping them in their own individual way, instead of uniformly in the way humanly easiest to Himself ; never forcing Himself or His teaching upon any *irresistibly*, as He could have done had He so chosen ; refusing—as in the case of the rich young ruler whom He allowed to go sorrowful away—ever to weaken the challenge to total self-donation which He knew to be essential for the development and fulfilment of the divine self in each.

In His use of language : utter lack of embroidery or exaggeration ; restraint resulting in power—in this connection His sparing use of adjectives merits deep pondering.

In His delivery of His message : He so made the heart of it His own that He could " get it across " in different forms for different occasions and people.

In His perspective of life, circumstances, and people.

In control of physical, mental, and spiritual moods : He disciplined body, mind, and spirit to serve Him to the uttermost in obeying the Father altogether irrespective of senses and emotion—weariness, sorrow, pain, nothing was allowed to interrupt or lessen His abandonment of Himself in entirety to the Father.

In His æsthetic sensibilities : He the supreme Beauty-lover to Whom ugliness, sordidness, and sin were uniquely repellent yet disciplined Himself to continue in the midst of it redeeming it *graciously*, e.g. His touching the leper, less to cleanse him physically—our Lord could easily have done that by prayer alone had He so chosen—than to restore his self-respect and banish the ingrained sense of his outcast condition.

In His inexhaustible patience with—and faith in—the disciples : all the depth of discipline, mortification, and self-denial implicit in His " Father . . . for their sakes I sanctify Myself, that they themselves also may be sanctified in truth " (Jn. xvii. 19).

In His deliberately heading His whole life towards Jerusalem knowing what awaited Him there.

In His silences (see pp. 116 ff.).

In His being unswerved by human success or failure.

In His never reacting to the fear, hate, opinions, or fanatical enthusiasms of others ; or to the prevailing moods—of which He was so conscious—of His " faithless generation".

In endurance and perseverance : " He spake a parable unto them to the end that they ought always to pray [Gk. has the connotation of worship primarily, rather than of petition] and not to faint " [Gk. = be cowardly, faint-hearted] ; this was experiential from His own persevering prayer, in spite of the apparent unyieldingness of circumstances, because anchoring in the power and Will of the Father to right all wrong. He denied Himself the right to give in : to fail in continuing appropriation of the Father's grace of enablement for the work given by Him to be done.

In His voluntarily laying aside the enjoyment of His uniqueness—uniqueness of Personality and uniqueness of relationship with God—to become supernaturally identified with the *ordinary* for its redemption and transformation.

His ' mortification ' was kept to Himself ; and never spilled over on others. He paid the cost Himself, and let others receive only fruits of graciousness and serenity. There was nothing fanatical or unbalanced in it : He was disciplined in His self-discipline. He had the humility to rest when weary—e.g. at the Well of Samaria ; in the boat on the Lake—and let the disciples " carry on ".

He felt no self-satisfaction nor self-complacency in His

self-denial, because He never regarded it as an end in itself. His self-denial was only the rejection of all that was less than perfect, in order to be inundated by, and remain in, eternal communion with the fulness of perfection.   Hence there was nothing morbid in His self-denial ; it was bound to be joyous —truly gain and not loss ; to be creative and not mere negation.

Born of the Spirit for the colossally creative task of reconciling to God all mankind, past, present, and future, there was no daring room for even one flash of disintegrating, vitiating thought of self-love, self-pity, or self-protection. What a DISCIPLINE, and daily, momently self-denial !

Our Lord's prayer of self-denial was the prayer of perfect fulfilment of God's Will in creation : that the soul should only exist selflessly to give back the love of its Creator, its Lover and Beloved.

Intercession

Jesus was on earth, and is now in heaven, the supreme intercessor—that is, one who goes between, who reconciles two enemies.   He is eternally " going between " God and Man, bringing God to Man, bringing Man to God ; and in Him God the Father, Whose Holiness is the implacable enemy of sin, reconciles sinful Man to Himself, Who cannot sin nor have any identification with that which is sinning. His earthly and heavenly intercessory ministries are one continuity, identical in aim and essence and differing only in form.   His ' high-priestly ' prayer on the eve of His death foreshadows for us His ceaseless high-priestly intercession in heaven.   (Here only His earthly intercessory ministry will be dealt with : for His heavenly intercessory ministry, see pp. 312 ; 315 f.) As intercessor our Lord mediated the Father's life to all souls deficient in it ; and offered to the Father on behalf of Man vicarious penitence and reparation (see pp. 113 ff.).

Our Lord's intercession was contemplative rather than petitionary ; although it could—and on occasion did—

embrace specific petition. His intercession was contemplative identification *with God* and with God's purposes for Man ; and never—even motivated by love of God, desire for the fulfilment of His designs, or compassionate anguish and yearning for souls—identification by spiritual intention *with Man*. Such human instead of divine identification, He fully réalised, would only have thrown His own soul an open prey to all the turbulent unrest and evil in Man ; and that not only without benefit to those for whom He desired to intercede, but to the *augmenting* rather than to the diminishing of sin which He so passionately desired to have annihilated. He refused to allow His imagination to rest in the sin and misery of Man *for Man's own sake* ; but anchored it instead in the all-sufficiency of the Father's love, holiness, and power ceaselessly at work transmuting that sin and misery ; and worshipped the Holy Spirit as ceaselessly pleading *within souls* their and the Father's cause.

His intercession was the practice of that which many centuries later His Holy Spirit taught that gloriously self-abandoned Carmelite, Mère Marie de Jésus, to teach her spiritual daughters : " Go after souls . . . not by going directly to them, but by going directly to God ". " He continued all night in the prayer of God " (Lk. vi. 12) was true of the night of His whole incarnate life. Ceaselessly He offered Himself in silence as an empty cup to be infilled with the Father's Love for all souls ; that through Him it might overflow to them in sanctifying and quickening.

The whole principle of His intercessory prayer is discernible in the sublime ' high-priestly ' prayer (Jn. xvii) breathed forth the night before He laid down His life. The core of it is there shown as identification with God ; and *for love of Him and His Will* travail for individual souls. The character of the father of the prodigal son (Lk. xv. 11 ff.)—in his quenchless prayer and faith-vigil for his sin-strayed son— was surely drawn in experience from His own intercessory travail for those of His spiritual children drifting, despite all His outpouring of love-gifts, far from Him. In His own experiential knowledge of the infinite day-to-day labour and cost of building the spiritual " house upon the rock ", His intercessory travail for souls was never spasmodic, confined merely to their *apparent* crises, but was steadily continuous —a perpetual leavening of life drawn for them from the Father according to their need—need gauged primarily in relation to eternity, rather than to time.   No soul once taken into Jesus' intercession was ever dropped from it. He kept serene and faithful intercessory tryst with God for it at every stage of its development, and through all its alternating fluctuations between response to, and rejection of, that which He mediated.

Our Lord's intercession for souls was the offering of Himself in entirety to the Father, not for some passing occasion, but for eternity.   His intercession was freely granted to any soul that asked it ; and since all souls ask it, if not explicitly, then implicitly by the interior misery of the divine image within them jeopardised by sin and self, the *boundlessness* of our Lord's intercessory prayer is borne in upon us—boundlessness which is the boundlessness of the Love of the Sacred Heart of the Trinity, which eternally embraces each and every soul ever created, or still to be created, by the Father.

We can never know *all* those souls whom our Lord's earthly intercession embraced ; but it stretches our imagination, deepens our realisation of the *immensity* and inexhaustibleness of Jesus' love and Very Self, and kindles faith and adoration, to know that—not as a flash in the pan, but as a deep continuously flowing tide of love—it *did* embrace :

His Mother ; Joseph ; His brethren James, Joses, Judas, and Simon, and His sisters ; the shepherds and Magi who came to worship Him at His coming into the world ; Simeon and Anna ; King Herod ; the Innocents martyred on His account ; John the Baptist ; each of the Twelve individually ; each single one of His disciples and of the multitudes who came to be healed of Him or to hear His teaching ; the bride and bridgroom of Cana ; Nicodemus ;

each of the Scribes and Pharisees and Sadducees who enter-
tained, opposed, or spied upon Him ; Herod the Tetrarch
and Herodias, who were responsible for the death of John the
Baptist ; the Woman of Samaria, and the Samaritans who
believed on Him then and those who later rejected Him.

All those in Nazareth—those in the synagogue who desired
to stone Him ; the nobleman and his son who was sick at
Capernaum ; the man with the unclean spirit in the
synagogue at Capernaum ; Peter's mother-in-law ; Zebedee
and his wife ; the leper whom He cleansed after the Sermon
on the Mount ; the centurion and his servant ; the widow of
Nain and her son : Mary Magdalene ; Joanna, the wife of
Chuza Herod's steward ; Susanna ; the Scribe who came to
Him saying : " Master, I will follow Thee whithersoever Thou
goest " ; and those others who said : " Suffer me first to go
and bury my father " ; and " . . . first suffer me to bid
farewell to them that are at my house " ; the Gerasene
demoniac, and those of His relations and acquaintance to
whom He sent him with tidings of God's mercy to him ; the
man sick of the palsy, and those who brought him to Him in
faith.

The publicans and others at Levi's feast ; Jairus and his
daughter and her mother ; the woman with the issue of
blood ; the impotent man at the Pool of Bethesda ; the lad
who gave Him loaves and fishes to feed the multitude ; the
man who said to Him : " Master, bid my brother divide the
inheritance with me ", and the brother ; the Syrophœnician
woman and her daughter ; the deaf man with the impedi-
ment in his speech ; the father and his epileptic son at the
foot of the Mount of Transfiguration ; the mothers who
brought Him their babes to bless, and each little one ; the
" one casting out devils in Thy name " whom John " for-
bade . . . because he followed not us " ; the woman taken
in adultery ; the man born blind ; the woman " which had
a spirit of infirmity eighteen years " ; the ten lepers ;
Martha, Mary, and Lazarus ; the rich young ruler who
" went away sorrowful " ; blind Bartimæus ; Zacchæus.

The children who acclaimed Him on Palm Sunday ; those buying and selling in the Temple ; the Greeks come up for the Passover who said to Philip : " Sir, we would see Jesus ".; Annas and Caiaphas ; Malchus and each of those who came to apprehend Him in the Garden of Gethsemane ; Pilate ; all the soldiers who took any part in His trials and Passion ; Simon of Cyrene ; the women who bewailed Him on the Via Dolorosa ; the two robbers crucified with Him.

What *sustained* travail He must have endured for many of these : and He is " the same yesterday, to-day, yea and for ever ", as many of us know as the deepest experience of our lives—fully recognising that but for His ceaseless intercession for us we should already have perished finally, as by our own inexcusable and humanly unforgivable doing we deserve.

Obviously, intercessory enfolding of all these—and many others of whom it happens we are not told—*could* not be at the level of *human thought* about each of them and all the needs and ever-changing circumstances appertaining to them, which is what all too often passes with us for ' intercession ' which it is not.   His whole penetration of effectual intercessory prayer is revealed by His : " See that ye despise not one of these little ones ; for I say unto you, that in heaven their angels do always behold the face of My Father which is in heaven " (Matt. xviii. 10) : intercession the abiding unitively with the Father in adoration of Him, and letting that adoration be a medium of His life and love to all His children as He wills.

Be it noted, and realised, that although it was our Lord's intercessory principle to pray, not in terms of temporal conditions, events, or needs at large, but in terms of individual souls, yet the public conditions of His time with Roman domination, over-taxation, and general unrest politically, socially, and economically, are just similar to those which we to-day let distract us from individual self-abandonment to Him, and enmesh our thought, time, and energy in prayer for secondary things which are basically dependent for their rightness precisely upon the degree of our individual and corporate voluntary belongingness to Him.

The ' high-priestly ' prayer of Jn. xvii. reveals unmistakably the whole twofold motive underlying all our Lord's intercessory prayer. " I pray . . . for those whom Thou hast given Me ; *for they are Thine* " (Jn. xvii. 9) ; " And for their sakes I sanctify Myself, that they themselves also may be sanctified in truth " (Jn. xvii. 19). He interceded for souls from pure love of the Father ; and He interceded for them, not primarily to relieve them of suffering as such, but, fundamentally, in order to mediate to them sanctification through the infectious quickening of supreme holiness, in order that in them might be unitively fulfilled the Father's purposes of love.

Our Lord's intercession for individual souls was all-embracing, and covered :

The sick and suffering : " This kind can come out by nothing, save by prayer and fasting " (A.V. Mk. ix. 29).

Sinners : " Neither do I condemn thee. Go thy way ; from henceforth sin no more " (Jn. viii. 11) : presupposing the continuing mediation of His enabling grace without which obedience would have been impossible.

" Father, forgive them . . ." (Lk. xxiii. 34) : recorded for us as uttered by our Lord on the Cross, this must have been a prayer perpetually welling up from His heart throughout the whole of His life.

Jerusalem : " O Jerusalem, Jerusalem, which killeth the prophets, and stoneth them that are sent unto her ! how often would I have gathered thy children together . . ." (Lk. xiii. 34).

The Church : " Neither for these [His immediate disciples] only do I pray, but for them also that believe on Me through their word ; that they may all be one ; even as Thou, Father, art in Me, and I in Thee, that they also may be in Us . . ." (Jn. xvii. 20 f.).

The Departed: In 1 Pet. iii. 18 ff., there is recorded for us the mystery known as " the Harrowing of Hell " : " . . . Christ also suffered for sins once, the righteous for the unrighteous, that He might bring us to God ; being put to death in the flesh, but quickened in the spirit ; in which also He went and preached unto the spirits in prison . . .".   None of our Lord's actions but was the outcome of an enduring disposition.   His post-Crucifixion " Harrowing of Hell " was but the natural sequence of His incarnate intercession for the departed.   He, so uniquely sensitive to the spiritual unrest of those around Him on earth, cannot but have been as sensitive to the needs of the departed not yet at peace ; and have interceded for them equally with those still on earth.   Our Lord's earthly intercessory ministry for the departed is implicit in at least three different passages in the Gospels.   " He is not the God of the dead, but of the living . . . " (Mk. xii. 27) : this He must have told the Sadducees out of experiential knowledge gained from God's response to His intercession for the departed.   St. Matthew (xiv. 13) records that Jesus, on hearing of the beheading of John the Baptist, " withdrew . . . to a desert place apart " : obviously for prayer—prayer which would inevitably include intercession for the soul of the murdered man whom He mourned.   He Himself declared to the Jews : " Verily, verily, I say unto you, The hour is coming, and now is, when the dead shall hear the voice of the Son of God and they that hear shall live . . ." (Jn. v. 25) : this was a revelation which must have been vouchsafed to Him by the Father, Whom later He thanked for " I know that Thou hearest Me always ", in response to His heartfelt intercession for the dead.

His intercession for souls was inexhaustibly patient, because fed, not by their response or apparent progress, but by the eternal Being and action of the Father, Whose Love and Holiness each and every soul will ultimately find irresistibly adorable.

Prayer of Penitence and Reparation

Our Lord's prayer of penitence and reparation began in Eternity with His " Fiat " for His Incarnation. Then, for sin's universal defraudment of the worship, and loving obedience, due to God, our Lord willed by sacrificial self-oblation vicariously to offer to the Father as from Man that *perfect* penitence and reparation of which no sinner—through the spiritual atrophy inevitably resultant upon sin—is capable. This offering, first made in intention in Eternity, was fulfilled practically in time ; and now again in Eternity is being offered to the Father as a *perfected* and plenary offering incapable of addition, and as such is also being ceaselessly applied to the transmuting of all Man's sin as he continues freshly to create it. In time, His prayer of penitence and reparation began at Bethlehem, and was maintained unbrokenly throughout His incarnate life until its consummation in the Agony and Passion. It was this lifelong *habitual* oblation of Himself, including all the thoughts, emotions, and sensory reactions which constituted His real self, at all times, in all places, under all circumstances, to the Father, which alone made possible the perfection of His supreme penitential oblation of Himself upon the Cross under circumstances of maximum and simultaneous physical, mental, and spiritual stress.

His penitence was borne solely of His innate sense of the sublimeness of the Majesty of the Father. His reparation was self-immolation to the Holiness of God in order to make up those dues of which sin had robbed the All-Holy.

By virtue of His sinlessness He felt such contrition for sin as is impossible of attainment by any sinner, be the sin never so great or never so slight. But this contrition He never dissipated in mere emotion as such ; but made it the disciplined foundation of concrete sacrificial deed and living, such as was the antithesis of sin and self whose outrage against Holiness He sought to offset by His pure and selfless love towards the Father. His prayer of penitence and reparation never dwelt emotionally or imaginatively upon the details of sin ; but was simply His " offering of a free heart ". " An offering of a free heart will I give Thee and praise Thy Name, O Lord " (Ps. liv. 6) : how often, sometimes with intensity of rapture, sometimes—in spiritual dryness or darkness—with only the set of His innermost will, He must have breathed this aspiration. His prayer of penitence and reparation offered to the Father precisely all that of which Man robbed Him by sin and self ; and especially obedience for his disobedience.

Our Lord's penitential offering of obedience was a gloriously progressive one. Obedience for Him was never a matter of passive resignation or mechanical response ; it altogether transcended even voluntary compliance with the dictates of another. It was an active disposition of deliberately willed union by self-oblation with the Mind and Will, i.e. intrinsic Personality, of the Father ; and it issued in a steady *development* of His whole Being, from childhood onwards, towards an ever-deepening perception of the essence of that Mind and Will, and consequently to ability to act in ever deepening conformity with them.

" Not disobedient unto the heavenly vision ", He was ready in action to follow the light right through to its most uncompromising end :

" Love your enemies " (Matt. v. 44) : the Cross.

" Be not afraid of them which kill the body, but are not able to kill the soul . . ." (Matt. x. 28) : the Cross.

" I seek not Mine own will, but the will of Him that sent Me " (Jn. v. 30) : Gethsemane—" Abba, Father, all things are possible unto Thee ; remove this cup from Me : howbeit not what I will, but what Thou wilt " (Mk. xiv. 36).

His obedience was perfect response to the Will of the Father *by identification* with Him.

This offering of consummate obedience was not only " well-pleasing " to the Father, but also wrought upon His disciples a deep impression which remained and was handed down—" For as through the one man's disobedience the many were made sinners, even so through the obedience of the one shall many be made righteous " (Rom. v. 19) : they recognised it as an effective medium for bringing others to Holiness.

Surely it was the intensity of our Lord's penitence to the Father on behalf of Peter denying Him that Peter divined in that look of His Master's, which brought him to penitence himself—penitence, as all else in the spiritual life, being strangely infectious.

His countering of the temptations in the Wilderness is a singularly illuminating revelation of the essence of offering in His prayer of penitence and reparation :

" Man shall not live by bread alone, but by every word that proceedeth out of the mouth of God " (Matt. iv. 4) : the offering not only of *obedience* for Man's disobedience ; but also of *faith in God* for Man's lack of trust in Him, of self-forgetfulness in the interests of God for Man's disregard of His claims and of Himself.

" Thou shalt not tempt the Lord thy God " (Lk. iv. 12) ; the offering of *reverence*, born of the quality of His perception of the essential Personality of the Father as perfect HOLINESS, and of His realisation of the legitimate demands of that Holiness upon Man and upon Himself as Man ; the refusal of less than perfection of love-offering.

" Thou shalt worship the Lord thy God, and Him only shalt thou serve " (Matt. iv. 10) : the offering of *exclusive allegiance* of the whole desiring spirit, mind, and will to the Father.

His cleansing of the Temple (Jn. ii. 14–16 ; Matt. xxi. 12–13) serves to show that His prayer of penitence and reparation issued in active effort, involving real moral courage, in order to get the Father's rights duly observed by others.

No merely negative non-committal neutrality with regard to sin is possible : either it must be being penitentially disannulled or else freshly created. " For he that is not with Me is against Me " (Matt. xii. 30) : if we are not with Jesus, in union with His prayer of penitence and reparation, then we are bound to be with sin against Him ; there is no other alternative open to us.   He " put away sin by the sacrifice of Himself " (Heb. ix. 26) ; and so only by the progressive sacrifice of self can we gradually enter into union with Him in His prayer of penitence and reparation for the satisfying of the Father in His Holiness and for the redemption of Man.

Prayer of Silence

Real silence is essentially an interior thing ; and may or may not involve abstention from speech.   Abstention from speech is not necessarily silence.   Interior silence is an inner detachment from self ; from the material ; from the senses and emotions ; from creatures ; from all that is temporal, in order to be invaded and possessed by the Eternal.   This interior silence it was—at times embracing verbal silence as well—which our Lord habitually offered as prayer to the Father : a prayer of desire for the Father's Self-communication to Him, and the medium for its reception in whatever way He chose to vouchsafe it.   He offered the Father interior silence always, and exterior silence deliberately from time to time, in order that the Father might at will be enabled at all times to impart to Him His life and Very Self—and also to evoke from Him reciprocal self-donation—for His own purposes and satisfaction.   Our Lord on earth prayer-offered to the Father that silence which is the counterpart of the silence of Eternity, in which alone are possible love's deepest interchanges.

Fundamentally our Lord's silence was receptivity to the Father.   He offered Himself to the Father in silence, that in that silence the Father might progressively bespeak Himself and His Will, and draw Him into deepening union with that Self and Will.   His silence was never idleness ; but the interior activity of self-offering to be infilled by the Father's Self, to be absorbed in the Father.

Jesus offered the prayer of silence for the Father's sake : that through it He might be truly known, loved, and obeyed. He offered it for His own sake : that through it energy of body, mind, and spirit might be ever freshly augmented for the fulfilling of His vocation, instead of dissipated and frittered away in false activity. He offered it for the sake of others : that through it there might be mediated to them the sense of the Companioning Presence of God with them in Holiness and Peace ; and the stilling which would leave them immersed in Reality.

" And in praying use not vain repetitions [Gk. = also, babble] as the Gentiles do : for they think that they shall be heard for their much speaking [Gk. = loquaciousness, volubility]. Be not therefore like them . . ." (Matt. vi. 7–8) : this advice He gave out of His experiential knowledge of the necessity of basic silence for creative prayer.

" . . . when thou doest alms, let not thy left hand know what thy right hand doeth : that thine alms may be in secret " (Matt. vi. 3–4) : He did not permit Himself ever to derive any self-satisfaction from His religious activities ; but preserved the virginity of offering—both spiritual and material offering—within the prayer of silence. Likewise He preserved within the prayer of silence " the virginity of suffering ". He never dilated upon either His offerings or His sufferings to others ; He never dilated upon them even to Himself or tried to analyse them : He refrained from drawing out their detail, not only to others or to Himself, but even to God. Silence but deepened as suffering deepened. When His suffering was at its most humanly intolerable, there was never more than a short sharp cry to God—and to no one else—in a seeking of strength for an intensified worship of, and abandonment to, the Father's Will, a fresh self-committal to Him in intensified faith.

Jesus' silence was experienced by others as something potent. " And the chief priests accused Him of many things. And Pilate again asked Him, saying, Answerest thou nothing ? behold how many things they accuse Thee of. But Jesus no more answered anything : insomuch that Pilate marvelled " (Mk. xv. 3 ff.) : marvelled less because of the negative quality of that silence—though under such circumstances merely to refrain from verbal self-defence and from retaliatory speech was in itself humanly wonderful—than for its creative quality of interior intercessory prayer for His enemies, the power of which prayer he could not help sensing, even although but dimly apprehending it for what it was.

Our Lord's prayer of silence was simply a continuous practice of the Presence of God.

Prayer of the Body

Jesus never made a cult of the physical as physical ; but neither did He ever affect to despise the body. For One at Whose Incarnation " a multitude of the heavenly host " had exultantly praised God, the body could not but ever be a sacred thing whose inner significance was primarily spiritual.

He disciplined His body always to be the servant of His spirit. He never pampered it ; indeed, He inured it to hardships and discomfort, and to strain of prolonged self-giving in many directions. But none the less, quietly— " Be not anxious . . . nor yet for the body . . ." (Matt. vi. 25)—He gave to it that modicum of care necessary to retain its perfection as an instrument of the Will of God.

Treating His incarnate body at all times as a divine *trust*, He was able to extract from it consistent service in mirroring and mediating the Divine. His prayer of the body, initiated by His " Fiat " for the Incarnation, was the steadfast immolation of that body to the redemptive purposes of God at the expense of denying it any natural gratifications outside those purposes : even gratifications lawful for others, if they did not happen to fall within the Father's vocational Will for Himself—" . . . and there are eunuchs, which made themselves eunuchs for the kingdom of heaven's sake " (Matt. xix. 12).

His prayer of the body was a perpetual drawing of energy from the Father ; and as perpetual an expenditure of that energy for God, and for Man for God's sake. His spirit ever exacted the uttermost of His body in self-donation, but never forced it to a point of inevitable recoil. He subordinated the flesh to the spirit, but in order that it might continue to contribute maximumly to the liberation of the spirit, He never overdrove or neglected it. Our Lord never played off body and spirit against one another as opponents. He deliberately allied them as yoke-mates whose perfection of holiness was each alike indispensable to the fulfilment of the Father's Will ; and so He established an harmonious and practical co-operation between the two. In Him the body never warred against the spirit, because never once was it yielded to self or sin or passion. His body was as consecrated in singleness to God as was His spirit.

Who but our Lord would ever have said to the disciples, fallen asleep in the hour of His Gethsemane Agony for which He had asked their vigil, the hour after that in which He had so sublimely imparted to them the essence of His Very Self of Love : " . . . the spirit indeed is willing, but the flesh is weak " (Mk. xiv. 38) ? Who but He would have credited them with anything but ingrate indifference ? But His words show experiential understanding of the practical difficulty of sustained reconciliation between the eager desires of the spirit and the natural *capabilities* of the body. It can have been no easy thing for the most ardent spirit Who ever lived not to outstrip—and overstrain to breaking-point—that body of flesh and nerves, which He deigned to take to Himself with all its inherent limitations as well as latent powers. But it may be said that, as He disciplined His body to His spirit, so no less necessarily did He discipline His spirit to His body while incarnate, that in co-agency with the body it might be enabled to make to the Father that complete offering of the whole Being, *impossible* to the spirit alone while indwelling a human body.

In connection with our Lord's perfect adjustment of relationship between body and spirit, Maurice Richmond has written illuminatingly : " The *poise* of Christ was won

9

physically by His fellowship with the mountains and olive-groves as well as by the mystic spring.   Incarnation is the perfect natural use of both means.   The achievement by the flesh of its call—" a body hast Thou prepared for me " —is by exposing that body to the conditions in which it can best be the receiver and transmitter of spiritual powers."

Jesus' prayer of the body was not only " a whole burnt-offering ", but was offered specifically by every part of that body as well.   " Praying hands " : how His prayed as none other have ever done—in manual labour in Nazareth ; in healing both bodies and souls by their touch ; in blessing children by their imposition ; in love-performing lowliest actions, e.g. the washing of the disciples' feet ; in pleading to God for Man's forgiveness as bound to the pillar at His scourging and nailed to the Cross at His crucifixion ; in inviting and pleading with all sinners to return to the Sacred Heart of the Trinity of Love and Holiness, of Life, Peace, and Beauty, as they were outstretched on the Cross.   The prayer of His feet : bearing Him ever in obedience along the way of God's Will, and in active service among men ; carrying Him steadfastly towards Jerusalem ; holding His ground in Gethsemane ;   treading the Via Dolorosa ; sacrificially exchanging His active ministry for " sin-bearing stillness on the Cross ", yielding those feet, which had carried Him " about doing good ", to agony and physical impotence in order to exercise love in its supreme activity of body broken and blood outpoured.   This " sin-bearing stillness on the Cross " was born of His lifelong spirit-stilling of His physical nature in order to enable it always and everywhere to be the vehicle of the Divine.

His Passion in its entirety was a prayer of Love's bodily self-donation in non-resistance to the utmost that sinners could inflict upon Him, in order to woo them from themselves to God, no matter how fast their imprisonment in the darkness of self.

He submitted His body to be seized and bound in the

Garden, and led thence at the will of His captors ; to be
struck by one of the officers at the house of Annas ; to
" Then did they spit in His face "—that Face which had
been transfigured on the Mountain—" and buffet Him : and
some smote Him with the palms of their hands " (Matt.
xxvi. 67), and to be beaten and blindfolded in the house of
Caiaphas ; His ears to hearing the clamorous uproar of the
mob shouting for His crucifixion ; to being scourged in the
palace ; to " they stripped Him, and put on Him a scarlet
robe. And they plaited a crown of thorns and put it upon
His head, and a reed in His right hand ; and they kneeled
down before Him, and mocked Him, saying, Hail, King of
the Jews ! And they spat upon Him, and took the reed and
smote Him on the head " (Matt. xxvii. 29–30) ; to dragging
along the Via Dolorosa spent with suffering of body and
mind and spirit, and without sleep ; to having His hands and
feet nailed to the Cross ; to enduring its agony undrugged,
literally unable to move hand or foot, to wipe away the
blood trickling down His face from the piercing of the Crown
of Thorns, to obtain any relief by even infinitesimal change of
position for His scourge-flayed back chafed by the rough
Cross. His submitting to all this unflinchingly, uncom-
plainingly, with the whole of His free will projected in
offering it in love as vicarious penitence to God, and as the
medium for Man's redemption, was a sublime penitential and
intercessory prayer, to which His body, by its silent embrace
of suffering, contributed as fully and creatively as His spirit :
body and spirit were absolutely unified in sacrificial self-
oblation.

On the eve of His Passion, our Lord instituted the
Sacrament of His Most Blessed Body and Blood. This
sacramental gift of His body to be the life of the world for
all time was only possible through His prayer of the body
having kept that body as a sacrament—as the outward and
visible sign of the essence of the Father's Being as Holy Love
—throughout His whole life. The real prayer of consecration was His lifelong prayer of the incarnate body perpetu-

ally immolated to identification with God's Will, which is Himself.

Our Lord's prayer of the body was a prayer of unbroken offering of His body to tabernacle the Father in His Love and Holiness—" Thou, Father, art in Me " : in Me incarnate.

Prayer of Active Service

Not all active service—however beneficent—is prayer ; for prayer lies in intention and not in activity as such.   But all Jesus' going about doing good, healing the sick, teaching, preaching, ministering to individual souls in need or sorrow, was prayer ;   since it sprang from, and was sustained in, love and obedience to the Father's Will.   His active service was undertaken only at the prompting of the Father—" the work which Thou hast given Me to do "—never haphazard.

Each single act of our Lord's active service for others was motivated solely by love.   It was the natural outcome of His prayer of ceaseless aspiration, in union with the Father's Will, that each and every soul should be freed from sin— and all its sequent trail of suffering and decay—into the glory of voluntarily chosen identification with God and His purposes of Love holy and beauteous.

Jesus' prayer of active service was the prayer of love ever at the disposal of the sick and suffering in body, mind, or spirit ;   the prayer of love expending all its energy, regardless of cost to itself, in mediating redemption to those in the toils of sin and self, so that the Father might ultimately have fulfilled to His satisfaction His original purposes in creating them.

Prayer of the Drinking of the Cup

Some of our Lord's very deepest words, during His last days before His Crucifixion, centre around the ' drinking of the Cup '.   To Him it was no metaphor ;   but a basic element of life—indeed, it might truly be said that it was to Him life itself.

His initial knowledge of what precisely the Cup was He

derived from His meditation on the Scriptures : exhaustive knowledge came only with His drinking of it.

" The Lord is the portion of mine inheritance and of my cup " (Ps. xvi. 5) : here He knew lay the whole thing. " The Lord . . . my cup " : this was the anchorage of all His thought and experience of the Cup.

Our Lord recognised that the Cup offered to Him by the Father was nothing less than to partake incarnate of the Father's Own Essential Nature of Love, Holiness, and Truth.

Love : unreserved self-donation for the satisfaction of the innermost being of the beloved.

Holiness : the purity of absolute selflessness, awful and annihilating to self and sin to which it eternally refuses any entrance to union with itself save by way of crucifying transmutation.

Truth : Eternal Reality, in face of which all falsity, and all distortion—whether through wilfulness or ignorance— of facts as they are, is simply shattered.

" For in the hand of the Lord there is a cup, and the wine foameth. It is full of mixture, and He poureth out of the same. Surely the dregs thereof, all the wicked of the earth shall wring them out, and drink them " (Ps. lxxv. 8).

" Awake, awake, stand up, O Jerusalem, which hast drunk at the hand of the Lord *the cup of His fury* ; thou hast drunken the bowl of the cup of staggering, and drained it . . ." (Is. li. 17).

" For thus saith the Lord, the God of Israel, unto me : Take the cup of the wine. of this fury [Septuagint omits " of this fury ", and has instead " of this pure " or ' unadulterated ' " wine "] and cause all the nations, to whom I send thee to drink it. . . . And it shall be if they refuse [Septuagint = " will not to receive " or " welcome "] the cup at thine hand to drink, then shalt thou say unto them, Thus saith the Lord of hosts : Ye shall surely drink " (Jer. xxv. 15 ff. ; Septuagint : Jer. xxxii. 15 ff.).

" For thus saith the Lord : Behold, they to whom it

pertained not to drink of the cup shall assuredly drink ; and art thou he that shall altogether go unpunished ? thou shalt not go unpunished, but thou shalt surely drink" (Jer. xlix. 12).

Inescapably must our Lord have realised, from deep meditation on these passages, a dread element in the Cup ; but that which was anthropomorphically styled—because so experienced by sinful Man—as the cup of God's "fury" He recognised as being no passion in God, but simply the implacability of Holiness towards sin ; the unyieldingness of Holiness to compromise with sin. The Cup of the Lord's fury he reverenced with His whole Being as the exaction of sin's dues by the intrinsic nature of Holiness absolutely— ·and as it were automatically—necessitating satisfaction. In the Cup of the Lord's fury He saw—and worshipped—the sublimity of God's invincible and all-pervading Holiness ; and also the compassion and generosity of God towards Man in bringing upon him the full play of His Nature, rather than submit lightly to his losing that bliss of union with Himself for which He created him.

On the way up to Jerusalem, He asked James and John, requesting of Him unique spiritual privilege : "Are ye able to drink the cup that I drink ? or to be baptised with the baptism that I am baptised with ?" (Mk. x. 38). The verbs in the Greek show very clearly that the drinking of the Cup was *a continuing process*, whereas the baptism was enacted once for all at a specific moment.

Our Lord's drinking of the Cup was not confined to Gethsemane ; its initial drops were sipped by infant lips. Lifelong was the draught whose dregs were reached in the Agony, but only completely drained in Crucifixion.

He drained the Cup drop by drop, not at one draught. None while on earth will ever be able to trace out the process in detail ; but His draining of the dregs the Holy Spirit has perpetuated for us in the Gospel records of the Agony and the Crucifixion. In this revelation of the draught at its intensest each of us may, in prayer of reverent silence, receive from the Holy Spirit that further light He wishes to give individually—for purposes of practical identification with it—on our Lord's earlier drinking of the Cup given Him by the Father.

Jesus recognised that there was no compulsion about the drinking of the Cup, save the inner compulsion of love to love. The Cup was not enforced upon Him : it was *proffered* Him by the Father freely to receive or to reject as He chose. His Agony in the Garden was the wrestling— to the point of bloody sweat—to assemble and force His whole Being, with every constituent particle of spirit, mind, and body, to a single will to continue the draught whose dregs in the actual drinking were proving of such scarifying bitterness.

The first prayer of the Agony to drain the Cup was His " Abba, Father, all things are possible unto Thee ; remove this cup from Me : howbeit not what I will, but what Thou wilt " (Mk. xiv. 36). This prayer for escape from the Cup, whose drinking had been the lifelong *choice* of His Will until now, reveals more poignantly than could anything else the intensity of horror in the draught towards its close. It caused such a recoil as almost to break down the habitual inner disposition which was essentially Himself ; and it caused Him for the first time in His whole life to *desire*—not to be confused with willing—something *on His own initiative* as distinct from the Father's. The horror was the progressive realisation *to the point of exhaustiveness* of the sum total of sin's outrage against the Holiness of the Father.

What seemed at first literally unendurable to our Lord— Who it must be remembered never refused suffering as suffering, however much in His perfect humanity He inevitably shrank from it—was that this understanding of sin's outrage against GOD came at this point by way of experience of *a sense of complete identification* with it. Mental and emotional consciousness were engulfed in *a felt oneness*—almost unhinging to the human brain, unutterably revolting to the spirit—with SIN. That which He sensed as the violation of His very nature—the substitution in Him of sin for sinlessness—was that from which He craved escape ; the only personal suffering from which He could ever even have desired to escape.

" O My Father, if this cannot pass away except I drink it, Thy Will be done " (Matt. xxvi. 42). This second prayer of the Agony reveals that the Father, Whom He knew always to hear His prayer, had answered the first by taking Him more deeply into His—the Father's—Own Secret Mind. Between the first and second prayers of the Agony the Father had, in unquestionable clarity, disclosed to Him His Will for the Cup to be drained.

As the Temptation in the Wilderness had been *multiple*, so too was the Agony, which was unspeakably intensified by the almost insupportable strain it put upon our Lord's faith in the Father. As man our Lord was not omniscient as—in another connection—He Himself has told us : " But of that day and hour knoweth no one, not even the angels of heaven, *neither the Son*, but the Father only " (Matt. xxiv. 36). By agonising prayer He had come to know that the Father willed Him to drink the dregs of what seemed complete identification of His whole self with sin. He did not then know *as did the Father* that it was no identification with sin *in will*, but only in thought and sense consciousness, as all sin's darkness was allowed to pass through His sinlessness that in Him, the Light of Light, it might cease to be. " And the light shineth in darkness ; and the darkness apprehended it not " (Jn. i. 5). Darkness cannot turn light into darkness ; but light can—and inevitably must—turn darkness into light. Darkness flood-lit by light is darkness no longer : it is itself become light. " Him Who knew no sin He made to be sin on our behalf that we might become the righteousness of God in Him " (2 Cor. v. 21). Only by Jesus' plunging into the abyss of Sin could it ultimately be annihilated.

To feel *Himself* identified with sin was horror indeed to Jesus beyond anything that we can imagine ; but even this was far from exhausting the dread Cup; there was yet worse. It was in the Father's seeming toleration of Sin that everything reeled for Jesus : the Nature and Very Self of the Father—Who was His Life, His Anchor, His Beloved, His All-in-All—being suddenly and dizzyingly at stake for Him. The bare idea of the possibility of the Father com- promising with sin was too appalling for Him to dare enter- tain ; for then indeed the foundations of earth and heaven, of very being—the immutability˙of the Holiness of the Father—would be demolished, and all life and experience given the lie irrevocable. Yet every present circumstance seemed to force it upon His brain and senses as inescapable fact. Only sheer against reason and against feeling, bereft of human support and of any consciousness of divine support, in a tempest of soul, such as is beyond our faintest concep- tion, by the stark faith of love in Love did He vindicate the Father, Whom then He had humanly altogether ceased to understand.

Later on the Cross, our Lord, in His vicarious penitence and reparation, paid the last dues of sin, and suffered *all the uttermost consequences of sin*, even although Himself sinless. This absolutely necessitated " the Dereliction " i.e. some experience of sense of that sundering from God which is inherent in sin : sundering which from Man's side seems— in anthropomorphic language—God's forsaking Man, rather than Man's forsaking God as has actually been the case. If the " Dereliction of the Cross " was the sense of Himself seemingly forsaken by the Father, the dereliction of the Agony of the Cup in Gethsemane was the even more tortur- ing sense of the Father's seemingly forsaking His own Father-Self. The sense of dereliction in the Agony of the Cup, and the sense of dereliction on the Cross, are both integral to the whole cycle of redemption ; because it is inevitable that all who come in any measure really to know God must, sooner or later, experience both that which causes them to feel that facts seem to belie His character as known to them, and that they themselves are forsaken of Him—" Wherefore in all things it behoved Him to be made like unto His brethren, that He might be a merciful and faithful high priest, in things pertaining to God, to make reconciliation for the sins of the people " (Heb. ii. 17).

The first prayer of the Agony had been an articulate petition for permissible escape ; in the second this was replaced by implicit petition for enablement for compliance. Not in escape, but in drinking is the only passing of any cup. But—infinitely precious inspiration deliberately recorded for us by the generosity of the Holy Spirit the Comforter, the Heartener—not even with our perfect Lord was the struggle settled once for all.   He had to go back to God on the same point of willingness and get Him to re-settle, and keep it settled.   " And He . . . went away, and prayed a third time, saying again the same words " (Matt. xxvi. 44).

After the prayers of the Agony of the Cup Jesus, with the royal freedom of a single will at one with the Will of the Father, said to Peter, when he had just cut off Malchus' ear : " Put up the sword into the sheath : the cup which the Father hath given Me, shall I not drink it ? " (Jn. xviii. 11). " The cup which *the Father* hath given Me . . ." ; so He regarded it—although all His external sufferings at that point were humanly entirely due to the sin and self-will of men—and therefore not only would He offer no resistance Himself : He would permit none to be offered on His behalf.

The predominant ingredient in the dregs of the Cup was suffering : suffering of the entire being.   But our Lord recognised that suffering was not of the essence of the Cup as given by the Father, but only the incidental medium whereby Love could prove in time its eternal unquenchableness.   " The cup which the Father hath given Me . . ." : the opportunity and privilege of partaking incarnate of the Nature of Eternal Love—by loving invincibly and undeviatingly through all suffering to the death and beyond (see also pp. 156 ff.).

" The cup which the Father hath given Me . . ." : the opportunity and privilege of partaking incarnate of the

Nature of Eternal Holiness—by suffering sin's outrage upon Holiness, and sustaining the full impact of Holiness upon sin.

" The cup which the Father hath given Me . . ." : the opportunity and privilege of partaking incarnate of the Nature of Eternal Truth—by undergoing Light's exhaustive exposure of darkness ; and penetrating Reality, which under the conditions of time is composed of Love, Holiness, and Sin (see also pp. 150 ff.). Even had our Lord's suffering for us fallen short of the Crucifixion, and ended with the Agony of the drinking of the Cup in Gethsemane, that alone would put us under an eternal debt to Him. We do well to ask the Holy Spirit to quicken in us realisation of the profundity of this debt until He inflame us to abandon our all in gratitude to Jesus, Who could have saved Himself the torturing sense of identification with sin had He chosen to repudiate His oneness with us. To James and John Jesus gave His assurance : " The cup that I drink ye shall drink ; and with the baptism that I am baptised withal shall ye be baptised " (Mk. x. 39). May He—for love of Himself, the Father, and the Holy Spirit—give to us, too, like enablement.

Prayer of Rejected Offering

Never has any man so deeply experienced the bitterness of rejected offering as did our Lord.

In reading the Gospels with their record of numerous responses made to our Lord by individuals and by crowds, it is easily possible to overlook two things : the self-seeking, which alone prompted so many of these responses, and the *repeated* rebuffs to which also He was subjected—again both from individuals and from crowds. It *ought* to be realised that " He came unto His own, and His own received Him not " (Jn. i. 11) is true, not only of the specific act of rejection by the Jews on Good Friday, but also of His whole public ministry in large measure, and probably—in lesser degree—even of the hidden years at Nazareth as well. The Gospel records of rejections are many ; and this because the Holy

Spirit has deemed it necessary for us to know how largely
rejection bulked in the incarnate life of our Lord :

Early in the public ministry, after our Lord had read and
spoken in the synagogue at Nazareth, " they were all filled
with wrath . . . and they rose up, and cast Him forth out
of the city, and led Him unto the brow of the hill whereon
their city was built, that they might throw Him down
headlong . . ." (Lk. iv. 28–29).

" But Simon Peter . . . fell down at Jesus' knees, saying,
Depart from me ; for I am a sinful man, O Lord " (Lk. v. 8).
Rather than pay the price of being conformed to the holiness
of our Lord, Peter felt he would rather dismiss Him.

" Give not that which is holy unto the dogs, neither cast
your pearls before the swine, lest haply they trample them
under their feet, and turn and rend you " (Matt. vii. 6).
This He taught only from personal experience of sacred
offerings of His to Man cast back at Him in antagonism.

" Then began He to upbraid the cities wherein most of His
mighty works were done, because they repented not.   Woe
unto thee, Chorazin !   Woe unto thee, Bethsaida ! for if the
mighty works had been done in Tyre and Sidon which were
done in you, they would have repented long ago in sackcloth
and ashes. . . . And thou, Capernaum, shalt thou be exalted
unto heaven ? thou shalt go down into Hades ; for if the
mighty works had been done in Sodom which were done in
thee, it would have remained unto this day " (Matt. xi.
20 ff.).

After His curing of Legion, and the drowning of the
swine, ". . . all the people of the Gerasenes round about
asked Him to depart from them ; for they were holden with
great fear " (Lk. viii. 37).

A second rejection in Nazareth : " And when the Sabbath
was come, He began to teach in the synagogue : and many
hearing Him were astonished, saying, Where hath this man
these things ? and, What is the wisdom that is given unto
this man, and what mean such mighty works wrought by His
hands ?   Is not this the carpenter, the son of Mary, and

brother of James, and Joses, and Judas, and Simon. . . .
And they were offended in Him. . . . And He could there
do no mighty work, save that He laid His hands upon a few
sick folk, and healed them. And He marvelled because of
their unbelief " (Mk. vi. 2 ff.). On their own testimony the
Nazarenes *recognised* something unique about Jesus, but
from prejudice and jealousy they refused to respond to it.

" I am come in My Father's name, and ye receive Me not "
(Jn. v. 43).

After His telling the Jews of the offering of His flesh and
blood for the life of the world : " Upon this many of His
disciples went back, and walked no more with Him. Jesus
said therefore unto the twelve, Would ye also go away ? "
(Jn. vi. 66–67).

On His last journey, the Samaritan village " did not receive Him, because His face was as though He were going to
Jerusalem " (Lk. ix. 53) : rejection from racial antipathy.

" O Jerusalem, Jerusalem, which killeth the prophets, and
stoneth them that are sent unto her ! how often would I have
gathered thy children together, even as a hen gathereth her
own brood under her wings, and ye would not ! " (Lk. xiii.
34).

It has already been pointed out (p. 25) that the excuses
with which He furnished the guests in His parable of the
Great Supper (Lk. xiv. 16–20) were representative of those
with which He was met during His own ministry. He and
His offers were rejected from inordinate attachment to
possessions, work, human relationships. His own prediction
of His Passion : " But first must He suffer many things and
be rejected of this generation " (Lk. xvii. 25).

The rich young man rejecting our Lord's advice for which
he had explicitly asked : " One thing thou lackest : go, sell
whatsoever thou hast, and give to the poor, and thou shalt
have treasure in heaven : and come, follow Me. But his
countenance fell at the saying, and he went away sorrowful :
for he was one that had great possessions " (Mk. x. 21–22).

" If the world hateth you, ye know that it hath hated Me

before it hated you . . . he that hateth Me hateth My
Father also. If I had not done among them the works
which none other did, they had not had sin : but now have
they both seen and hated both Me and My Father " (Jn. xv.
18 ff.).

Peter rejecting our Lord's prayer and warning offered
before his denial of Him (Lk. xxii. 31–34).

Scribes and Pharisees rejected Him *passim*.

Individually and collectively men rejected His offering of :

    Himself as the Light of the World.

    Himself as the Life of the World.

    Himself as the ' Door ' to the Father, Whose Name, i.e.
        Personality, He revealed.

    His teaching.

    His mighty works as interpreters of God's Eternal
        purposes of Love and Holiness.

Men rejected Him at all points of His vocation ; as :

    Son of God : preferring a God of their own imagining.

    King : preferring the rule of Self.

    Saviour : preferring to continue in darkness rather than
        face the cost of yielding themselves to be embraced
        by Light.

Yet never once was there " a hurt self " reaction to any
of this. He was in the world, not as His own trumpeter, but
only as the ambassador of the Father ; and therefore He
recognised that " he that rejecteth Me rejecteth Him that
sent Me " (Lk. x. 16). Herein lay for Him the bitterness of
rejected offering : the knowledge that the *Father's* overtures
of love were being repulsed ; and that Man by his own free
will—and to his own destruction—was deliberately cutting
himself off from his Creator, Father, Lover, and only
Satisfier.

It was increasingly borne in upon Jesus that though He
might *offer* His all to Man, it yet might not be accepted, and
could not—in the nature of Love—be forced. " I am the
living bread which came down out of heaven : *if* any man
eat of this bread, he shall live for ever : yea and the bread

which I will give is My flesh, for the life of the world " (Jn.
vi. 51). He *is* the true " bread of life " ; " but the Jews
murmured concerning Him ".   Yet, in face of all this repeatedly renewed in one form or another, He continued to go
on giving freely, ungrudgingly, expectantly. He had to
come inescapably to realise that the highest would not
always be *wanted* by Man even when offered to him. None
the less, He not only remained uncynical ; but retained a
supernatural faith for human nature.

Man's refusal of what He offered never made our Lord
alter or diminish His ceaseless outpouring of love. No
ingratitude ever soured or embittered Him.   Time and again
He followed up men's rejections with a fresh offering ; and
many of us have deep cause to know He does the same
to-day. So with Judas, to whom He extended more than
one ' last chance '. When Jesus knew him to be on the verge
of betraying Him, *for Judas' sake and not His own*, He sought
to woo him from sin by a favour, a courtesy, a graciousness
such as was customarily offered to an *honoured* guest :
" . . . So when He had dipped the sop, He taketh and giveth
it to Judas, the son of Simon Iscariot " (Jn. xiii. 26). Again,
in the Garden of Gethsemane, although he had previously
rejected what was offered him at the Last Supper, i.e.
enablement to resist temptation if he chose, Jesus renewed
offering to him—this time enablement for repentance if he
chose. "Friend, wherefore art thou come ? " (A.V. Matt. xxvi.
50).   Judas, *think* what it is that *you, who have companioned
Me*, are doing !   There must have been in Jesus' eyes that
same look of vicarious penitence, which later melted Peter
after his denial of his Master.

Rejected offering became prayer in our Lord by the
exercise of love and faith.   Rejected offering only released
further outpouring of His love and intercession for those
who failed or refused—be the motive what it might—to
accept what was proffered them by Him.   In love and faith,
He offered to the Father His desire *in place of their lack of
desire* that they should be " sanctified in truth ", that so in

His prayer the Father might have a channel for the Holy Spirit's eventual kindling of this desire in themselves. By faith our Lord set at naught rejected offering. He knew that no offering of Love, even although temporarily rejected, *could* go for nothing ; and so that love which underlay specific offers which had been rejected He again offered to flow into the one great Ocean of Love, thence to overflow, as, when, and where, the Father willed.

Prayer of Peace and Serenity

On the eve of His death our Lord gave to His disciples the greatest gift He had to give—His peace, which was essentially Himself. " Peace I leave with you ; My peace I give unto you ; not as the world giveth, give I unto you . . ." (Jn. xiv. 27). These words of bequeathal—as also earlier words of His to the Twelve : " Think not that I came to send peace on the earth : I came not to send peace, but a sword " (Matt. x. 34)—showed clearly that it was not a peace which would equate with ease or undisturbedness of circumstances.

Peace as achieved—and given—by our Lord was a freedom from self, not from difficulty, suffering, or even from sorrow. He attained peace, not by a negative, self-protective withdrawal from the hard realities of daily life, but by immersing His whole Being in the Father and—simply from sheer love of Him—actively co-operating with His Will.

Our Lord's prayer of peace was the deliberate anchorage of His Will and desire in Love. His serenity was worship of the Father All-Sufficing. Our Lord's incarnate prayer of peace was a correspondence in the flesh with the immutability of Eternal Love, ceaselessly generating and evoking fresh love. It was the unreserved givenness of His whole Being, body, mind, and spirit, to Love for the exercise of love to the uttermost under all circumstances, be these what they might.

" Jesus knowing . . . that He came from God, and goeth unto God . . . began to wash the disciples' feet, and to wipe them with the towel wherewith He was girded " (Jn. xiii. 3–5). Here the Holy Spirit has revealed the whole of Jesus' incarnate prayer of peace : faith and love habitually abiding in the Father as Source, Goal, and Companion ; and serving men in radiant humility for love both of Him and of them.

Our Lord's incarnate prayer of peace was the perfect and unbroken committal of Himself to a life of union with God in the Holy Spirit, simply because of His being what He is. It was, therefore, a prayer of worship ; glorifying the worth-ship of the Father the All-and-Only-to-be-Desired : a prayer of faith anchoring in the invincibleness of the Father's Love and Holiness. It was the supreme prayer of Sonship ; glad, unquestioning, confident dependence upon a Father known—by His essential Nature—to be infallible. It was a prayer of rejoicing : rejoicing to be possessed of, and by, *such* a God and Father of Love, Beauty, Wonder, and Holiness ; a God and Father alike to and for all mankind, because He cannot be other than All-Loving, All-Beauteous, All-Wondrous, All-Holy, be men what they may to Him. This prayer of peace—an abiding interior disposition of anchorage in the Father—expressed itself exteriorly in a variety of ways.

The hidden years in Nazareth, years of even—doubtless often monotonous—routine in home and craft, years free from external crises or circumstances of undue whirl or excitement, served to root our Lord in a *quietness*, a *stillness* of spirit drawing its life solely from God, and living it for Him alone. Then, at thirty, the Father changed the whole external setting of His life, calling Him to emerge from the externally peaceful routine of a comparatively sheltered private life into a public life, which necessitated constant fresh adjustment to circumstances ever changing and for the most part externally the very reverse of peaceful.

In the Temptation in the Wilderness preluding the public ministry it is impossible not to see—among other things—a diabolic assault upon the peace of our Lord : a supreme

10

testing of that peace which had come to be the habitual prayer of His life. Hitherto peace had been achieved amid external circumstances more or less favourable to it : now its reality was to be tested by circumstances which made—and would continue to make—rude assault upon it both exteriorly and interiorly. Exteriorly, peace had henceforth to be maintained—if maintained at all—amid crowds and movement from place to place, ceaseless encroachment upon His time and privacy; continuous pressure of human criticism, opposition, and wilful hostility. Interiorly, it had to be maintained amid all the problems and stress involved in the active dealing with the universal consequences of sin to which His baptism of vicarious penitence had committed Him.

Our Lord's prayer of peace during the ' hidden years ' was a life of love drawn from, and offered back to, the Father in trustful obedience, reverence, and worship. It was precisely in this same trustful obedience, reverence, and worship, that our Lord made His stand in repelling the Temptation—as is clearly shown by His ' answers ' to the Tempter, i.e. by the principles of His resistance—and also in embarking upon the new phase of the Lamb's progressive process of taking away the sin of the world. This phase entailed for Him a fresh and ever-intensifying degree of bearing our sins in His own body, mind, and spirit, until the binding-power of sin was finally annulled in the consummation of His perfect oblation of Himself to the Father.

The impact of the full force of the world's sin upon our Lord's Nature strained His peace almost to breaking-point more than once—as in His Palm Sunday anguish of spirit ; the Agony ; and the Dereliction—but although impinging upon it at surface level, it was never able to penetrate its inner citadel, i.e. that impregnable givenness to God of the very essence of His Being, which nothing earthly, or even diabolic, could ever undermine.

The fact that our Lord's peace was assailable at surface level—as He Himself has by His Holy Spirit expressly left

on record for us—makes us realise with all the more wonder
and worship that His prayer of peace was no effortless,
almost automatic state, natural if not inevitable to Him ;
but one which *needed achieving* just as much by Him as by
any who ever feel drawn to it by the Father as He was.
Only by perfect correspondence to the grace given by the
Father, through the Holy Spirit, was our Lord enabled to
persevere in that prayer of peace which is the prayer of
prayers, since it contains within itself the seed and heart of
all prayer. Expressed or dumb, it matters not ; since
basically this prayer of peace is the soul's exclusive allegiance
to God ; the fusion of the will of the created with that of
the Creator ; the one-ing of spirit and Spirit.

Such was the reality and potency of our Lord's prayer of
peace that neither men's intrusion upon His privacy or
time; their hostility or ununderstanding; personal danger or
suffering ; nor humanly insurmountable difficulties had
power to dispel His peace. He worshipped the Father by
imperturbability. Perhaps one of the most glorious instances of this was His healing of Jairus' daughter (Mk. v.
22 ff.).

" Some came from Jairus' house saying, Thy daughter is
dead ". Nothing was more probable than that the news was
true—since Jairus had already told Him that she was at the
point of death—and that things were humanly irremediable.
But " Jesus, not heeding the word spoken, saith unto the
ruler of the synagogue, Fear not, only believe ". His knowledge of the character and power of the Father bulwarked
Him always to rule out the *finality* of sorrow, evil, or death,
the worst-seeming human appearances notwithstanding.
He knew that the Father's Will was for life, and for peace,
and for joy: and He banked and acted on this always in
calm and steadfast confidence. No apparently irrevocable
calamity could imperil for Him the certitude of the redemptive power of God. He knew the Father equally almighty
in human extremity as in easy fortune. " And when He
was entered in, He saith unto them . . . the child is not

dead but sleepeth. And they laughed Him to scorn ". As
He was unshaken by circumstances, so neither was He shaken
by human opinion conflicting with His own : God, God's
good-will and power were His surety and His driving-force.
Neither circumstances nor opinion ever deflected Him from
the God-appointed task in hand. This imperturbability in
God resulted in the humanly miraculous, and—as in this
case of Jairus' daughter—brought life out of death, joy out
of disaster, peace out of distraction.

His prayer of peace bore fruit in wonderful poise. He was
able to rest disciplinedly and trustfully in the heaviest press
of work and claims of need upon Him : no small achievement
in itself. He never let Himself be stampeded or swept off
His feet by any external clamour, mob emotion, or force,
e.g. the people, after His feeding of the five thousand, wanting to make Him king.

" . . . Did not we cast three men *bound* into the midst of
the fire ? . . . Lo, I see . . . men *loose*, walking in the
midst of the fire, and they have no hurt . . ." (Dan. iii.
24–25) : a practical illustration of the eternal truth that
only in, and through, the furnace can come that final freedom
which is unassailable. So it was with our Lord. The
liberation following upon the furnace of the Agony in
Gethsemane found expression in the transcendent SERENITY
which was outstanding in His Passion : the Passion which,
in vicarious penitence, He made in its entirety an offering of
peace to the Father, offsetting the turbulence of men out-
raging His Nature and Purposes.

When in the Garden His would-be captors had Him virtually in their hands, they were so unnerved by the majesty of
His serenity as to be unable to take Him. " Jesus therefore,
knowing all the things that were coming upon Him, went
forth, and saith unto them, Whom seek ye ? They answered
Him, Jesus of Nazareth. Jesus saith unto them, I am He
. . . When therefore He said unto them, I am He, they went
backward, and fell to the ground. Again therefore He asked
them, Whom seek ye ? And they said, Jesus of Nazareth.

Jesus answered, I told you that I am He . . ." (Jn. xviii.
4 ff.).   He Himself had said earlier : " . . . I lay down My
life. . . . No one taketh it from Me, but I lay it down of
Myself " (Jn. x. 17 f.).

Truly this was so.   None could, against His will, pierce
through a serenity so profound as to be perceptibly inviolable
even to those bent on violence.   No cross-questioning in the
dock ; no false witness against Him ; no outrage, physical,
mental, or spiritual, against Him, could shake His serenity,
even when both His body and His emotional nature were
spent with exhaustion.   Total absence of self-defensive
anxiety it was, in large part, which made possible His unbroken continuity of the prayer of peace even throughout
the whole process of being stripped of everything even to life
itself.   The Cross was the consummation of our Lord's
perfect prayer of peace ; for His was the perfect peace of
self-naughting in obedient, trusting, generous, love-fired
co-operation with the purposes of the Father.

Jesus incomparably beautiful !   Many are the titles which
have been given to Him in love and adoration.   One of the
loveliest of these is " Prince of Peace ".   He is the Prince of
Peace because He is the Prince of Lovers : Himself unutterably lovable, and having in His deathless love the ring
of immortal youth.

Prayer of Compassion, Patience, and Understanding

" Now after that John was delivered up, Jesus came into
Galilee, preaching [Gk. = proclaiming, publishing abroad]
the gospel of God, and saying, The time is fulfilled, and the
kingdom of God is at hand : repent ye, and believe in the
gospel " (Mk. i. 14–15).   It was our Lord's prayer of compassion, patience, and understanding which in large measure
effected this proclaiming of God as Himself the good news.

Man by his sin had forfeited the power truly to perceive
the Nature of God.   Guilty conscience had begotten in him
the fear of God as a ruthless Judge—if not an Enemy—
finding His satisfaction in punishing him.   On the basis of

this misconception of God, Man—himself utterly incapable of breaking with sin—was in a literally hopeless state, with no prospect of anything but ultimate perdition ahead of him. From Man's side there was—and could be—no hope. Hope—if any at all—could only come from God. To make Man know the surety of this hope from God—God Himself as the One Hope, the Saviour and not the Condemner of Man—it was essential that there should be a true interpretation of God's intrinsic Nature. This interpretation the Father Himself gave, through the Holy Spirit, in the Person of Jesus, Whose Nature was at all points identical with His own. Our Lord's prayer of compassion, patience, and understanding was a perpetual prayer of glorifying the Father, i.e. making Him known as He is.

Our Lord's compassion was fundamentally an innate disposition drawn from His sharing of the Nature of the Father, of Whom He Himself declared: " the Most High . . . is kind toward the unthankful and evil " (Lk. vi. 35). His prayer of compassion was the revelation—in intention, in word, in deed, and in teaching—of this disposition of compassion, patience, and understanding as eternally inherent in God. It was, moreover, an intense appeal to Man to take his stand on God being what He is changelessly and for ever ; to turn from self where is only despair and ultimate madness, and to dare to believe the good news of a God desirous and able to save him.

Only a God Whose Holiness is such as to make absolutely impossible and unthinkable any compromise with sin, could dare reveal Himself so clement to sinners as, in and through Jesus, the Father has done. In more than one parable our Lord portrayed the divine compassion, patience, and understanding as altogether beyond any reasonable human expectation. In the parable of the Unmerciful Servant (Matt. xviii. 26 ff.), He enshrined the sublime utterance— and every utterance of His is eternal truth—" I forgave thee all that debt *because thou besoughtest me* ". Surely these words of a Master to the servant hopelessly indebted to him are a revelation of God to inspire confidence, even in those of us most conscious both of our sin and of the extent of our indebtedness to Him in His Love and Generosity. In the parable of the Good Samaritan (Lk. x. 30 ff.), our Lord illustrated the concrete exercise of the divine compassion. First the strong tenderness in face of suffering as such, *without any analysing of the deserts of the sufferer.* (How easily the Good Samaritan might have argued that had the traveller not been deserving of it he would never have been reduced to such a plight ; or, had he not been a fool he would have avoided laying himself open to it !) Then practical help given at personal inconvenience and cost for just so long as necessary ; and subsequently, provision against future need. The sense of responsibility for the continuance of help in building up the sufferer, even after the initial crisis has been met.

In the matchless parable of the Prodigal Son (Lk. xv. 11 ff.), there is the divine compassion not only for the sower of wild oats—" But while he was yet afar off, his father saw him, and was moved with compassion and ran, and fell on his neck and kissed him "—but also the patient, loving understanding with the elder brother, who " was angry, and would not go in : and his father came out, and intreated him. . . . Son, thou art ever with me, and all that is mine is thine ". In the joy of welcoming the returned prodigal there is no neglect of love toward him who wilfully refuses to enter into that joy. Each is compassionated according to his own need : love ever seeking to draw all—however humanly unattractive—within the circle of its own blessedness.

Our Lord's prayer of compassion, patience, and understanding was a life-practice of the disposition which He portrayed in the Lord of the Unmerciful Servant, the Good Samaritan, and the Father of the Prodigal Son.

The compassion of Jesus was always balanced : wide and diverse as well as deep and intense ; peaceful as well as energetic. It never lost sight of the individual in the multitude, or of the multitude in the individual. His sympathy was never limited to one or two particular kinds of suffering, but embraced all alike—whether physical, mental, moral, or spiritual misery, material anxieties, ignorance, bewilderment, or fearfulness. His delicacy with regard to the feelings of others was a courtesy unutterably beautiful in itself, and singularly potent in evoking from them a better self surprising even to themselves. His acts of compassion had never a trace of patronising condescension. The feelings of others were for Him sacred ; and never to be hurt from carelessness, lack of consideration or imagination, but only —and then unflinchingly—where it was unavoidable in their deepest spiritual interests. He placed Himself alongside each and all, and by the consecrated and prayerful use of His imagination made understanding allowances for them where so to do was creative. Yet He was none the less able, whenever necessary, to make ruthless supernatural demands upon ordinary men and women.

Our Lord's compassion was never a barren sentiment, but always a practical and immediate lifting of the suffering or need, to the Father by prayer, so that through Him the Father might' liberate His own redemptive power, always unfailingly sufficient for the meeting of any and every need, however humanly taxing. Hence it was that His compassion was always bracing, and invariably pierced through surface symptoms to root needs. It was never a mere expression of condolence, acquiescing in continuance of the trouble ; but quickening faith in the Father's Will for perfection, introduced to transmute the whole situation.

At bare sight—or sensing—of need, even before any appeal for help was actually made to Him, our Lord's compassion flowed spontaneously, and its flow was effective intercessory prayer. There are many recorded instances of this in the Gospels, both with regard to individuals and to crowds, e.g. the Widow of Nain (Lk. vii. 11 ff.) ; the Impotent Man at the Pool of Bethesda (Jn. v. 1 ff.) ; the shepherdless and hungry multitude in a desert place (Mk. vi. 34 ff. ; Matt.

xv. 32) ; Jerusalem in its blind self-destruction (Lk. xiii.
34 ; xix. 41–42) ; the Woman which had a spirit of infirmity
eighteen years (Lk. xiii. 10 ff.), etc. No suffering, however
loathsome physically, mentally, or morally, ever repelled
Him from those in its toils. This was because love was the
sole source of His compassion, and love cannot be repelled ;
by its very nature it yearns to—and must inevitably—
share the miseries of the beloved until such time as the
beloved is freed to share its own wholeness.

Never did any experience of His own, however exalting or
desolating, make our Lord even temporarily oblivious to the
needs of others. After the multitude have wanted to take
Him by force and make Him king (Jn. vi. 15), He withdrew
alone to a mountain to pray. There, as He knelt rapt in
communion with the Father, was vouchsafed to Him
a wondrous vision of the true nature of the Kingdom
promised to Him. But even thus gloriously caught up into
Eternity, there broke in upon Him the sense of His beloved
disciples in need, " distressed in rowing, for the wind was
contrary unto them" (Mk. vi. 48 ff.).

Then—since Love's essence is identification with the
beloved ; is instantaneous forthgoing to the joy or sorrow of
the beloved ; is compassionate meeting of the need of the
beloved—" about the fourth watch of the night He cometh
unto them, walking on the sea . . . and saith unto them,
Be of good cheer : it is I ; be not afraid. And He went up
unto them into the boat ; and the wind ceased. . . ".
This walking on the sea was no spectacular " display " of
power over Nature, as has sometimes been assumed quite
unjustifiably, since such a motive for the exercise of His
miraculous power would have been entirely incompatible
with all that He had rejected, once and for all, in this connection in the Temptation in the Wilderness. It was something unself-consciously, unthinkingly accomplished by
Love Omnipotent and Compassionate, which neither heeds
nor notices obstacles arising in the path of its self-donation.
How should it be any more difficult for Jesus then—caught

up into the vision of the consummated Kingdom of Love Invincible—to walk on the sea than on land ?   If human love faced by need or danger can—as it does—rise to feats ordinarily impossible in cold blood, how much more so then Divine Love !   That Jesus as man should walk on the sea was merely a ' miracle ' *incidental* to the infinitely profounder and more miraculous miracle that He as man should so *love* as He loved, with a love thus infinitely compassionate.

Similarly, all through the stress of the Agony and the Crucifixion His prayer of compassion still flowed ceaselessly, embracing alike the individual and the mass, lifting their need to the Father in self-forgetfulness of His own.

" He Himself knew what was in man " (Jn. ii. 25).   He knew that in man was the Divine Image in which God had created him.   He knew also that Man had sold himself a bond-slave to sin, and thereby so warped the divine nature implanted in him, that only by slow way of blood and tears to the nature he had misbegotten for himself *could* he receive the redemption wrought for him by God.   Jesus' under-standing of men was derived from His union with the Mind of the Father : it was *the Creator's understanding of that which He has created*.   Jesus' complete understandingness both of good and evil in Man it was which made Him so patient with him.   He knew from how far a country each and all had to return to the Father : and knowing the full extremity of Man's plight, He never despised even his most pitiable and unstable efforts to turn from darkness to light. But above all He knew the Father, and so He could never despair for any man or woman.

It was this complete understandingness of His both of the good and of the evil in them, which, sensed by those who were sick in body, mind, or spirit, was as a magnet drawing them to Him and evoking their unreserved confidence.   All, however diverse in temperament, knew themselves exhaus-tively understood by Him as even they could not under-stand themselves.   Each felt that His compassion unriddled every fact to its depth, and in full cognisance of it still conveyed the absolutely convincing assurance—which centuries later He Himself articulated to Julian of Norwich —" I may make all thing well, I can make all thing well, I will make all thing well, and I shall make all thing well ; and thou shalt see thyself that all manner of thing shall be well."

In the synagogue at Nazareth (Lk. iv. 16 ff.), our Lord claimed for Himself : " The Spirit of the Lord is upon Me, because He anointed Me to preach good tidings to the poor : He hath sent Me to proclaim release to the captives . . . to set at liberty them that are bruised ". His prayer of compassion, patience, and understanding was the fulfilling of this vocation. *His prayer of compassion liberated without condemnation.* " Neither do I condemn thee : go thy way ; from henceforth sin no more " (Jn. viii. 11) ; this—said to the woman taken in adultery—was His attitude to all : " I came not to judge the world, but to save the world " (Jn. xii. 47). He was patient with the disciples even when they were most flagrantly in the wrong. His way with them was not that of denunciation, but of love's ceaseless bestowal of the alluring vision and example of perfection at each point where they fell short.

Our Lord's prayer of compassion was basic union with the redemptive Will of the Father for all mankind. " The Son of Man came to seek and to save that which was lost " (Lk. xix. 10) : it was for this that He was ' sent ' by the Father. Boundless was His understanding of Man's need : boundless was His compassion in self-donation to meet that need. The prayer of compassion offered throughout His incarnate life continues now as part of His High-Priestly prayer. The prayer of His compassion—of His self-donation—is for all time : like Himself it is " the same yesterday, and to-day, and for ever " :

" Come unto Me, all ye that labour and are heavy laden, and I will give you rest " (Matt. xi. 28).

" If any man thirst, let him come unto Me, and drink " (Jn. vii. 37).

" Take, eat ; this is My Body . . . Drink . . . this is My Blood of the Covenant, which is shed for many unto remission of sins . . ." (Matt. xxvi. 26–27).

" Father, forgive them . . ." (Lk. xxiii. 34) ;
and He Himself, the Word of Truth, has declared that His prayer is always and unfailingly heard by the Father—by " the Most High . . . kind toward the unthankful and evil ".

How great then—in spite of all our undeserving—is our hope in Him. " With man it is impossible " that he should be saved ; " but with God all things are possible ", because He is Love and Love never fails.

" His compassions fail not " : this is perhaps *the* truth of which life's experience has most profoundly convinced many of us, as inescapably we recognise, with awe and thankfulness of our innermost being, how altogether otherwise from the mercies God has vouchsafed are our deserts. It is to Jesus' prayer of compassion—ever releasing, through the Holy Spirit, the redemptive and sanctifying love of our Father— that we owe all these mercies.

Prayer of Sanctity

Our Lord's prayer of sanctity was a progressive abandonment in the Holy Spirit for exhaustive identification with the Being and Will of the Father. It was a prayer ceaselessly liberated by His consistent and unbroken resistance to temptation ; and offered back to the Father both in vicarious penitence and reparation, and in intercession for souls.

This prayer was motivated by His twofold desire :

" Father, glorify Thy Name " (Jn. xii. 28)—Reveal Holiness Thyself ;

" . . . that they themselves also [i.e. " which Thou hast given Me "] may be sanctified in truth " (Jn. xvii. 19) ;
it may, therefore, be said to be the composite prayer of His Sonship and of His Saviourhood.

On the eve of His death, Jesus, Truth Incarnate, declared :

" The prince of this world cometh, and hath nothing in Me "
(Jn. xiv. 30). These quiet words enshrine a stupendous
reality which we shall only be able really to *fathom* in
Eternity. In this sublime declaration the Holy Spirit has
revealed to us the fruit of Jesus' prayer of sanctity : imperviousness to sin—and imperviousness to sin creating for
sinful Man an eternal sanctuary, inviolable by the powers of
evil which he has loosed to his own destruction. Jesus'
prayer of sanctity is Man's *sole* inviolable sanctuary from
sin ; his sole impregnable refuge in time of temptation ;
because the citadel of His Incarnate Nature is the sole
human citadel which has never capitulated to evil. In
worship of Jesus, in Whom the prince of this world hath
nothing, is the sinner's liberation.

Jesus' prayer of sanctity is not separable from Himself :
He Himself is that prayer, and that prayer is Himself.
Therefore to refuge in His prayer of sanctity is not only to
refuge in His intercession, mediating the desire and the
enablement to resist temptation ; but to refuge in Himself,
in His Sacred Heart, the Holy of Holies, in Whom—and in
Whom alone—is safe-keeping from renewal of sin. Jesus'
prayer of sanctity sunders the sinner from his sin. It
gradually consumes and annihilates sin ; and restores unimpaired in the sinner the original image of God in which he
was created, i.e. quickens in him the perfect functioning of
the divine nature and life for which he was designed—fulfils
the soul's unique vocation.

Prayer of His Blood

So absolutely as ' one of ourselves ' does our Lord come.to
each and all—whether race, class, or temperament—that it is
often difficult for non-Jews to remember that incarnate He
was essentially a Jew, rooted and grounded in the whole body
of Jewish tradition and law—His mind and spirit saturated
with it. But so it was.

All our Lord's conception of the unique significance of

blood was derived from the Scriptures, where it equates with :

Life : " . . . flesh with the life thereof, which is the blood thereof . . ." (Gen. ix. 4 ; cf. Septuagint : " . . . flesh with blood of life . . .").

Salvation : The divine command at the Institution of the Passover—" And the blood shall be to you for a token upon the houses where ye are : and when I see the blood, I will pass over you, and there shall no plague be upon you to destroy you, when I smite the land of Egypt " (Ex. xii. 13 ; cf. Septuagint : " . . . I will see the blood, and will protect you ").

Sanctification : The divine command for the consecration of priests—" And thou shalt take of the blood that is upon the altar, and of the anointing oil, and sprinkle it upon Aaron . . . and upon his sons . . . and he shall be hallowed . . . and his sons " (Ex. xxix. 21).

Offering for Sin : for the shedding of bullocks' and rams' blood in this connection, see Ex. xxix.–xxx. *passim.*

But deep meditation upon the whole mystery of ' blood ' as enshrined in the Scriptures must humanly have given Him to pause, and caused Him to draw upon the Holy Spirit for further revelation concerning it.

" Hear, O My people, and I will speak ; O Israel, and I will testify unto thee : I am God even thy God . . . thy burnt offerings are continually before Me . . . Will I eat the flesh of bulls, or drink the blood of goats ? " (Ps. l. 7 ff.).

" . . . with the blood of the sin offering of atonement once in the year . . . make atonement . . . throughout your generations . . ." (Ex. xxx. 10).

An endless renewal of offering of blood of bullocks and goats for sin ! Patently this was only a symbolic prototype of an effectual reality yet to be achieved—a yearning aspiration towards the fulfilment of a most deeply recognised and basic need.

Our Lord's prayer of His blood completely fulfilled **every** uniquely sacred function of blood as revealed in the Scriptures ; that is to say, it was life, it was redemption, it was sanctification, it was offering for sin ; and in the Holy Spirit's further revelation to Him of the Will of the Father it realised all that had but been typified before.

Blood as Life : Our Lord's prayer of blood as life was twofold. It was the Word being made flesh in order to take to Himself human life as well as divine—" Since the children are sharers in flesh and blood, He also Himself in like manner partook of the same . . ." (Heb. ii. 14)— and therefore His whole incarnate life was a prayer of His blood. It was also His *imparting* of life to men—" Jesus therefore said unto them, Verily, Verily, I say unto you, Except ye eat the flesh of the Son of Man and drink His blood, ye have not life in yourselves " (Jn. vi. 53).

Blood as Salvation : " For it was the good pleasure of the Father . . . through Him to reconcile all things unto Himself, *having made peace through the blood of His Cross* " (Col. i. 19–20) : the reconciliation of Man to God that is Man's salvation was the fruit of the prayer of Jesus' blood.

Blood as Sanctification : " Wherefore Jesus also, that He might sanctify the people through His own blood, suffered without the gate " (Heb. xiii. 12) ; " . . . the blood of Jesus His Son cleanseth us from all sin " (1 Jn. i. 7) ; " . . . These are they which come out of the great tribulation, and they washed their robes, and made them white in the blood of the Lamb " (Rev. vii. 14).

Blood as Offering for Sin : " Nor yet that He should offer Himself often ; as the high priest entereth into the holy place year by year with blood not his own ; else must He often have suffered since the foundation of the world : but now once at the end [Gk. = consummation] of the ages hath He been manifested to put away sin by the sacrifice of Himself " (Heb. ix. 25–26). This prayer of Jesus' blood was part of His vicarious penitence and reparation.

A deliberate free-will offering was Jesus' prayer of His blood. It was not self-chosen, nor yet was it making a virtue of necessity. It was a voluntary union with the Will of the Father at all points, from the Pre-existent "Fiat" for the Incarnation with which it came into being, through the laying down His life of His own will, i.e. at the Will of the Father and not at the will of men, to His ever fresh, "This is My Blood of the New Testament, which is shed for you and for many for the remission of sins", which moment by moment as long as time shall last the Divine Generosity and Compassion bespeaks through the lips of some priest somewhere in the length and breadth of the world.

"So when Pilate saw that he prevailed nothing, but rather that a tumult was arising, he took water, and washed his hands before the multitude, saying, I am innocent of the blood of this righteous man : see ye to it. And all the people answered and said, His blood be on us, and on our children" (Matt. xxvii. 24–25). Instantaneously must the prayer of His blood have transmuted their "His blood be on us, and on our children" to "Father, let My blood be upon them and upon their children—till time shall end—only for redemption and for sanctification". May *we* all be redeemed and sanctified by this prayer of His blood, the supreme prayer of His love—"Greater love hath no man than this, that a man lay down his life for his friends" (Jn. xv. 13).

Prayer of Truth

Our Lord Himself summed up His incarnate life, on its last morning, in terms of truth : "To this end have I been born, and to this end am I come into the world, that I should bear witness unto the truth" (Jn. xviii. 37) ; and on the previous evening He had explicitly claimed *Himself* to *be* the truth—"Jesus saith . . . I am the way, the truth, and the life" (Jn. xiv. 6). All His teaching was a part of this ' witness unto the truth ".

God's " I AM THAT I AM " : this was His prayer of truth—

the manifesting to men of the Holy Father with Whom He was completely identified in mind, will, and spirit. It was also an unbroken correspondence with the Essential Nature of the Father in the innermost citadel of His Being, in order that the Father might in intercommunion of Reality with reality find plenary satisfaction for His love.

His prayer of truth was contemplative : the continual beholding, listening to, and reflecting of, the Father in the Holy Spirit. It was the courage of unflinching willingness to see true, i.e. to see God as Light, and also to see " the thick darkness " round about Him, and the full exposure of sin in the light of His Holiness. It was the consistent living of a life of such perfect moral integrity as to make true vision possible. It was life lived on the basis of an ever-worshipping avowal of God the Alone Perfect inherently without beginning and without end. It was supreme worship offered in exultant humility : the avowal and enthroning of Love, Beauty, and Holiness as alone eternally all-in-all and invincible. It was the habitual stilling of self in loving reverence before the immensity, beauty, and transcendent rightness of the Will of the Father.

Our Lord's prayer of truth was a prayer of the mind as well as of the spirit. It was a rigorous disciplining of the imagination, involving the total rejection of day-dreaming round self, the total elimination of any working up of the emotions as an end in itself. It was, from His earliest years till the very day of His death, a ceaseless *questing* of mind and spirit to know progressively, by all means at His disposal, the fulness of spiritual truth. Even as a child He took the opportunity of ' consulting '—off the ground of all He had already penetrated in prayer and meditation upon the Scriptures—with the doctors in the Temple.

It was the perpetual fresh appraising and dealing with life in right perspective—the perspective of facts as they are in relation to God and Eternity—unbiased by self and its desires. It was anchorage in Reality by dint of an unremitting " No " to all else. It was the bringing everything

II

always and instantaneously to the bar of God in Whom alone is perfect, enduring Reality. It was a *plunging* into the abyss of Reality *in readiness to sustain its consequences*, instead of deliberately trying to escape suffering by merely skimming only its surface. It was a plunging to the heart of Reality in order to correspond with it. This anchorage in Reality was the heart of our Lord's incarnate joy, and the heart of His incarnate suffering : the joy in God being what He is ; the untold suffering in the fact and effects of sin.

Costly to our Lord, beyond power of human imagination or even love to conceive, was His prayer of truth, because it involved His facing, up to the hilt, all the facts of time as well as of Eternity, i.e. the seeing *with exhaustive understanding of its significance* the whole abyss of sin together with all its concomitant suffering, as well as the depths of the abysses of Love and Holiness. The minds and spirits of *sinners*—who can never truly see or realise sin for what it is —can at times come to reel literally to, if not over, the verge of insanity at realisation simply of their own individual sin, an infinitesimal fraction of the whole body of universal sin. *Think*, then, what must have been the impact upon the *sinless* human mind and spirit of Jesus of the sin of the whole world in its stark reality as it appears to God ! Jesus' " I am the truth " means that He is the One Who has the power not only of courage to plumb all the secret recesses of sin in each and every soul, but also of inundating them with transmuting Love and Holiness from the abysses which alone are eternal.

His prayer of truth ceaselessly consumes—and *liberates* us from bondage to—the unreal, until Ultimate Reality, i.e. Love and Holiness, alone remains. Through our self-perverseness this liberation can only be wrought by Him at cost to us of blood, tears, and fire ; but even this is but a small price to pay for the unutterable gift of being rescued from the nightmare quicksands of falsity to the security of eventual grounding on a rock-foundation of unassailable reality in Him.

" Howbeit when He, the Spirit of truth, is come, He shall guide [Gk. = lead on one's way] you into all the truth " (Jn. xvi. 13) : this farewell promise of our Lord's to His disciples is an open promise to all who will accept from the Father the gift of His Holy Spirit. It is also the laying bare to us the key to His own incarnate prayer of truth : perpetual abandonment to the Holy Spirit to be taken on step by step in the way leading back to the bosom of the Father. His prayer of truth was anchorage in the Holy Spirit in " knowing . . . that He came forth from God, and goeth unto God " (Jn. xiii. 3) ; and for our union with Him in this prayer He now ceaselessly intercedes.

Prayer of Life

Jesus declared : " For as the Father hath life in Himself, even so gave He to the Son also to have life in Himself " (Jn. v. 26). His prayer of life was the perfect exercise of that gift—the well-spring of love—entrusted to Him. All the inexhaustible powers of loving given to be inherent in Him, He directed first and foremost back to the Father Himself, and from thence radiated them to embrace all souls already—or still to be—created by Him. His prayer of life was an energy of love ceaselessly and solely expended for the glory of God and the redemption of men—" . . . I love the Father, and as the Father gave Me commandment even so I do " (Jn. xiv. 31) : " For verily the Son of Man came . . . to give His life a ransom for many " (Mk. x. 45) ; " I lay down My life for the sheep " (Jn. x. 15).

' Life ' to Jesus was synonymous with ' Father ' : the Father eternally loving and evoking love. Union with the Father in His Holy Spirit, that—and that alone—was life. The abandonment to the Holy Spirit for this union was His prayer of life and His life of prayer. " I am come that they may have life, and may have it abundantly " (Jn. x. 10) ; His prayer of life was offered in order to reveal the Father to men, and to draw them into like abandonment to His own to the Holy Spirit for union with Him. It was offered also in order to give back to the Father a redeemed humanity. His Prayer of life was the bringing down from heaven of the Divine Nature into human flesh ; and the taking up—at the Ascension—of perfect humanity into the Godhead.

Paradoxically, Jesus' prayer of life was limitless and inexhaustible, and yet, as He Himself has told us, it was " narrow . . . and straitened " (Matt. vii. 14). An energy of love functioning invincibly in Eternity : *in time* it was a perpetual laying down of self-life in order to take again— and release for others—the Divine Life ; the perpetual rejection of self-will making possible a perpetual choice of the Will of the Father, itself the functioning of Love flamingly alive without beginning and without end.

Prayer of Simplicity

Our Lord's prayer of simplicity was a prayer of integrity, i.e. of singleness, of trust, and of liberty. It was the harmony of a spirit, mind, and body voluntarily functioning but as one sole, ceaseless, and unquenchable impulse of love towards the Father. It was a Son's confident resting in His Father—utterly content quietly to trust the Wisdom and Power of the Father's love, and to make that trust the practical basis of all His action and conduct. It was the complete liberty of objective living for God instead of subjective living for self ; the liberty of a mind knowing no complex labyrinths of self-preoccupation because deliberately merged in the infinite purity of the Mind of the Father ; the liberty of a dependence upon the Father so absolute as to preclude any other bondage whatsoever— whether to self, to circumstances, or to other people ; the liberty of sinlessness immune from sin's trail of complexities.

Jesus' prayer of simplicity was life—and being—solved and motivated solely by love.

Prayer of Changelessness

" I am the Lord, I change not " (Mal. iii. 6). How often, and how deeply must our Lord have both meditated and experienced this changelessness of the Father, eternally Love, eternally Holiness, eternally Truth. His own prayer of changelessness was an identification in the Holy Spirit with the Unchanging Father, ever essentially one and the same. Jesus Himself said : " Every one that committeth sin is the bondservant of sin. And the bondservant abideth not in the house for ever : *the son abideth for ever* " (Jn. viii. 34–35) ; this was His prayer of changelessness : the prayer of the Son abiding in the Father's house—in the Father's bosom, in the Father's Very Self—for ever.

Our Lord's God-anchored serenity resisted the swirl of human unrest all about Him, and rendered Him immune from the contagion of fluctuating thoughts and emotions ceaselessly flickering and guttering in men and women everywhere. His prayer of changelessness was in part made possible by the self-denial and discipline which rigorously excluded any moral or spiritual capitulation to moods whether of body, mind, or spirit ; and in part by His constant subordination of the natural to the supernatural, and of the temporal to the eternal. *Interiorly* there was habitual withdrawal from the restless flux of the world and of Man in order to plunge into the stillness of the eternal—i.e. through the Holy Spirit into the Heart of the Father—so that there might be mediated to Man the knowledge of the Unchanging Father, Whose Heart is Man's only possible Abiding-place of Peace.

Our Lord's prayer of changelessness was a prayer of loyalty and reliability : a prayer of unswerving loyalty to the Father ; a prayer of self-donation to Man as " Jesus Christ the same yesterday, and to-day, and for ever " (Heb. xiii. 8). It was a prayer of impenetrable stability. This prayer of His changelessness is the sinner's final hope, and ground for our inexpressibly deep thanksgiving. Jesus, " Him with Whom we have to do "—to use the thought-provoking phrase of the writer of the Epistle to the Hebrews (Heb. iv. 13)—is utterly dependable ; such as He was He is, and such as He is He ever will be. Never can His mercy and com-

passion diminish, His generosity abate, nor His love stale ;
so neither can there be any slacking of His inexorable demand upon us to abandon ourselves unreservedly to be made
one with Him in holiness, if we would be brought into eternal
life in God and not die in our sins.

The Pre-existent Word ; the adorable incarnate Jesus of
the Gospels, " full of grace and truth " ; the Risen and
Ascended Christ ; the Great High Priest ; the Lamb of God ;
Jesus of the Mystical Body ; by His prayer of changelessness will to-day and for eternity be *all this* in any soul who
will let Him.   " Behold, I stand at the door, and knock : if
any man hear My voice, and open the door, I will come in to
him. . . ." (Rev. iii. 20) ; so in His changelessness He perpetually renews this promise to each one of us until—for
very love of His love and patience—in contrition and joy
we belatedly embrace it.

All the ' interior methods ' of our Lord's prayer were
gathered up in :

Prayer of Love to the Uttermost

Love incarnate in a fallen world inevitably suffers.
Hence our Lord's exercise of love to the uttermost entailed
for Him companionate suffering likewise to the uttermost.
(For the extent and nature of this suffering see pp. 124 ff. ;
164 ff. ; and 258 ff.)

No suffering could, however, dam up the flow of Jesus'
love, ever ceaselessly new as well as ever eternally the same.
The exercise of His love was never limited by the keeping of
any preserves from physical, mental, or spiritual suffering
as beyond what was to be expected or endured.   This love
of His was without reservation ; inextinguishable ; many
faceted ; and inexhaustible : and to its all-pervasiveness
nothing can ultimately remain impermeable.

Through all suffering our Lord rested in the certain
knowledge that nothing, and no one, but self can ever
prevent Love from functioning.   All of which His incarnate
love was stripped—material for gift ; response from the

beloved—was but so much fuel for its intenser, wider, deeper functioning in the unadulterated self-donation of its own essential being. It was precisely when the sole activity left open to Him was to love through suffering that fettered His body to immobility, and strained His mind and spirit to the uttermost, that His supreme fruit-bearing was effected.

It was in Jesus' Words from the Cross that the cumulative loving of a life-time found supreme expression : " Father, forgive them ; for they know not what they do " (Lk. xxiii. 34) : unelicited and all-embracing Love, gloriously vindicating the possibility of fulfilment of His own dictum : " Love your enemies, do good to them that hate you, bless them that curse you, pray for them that despitefully use you " (Lk. vi. 27–28). *What* a trail of injury and outrage there was needing His forgiveness ! Yet Love amply covered it all. Just nothing in the way of unloveliness or human unlovableness—no perpetration of sin or multitude of sins—ever excluded any from His love. No outrage whatsoever, no series of outrages, could ever poison His love to impatience, disgust, lukewarmness, or despair. He could —and did—love everyone *in the raw*, even at the very time of their sinning and before they evinced any intention of repentance.

" Verily, I say unto thee, To-day shalt thou be with Me in Paradise " (Lk. xxiii. 43) : Love's *listening*. Selfless listening—absolutely unimpaired and undeflected by His own personal, intensely acute, *present* suffering, weakness, and problems—not only *to*, but *for* expression of, the need of the beloved. Listening : compassionate, divining, recreative. Love's *responsiveness* : in excess of all demand or imagining. Love's *generosity* : offering the uttermost—i.e. identification with Himself : " Thou . . . with Me . . ."—in spite of personal injury previously received. Love's *humility* : willingness to be identified with one who had been malefactor, robber, and mocker.

" He saith unto His Mother, Woman, behold, thy son !

Then saith He to the disciple, Behold, thy mother ! "
(Jn. xix. 26–27) : Love's *drawing-power* in life and in death.
Love drawing others, not only to Himself, but also to one
another in Him.   The perfect trinity of love between Jesus,
His Mother, and the beloved disciple John in life, that He
could, at death, with confidence and certainty bequeath
them to one another to fulfil His own relationship to each.
Love's *thoughtfulness* : occupied with the needs of others in
the very midst of His own extremity, He left nothing un-
provided for ; but rounded everything through storm and
stress to peace.   Love's *insight* : there were others to whom
Jesus could as, and perhaps more, easily have committed
His Mother ; others more conventionally suitable—Martha,
Mary, and Lazarus ; Mary Magdalene ; some of the richer
women who followed Him—all of whom would have been
more than glad to care for her, both for His sake and for
her own.

But Love knew the need of heart and spirit.   Between no
other two in the world could there be such comforting, vital,
and fruitful spiritual fellowship and communion, as between
the two nearest His heart in love and understanding.   The
commitment of His Mother to John, and of John to His
Mother, was for their *mutual* welfare : He foresaw what each
could be and do for the other.   John had even greater
spiritual need of the Mother of Jesus than she of him in any
way whatsoever : there was still so much that John hungered to know of Jesus which Mary could satisfy.   Jesus
knew that in giving John His Mother He was equipping him
uniquely for the fulfilment of his vocation as the apostle and
evangelist of love.   Love's *faith* : implicit trust.   He did
not question their willingness ; but took it for granted, and
was justified in His faith—" And from that hour the disciple
took her unto his own home " (Jn. xix. 27).

" My God, My God, Why hast Thou forsaken Me ? "
(Mk. xv. 34) : this cry from the darkness was the supreme
articulation of Christ's love for the Father.   The intimacy
of personal relationship : *My* God ; the adoration and

wealth of yearning aspiration : My *God*. It was not His
own sense of dereliction that was to Jesus the sting of the
forsakenness, but its incompatibility with the known
character of the Father as worshipped in a life-time of
Fatherly protection, direction, sustaining, and above all in
the communion of mutual unreserved self-donation. The
profundity of Love's sense of identification with the
Beloved : it was incomprehensible to Jesus how anything
could come between Himself and the Father.

" I thirst " (Jn. xix. 28) : Love's yearning for Love.
Primarily the cry of our Lord's soul for His Father, this
Word voiced also His quenchless passion for souls. Love's
universality : all-inclusive. His passionate love yearned to
go on expending itself even beyond the uttermost were that
possible, in order to win back to the Father every single man
and woman, despite anything they might be or do that was an
offence against Love. Love's *insatiableness* : there must be
ever more and more of Love ; ever more and more loving.
Love's *invincibleness* : ever generating its own unceasing
faith, and loving always *in the present*.

" It is finished " (Jn. xix. 30) : Love's *satisfyingness*—" It
is fulfilled." Love's unswerving obedience : Love's tireless
perseverance. Love's concentration upon the task in hand
for others, regardless of cost to self. Love's faith to apprehend God's vision as *completed*, before results are humanly
visible.

" Father, into Thy hands I commend My spirit " (Lk.
xxiii. 46) : Love's *imperishable trust*. Our Lord's adoring
trust in the Father was in no slightest wise diminished by
the extremity of physical and spiritual suffering which was
the outcome of His filial obedience. Love's glad abandonment to Love was in utter content, and altogether peaceful
despite the human horror inherent in the external circumstances.

Our Lord's prayer of Love to the uttermost was Love to
the uttermost *in degree of self-donation* : it was also Love to
the uttermost in *filling all Eternity*—the life of all that lives

enduringly in union with the perfect Will of the Father.   It
was the prayer of the Pre-existent Son of God, One in
essence with the Father Who is Love.   It was the prayer of
" the Word . . . made flesh ".   Jesus " came forth from
God " ;   dwelt among men ;   and " goeth unto God " in
Love.   His prayer of Love to the uttermost is the whole
eternal cycle of Love without beginning, and without end :
Love in the Blessed and glorious Trinity ;   Love from God to
Man ;   and Love from Man to God.   Jesus' prayer of Love
to the uttermost is the source, significance, and goal of all
that has been, is, or ever shall be, because it is nothing less
than His whole, entire, and perfect Self, Very God of Very
God, of one substance with the Father, by Whom—and in
Whose Holy Spirit alone—all things subsist.

The essence of this prayer of Love to the uttermost has
been revealed to us by the Holy Spirit in words of Jesus'
own, spoken to His disciples on the eve of His death :
" Even as the Father hath loved Me, I also have loved you "
(Jn. xv. 9).   Eternity will be the progressive and inexhaustible fathoming *in experience* of this transcendent Love.

. To all who will accept it, Jesus offers union with Him in
His eternal prayer of Love to the uttermost :   and only in so
far as we do accept it do we truly *live* at all.

" I and the Father are one " :   *this* is Jesus' prayer of
Love to the uttermost ;   and this is the sum of His entire
prayer-life both incarnate and heavenly.

OUR LORD'S PRAYER-PENETRATION TO THE SIGNIFICANCE OF LIFE

L IFE is an enigma exacting from every individual some attempt at solution. Raw material for this solution is furnished by the personal experience and environment with which life confronts the individual. Our Lord was in no wise exempted from this universal compulsion experimentally to *work out* as far as possible the ultimate meaning of life.

The facts of life as personally experienced, and as witnessed in the lives of others, commonly assail brain, heart, and soul, with many an inescapable problem, both individual and corporate :

Whence, why, and whither ?

Design or futility ?

The function of the individual in relation to the whole.

Relations of individuals, sexes, classes, communities, sects, nations, one to another.

The fact of sin, and the problems of its consequences and cure.

Death : survival or annihilation ? And if survival, survival to what ?

Is life worth the suffering it inevitably entails ?

What is the best that can be made of life ; and how can this best be achieved ?

How can the practical difficulties and temptations of life be met and dealt with ?

All these are problems inherent in incarnate life, and therefore sustained in their full impact by our Lord.

Our Lord's " Fiat " for His Incarnation involved the voluntary laying aside in time, not only of His Pre-existent Glory as Very God of Very God, but also of His Pre-existent Omniscience. The Pre-existent Omniscience of the Son of

God absolutely precluded for Him anything in the nature of *problem*, since to God all is open and without mystery because the Truth of His Own Being, completely and exhaustively fathomed in the Eternal flux and reflux of Simplicity which is the Love-life of the Blessed Trinity. The taking upon Himself our human flesh and human nature did, in effect, commit Jesus to travail with every problem of life by which man is ever liable to be assailed.

Senses, emotions, reason, or external appearances, are commonly the mediums upon which man relies for his attempted elucidation of life. Our Lord, whilst making use of these, relied upon none of them ; but for His final interpretation of life depended solely upon knowledge infused in prayer. He abandoned Himself to the Holy Spirit to be guided into all the truth—that is, into God's Reality—about life. The Holy Spirit anchored Jesus in the Father as Source and Goal, as the beginning, the way, and the end ; and interpreted all else only in the light of the Being and Will of the Father. God, for Jesus, was not—as for so many—one among a number of factors, but the all-embracing One apart from which nothing else was ever considered. Jesus assessed life only in God, and never as an isolated entity in itself ; and because of this He was able, without blenching, without false sentiment, without despair, to take into steady account all the facts of fallen earth.

Our Lord accepted the raw material of experimental facts with which life confronted Him as coming from the Father, and as forming—however humanly perplexing they might seem—a lucid whole within His Will.

Jesus' prayer-penetration of the significance of life was not merely illuminative, but was also intensely practical. It was such as to enable Him to deal perfectly with life at all points, e.g. to deal with the material as well as with the spiritual ; the temporal as well as with the eternal ; external circumstances, human relationships, suffering, sin, death. He read life aright, because He enthroned God centrally, and never divorced the eternal and the temporal.

He came to a true understanding of Himself, and of others, because God's original design for each soul was taken as the interpretative norm.

There emerge from our Lord's teaching certain dominant ideas which enshrine that significance of life unveiled to Him in prayer :

The All-Sufficingness of the Father ; Holy, Omnipotent, Omniscient, All-Loving, and All-Lovable ;

The Nature of His own Personality and Vocation, in relation both to God and to Man ;

The Brotherhood of Man in the Sonship of God.

Life unfolded itself to Jesus as potentially a glory of voluntary human self-abandonment to co-operation with the indescribably beautiful Holy Will of the Father.

There also emerges no less clearly from our Lord's teaching the fact that there are *things which He is content not to explain* exhaustively—e.g. the mystery of suffering ; the fact of sin —or even to explain at all, e.g. the reason for certain fates befalling certain people (Lk. xiii. 1–5) ; the disproportionate distribution of spiritual gifts (Jn. xiv. 22–23 ; Matt. xiii. 11–12).   A question put to our Lord about choice of recipients for spiritual revelation was met by Him with a personal challenge to leave off questioning, in favour of obedience. He was concerned for attention to the ' how ' rather than to the ' why ' of things.   Not the ' why ' of vocation, but *surrender, self-abandonment* to it He recognised—from His own personal experience—as the business of the soul.

Our Lord's incarnate prayer-penetration of the significance of life left *reverent room for mystery*, i.e. the worshipful acknowledgment that God alone is omniscient.   He accepted as a wholesome and God-ordained fact that in time understanding of life could only be partial ; and that it was no more desirable than possible to formulate its meaning exhaustively.   He recognised life, not as an intricate enigma to be solved intellectually, but as an opportunity to grow in the simplicity of unitive knowledge of God Who alone is in possession of—and responsible for—the why and where-

fore of everything, and Who is, moreover, dealing with it
all ceaselessly and effectively.

In prayer our Lord knew God to be the Whence, the Why,
the Whither of all life. He knew that every tiniest fragment of life was a creative part in a Divine Plan so gloriously
purposeful as to exclude even the possibility of any futility.
He knew that every soul is created by God with a unique
vocation defining its relationship both to God and Man ;
and that every relationship, individual or corporate, is
fructified and made luminous in Love.

Experimentally our Lord fathomed, in spirit, mind, and
body, the very depths of the perpetual mystery of suffering
as none other has ever done, or could do (see pp. 124 ff. and
258 ff.). He penetrated to its hid treasure—which has been
called " the mystic benefits of pain "—because neither
mentally nor emotionally did He ever treat of any suffering,
whether His own or that of others, apart from its God-
related context.

The Gospel accounts of the Temptation in the Wilderness
—of necessity ultimately derived direct from our Lord
Himself—nowhere take stock of it in terms of personal
suffering. Our Lord treated suffering objectively rather
than subjectively. He dealt with the fact and causes of
suffering, but refused to immerse Himself in contingent
feelings or analytical speculations. He never either avoided
or courted suffering for its own sake ; but simply dealt with
each fresh facet of it, as it occurred, according to the way
in which it fell into the redemptive purposes of God.
Neither mentally nor emotionally did He interest Himself
in, or attach any importance to, His own personal suffering
as being *His* ; but always subordinated it to the Will of the
Father, and utilised it simply as a medium for expressing
His obedience and love. For the suffering of others He was
ever compassionate, suffering with them in their suffering
in an intensity precisely in proportion to His inattention to
His own. But for those with apostolic—priestly—vocation,
those conscious of a drawing of will to union with Him, He

serenely accepted suffering as incidentally basic to vocation, as He so accepted it for Himself.

Jesus did not so much concern Himself with the ' why ' of suffering as with the ' how ' of its acceptance. His own personal suffering He made a love-offering to God in reparation for the sins of the world, and with intention for the redemption of souls ; the suffering of others He regarded as either to be alleviated, or else—as, for instance, in the beatitudes of the Sermon on the Mount (Matt. v. 3–12)— interpretatively accepted on their behalf in union with the redemptive purposes of God.

Our Lord never Generalised about Suffering. He recognised it as God-permitted in love, sometimes to holiness and sometimes to sin in the sufferer ; sometimes for sanctifying, sometimes for discipline ; sometimes for chastening ; and sometimes for releasing the redemptive love of God.

" Blessed are they that have been persecuted for righteousness' sake : for theirs is the Kingdom of heaven " (Matt. v. 10) : experimentally Jesus had proved in His prayer of sanctification that peace and joy are not incompatible with simultaneous suffering.

" . . . Love your enemies, and pray for them that persecute you " (Matt. v. 44) : experimentally our Lord had proved that suffering could be a well-spring intercessorily transmuting everything for those who had been inflicting the injury.

In spite of all His forthgoing compassion towards suffering (e.g. His unsought raising of the widow of Nain's son—Lk. vii. 11 ff.), Jesus not only accepted but demanded it inexorably from those who would be His followers. His standard of sacrifice was ruthless from having proved its necessity in His own life. For His so dearly beloved disciples He could serenely permit that they should know ahead that they were to be delivered up to councils and scourged in the synagogues, and brought to trial before kings and governors, and hated of men for His sake (Matt. x. 17 ff.).

Our Lord's methods of alleviating suffering differed—at

the prompting of the Holy Spirit—with different individuals. To some relief was given unasked ; to others in immediate response to a first request ; others again were initially tested to the uttermost, e.g. the Syrophœnician woman (Mk. vii. 24 ff.). He was ready to delay alleviation of physical or mental suffering in order to evoke in the sufferer ability to receive a greater spiritual gift over and above the alleviation of suffering as such.

Jesus specifically denied outstanding suffering as necessarily a proof of greater measure of sinfulness in the sufferer, e.g., " Now there were some present . . . which told Him of the Galilæans, whose blood Pilate had mingled with their sacrifices. And He answered and said unto them, Think ye that these Galilæans were sinners above all the Galilæans, because they have suffered these things ? I tell you, Nay ; but except ye repent, ye shall all in like manner perish. Or those eighteen, upon whom the tower in Siloam fell, and killed them, think ye that they were offenders above all the men that dwell in Jerusalem ? I tell you, Nay . . ." (Lk. xiii. 1-4). Although in certain cases our Lord deliberately connected physical illness with the personal sin of the sufferer, He yet in another instance as deliberately refused to countenance the theory of personal or parental sin put forward to account for the case of a man born blind (Jn. ix. 1-3).

The parable of Dives and Lazarus (Lk. xvi. 19 ff.), with its : " But Abraham said, Son, remember that thou in thy life-time receivedst thy good things, and Lazarus in like manner evil things : but now here he is comforted . . .", showed that our Lord's compassion had led Him through to the vision of Love's *eternal* comforting, i.e. compensation in strengthening due to earthly suffering in time.

In spite of the implicit faith of Martha and Mary, our Lord delayed in going to their brother Lazarus after receiving news of his sickness (Jn. xi. 1 ff.). It is precisely those whom He can most trust to whom Jesus often permits longest and deepest endurance of suffering for the greater glory of God, and in order that they may learn the farthest reaches of spiritual truth which *can only be learned in the furnace.* Around their suffering He mediates from the beginning the serenity of His faith-vision of the end—the glory of God— and of their more than compensatory eternal joy and en- richment ; and at the right and creative moment He mediates also the immediate comfort of an intensely under- standing personal grief-sharing sympathy.

Jesus, out of His own experience, taught that steadfast endurance of suffering, of the worst that can be inflicted from without, of the most acute physical, mental or emotional suffering, transmutes it to the gain of spiritual personality. He taught that suffering as such is not in itself injurious, even though it literally kill the body (Lk. xxi. 16 ff.).

Our Lord, in the Holy Spirit, foresaw the most fearsome depths of tribulation as one sign of the coming of the Son of Man (Mk. xiii. *passim*).

In Christ's description of the Last Judgment (Matt. xxv. 31 ff.), He reveals the suffering of each and every individual to be His own personal suffering ; and response or indiffer- ence to their suffering as likewise personal to Himself. Human suffering stands here unveiled as the direct oppor- tunity for personal ministry to our Lord.

Our Lord never complained of His own suffering, though He did *admit* to it more than once, mentally, emotionally, spiritually, and even physically.

One of the earliest truths proclaimed by our Lord after His Resurrection was the unreserved and exultant recog- nition : " Behoved it not the Christ to suffer these things and to enter into His Glory ? " (Lk. xxiv. 26).

Every sorrow and perplexity Jesus took straight to God and not to men, e.g. the death of John the Baptist (Matt. xiv. 10–13), which when He heard of it He departed into a desert place apart for prayer.   All suffering was for Jesus the *open sesame* to fresh union with the Father, and to fresh redemptive offering for suffering mankind.   All He suffered, whether in spirit, mind, or body, led Him deeper and deeper

12

in self-commitment to the Father in trust, consecration, obedience, and thanksgiving for the Father's Self.

" Though He was a Son, yet learned He obedience by the things which He suffered, and having been made perfect, He became unto all them that obey Him the author of eternal salvation " (Heb. v. 8–9). Suffering for Jesus was illuminating ; it was maturing, i.e. it was equipment for His vocation ; and it was a source of salvation to others.

Our Lord's reaction to suffering was always selfless, e.g. on the Via Dolorosa, ". . . there followed Him a great multitude of the people, and of women who bewailed and lamented Him. But Jesus turning unto them said, Daughters of Jerusalem, Weep not for Me, but weep for yourselves and for your children " (Lk. xxiii. 27–28). He never saw His own personal suffering as central, but the suffering of others. Neither His own physical, mental, nor spiritual suffering ever blunted His passionate concern for the welfare of others. His own suffering occupied Him not at all in face of the spiritual danger or human need of others.

The fact of sin could never be ignored by One Whose unique holiness made for unique perception of sin. In His sinlessness Jesus recognised as sin that which was inevitably imperceptible as such, or at any rate in anything approaching the same degree, to any who had ever once harboured sin within themselves. Jesus, *by the purity of His love for the Father*, knew exhaustively the sinfulness of sin as no other human being has known, or ever could know, it. But despite this fact He never despaired of any sinner, as sinners all too often despair for themselves or for others.

All our Lord's dealing with sin—whether as a universal fact, or specifically in an individual sinner—was in invincible confidence, because it was based upon the fundamental promise of the Father, vouchsafed in angelic prophecy before His birth : ". . . thou shalt call His name Jesus ; for it is He that shall save His people from their sins " (Matt. i. 21). Jesus grew up in the innate conviction of the Father's Will and power to deliver sinners. This con-

viction so vitally impregnated His mind and spirit as
absolutely to exclude thought of any sin however vile,
however wilful, however habitual, as irremediable.   Jesus
knew that love alone—and not sin—is indestructible.

Our Lord viewed sin, not as we do through the maze of
time in which its apparent triumph and endless trail of
renewal, complexities, and resultant suffering seem most
often to predominate.   He viewed it through the Eternity of
God—sole Shedder of Truth—God the Consuming Fire in
Whom Love's provision for the ultimate annihilation of
Man's sin was assured at its very origination : assured from
God's side completely and instantaneously, though only
gradually and progressively to be responded to and appropriated from the side of Man.

Jesus was unfailingly sensitive to the moral and spiritual
state of others, e.g. the Woman of Samaria (Jn. iv. 7 ff.) ;
and the man sick of the palsy (Mk. ii. 3 ff.).   Intuitively,
through His prayer of union with the Father and of love to
the uttermost, in the Holy Spirit " He Himself knew what
was in man " (Jn. ii. 25) both individually and corporately.
He recognised the deep root of sin in all men, but was *never
shocked* at it because He realised to the full both its inevitability in the Fall, and its entire remediableness in the
Divine Economy of the Father.   Jesus came " preaching
the Gospel of God " (Mk. i. 14) ; and that Gospel had at its
heart the call to repentance.   This call, which was in actual
fact a gloriously liberating invitation, was issued serenely,
confidently, joyously, and with prodigal generosity, in the
knowledge unshakable—because divinely imparted—that
" the Son of Man hath power on earth to forgive sins " (Mk.
ii. 10).   But it was also issued absolutely uncompromisingly,
because although He knew that not a single sinner upon
earth could ever pass beyond the bounds of potential
reclamation in Himself, He knew likewise that only through
sincere repentance could this potential reclamation become
actual.

Jesus' travail for sinners to become morally and spiritually sanctified never slackened, even when their own faith or desire for it wilted or ceased. When Peter articulated his unreadiness to die to self in order to become holy in oneness with Jesus, Whom He recognised as All-Holy—"Depart from me ; for I am a sinful man, O Lord " (Lk. v. 8)— precisely then did our Lord choose to re-define his vocation more particularly, more challengingly, more aweingly, and with trust for Peter that Peter dared not then have for himself. *Jesus never withdrew the vocation of any sinner because of sin.* Instead, He mediated confidence in His power to deal with sin in such a way as to enable ultimate perfect correspondence with the God-designed vocation, whose vision His generosity would from time to time renew, and freshly and ever more deeply interpret and simplify.

The Lord's Prayer contains our Lord's explicit recognition of the universality of sin as a reality to be acknowledged centrally in prayer. Likewise, it contains His recognition of the duty of the individual to pass beyond obligation of concern and contrition merely for his own personal sin, to that on behalf of all mankind in whose whole body of sin he himself shares most concretely.

Jesus knew to the full the properties of sin. Plainly He showed sin as moral and spiritual *auto-intoxication* : " Hear Me, all of you, and understand there is nothing from without the man, that going into him can defile him : but the things which proceed out of the man are those that defile the man " (Mk. vii. 14–15). He recognised in all men sin's power to deceive, and to foster unreality ; and also its tyranny of enslavement : " Every one that committeth sin is the bondservant of sin " (Jn. viii. 34). He realised man's absolute inability to extricate himself from the quagmire of sin, be it personal, family, social, national, or racial— " . . . except ye believe that I am he, ye shall die in your sins " (Jn. viii. 24). But for all this, *sin had no dominion over His faith* because of His deep interior identification in the Holy Spirit with the Father's Will to wipe out sin and redeem Man. He knew Himself empowered by the Father to save men by virtue of a love one with His, a love that brooked no limiting from self-cost ; and He knew that Love would continue ceaselessly to draw men to desire and to accept the salvation made possible and freely offered to them. There was, therefore, in Jesus no impatience with sin, but a serenity born of the *surety* of the ultimate destruction both of itself and of all its fruits, as enshrined by Him in His parable of the Wheat and the Tares : " . . . Let both grow together until the harvest : and in the time of the harvest I will say to the reapers, Gather up first the tares, and bind them in bundles to burn them : but gather the wheat into my barn " (Matt. xiii. 30).

Despite our Lord's unique perceptiveness towards sin, He, the Truth, in transparency of conscience was able to—and did publicly—issue the stupendous challenge : " Which of you convicteth Me of sin ? " (Jn. viii. 46). Jesus had no guilt in common with sinners, but none the less He had a perfect experimental understanding of the danger and hardness of their plight, through His own renewed personal temptations. His heart overflowed with pity for sinners ; and yet at the same time—from the ground of His knowledge of the Father, and in the invincible confidence possible only to absolute Love and Holiness—it overflowed also with serene *expectancy* of faith for them. Jesus, in God, identified Himself with sinners to save them from their sin by the holiness of His sacrificial love. To the woman taken in adultery Jesus said : " Neither do I condemn thee : go thy way ; from henceforth sin no more " (Jn. viii. 11). This was His consistent attitude towards sinners : not condemnation for their sin, but liberation into holiness through the enablement of His sacrificial love and intercessory prayer.

" He is gone in to lodge with a man that is a sinner " (Lk. xix. 7) : this was said in bitter complaint and disapprobation by a crowd at Jericho, when Jesus entered the house of Zacchæus the publican. But this " He is gone in to lodge with a man that is a sinner " is more than a human jibe with reference to one specific incident. it is *a timeless truth* ever freshly experienced, in countless ways, by myriads of souls all down the ages. Many of us, sinners, there are now to-day, for whom He has repeated this gracious, loving condescension *and Himself made it known to us*, sometimes in the Blessed Sacrament ; sometimes when silently and alone we have betaken ourselves to Him again in genuine repentance ; sometimes in Love's generosity instantaneously enveloping us afresh even whilst freshly sinning.

In His exquisite ' sinner ' parables (i.e. the parables of the Hundred Sheep, the Ten Pieces of Silver, and the Prodigal Son, recorded for us in Lk. xv.), Jesus gloriously revealed :

(1) Sinners are precious, and not abhorrent, to God— from which it follows that since *sin* is abhorrent to Him, sinners, in His Heart and Mind, are eternally separated from their sin, which is never at any time part of their intrinsic self as beloved by Him.

(2) Any sinner can by penitence kindle joy in heaven.

(3) The Divine readiness instantaneously to forgive is ever greater than the human readiness to repent and to trust to God's mercy and generosity.

(4) Repentant sinners never run any risk of even the possibility of rebuff with God, but can invariably be sure of welcome from Him *whenever*, and from *whatever*, they turn to Him again, because it is not in His Nature to be other than even more prodigal of fresh love and forgivingness than they of squandering and misusing in sin all that He has previously lavished upon them.

(5) THE COMPLETE REINSTATEMENT OF THE SINNER.

The original Beauty of Holiness in and for which each soul was created by the Father can be given back *unimpaired* by Him, despite its temporary loss due to sin. The prodigal son, on recognising his destitution from sin, deems himself to have forfeited his vocation of sonship. He plans, not only his confession to his father—" Father, I have sinned against heaven, and in thy sight : I am no more worthy to be called thy son . . ."—but also the relinquishing of his high vocation for a lower involving an altogether different relationship to his father : " make me as one of thy hired servants."

The prodigal's verbal confession is forestalled by the father's kiss of peace and welcome. Then, and then only, is he allowed to acknowledge his sin and unworthiness, but the Father will not allow him to add his " make me as one of thy hired servants ", i.e. he will not allow his son to plan for himself a future state lower than that to which he was originally destined. The father has ceaselessly been holding in his heart and mind the son's vocation even whilst he himself has withdrawn from it ; and has been keeping it open for him although the son had deliberately turned his back upon it even after initial experience of it. The father's *first words* on the prodigal's return are the command to his servants : " Bring forth quickly the best [Gk. πρώτην = first] robe, and put it on him . . ." i.e. a command for his instantaneous reinstatement to his former, his original, estate.

In the parable of the Prodigal Son Jesus set forth in story form not only the *eternal* lover-attitude of God towards the sinner ; but also the fact that *no sinner's moral past is irreparable, be it what it may.*

A concrete instance of Jesus' power absolutely to cancel past sin is recorded for us by St. Luke (iv. 33 ff. R.V.), in connection with His healing of the man with the unclean spirit in the synagogue at Capernaum :

" And Jesus rebuked him, saying, Hold thy peace, and come out of him. And when the devil had thrown him down in the midst, he came out of him, *having done him no hurt.*" Here is factual illustration of the truth—of such fathomless comfort and re-encouragement for us in our need—that Jesus, " the same yesterday, and to-day, and for ever ", can restore *untainted* the whole personality of any sinner, and enable the soul to become in Him that for which the Father created it.

Jesus preached and mediated the mercy of God towards

sinners.   His gentleness with sinners was the outcome not
of any easy tolerance of sin, but of His inveterate hostility to
it.   His gentleness towards sinners was born of His prayer-
dealing with them always in the light of the knowledge of
God's Will and power to save them ; in the cost of His own
vicarious penitence and atonement for them ; and in faith's
anticipation of their final reinstatement in union with His
holiness—" For their sakes I sanctify Myself, that they themselves also may be sanctified in truth "—in " the liberty of
the glory of the children of God ".

The human problem of death, like every other problem,
resolved itself for the praying Jesus in God.   " He is not the
God of the dead, but of the living " (Mk. xii. 27).   Our Lord
in His incarnate union with the Father experienced such a
superabundant life as must needs, He knew, be unquenchable, eternal, unassailable by any cessation of mere physical
functioning : a life indestructible, inexhaustible, all-sufficing
for the needs of all souls eternally alive in Him.   Through
Jesus' perfect worship of the Father's Will there was vouchsafed to Him by the Holy Spirit the inner knowing that
survival was survival in Love, survival to love and to
worship Love, to be immersed in Love, to be utterly
identified with Love, and to live eternally in the ceaseless
exercise of love.

On the eve of His death, Jesus imparted to His disciples the
certain knowledge previously gained by Him in prayer :
" In My Father's house are many mansions " (Jn. xiv. 2),
and promised, " I go to prepare a place for you ".   Death He
recognised as the *open sesame* to an eternity of diversity and
liberty in loving, in which Love's provision embraces every
single soul, freeing it to love *in her own unique way* as divinely
designed before time and to outlast time.   Our Lord apprehended and taught the survival of personality ; but He left
all detail of conditions in the Father's " many mansions "
shrouded in reverent mystery, where we, too, trustfully
resting in the Father's Love and Mercy, best leave it in
humble adoration of His Wisdom.

Life, as a whole, as revealed to our Lord by the Holy Spirit in prayer, was a perfect creation of the Father's, marred in time by the sin of Man, but ceaselessly being re-created by His transcendent Love into an eternity of Perfection, Beauty, and Satisfyingness, one with His original design : a harmony of Love and Holiness embracing all created things.

Suffering in no wise detracted, for Jesus, from the " worthwhileness " of life. He saw suffering only as potential offering to the Father for penitence and for a medium of His redemption to the world. He recognised it as often *beneficial* in a fallen world, both as a cleansing fire and as material for love-offering from Man to the Creator Whom by his sin he has outraged.

Life for the individual, as revealed to our Lord by the Holy Spirit in prayer, was none other than specific vocation as bestowed by the Father ; no single soul ever created by Him throughout time being without her own unique vocation of indescribable beauty—and in His Mind—of inexhaustible wonder. Through perfect self-abandonment in the Holy Spirit to His own vocation, Jesus knew that for each and all " the best that can be made of life " is like self-abandonment to vocation, however perplexing, dim, or even *irreconcilable with circumstances* that vocation may humanly seem at times. Experimentally He knew vocation progressively to unify all the apparently unrelated and contradictory facts of incarnate life ; to impart dignity and worth to the otherwise trivial and insignificant ; and to transmute to the purposes of Love and Holiness all that which is essentially contrary to them.

Life—as to its practical difficulties and temptations— Jesus proved experimentally could only be dealt with victoriously by unbroken correspondence to grace. The indwelling of the Holy Spirit ceaselessly uniting the soul to the Father Who is Love inexhaustible and Holiness invincible, this, and this alone, He knew could—and would unfailingly—meet perfectly life's multitudinous taxing demands. So in His own life He has triumphantly shown us this : " In the world ye shall have tribulation ; but be of good cheer ; *I have overcome the world* " (Jn. xvi. 33). But not at *example*—however glorious—does it rest.

Jesus leaves us not alone an example, an example impossible for us in our own strength to follow, but Himself freely offers us *for the taking*—for which taking the inescapable price is death to self—His own life victorious at all points in love and holiness to be our life ; and also offers *Himself* to live life in us as the Father created us to live it in Him.

THE MIND OF CHRIST

THE dominant characteristic of our Lord's Mind was harmony : harmony in itself, with God, and with His environment. It was the harmony of a mind unbrokenly God-centred and utterly free from self-preoccupation.

He was never muddled, never hurried ; neither was He ever perturbed by interruptions.

He always saw things in perspective : the material and the spiritual ; the human and divine ; the physical and spiritual ; His own spiritual experiences, e.g. His prayer to God : God's voice to Him (as recorded in Jn. xii. 27–30) : " This voice came, not because of Me, but for your sakes " ; time and eternity. This was because with Him always God was first ; others linked to Him by prayer ; and self nowhere except as a medium to love, pray, and suffer creatively for a universal one-ing to God in love.

His Mind was both receptive and creative : very sensitive both to God and Man.

His Mind was steadfast, because it was anchored outside Himself.

His Mind dwelt on facts and realities, not in emotionalism —although He was a man of powerful emotions. He never exaggerated. He never divorced conviction from action. He *lived* what He *saw* as God's Will. He always saw clearly.

The bent of His mind was inclusive and not exclusive.

His Mind was always crystal clear : undeceiving of self or others.

He was possessed of sound judgment and insight ; and was never wrongly swerved by public opinion.

He never resorted to expediency : He never compromised.

He never confused the real issue, but let it emerge clear and untrammelled.

He never ran a thing to death, nor explained it thread-bare ; but always left spice and intrigue in it.

He never forgot details in the general scheme, nor lost sight of the whole by over-absorption in detail.

He never gave superficial attention to any one or any-thing, but backed His attention with His whole being. He was never bored ; and never indifferent.

He never departmentalised.

His Mind was both logical and imaginative at one and the same time.

His was the Mind of the poet and artist, fertile in imagina-tion, working pictorially but never flamboyantly. He ever combined freedom and restraint.

His ideas and beliefs were so interwoven into His inner-most being that He could readily and easily find for them fresh forms of expression to fit varying occasions and needs.

The Mind of Christ is the eternal expression and reflection of the adorable, All-Holy Trinity : as such may we each and all be progressively enabled, by the Holy Spirit, to " Let this Mind . . . which was in Christ Jesus " be in us also a perpetual exercise of selfless love to the glory of the Father, Son, and Holy Spirit.

"BEHOLD, THE MAN!"

" BEHOLD, THE MAN ! "

" BEHOLD, the man ! " (Jn. xix. 5). Thus, after His trials, was Jesus—" wearing the crown of thorns, and the purple robe "—presented by Pilate to the chief priests, the elders, and people of the Jews outside his palace : presented in hopes that the bare sight of any human creature reduced to so pitiable a plight must inevitably evoke compassion.

To outward seeming

A man on trial for His life, stripped of all the externals of human dignity, His whole self the butt of ridicule, and His body a bleeding victim of physical cruelty ; yet nevertheless a man completely fearless and uncowed, attempting no plea for Himself.

To human knowledge

A Galilean peasant carpenter turned itinerant teacher and healer, with pretensions to being—
    Son of God ;
    King ;
    Saviour of the World.

To human opinion

Over and above the external facts of His life, which were simple and not in dispute, opinion even among those who saw Him brought forth by Pilate was divided.
To some He appeared as :
    A fanatic, possibly self-deceived, certainly dangerous.
To others as :
    One possibly justified in His claims, but none the less to be feared on that account.

To yet others, who dared not then attempt to defend Him, as :

> One Who had undoubtedly, and only, gone about " doing good " and working miracles ; a friend of sufferers and sinners, and of " the common people ".

But to all, in varying degree, because they were unable to unriddle the paradox of His personality, He appeared as :

A Mystery.

In Eternal Reality

Jesus was not only :

The country carpenter ⎫
Teacher ⎪
Healer ⎬ as incarnate in time ;
Lover of God and Man ⎭

and :

Son of God ⎫
King ⎬ as He claimed to be ;
Saviour of the World ⎭

but also :

PERFECT MAN : glorious, unfallen creation of God.

Christ and Paradox

The paradox in Christ's teaching is an accepted fact of common knowledge. It has intrigued men and provoked their deepest thought. It has brought them increasing fulness of understanding as shafts of light from every angle illuminate the central truth. Yet strange it is that men seem, while thinking through the paradoxes Christ *taught*, largely to have ignored those He *lived*. There is, however, every bit as much paradox in the human character and personality of Christ as there is in His teachings ; and it is this very paradox—of traits seemingly antithetic but in reality complementary—which makes for its glorious harmony, poise, and completeness.

Jesus of Nazareth simultaneously and harmoniously

united in Himself qualities which seem, humanly, certainly
disparate if not incompatible. Here bare suggestiveness
alone is possible, or indeed desirable, for Jesus Christ is, and
must finally remain, His own direct interpreter—" No man
can say that Jesus is the Lord, but by the Holy Ghost."
His love knew the extremes both of compassion and of
sternness. He had an equal capacity for joying and suffering with and for others. He could be interested in, and
make Himself interesting to, the most learned and the
simplest alike, the spiritual and the worldly, the lovable and
the unlovable, the rich and the poor, the success and the
failure.

He had an inextricable sense of the eternal and of the
immediate. He harnessed white-hot passion and sanity.
He displayed both conformity and non-conformity to custom
and ceremonial. He combined intense mysticism with exceptionally practical and potent activity ; utter givingness
with utter demandingness ; seeming effortlessness with
rigorous man-hidden discipline ; abhorrence of sin with love
and reverence for the sinner ; strength with tenderness ;
authority with humility ; implicit faith in the spiritual
future of men and women with exhaustive knowledge of
their past and present abysses of weakness and sin ; concern
for the multitude with concern for the individual ; concern
for God with concern for Man ; concern for a cause with
concern for its adherents ; concern for the spiritual with
concern for the physical and material. He absolutely fused
the sacred and secular, the human and divine.

He Who healed the woman bowed under " a spirit of
infirmity " for eighteen years, and recalled to life a widow's
only son simply at sight of their distress, and without so
much as one appealing word to Him, was the same Who for
a time withstood with apparent harshness the poignant entreaties of an agonised Syrophœnician mother. He Who
accused not " the woman taken in adultery " was the same
Who poured forth vials of invective upon the Scribes and
Pharisees in all the meticulousness of their observance of the

13

Law. He Who at special pains sought out the man born
blind, whom the Pharisees had cast out after He healed
him, in order verbally to reveal Himself to him as Son of
God, was the same Who let His disciples grow painfully into
gradual recognition of His Messiahship through such
bewilderment and mental anguish.

The hands whose touch gave sight to the blind, healing to
the sick, raised the dead, blessed little children, brake bread,
gave courage to the fearful, and restored a leper's self-respect
and sense of human kinship, were the same which " made a
scourge of small cords " and drove out all " that sold oxen
and sheep and doves in the temple . . . and poured out the
changers' money, and overthrew the tables ". He pierced
to the heart of every need and met it effectually, and in the
appropriate manner. His compassion was always bracing ;
and His sternness was never to the weak or those already
' down '—it launched itself only on those with otherwise
impregnable citadels of self-righteousness and hypocrisy.

Mourners and merry-makers, jubilant and afflicted, triumphant and defeated, alike desired His presence. He
could by His learning astonish the doctors in the Temple ;
amaze Nicodemus, " a master in Israel " ; outwit lawyers,
Scribes, and Pharisees ; and astound the rabbis by the
' authority ' of His doctrine ; and yet such was the simplicity—inexhaustibly deep like all simplicity—colourful-
ness, imagery, and homeliness of His teaching that " the
common people heard Him gladly ".

He Who was upbraided for plucking ears of corn and
healing on the Sabbath, and eating with unwashen hands, was
the same Who " as His custom was . . . went to the synagogue on the sabbath day " ; paid tribute money ; came to
" fulfil the law " ; and said, when John demurred about
baptising Him : " Suffer it to be so now : for thus it
becometh us to fulfil all righteousness ".

He Whose instantaneous and apparently natural power
over " wind and wave ", unclean spirits, sin, disease and
death, men saw and marvelled at, was the same Who

utterly denied Self and spent whole nights alone in prayer and communion with the Father, drawing in supernatural strength for superhuman tasks.

He Who exchanged the fulness of heaven for earth's most abject poverty ; gave His all, Himself, to save men from pain, from their own foolishness and sin ; for Whom no sacrifice, no condescension for even the humblest, poorest, vilest, most humanly repulsive man or woman was ever too great ; for Whom no gift was too precious or costly to shower freely, joyously, without trace of patronage or sense of benefit conferred ; was the same for Whom nothing was too much, too hard, too dangerous, too exacting to demand of others. He Who *gave* His " body broken " and His " blood outpoured " was the same Who said : " If any man will come after Me, let him deny himself and take up his cross *daily* " ; and " Whosoever he be of you that for-saketh not *all* that he hath, cannot be My disciple ".

He Who lived in God as God, with an ' authority ' that was equally incontestable to friend, critic, and foe ; Who forgave sins ; stilled storms ; exorcised evil spirits ; ful-filled the Law by transcending it, and justly claimed that " all judgment " had been " committed " unto Him by the Father, was the same Who was " meek and lowly in heart ", and said of Himself as simple truth : " The Son can do nothing of Himself, but what He seeth the Father do . . . I can of Mine own self do nothing . . . I do nothing of Myself : but as My Father hath taught Me, I speak ".

It was to the same man to whom he said : " Get thee behind Me, Satan : thou art an offence unto Me, for thou savourest not the things that be of God, but those that be of men ", and " Before the cock crow, thou shalt deny Me thrice ", that He also said : " Thou art Peter, and upon this rock I will build My church ; and the gates of hell shall not prevail against it." He chose among His disciples Matthew, whose whole business was with money and material things ; Simon the Zealot, bent only upon national revolt against Roman domination and the forcible establishment of a

Jewish kingdom ; Galileans and Nathaniel, who despised all things Galilean ; men ignorant, obscure, often cowardly, wrapped in dreams of self-aggrandisement and the wiping out—if necessary by fire from heaven—of their enemies and their Lord's. He had faith in the ability of these men individually and *corporately* to become understanding recipients of supreme spiritual truths, sharers with Him in the active service of the Kingdom, and His effective witnesses after His death.

He Who " taught daily in the temple " also consorted with those considered beyond the pale of respectability. He accepted the invitations of publicans and sinners, and even in the case of one publican invited Himself—*what* graciousness—to his house. He Who instituted and *gave* the Sacrament of the Last Supper invested and *accepted* as a sacrament a woman's love-offering of precious ointment. He made the commonplace sacred ; and the sacred He made natural. He expressed and consecrated every emotion ever known to Man : joy and gaiety, sorrow, solemnity, and reverence alike among them.

Really to try to think and pray through *for ourselves* the paradoxes that Christ *lived* is first to be dismayed, and then inspired : dismayed at our indescribably lack-lustre reflection of His boundlessly rich personality ; and then inspired that His fulness *can* flood and float even *us* off any rock on which we may blindly or wilfully have run aside, and fill our sails and set us—under an open sky—straight for a limitless horizon.

JESUS THE COUNTRYMAN

(refer to pp. 42 ff. and 80 ff.)

JESUS visited and dwelt in towns from time to time, but He was essentially countryman rather than townsman; and we feel that fittingly this must needs have been so.

"Behold, the man!"—One Who lived close to Nature and Who steeped Himself in the country's elemental and universal cycle of life and death, rather than in the ephemeral artificialities always incidental to, and inextricable from, town life. Wonderingly, worshippingly, with a deep inner thrill, Jesus watched the timeless revelation of the country: the eternal mystery of growth from hiddenness to manifested beauty, from seeming-nothingness to perfect fulfilment.

By close observation and warm understanding Jesus was one in knowledge and sympathy with all who laboured—under varying conditions and difficulties—to bring forth the fruits of the earth. The whole process of growth had an irresistible fascination for Him, as is evidenced by the illustrative and interpretative use He made of it in His parables.

Jesus had an affinity with Nature in all her moods. His commands evoked perfect response, not only from the elements, but from the animal creation as well. Superbly did He, on Palm Sunday, ride—no easy task—an unbroken colt "whereon no man ever yet sat" (Mk. xi. 2); the colt instinctively—as animals will—sensing a master and lover. No less than with children, or with grown men and women, Jesus "had a way" with animals and birds: the true countryman's way of fearless love, tenderness, patience, and sacrifice towards beast and bird, evoking their love and trust in return.

Jesus was a countryman through and through, with all that implies of simplicity, serenity, reality, appreciation of beauty, and reverence for life and labour.

187

" BEHOLD, the man ! " skilled of hand and eye ; a craftsman with the soul of poet and artist.

Innate in Jesus, and expressed from a child upwards, was a passionate love of beauty with its companionate urge to create and ceaseless, insatiable yearning for perfection. He loved beauty in any and every form. He once bade His disciples " Consider the lilies of the field "—orange Palestinian lilies—if they would truly understand the character of God their Father. This He told them because He Himself revelled in *colour* and found God in it. He loved colour because the Father created it : created it simply for sheer delight in it, but also in His generosity to give joy to Man. He loved the prodigality of love and life and power in its vividness ; and the purity of its transparency. He loved it for itself. Beauty of form entranced Him no less.

With what fascination must Jesus, as a child, have watched Joseph plying his trade, have seen article upon article emerging from shapeless wood to finished form perfect for its purpose ! With what eagerness and interest must He have applied Himself to learning the laws of His craft, and with what exhilaration—passing through initial unswerving obedience to rule to disciplined freedom of technique—mastered and transcended them ! All our Lord's handicraft must have borne upon it—in absolute *loveliness* of form and finish, and in that unique rhythm that can be captured in wood alone—the impress of His soul's innate poetry and artistry, which found its highest expression in His prayer and then in His teaching (see pp. 194 ff.).

The *creativeness* of the WORD by Whom all things were made persisted both in the imaginative and executive genius of Jesus of Nazareth. Perfect in beauty was all He ever conceived in mind and spirit ; and its concrete realisation—

whatsoever the medium—was no less perfect than the original conception. Perfect was His mastery over every medium in which He ever worked, making it always in some way or another a glorious revelation of some facet of the Father's Being and of His Eternal and Universal Will. Wood, words, imagery, bodies, minds, souls, were the mediums through which at different times He progressively unfolded this inexhaustible revelation of the Essential Nature of the Father as eternally expressed in the fathomless life of the Holy Trinity.

Wood was the medium in which Jesus so largely wrought in the ' hidden years '. He so wrought—uniting His manual labour by prayer to the divine creation of the world and all that is in it—as to consecrate all labour for all time and for all men, infusing into it as its dominant motif perfection and heartwhole effort to the glory of God, Who wills all things from greatest to least to be perfect according to their destined purpose. No pains can He ever have spared in thought, time, or energy, over any single one of the many tasks that fell to Him as carpenter, never letting the monotony of mechanical routine detract from the offering of His whole being to God through manual labour for just so long as ever that should be His God-appointed work. His manual labour He made worship of God, and intercession for those who were to receive and use His handiwork and also for all others labouring like Himself. Nothing in His carpentry was trifling or insignificant ; all was a love-offering to the Father, and also a love-offering towards the material necessities of Man : His natural strength offered up in hard, contented, systematic labour.

As in the ' hidden years ' Jesus wrought with wood as His medium, so at His life's end He came back to it. At Nazareth He shaped the wood to His design : on Calvary He shaped Himself to the wood's design—the Cross which He chose to accept as His life's supreme medium for the expression and manifestation of the infinite Love, Holiness, and Truth, the I AM THAT I AM our Eternal God and Father.

JESUS THE TEACHER

ONLY after a long, hidden, intensive, and for the most part silent, preparation, and not until He was about thirty, did Jesus publicly emerge as a teacher. All output in teaching was preceded by years of concentrated intake in learning—in terms of the Holy Spirit's interpretation—from :

The Father.

The Scriptures.

Nature.

Life :

(a) As personally experienced in His own body, mind, and spirit ;

(b) As witnessed in human nature and affairs at large. Jesus was a learner—and a *thorough* learner—before ever He was a teacher.

Deeply and prayerfully, year in year out, did Jesus investigate the cumulative deposit of teaching in the Law and the Prophets—as a child eagerly listening to, and questioning, those most expertly versed in them—before ever He embarked on any teaching of His own.

He studied His subject—God, and Man.

He studied His pupil—Man.

He meditated upon the revelation of God, and of His purpose for Man, as explicit and implicit in the Scriptures ; and His entire life—by love, by prayer of communion, by obedience—was one unbroken study of God, i.e. a striving to grow in progressive knowledge of God. Ceaselessly He studied God's good pleasure also, in order so to understand it that He might be enabled to satisfy it to the uttermost. His was indeed first-hand knowledge of the ' subject ' He had to teach. He identified Himself so completely with His ' subject ' that His teaching was Himself, Himself His teaching. Jesus was Himself the " express image " of the Father, Who in His own Self was the " good news " absolutely central in the teaching of our Lord. Likewise did Jesus identify Himself with those whom He had to teach, so that by prayer and love He learned their innermost needs and their capacity for assimilating the Truth as it was in Him to impart to them for their salvation.

The manner of His teaching was with :

    Simplicity.

    Sincerity.

    Authority.

The authority of Jesus' teaching lay in the fact that it derived not from rabbinic authorities—as did all other contemporary Jewish teaching—but from the sole incontrovertible authority (i.e. weight of testimony) existent : the perfect union of the soul with the Living God, Maker of Heaven and Earth, and of all things visible and invisible.

His method :

    Example first and foremost.

    Direct instruction.

    Parabolic teaching.

In thought, word, and deed, Jesus was one with the Father in the Holy Spirit always ; so that not only all He said, but also all He was and did perpetually *conveyed* God to men whether they recognised it or not. His sheer personality drew people to hear Him teach, because *in perfectly ordinary circumstances* such as were their common lot, *He lived life as they had never imagined it could be lived* : lived it with a reality, power, and beauty that were magnetic. The beauty and significance of *His* life—for those with inner seeing—was a revelation of potential, but hitherto undreamed, transformation of *their own lives* from ugliness, sordidness, and superficiality, to a like beauty and significance.

All His precepts were delivered from His own practical experience of conduct *as enjoined by the Holy Spirit* under

varying given circumstances, but as general principle, and
for general application.   His Passion was the supreme fulfilment in personal example of fundamental principles of
conduct already—from previous habitual exercise of them—
enunciated in His teaching, e.g. :

" Love your enemies, do good to them which hate you,
bless them that curse you, and pray for them which
despitefully use you " (Lk. vi. 27).

" And be not afraid of them which kill the body, but are
not able to kill the soul " (Matt. x. 28).

His prayer of the drinking of the Cup, especially the
draining of its dregs in Gethsemane, along the Via Dolorosa
and on Calvary, was the unsurpassable fulfilment of the
teaching in the parable " He spake . . . .to the end that they
ought always to pray and not to faint " [Gk. = be cowardly,
faint-hearted] (Lk. xviii. 1) : victorious prayer never for one
moment giving quarter to self even in the face of humanly
terrifying ordeal upon ordeal, mentally, spiritually, or
physically.   Never once did the witness of His life detract
from His spoken word, however sublime, but rather did
being and action transcend even His sublimest teaching, and
veritably constitute its living core.

Our Lord's teaching was delivered under very different
circumstances at different times : sometimes in the synagogues or even in the Temple itself ; sometimes in the open
air, on the hillside, or from a boat on the lake ; sometimes
to a multitude ; most often privately to His chosen
disciples ; sometimes to a single individual who deliberately
sought—or whose need occasioned—some particular enlightenment.

In all His direct teaching Jesus confined Himself always to
eternal principles and truths ; and even when solicited by
any one in specific difficulties He never let Himself become
enmeshed in the detail of passing human circumstances or
problems, only pointing a swift and conclusive challenge on
that level where necessary, e.g. " And one of the multitude
said unto Him, Master, bid my brother divide the inheritance

with me. But He said unto him, Man, who made Me a judge
or a divider over you? And He said unto them, Take heed,
and keep yourselves from all covetousness : for a man's life
consisteth not in the abundance of the things which he
possesseth " (Lk. xii. 13–15) ; and this He followed up with
still further teaching of universal and timeless application,
which incidentally was all directly applicable also to the
individual problem which had initially evoked it. There was
no " going into the case " in detail ; no probing the human
rights and wrongs of the affair, a process which He knew
would only stir up and augment all the already existing ill-
feeling in the matter ; but simply a clearing of the underlying principle in which, as He realised, all problematical
detail would necessarily find its solution.

Common sense and imagination were equally employed
by our Lord in illustration of His teaching. He made
frequent use of the argument from ordinary and universal
experience, e.g. " Neither do men light a lamp and put it
under the bushel, but on the stand ; and it shineth unto all
that are in the house " (Matt. v. 15). Likewise with the
reticence of true imagination again and again He lit up the
seemingly commonplace, thereby releasing its hidden glory
and beauty. He intimated beauty to others, not by
enthusing upon it as an abstract quality, nor by trying to
draw verbal attention to its detail in any given object, but
rather by sharing with them the vision-analogy with which
in tranquillity it had inspired Himself, e.g. " Consider the
lilies, how they grow : they toil not, neither do they spin ;
yet I say unto you, Even Solomon in all his glory was not
arrayed like one of these " (Lk. xii. 27). Here without any
adjectival effusion Jesus has conveyed—and for ever un-
forgettably—maximum splendour and thrill of colour and
sheen and delightsomeness.

Jesus challenged the hearts and wills of men by uncompromising demand for total self-abandonment for the sake of
God's Kingdom. No less did He challenge their *minds* by
the paradoxes in His teaching ; by countering question with

question, or by meeting it with an answer whose relevance did not immediately appear upon the surface.

All Jesus' moral teaching penetrated the circumference of acts and words and secondary feelings right to the central disposition of the heart. Thought-life and motive rather than their resultant actions He brought to light as of prime importance, and made them the touchstone of everything.

Jesus knew that deep down in every man and woman is the child, story-loving as are all children ; and so, much of His teaching He deliberately cast into parabolic form, knowing that this would intensify its appeal, and that both narrative and imagery would act as invaluable aids to memory. As a story-teller He surpassed in genius any and every other whose sole *métier* it has even been, although for Him it was but one of many forms of creative expression. The Prodigal Son, and the Good Samaritan, are the world's stories of all stories, once heard impossible ever to be forgotten.

The " Sermon on the Mount " may be thought of as Jesus' ' collected ' direct instruction. The innate poetry and artistry of His soul are perhaps in no way more apparent than in the fact that all the teaching of this " Sermon on the Mount " overflowed in the poetry and imagery of illustrative parables delivered on quite other occasions, e.g. :

Teaching in the " Sermon on the Mount ".	*Parables.*
" Ye are the salt of the earth : but if the salt have lost his savour . . . it is thenceforth good for nothing, but to be cast out . . ." (Matt. v. 13).	The Barren Fig Tree (Lk. xiii. 6). The Talents (Matt. xxv. 14).
" Ye shall know men by their fruits " (Matt. vii. 16).	
" Blessed are the poor in spirit " (Matt. v. 3).	The Pharisee and the Publican (Lk. xviii. 9).

" Blessed are they that hunger and thirst after righteousness " (Matt. v. 16).	The Hid Treasure (Matt. xiii. 44). The Pearl of Great Price (Matt. xiii. 45).
" Blessed are the merciful " (Matt. v. 7).	The Unmerciful Servant (Matt. xviii. 23).
" Love your enemies . . ." (Matt. v. 44).	The Good Samaritan (Lk. x. 30).
" And when ye pray ye shall not be as the hypocrites are . . ." (Matt. vi. 5).	The Pharisee and the Publican (Lk. xviii. 9).
" Lay not up for yourselves treasures upon the earth..." (Matt. vi. 19).	The Rich Fool (Lk. xii. 16). Dives and Lazarus (Lk. xvi. 19).
" Ask, and it shall be given you " (Matt. vii. 7).	The Importunate Widow (Lk. xviii. 1).

Jesus taught by parables intriguingly, thought-provokingly, vividly, pictorially. His parables were for the most part taken from within the everyday experience of His hearers, and would therefore come home to them intelligibly and in such a way as to create associations which would readily and lastingly recall His teaching. To those who heard His parable of the Sower the sight of any sower, of stony ground, of thorns, of fruitful crops, could not but be ever afterwards inseparable from that parable and the truths it enshrined. *His parables breathe for all time His identification of Himself with the common round and ordinary person.* Rich and poor, labourer, housewife, and unemployed, alike cannot help knowing from them His complete understanding of their own peculiar difficulties, temptations, joys, and sorrows ; and cannot help knowing, moreover, that He possesses the key to them all. Jesus took many of His parables from Nature : and thereby illustrated the root principle of God the Source of all life, and of gradual growth under His blessing, and in active co-operation with the fulfilment of His laws and Will.

The attention of His hearers was challenged from the first : " Hearken ; Behold . . ." (Mk. iv. 3). " Hearken " : He called into play all their faculties of attention. Then with the *first* word of this first parable of the series delivered on this particular occasion, He called into play the whole of their perceptive and imaginative faculties as well : " Behold ". Thus He addressed Himself to the entire personality of His hearers. His parables are all the acme of simplicity ; and are therefore inexhaustible as is all simplicity. There is in them no redundancy, for all their fertility of imagery. They contain no artificial heightening by means of superlatives ; they are living and strong in the predominant usage of verbs rather than adjectives.

The poetry and artistry of our Lord's parables defy analysis : each one must divine for himself what he is able, knowing full well that it is but a fragment of the entirety of Beauty that has been captured and expressed in them by Him, Who has mastered words and images in a degree never paralleled before or since.

The Content of His Teaching

Jesus' teaching on examination falls readily under diverse headings :

The Father.
The Son.
The Holy Spirit.
The Kingdom :
    (*a*) Its nature, i.e. the Life and Being of the Blessed and glorious Trinity constituting and embracing the life of Man according to the original Will of the Father.
    (*b*) Conditions of entry.
    (*c*) Characteristics of its citizens.
Prayer, and devotional life.
Faith.
Renunciation and Self-abandonment.

Human relationships, including :

(a) Compassion ;
(b) Forgiveness ;

but it is none the less essentially a *unity* : one central Truth
—God's Nature and Will—reflected from varying angles.
Jesus' teaching comprised the completest revelation *possible
in time* of the Father and His Will, and the revelation of how
Man could become conformed to—and transformed in—that
Will. This was the body of His teaching, and as such
remained static ; but it was progressively adapted to His
different hearers in the form in which they would find it
most assimilable.

Every fragment of Jesus' teaching comprised a surface
truth, and also several deeper and hidden planes of Truth
one and inexhaustible. Many hearers never perceived
more than the surface truth, whilst others were enabled
eventually if not immediately to plumb some at least of the
other deeper and hidden planes. This is equally applicable to '' hearers '' all down the ages, including ourselves,
who have access to the teaching of Jesus as preserved by the
Holy Spirit in the Gospels.

An outstanding instance of this depth upon depth comprised in Jesus' teaching is the Lord's Prayer. Never in
time, or even in eternity, can its Jesus content be exhausted.
Only after years of trying really to *pray* this prayer can we
be brought within the fringe of its sub-surface significance.
'' Hallowed be Thy Name '' : only gradually do we come,
by love and not by thinking, to learn something more of the
Father's Name, i.e. His I AM THAT I AM ; and to learn how
we dishonour It more than ever we had realised, and thence
by contrast to begin to understand something more of what
is involved in hallowing It . . . '' Thy Will be done . . .''
takes every moment of life, and death itself, to teach us, so
slowly as for the most part to be almost imperceptible, the
true essence of this Will, and how, *concretely*, it may be
embraced and fulfilled ; and eventually the time must come
when this teaching has to take the form of unlearning all our

previous notions, and having them exchanged for the *unknowing* which is the only true and safe knowing, i.e. the unbroken and all-pervading realisation of " My thoughts are not your thoughts, neither are your ways My ways, saith the Lord. For as the heavens are higher than the earth, so are My ways higher than your ways, and My thoughts than your thoughts ". " Give us this day our daily bread " : the material necessities of daily life we first imagine—and not wrongly, since our Lord desired and meant us consciously to depend upon the Father Who knows all our needs even before we plead them. But then we come gradually to include the *spiritual* as well as material necessities ; and to embrace in that " us " and " our " the whole world, not as a phrase or vague idea, but in a living sense of our identification with each and all whoever or wherever they may be.

Next there dawns the transforming day when the Holy Spirit Himself interprets for us this petition for " daily bread " in Jesus' own words : " . . . the bread of God is that which cometh down out of heaven and giveth life unto the world . . . *I am the bread of life* . . . Yea, and the bread which I will give is My flesh, for the life of the world " (Jn. vi. 33, 35, 50 f.) ; and so it becomes a prayer for the daily indwelling *in all souls* by Jesus Christ their Redeemer and their Life : a prayer best offered, in union with His high-priestly intercession for all souls, through the daily offering in the Sacrament of His Most Blessed Body and Blood of the one " full, perfect, and sufficient sacrifice, oblation and satisfaction for the sins of the whole world ". It thus becomes a prayer, not only of petition on behalf of all men, but also on their behalf a prayer of faith and thanksgiving ; and, moreover, since we *are* all inextricably one far more than we thoroughly realise, a receiving of this Living Bread not only within ourselves, but also on behalf of all others who come not for themselves to receive Him in the Sacrament, be the reason what it may -prevention by sickness, service for others, lack of opportunity, or lack of desire simply through ignorance of the adorableness and all-satisfyingness of Jesus *their own* Saviour as well as Saviour of those who consciously recognise something at least of their debt to Him.

Jesus adapted His teaching to His hearers in accordance with what He knew to be God's vocational design for them ; and also in accordance with the mental and spiritual background they already possessed. He taught always with love and compassion as well as with insight and patience, no matter how great the suffering entailed for Him by the blindness, dulness, obstinacy, cowardice, or antagonism of His hearers.

Our Lord's whole dealing with the Scribes and Pharisees showed uttermost resource as well as generosity in His teaching. Again and again, first in one form, then in another, trying always to compute the spiritual in terms of outward observance, they raised with Him the issue : " Why walk not Thy disciples according to the tradition of the elders . . . ? " He met their problems in a variety of ways so as to afford them maximum opportunity for satisfaction, e.g. :

(*a*) By teaching *along their own lines,* i.e. referring them to the very Scriptures by which they professed to set such store, and freshly interpreting for them divers passages relevant to the specific problems in question.

(*b*) By making His own fearless action in transcending man-made ' traditions ', *where charity and compassion required it*, an illuminating commentary upon their projected difficulties.

(*c*) By exposing the unspirituality of formalism : " And He said unto them, Well did Isaiah prophesy of you hypocrites as it is written,

> This people honoureth Me with their lips
> But their heart is far from Me.
> But in vain do they worship Me,
> Teaching as their doctrines the precepts of men.

Ye leave the commandment of God, and hold fast the tradition of men " (Mk. vii. 6–8).

(*d*) By sharing with them explicitly, in order that " they

14

might be saved ", the truth of His relationship to the Father
(e.g. Jn. v. 19 ff. ; Jn. viii. 13 ff.), regardless of the fact that
these men with whom He had to deal were utterly, often
wilfully, out of sympathy with Him, and could not humanly
be expected to apprehend any spiritual truth or vision
cutting across their own traditional and ingrained beliefs.
What humility ; what generosity ; what love ; for their
sakes to risk almost certain bitter misunderstanding of
Himself and of His vocation as their King and Saviour.

Tirelessly He tried every means of teaching them the
truth, and exhausted all Love's devices in attempting to
woo them to the light.

Our Lord's teaching of the disciples aimed—both for their
own souls' sakes, and for the sake of those who all down the
ages should believe on Him " through their word "—at
equipping them to found and raise their own spiritual
edifices, as He did His own, on the ' rock ' of the Father
Eternally Changeless in Love, Holiness, and Truth. His
teaching equipped them not only for their own individual
relationships to God, furnishing them with " treasure . . .
new and old " ; but also revealed to them " the faith . . .
once for all delivered " in trust for all succeeding generations.

Jesus Himself declared that He was never " alone " ; and
this was essentially true of Himself as teacher. Not only, as
He said, did He teach nothing of Himself, but " as the
Father taught " Him (Jn. viii. 28) ; but in His teaching *He
relied absolutely upon the Holy Spirit.* On the eve of His
death He prophesied to His disciples that not only would
the Holy Spirit interpret to them His words—" He shall
take of Mine, and shall declare it unto you " (Jn. xvi. 14)—
but would also recall them after His Ascension : " These
things have I spoken unto you, while yet abiding with you.
But the Comforter, even the Holy Spirit, Whom the Father
will send in My Name, He shall teach you all things, and
bring to your remembrance all that I said unto you "
(Jn. xiv. 25–26). What a vindication of this prophecy are

the Gospels, which save by the inspiration of the Holy Spirit could never have come into being, perpetuating the teaching as well as the personality of Jesus for all time.

Our Lord's teaching was an integral part of His vocation to reveal God to Man, Man to himself, and to redeem Man to God. Designedly no attempt is here made to recapitulate that teaching. The gift of such understanding of the Master's teaching as is possible in time can only gradually be received by way of direct and persevering recourse to the Gospels, day in day out, each for himself or herself, in a life-abandonment of the entire self to the Holy Spirit, the Revealer and Interpreter of the Mind of Christ, Who alone can—and will—progressively satisfy all sincere desire to penetrate the truth as it was taught by Him Who Himself is Eternal Truth.

JESUS THE HEALER (see also pp. 164 ff.)

OUR Lord Himself said : ". . . blessed is he, whosoever shall find none occasion of stumbling in Me " (Matt. xi. 6). This He said, knowing full well that for many certain aspects of His Person and work would inevitably present such serious intellectual and moral difficulties as must appear humanly insuperable. It is in Jesus as healer that occasion of stumbling has, perhaps, been felt most acutely and by the largest number of persons ; and this for a variety of reasons, of which only a few can here be mentioned.

There have been those, largely of a scientific or so-called ' realist ' bent of mind, for whom the miraculous—including the healing—element in the Gospels has seemed untenable either in part or in entirety. Some have rejected all the miracles *qua* miracles. Others have accepted such as their reason could approve in the light of the latest scientific knowledge available, and rejected the remainder. Others again have tried to leave the miraculous element in abeyance, so to speak, as a moot-point non-essential one way or other to the rest of the Gospel revelation—an attempt which, it may be said in passing, cannot be carried through in practice.

There are, on the other hand, those who freely accept the miraculous element in the Gospels because, after prolonged prayer and the deepest intellectual and moral testing of which they are capable, they are unable to reject it. These are, therefore, committed fully to believing in Jesus as healer ; and hence their point of stumbling is on shifted ground. They know from the Gospels that He is never recorded to have refused healing to any in the days of His flesh ; and they know with equal certitude born of experience that He is " the same yesterday, and to-day, and for ever ". What they do not know is how to reconcile this unquestionable double truth with facts as they have emerged all down the ages and appear to-day.

Our Lord's healing ministry, although effectually carried on by the apostles, none the less virtually died out in later times ; and eventually sickness came to be regarded as the " Will of God ", His visitation to be accepted at least resignedly by all those who acknowledged Him. To some—and many of those His greatest saints and lovers—physical suffering seemed, if not positively a vocation in itself, at least under the permissive Will of God an integral part of vocation, and potentially a consecrated offering well-pleasing to God and a channel of redemption for the world, just in as far as it was genuinely united to the Passion of the Saviour.

Then within our own times has come a further change of attitude in regard to the whole question of physical suffering. Whilst there are not lacking those who still hold to the vocation aspect of it, this is increasingly being abandoned. The Church has, in part at any rate, resumed her healing ministry. " Resignation " to illness as the Will of God is now considered by many as equally—if not more—sinful than " rebellion " would formerly have been by those who advocated " resignation ".

It is an unquestionable fact that numbers have been spiritually healed, and that in many cases which cannot be classed as neurotic, and where medical and psychological treatment had either failed completely or but partially succeeded. But it is no less unquestionable that many who have sought spiritual healing have not *physically* been permanently cured, even in cases where from time to time there has been great relief and apparent improvement. These cases provide many occasions of stumbling alike to patients, intercessors, and to those who seek to mediate the healing. *Why* is there failure on the physical plane ? Is there more than common sin or lack of faith in the individual sufferer who continues ill ? or is the sin or lack of faith *corporate* rather than individual ? Is failure on the physical plane possibly not an index of *essential* failure at all ? Is the suffering of some, for a time at any rate, within the permissive Will of God, whilst it is His designed Will to heal that of others ?   And if so which ; for how long ; and why ?

There are many who have experienced deep and lasting blessing through *physical* cure by spiritual healing. There are those also who have again and again in all spiritual gratitude received—either direct, or mediated within His Church's ministry, or through some consecrated doctor or nurse His whether professedly so or not—our Lord's stilling touch, giving freedom from physical pain all but overwhelming mind as well as body ; peace for the all but intolerable fear and restlessness of utter physical exhaustion ; an inflow of energy dispelling the physical prostration that is neither life nor even merciful death, but simply a paralysing and en-shrouding horror.

Yet some of these there are who—without shadow of hesitation—know that by far their deepest cause for adoring thankfulness is in physical cure delayed, or even, it may seem, withheld altogether. They have *proved*—more incontestably than would perhaps have been possible in any other way—the LOVE of God precisely in the companioning of Jesus, literally realler and closer than all else, self included, in the fire of fierce unabating physical pain ; and also His patience, sufficiency, and more than generosity in His daily sustaining of them through the prayer and loving care and help which He Himself has evoked from others on their behalf.   Such as these—even whilst knowing that sickness was never included in the original Will of God—simply cannot regard it as unmitigatedly evil *in a fallen world* where all, well or sick, are sinners. They have too undeniably experienced, within the veriest depths of their innermost being, its potential blessing in enlightenment and closer one-ing to Him, Whom to come to know is to count trifling even the uttermost cost to body, mind, or spirit, involved in the process.

Any and all problems arising either at large or in particular in spiritual healing can only find their solution in Jesus the

Healer eternally the same as revealed by the Holy Spirit in the Gospels.

It is a striking fact, not without deep significance, that the synoptic gospel which treats most fully of our Lord's miracles of healing, and is alone in recording such outstanding ones as the raising of the Widow of Nain's son ; the healing of the woman with a spirit of infirmity for eighteen years ; and the cleansing of the ten lepers, should be that of St. Luke who—both as a *physician* and as a man innately given to the sifting and scrutinising of the reliability of facts, records, and testimony—would naturally be infinitely more critical with regard to them than would either of the other synoptists.

In those healing miracles which St. Luke relates in common with St. Mark, or with the author of the Gospel according to St. Matthew, he adds details peculiar to himself which prove the pains he has taken to investigate each case and to assure himself of all the facts, e.g. he alone tells : of the man with an unclean spirit in the Synagogue at Capernaum that when the " *devil had thrown him down in the midst,* he came out of him, *having done him no hurt* " ; of the leper that he was " a man full of leprosy " ; that it was the *right* hand which the man in the synagogue had withered ; that the centurion's servant was " at the point of death " ; of Legion that " for a long time he had worn no clothes " ; of the woman with the issue of blood that before she came to our Lord she could " not be healed of any " ; that it was the *right* ear of the servant of the high priest which was smitten off by Peter in the Garden of Gethsemane.

All St. Luke's minute investigation of facts led him, not only to accept the genuineness of our Lord's miracles of healing, but also to *account* for them : " The power [δύναμις] of the Lord was with Him to heal " [R.V. margin " that He should heal "] (Lk. v. 17) ; " And the whole multitude sought to touch Him : for there went virtue [δύναμις] out of Him, and healed them all " (Lk. vi. 19) ; " Jesus of Nazareth . . . God anointed Him with the Holy Ghost

and with power [δυνάμει] : Who went about doing good and
healing all that were oppressed by the devil ; *for God was
with Him* " (Acts x. 38). God with Him : here St. Luke
has plumbed the heart of Jesus as Healer. His power to
heal was born of His perfect union with the Father in
adoration of His Will—His original Will for the perfection
of the world, and His re-creative Will to restore all things
after the Fall. This ' power ' expressed itself in different
ways on different occasions, but always it was solely and
equally the fruit of His union with the Father in love and
obedience.

Our Lord, illuminated by the Holy Spirit, maintained
always a true perspective in all things. The study of Jesus
as Healer particularly necessitates similar perspective if it
is not to become positively misleading. To detach, as it
were, His miracles of healing from the fulness of His entire
ministry and vocation in such a way as to conceive a ministry within a ministry, a " healing ministry " as almost a
separate entity and end in itself, is to set up a false division
and a false emphasis which He Himself absolutely and
deliberately rejected. No matter what the consequences
involved, in publicity, inconvenience, or flocking crowds,
invitation to such healing would have been extended unreservedly to all—just as was His invitation to men to come
to Him as teacher, Saviour, and Giver of Eternal Life—
had it been the Father's Will *and best gift.*

It is significant that Jesus never invited the sick in body
or mind to come to Him purely as such, and in order that
they might be released from suffering or disability. Neither
has the Holy Spirit recorded for us any systematic teaching
as ever having been given by Jesus upon this whole " healing
question " : nothing more than a few bare—almost, it
might be said, cryptic—answers evoked by definite questions
put to Him by His disciples in regard to specific cases by
which they had found themselves particularly bewildered.
Surely this is because " healing " is, as Jesus fully recognised,
but a part—albeit an integral part—of His whole eternal

ministry of atonement : an *offshoot* rather than a *goal* in His ministry on earth, whether that of the days of His flesh two thousand years ago, or that of His Mystical Body to-day. It is one of the " signs " of His Messiahship as He Himself attested for John the Baptist questioning in prison —" Go your way, and tell John what things ye have seen and heard ; the blind receive their sight, the lame walk, the lepers are cleansed, and the deaf hear, the dead are raised up, the poor have good tidings preached to them " (Lk. vii. 22)—but it is *not* the whole content of salvation, neither is it in itself " the good news ".

" Behold, I make all things new " : to this end was Jesus sent by the Father—to make at-one with His original Perfect Creation all that was resultant upon the Fall. Resultant upon the Fall—the rebellion of the creature against the Creator—was the coming into existence of :

(1) Principalities and Powers of Evil (where before had been only principalities and powers of good).

(2) A Body of universal and self-generating Sin.

(3) Intermittent Chaos and Destructiveness in Nature.

To one or more of these three sources—and to these alone —every single sickness or impotence of body or mind is traceable. Such sickness or impotence may or may not— certainly need not, but all too often does—have its development within the spirit of the individual sufferer ; sickness of body or mind not infrequently being the result of the spirit's will deliberately divorced from the Will of God. At other times, sickness of body or mind, whilst not apparently orginally developed within the spirit of the individual sufferer, yet seems ultimately to penetrate and disintegrate it.

Speculation as to the *immediate* cause underlying specific suffering is the almost universal human reaction to it, whether in the sufferers themselves, in those who love them, those who minister to them, or those who perpetuate the rôles of Job's friends. The frequent tendency is to try to analyse the origin of specific physical or mental sickness *as though isolated within the individual* in whom it shows itself ; but it was never our Lord's way to confine Himself to this, nor even generally, it would seem, to concentrate upon it much at all.

He dealt with sickness as He dealt with other results of the Fall, simply in the course of His ministry of at-one-ment, which at-one-ing was a *process*, and not an instantaneous act either as wrought by Him or as appropriated by Man. Jesus lost Himself in no maze of secondary causes and effects. All His exercise of healing power was broad-based upon the Father's loving Will to restore the Perfection ruptured at the Fall. He dealt with the physical as a component, but not as a primary, factor in healing ; and distinguished—as in the case of the ten lepers—between mere physical restoration and the further wholeness of personality entirely well-pleasing to Him. All ten lepers were physically healed, but only the one was—through worship—" whole ", i.e. in harmony in the whole of his being functioning according to the design of God.

Our Lord's attitude towards the individual sufferer was always one of compassion and reverence rather than of analysis, or of condemnation even where humanly it seemed most patently deserved. He had " rebuke " for the disease, e.g. for the *fever* from which Peter's mother-in-law was suffering ; or for *the evil spirit* dominating the sufferer, but never for the sufferers themselves. His strength of body and mind and His own personal holiness were ever at the service of those who suffered, in such a way as to exclude any possibility of their feeling themselves despised on the grounds of their infirmity, or condemned on the grounds of what it might connote.

It must be noted that *never* did He attempt to draw the sufferers into a search for the causes underlying their diseases, and that where, by the illumination of the Holy Spirit, He knew there to be a direct connection between their sickness and their own personal sin, all He saw fit to do was either to precede the gift of physical healing by

that most wondrous of all gifts, His limitless absolution—
" Son, thy sins [into which He did not even enter] be forgiven thee " (Mk. ii. 5)—or else to follow up the physical
healing with a loving and compassionate warning : " Behold,
thou art made whole : sin no more, lest a worse thing befall
thee " (Jn. v. 14).

Jesus' motive was to *free* the entire being and personality
to function holily in perfect accord with God's original—
and unique—Will for it.

Jesus' miracles of healing, as selected by the Holy Spirit
for permanent record, show an astonishing variety in content
which proves once for all time that no disease or infirmity,
nor even any disposition of mind or spirit, is beyond His
power to heal. They show a no less astonishing variety in
method. Some He performed in public, some in private,
some by the laying-on of hands, some by word, some by
touch, some by prayer alone and at a distance from the
unseen patient, some by making clay of spittle and anointing
with it. Some of His miracles were, as He Himself stated,
conditioned by the faith of the sufferers or their friends.
In some instances faith effectually drew upon that healing
virtue proceeding from Him. In other instances—such as
the healing of Malchus' ear (Lk. xxii. 50–51)—there is
nothing at all which presupposes such faith, but rather the
contrary. So many of His healings were instantaneous that
it is often loosely thought—even on occasion said—that
they all were ; but study of the Gospels shows that this was
far from being the case, and that where it was not so it
was due on His side to obedience to the dictates of the all-
wise Holy Spirit, Who designed blessing not only for those
immediately concerned, but far beyond them to others also.

The non-instantaneous healings of the Gospels need deep
pondering, for each has even more treasure to yield than
those which were instantaneous. So great is this treasure
that all must ponder it for themselves, for no one person
can receive more than a fragment of the whole. Hence only
a few selective suggestions are here possible.

Jesus never ultimately refused to heal any who came and asked healing of Him either for themselves or for those they loved, but to more than one for a time—short perhaps as time goes, but infinitely long to faith and love—it must fully have seemed as though healing was not to be granted. In each case, even if not immediately then certainly after the healing had been received, looking back, there must have been recognition that through the very delay itself Jesus had given the greatest gifts of all : gifts greater even than the actual healing which alone had been desired when first His help was sought.

The Healing of the Nobleman's Son (Jn. iv. 46–54)

The nobleman came to Jesus at Cana and " besought Him that He would come down, and heal his son ; for he was at the point of death " at Capernaum.   The nobleman expected that Jesus would come and perform for his son a miracle no less wonderful in manner than that of His turning water into wine in this very same Cana.   He in no way doubted either Jesus' power or will to do so.   How startlingly then must Jesus' sole reply—given out of His intuitive knowledge in the Holy Spirit of the inner state of the man's mind and heart—have fallen upon his ears : " Except ye see signs and wonders ye will in no wise believe ". Surely this *could* mean nothing else than tacit refusal to work any sign or wonder for his son !   Either he must abandon all hope of help for his son, or else recast that hope.

Jesus' answer forced him to seek anchorage elsewhere than in His miracles ; and he found it in Jesus' Very Self apart from His signs and wonders.   Increasing respect slowly deepened to worship, and he but clung the more to Jesus in spite of—or rather, more probably precisely because of— His refusal to help in the expected and desired way.   " Sir, come down ere my child die " : now it was in Jesus *being with*, rather than *doing for*, his son that he anchored his hope of cure.   He was content to leave Jesus' presence to operate in the way of His own choice, be that as unspectacular as might be. He had ceased to appeal to Jesus as wonder-worker, and re-directed that appeal to His pity and to His responsiveness to love's distress, which are amongst the constituent elements of His essential Self. " Go thy way, thy son liveth." So, not even Jesus' presence with his son was to be granted.   There was humanly nothing to minister either to brain or senses any plausible ground for cure, yet " The man believed the word that Jesus spake unto him, and he went his way " ; and in due time he found Jesus' promise tangibly vindicated, and knew that signs and wonders had not been refused, as undoubtedly appeared at first and for some while after.

" This is again the second sign that Jesus did . . ." says St. John. This miracle of prayer prevailing at a distance was infinitely more wonderful and more limitless in poten-tiality than any miracle wrought on the spot and through external media. Here was no possible room for doubt that the spiritual and the spiritual alone was all-sufficing. The nobleman had received his son's cure ; but not that only—he had, through delay in proof of that cure, received the yet greater gift of Jesus' re-creative understanding of himself, drawing him on to truer knowledge of Jesus' Self and limit-less power and the marvellous diversity of His working, in such a way as permanently to gain his unshakable trust in the Person and bare word of Jesus unsupported by any external evidence whatsoever, and to enable him to infect others with like faith.

The Healing of the Syrophœnician Woman's Daughter
    (Mk. vii. 24–30 ; Matt. xv. 21–28)

The Syrophœnician mother, who came to our Lord on behalf of her daughter, initially met with what seemed nothing less than complete rejection. To her genuinely worshipping appeal to His pity, to her faith in His power, " He answered her not a word ". Undaunted, she continued appealing to Him for help ; but all that was vouchsafed her in reply was His : " I was not sent but unto the lost

sheep of the house of Israel ". Still refusing to be cast off,
" she came and worshipped Him saying, Lord, help me ",
appealing confidently to a love and compassion in Him that
she sensed as all-embracing ; but even this only met with
what seemed deepening rebuff : " Let the children first be
filled : for it is not meet to take the children's bread and
cast it to the dogs ". He seemed to have no concern for
her daughter ; only for the right exercise of His own
ministry—and so she tried genuinely to enter into things
from His side instead of her own, to understand His point
of view, piteously irrelevant as it must have seemed to her
mother-love. Infinite was her reward : the Holy Spirit
Himself replied through her : " Yea, Lord : even the dogs
under the table eat of the children's crumbs "—and His
reply was the Father's first commissioning of the extension
of Jesus' ministry beyond the bounds of His own nation to
embrace all peoples everywhere.

The woman ultimately received the healing petitioned for
her daughter, but the delay in its granting had spurred
her—as nothing else could have done—to an effort to
understand the mind of Christ, and in this effort laid her
open to become the mouthpiece of the Holy Spirit's further
unfolding of the Father's Will. Thus was she linked
intimately and creatively with each of the Persons of the
Blessed and Glorious Trinity, and also as a channel for the
extension of our Lord's redemptive ministry with all the
numberless thousands of Gentiles of all succeeding time
who should follow her in finding Him as their Saviour and
Lord. The great gift of delay was for her less in the invaluable spiritual blessing which she received for herself,
than in the fact that during her time of anguished waiting
she was chosen by the Father to be one of the blessed to
whom it is given to be the medium of rich gift and joy from
Himself to the well-beloved Jesus, and also the medium
whereby countless others might receive Him as their own.
Surely she could not but recognise all this as infinitely more
thankworthy than would even have been the healing of her

daughter wrought instantaneously without the eternally fruitful travail which had been involved for her in the process.

The Raising of Lazarus (Jn. xi. 1 ff.)

Admittedly a " difficult " miracle which has been interpreted in numberless ways so different as often to be absolutely contradictory one to another, there yet emerge certain facts which are as incontrovertible as they are illuminating.

Jesus' comment on receiving the news of Lazarus' sickness was one which appeared to admit of no ambiguity whatsoever : " This sickness is not unto [the Greek emphasises the *issue*] death, but for [Gk. = in behalf of] the glory of God, that the Son of God may be glorified thereby." His immediate reaction to this sickness of one whom, together with his two sisters, He especially loved, and for whom He would, therefore, particularly desire complete immunity from any and all evil, was not one of dismay or sense of tragedy or evil, but of vision of limitless and unsurpassable blessing. In this sickness He perceived infinite and eternal cause for thanksgiving, knowing that nothing could be more thankworthy for anyone than that what they experience in time —be it sickness or health, joy or sorrow, darkness or light— should be drunk from the cup of life with single intent for God's glory, in such a way as to provide Him with yet another medium in and through which eternally to glorify Himself in His Beloved Son.

" When therefore He heard that he was sick, He abode at that time two days in the place where He was." There has been great diversity of opinion as to what really underlay this statement. Some hold that He deliberately waited to let Lazarus die and an appreciable time pass after His death in order finally to work a greater miracle. Others cannot reconcile this with the tenor of His mind and methods as apprehended by them. Probably more will be satisfied by what Bishop Westcott here advanced : " The journey

would occupy about a day. Thus Lazarus died at the time
when the message came. Christ therefore did not wait
for the death, but knew of the death. . .".

However this may have been, it remains indisputable that
had such been the Will of the Father, Jesus could immediately
have healed Lazarus, whether then at the point of death or
actually dead, by prayer at a distance ; or He could at
once have set out for Bethany so as to shorten the suspense
of the sisters, and sooner be with Lazarus if his healing
necessitated His actual presence in the flesh to give the
physical word or touch of life. He did neither, because in
the fulness of the Father's love and wisdom the time appointed for Lazarus' healing was not yet come : delay was
a deliberate and purposeful part of the all-embracing sweep
of the Divine economy dealing with the sick man, not in
isolation, but in association with all in any way bound up
with him so as to be affected by him. This " all " was not
merely his sisters, friends, acquaintance, nor even his con-
temporaries, but was co-extensive with the whole human
race throughout time, a body more compact and universally
interactive than we are wont to realise as inescapable fact.

After the two days, Jesus, regardless of His own personal
danger, proposed to go to Lazarus, and told His disciples :
" Our friend Lazarus is fallen asleep ; but I go, that I may
awake him out of sleep." The disciples were perplexed ;
and their perplexity was in direct ratio to their implicit trust
in His earlier declaration : " This sickness is not unto
death ". To their articulate bewilderment He replied uncompromisingly : " Lazarus is dead. . . ".

What must have been the mental and spiritual confusion
of the disciples ! Their Jesus, Whose every word they
knew as promise and impossible for them to doubt, had
given utterance to two explicit statements equally devoid
of loophole for ambiguity, yet which no human reason,
experience, nor imagination, let alone understanding, could
possibly reconcile. " This sickness is not unto death " ;
" Lazarus is dead " : that both could be true appeared

absolutely incredible and impossible. Yet that He the Truth could fail in truth was more incredible and impossible. Reason and senses were dumbfounded, and all the more so because of His adding : " I am glad for your sakes that I was not there, to the intent ye may believe ". They *had* believed in His will and power for immediacy of healing, yet it seemed that He rejoiced that through His non-intervention an opportunity was afforded them of learning to believe something over and above this. What this ' something ' might be was utterly beyond conjecture.

Their deepest and most torturing problem must then have lain less in the seeming irreconcilableness between facts— " Lazarus is dead "—and Jesus' promise : " This sickness is not unto death, but for the glory of God . . .", than in the seeming irreconcilableness in love between the suspended action of Jesus and His known power to mediate instantaneous healing *at will*.

Time was to vindicate the truth of both the apparently conflicting statements of Jesus. Lazarus had died ; but the final issue was not death, because he was raised again by Jesus four days later, and the whole mystery instinct with the glory of God for all eternity. This vindication disclosed—and not for the disciples only, but for all throughout time—an area of Divine truth, i.e. knowledge and operation existing beyond the utmost reaches of human reason, senses, imagination, understanding, or expectation based upon previous experience. It also established once and for all as a perpetual reality—in despite of the seemingly irrefutable lie given in concrete instances by human intellect, appearances, or facts—that *with Jesus absolutely nothing is irretrievable*. The ' something ' more—which had to be conjoined to the disciples' unweakened belief in Jesus' power to heal instantaneously at will—was belief in the certain reality that delay in its exercise was not inconsistent with love *because He could never be other than Love*.

So, gradually for us all, preconceived notions as to how His love ought necessarily to express itself in any given circum-

15

stances must yield to a complete faith in the lovingness and wisdom of that love, even where it runs counter to all human understanding and expectation. Delay and immediacy must be recognised as indistinguishable within the infinity of God's eternal love, which, timeless itself, yet makes use of our creaturely time-sense as a medium for revealing to us the actuality of its ceaseless exercise with redemptive and healing intent. Our " not yet " is as much " now " with God as our own " now " ; and with the inflooding of His " now " become ours too—our time-bondage is annihilated in His Eternity in which alone is the true perspective of perfect Reality.

Each of our Lord's healing miracles has an eternal and universal application over and above its temporal application for the individual sufferer concerned, because each involved the expression of some thought of the Father's, Whose every thought is an eternal disposition in Jesus. His " . . . Come forth " first articulated for the grave-bound Lazarus is repeated again and again as He frees soul after soul from its bondage of body, mind, and spirit, at the time appointed by the Father in His knowledge that that soul has " touched bottom ", i.e. has plumbed the thick darkness of complete human stripping which is the indispensable prerequisite for its resurrection in Jesus. It is precisely when the human wreckage is seemingly exhaustive, unlifting, and final, that Jesus by His " Come forth " can—and does—prove to the soul the invincibility of Love, which is the Glory of God that casts out all need for fear of anything in earth or beyond it because in Him all is ultimately reperfected in conformity with His original Creation.

There is in the Gospels at least one passage which proves unequivocally that our Lord did not regard wholeness of the physical body upon earth as the *summum bonum* : " And if thy hand cause thee to stumble, cut it off : it is good for thee to enter into life maimed, rather than having thy two hands to go into hell. . . . And if thy foot cause thee to stumble, cut it off : it is good for thee to enter into life halt, rather

than having thy two feet to be cast into hell. And if thine
eye cause thee to stumble, cast it out : it is good for thee to
enter into the Kingdom of God with one eye, rather than
having two eyes to be cast into hell . . ." (Mk. ix. 43 ff.).
Jesus here expressly showed that physical wholeness as such
is not an indispensable qualification for eternal life, but that
physical *limitation* may be, and is, in certain cases.

It is very significant that these words of our Lord's on
physical limitation—limitation which, be it noted in passing,
necessarily involved acute physical suffering as well—should
have for calculated climax His : " For every one shall be
salted with fire " [R.V. marg. Many ancient authorities
add : " and every sacrifice shall be salted with salt "]. This
Moffatt luminously renders as " Everyone has to be consecrated by the fire of discipline ", thereby instantaneously
calling to mind two truths recorded of our Lord in the
Epistle to the Hebrews which give point—it is the sense of
waste or futility, and not of pain, which is the real sting—
to all suffering, whether it be physical, mental, or spiritual :
" For it became Him, for Whom are all things, and by
Whom are all things, in bringing many sons unto glory, to
make the captain of their salvation *perfect* [Gk. implies
completeness, maturity] *through sufferings* " (Heb. ii. 10) ;
" Though He were a son yet learned He obedience by the
things which He suffered " (Heb. v. 8).

Physical suffering may often unfold itself as a creative
process of learning obedience, i.e. filial response at deep
levels not yet sighted, let alone learned, by all who are whole
in body. It is also a maturing process : a process which
tends to ' complete ' the sufferer's personality in so far as it
draws it out into union with God, and to " remember them
that are in bonds, as bound with them ; and them which
suffer adversity . . .", and merges what is purely individualistic into conscious oneness with the whole travailing human
race taken both individually and corporately.

The " healing question " is one about which no human
being dare presume to dogmatise. Certain truths we know ;

and one is that suffering is a mystery.   It is a mystery in the
sense that much about it must perforce remain humanly
baffling until finally all hid things are exhaustively brought
to light in Eternity.   But it is also—and this is far more
important—a mystery in the sense that it is *sacramental* and
has implicit in it all the potentialities of the mysteries of our
Lord's own life, just in so far as it is offered in union with
them.

It is instinctive to human nature to wish to understand
things to the satisfaction of the intellect, but as we cannot
know God *by thinking*, only *by loving*—as is made abundantly
plain in " the Cloud of Unknowing "—so neither by thinking
can we work out any " healing formula " which shall be
adequate for every contingency, only by loving.   Every
human theory of how and when God will or ought to heal
will be confounded by fact in case after case.   Only by loving
Jesus so as to know more really than anything else that He
is LOVE can we resolve the " healing question ".   Jesus the
Healer is Love :   this—remembering that Love is All-Holy,
All-Wise—and this only is the sole ' formula ' which can,
and will, infallibly cover every healing problem that can ever
arise.   Let time or method, human cause or issue, once
creep into the ' formula ', and it breaks down at once.

Time, and comparison between individual cases, are the
two chief stumbling-blocks alike for those who seek to
mediate healing, and for those who seek to be healed ; but
they are stumbling-blocks which our Lord Himself explicitly
dealt with in principle, albeit in differing contexts.

Peter, having learned of His Risen Lord the way in which
He desired him to work out his own vocation, promptly
turned to comparison with another—John, the beloved
disciple—and asked Jesus : " Lord, and this man, what ? "
(Jn. xxi. 21).   Jesus' reply to him was uncompromising :
" If I will that he tarry till I come, what is that to thee ?
follow thou Me."   This answer is intended equally for us all
as well as for Peter.   It is our Lord's solemn charge that we
recognise that His dealing with each soul—which includes

His dealing with the body in which that soul is templed—
is solely His affair ; and is *peculiar to it* according to His
Will, which is for its perfect fulfilment of the unique vocation destined for it by the Father.

In His dealing with souls He is absolutely unfettered by
any necessity for conformity of method, or for visible human
result at any given stage in time ; and He calls upon us to
trust His Wisdom, to worship His Love in this by abstaining
from all comparison between His dealings with one and
another—comparison which cannot but lead to perplexity,
discontent, and dejection—in order simply to companion
Him with single heart and mind in the way which He
appoints for us personally, which will be altogether different
from that which He appoints for others.   All that is wrought
by Him is to the glory of the Father.   In one He may be
glorified by what—time-bound—we sense as instantaneous
healing ; in another, such is the inexhaustible diversity of the
manifestation of His glory, He may be equally glorified
in what seems to us deferred healing, even it may be in healing apparently altogether withheld.

The time question He dealt with from two angles ; and
there again the outcome was to show unmistakably that it is
solely His—and not our—affair.   We may not know what
He intends for others, because with each soul He holds secret
tryst which no other may penetrate, and which even the soul
itself can only fully fathom in Eternity.   So neither may we
know *when* He intends any specific consummation.

The disciples asked their Risen Master : " Lord, dost
Thou at this time restore the kingdom to Israel ? "   And
they received for sole answer, His : " It is not for you to
know times or seasons, which the Father hath set within His
own authority " (Acts i. 6–7) ; and this answer is to make us
all, equally with the disciples, realise that in nothing—be it
national, social, or physical restoration—are we either
entitled or able to lay down, whether for ourselves or for
others, any time limit whatsoever.   We have no gauge by
which to assess His processes in terms of time.   He does all

as and when He sees fit ; and it is only after His consummated action, and not before, that we shall—or can—understand the perfection of its fitness.   Our not knowing times
and seasons of His restoration of things at large or in
particular is His gift of opportunity to offer Him well-
pleasing faith, and serenity grounded solely in anchorage in
His I AM THAT I AM.

The other angle of our Lord's dealing with our " time-
complex ", as it has so aptly been called, is in His parable of
the Labourers in the Vineyard (Matt. xx. 1–16).   In this
parable He reduces the time-factor to an absolute non-
essential in ultimate spiritual issues.   The first hour, the
third, the sixth, the ninth, even the very last : it is all one.
So with those who seem from physical suffering or limitation
to be " idle " in so far as so-called " active work " is concerned : it will be *all the same in the end* whether He has freed
them for bodily activity in the first or the last hour.   The
end is that all receive from Him the identical gift : the gift
of Himself as the fulness of Life.   A little more heat or less,
a little more travail or less, will then be irrelevant : His purposes will have been consummated ; our joy fulfilled in
Him ; and His glory manifest in all.

In this same parable of the Labourers in the Vineyard,
Jesus has provided what must, under time-conditions, surely
be His final word for us as Healer : " Is it not lawful for Me
to do what I will with Mine own ? or is thine eye evil, because I am good ?   So the last shall be first, and the first
last."   All in need of healing have to receive it from Him as
and when He chooses to give it.   As with the labourers in
the parable there seems manifest inequality both in the degree of " burden . . . and scorching heat ", and in the *length* of
what has to be endured.   It may humanly appear unfair ;
but all is vindicated by His *generosity* which gives to all alike
" whatsoever is right ".

On another occasion Jesus said : " What I do thou
knowest not now ; but thou shalt understand hereafter."
The Jesus Who said this was the same Jesus Who is the

Healer of us all in His way and not ours, His time, not ours—
that is, in the Father's way and time. The healing is His
affair, not ours : our only part is freely from love and in
penitence to abandon ourselves to Him as " His own " in
body, mind, and spirit ; and He will then in His boundless
generosity give to each " whatsoever is right " i.e. He will
by " even . . . come " consummate in each the Father's
Will which stops not short of perfection in the whole being
for all eternity. This and nothing less is true healing, and
to this each and all must sooner or later hear His " . . .
Come forth " ; and in Eternity the thanksgiving of—and on
behalf of—those healed at the first or the last hour will be
equal, because it will be the flowing forth of their whole
being in a ceaseless energy of worship of our Healer and
Redeemer in His oneness with the Father Who created us
perfect, and with the Holy Spirit Who in and through His
perfection re-created us in holiness.

LOVER OF GOD AND MAN

LOVER of God : see pp. 46 ff.
Lover of Man : see pp. 106 ff. ; 139 ff. ; 156 ff.

There was born on the first Christmas night in Bethlehem of Judæa a Child Who was, by the gradual unfolding of Perfect Love in word, deed, and person, to revolutionise Man's understanding of God, and necessarily thereafter to revolutionise Man himself for God.

The love lived by Jesus was never less than perfect, but it was essentially an ever-developing, ever-widening love perfect in each stage of growth rather than full-blown at birth. Jesus first manifested and *was* love in His own home. He was " subject " to Mary and Joseph, not grudgingly, but with charm and generous self-abandon, and was for thirty years content to remain within the small home-circle, supporting it by His flawless work, and beautifying and enriching it by the lavishness of a love perpetually expressed in tenderness.

Our Lord's whole love of humanity converged in special love for His Mother, who was the means under the Holy Spirit of conferring that humanity upon Him. He loved her devotedly for herself, in all the beauty of holiness flowing from her life-abandonment to the Father through perfect and sustained responsiveness to the operations of the Holy Spirit within her. He loved her too for having given Him His humanity ; and also for having given Him to humanity in the flesh, thereby enabling humanity to be given back to the Father. He was infinitely thankful to her for so co-operating with God as to enable Him to fulfil His vocation as Son of Man as well as Son of God. He loved her not only as His own Mother in the flesh, but as Mother also of His Mystical Body by the perpetuation of her " Fiat " throughout Eternity with intent that He might be born not only of her in the flesh, but also of her—*and of all souls*—

within the citadel of the soul to the glory of the Father
throughout all Creation.

There came a glorious day when Jesus' love broke through
home confines and little by little radiated far and wide, inspiring and making glad first chosen friends and after a
countless multitude who either followed or sought to know
Him. This Love, never for an instant losing sight of the
individual in the multitude or the multitude in the individual, scaled successively the barriers of dissimilarity in
interest, temperament, class, nationality, and race, until it
reached a world-embracing climax on the Cross, when
humanly expressed in uttermost completion it merged again
into the purely Divine Source from which it first came forth.

Sentimentality and emotionalism all too often masquerade
as love ; but Jesus once for all refuted their claims to Love's
stupendous title, by His revelation of the utter selflessness
of Love as expressed by Him in understanding, compassion,
power, loveliness, and trust.

Jesus, simply by virtue of unique understanding, was—
and is—the most perfect friend the world has ever known.
He knew what was in men's minds ; sensed the unspoken
need or fear ; justly appraised the motive ; adjusted the
disparity between ideal and achievement ; appreciated the
seemingly unsuccessful effort ; divined the hitherto unformulated hope ; and—as at His Presentation Simeon
foretold—revealed the thoughts of many hearts, laying bare
to countless men and women better selves till then un-
suspected, either by themselves or by others, merely because
stifled beneath anxiety, indifference, trouble, or recklessness.
To see a need was with Jesus invariably to answer it—though
not necessarily always in the way expected or desired. A
Man to Whom men readily confided their troubles, His comfort was refreshing, His strength invigorating, but He was
inexorable in His demands : help could only come in answer
to faith, and must find repayment in transmission of service
to others. To divine an aspiration was, in the same way,
with Jesus invariably to fan, encourage, and nurture it—

provided always it was rooted in singleness of motive. It was just the fusion of this intuitive understanding with a singularly keen imagination that kindled the creative compassion which was the dominant note of Jesus' love.

Few of us grasp the reality of suffering from the written or spoken word, we need to *see* in order to comprehend it ; but it was otherwise with Jesus. His imagination rendered unseen suffering no whit less real or urgent than that actually beneath His eyes ; and this automatically widened immeasurably for Him the sphere of potential helpfulness and inspiration. He could enter into all the mental anguish ever experienced by Man. He enlightened the doubtful— as He does for all time in His special reappearance after the Resurrection to reassure, and convince, a man agonising in a would-be belief that refused to yield intellectual satisfaction. He heartened the fearful at no small self-expenditure of energy and trouble. He yearned over the lonely, as His wondrous and beautiful solicitude for both His Mother and the Beloved Disciple even in the agony of His Crucifixion radiantly affirms for ever. He plumbed and shared the throes of penitence ; salved the unspeakable agony of self-appalled remorse that dares not even dream of forgiveness ; restored self-respect ; gave peace for torture of mind and heart ; and blessed with hope and courage as with Mary in the house of Simon. Wonder-fraught is the compassion of Jesus' love, so too are its power, loveliness, and trust.

The power of Jesus' love is not only absolutely without parallel in human history, but it also literally staggers human understanding with its intensity. It triumphed in every realm, physical, mental, moral, and spiritual. The blind received sight, the deaf heard, the dumb spake, and the lame leapt for joy, even lepers were cleansed and the dead raised to life. Time and again doubts, fears, and delusions fled ; and demons of desire and jealousy were impotent before it. It revolutionised the characters of men : liars became truthful ; thieves honest ; the unthankful grateful ; the suspicious trusting ; the proud meek ; the mean generous; the timid brave; the savage tender, and the wanton chaste. It transcended intellect and reason, and fired visions alike in scholar and in humble fisherman, revealing heaven's heart-hid secrets to spiritual babes. The power of Jesus' love was not, however, more manifest in the wealth it bestowed than in the riches it evoked: it drew forth response from lukewarm hearts; consideration from carelessness; and from the shroud of self echoing love and sacrifice.

Loveliness was one of the secrets of the power of Jesus' love—loveliness so exquisite and divers-hued as to evade all earth-born words. Jesus accomplished an incalculable amount just by doing seemingly little things in a great and unforgettable way. He helped people warmly and ungrudgingly always for *their* sakes and from love of them, never, as we perhaps are sometimes apt to do, coldly from half-rebellious sense of duty, self-respect, or would-be self-improvement or self-expression. He invariably gave far more than was ever asked or even expected of Him—as to the Penitent Thief who asked a thought and received an eternity of Love's companionship—and He gave in such ways as to enhance His gifts a millionfold. He gave unreservedly with never a hint of condescension or desired reward; He gave joyously and unstintingly; He gave continuingly; and with signal grace He gave to others—perhaps best gift of all—the chance and the wish to give of their best themselves, both to Him and, for love of Him, to all with whom they came in contact. He gave deepest joy and never-ending inspiration to the despised and hated Levi and Zacchæus simply by gracing their boards, and making them feel that they had something to give which He both wanted and needed, thereby arousing in them a desire to go on giving grandly both of their substance and themselves.

But in nothing was the loveliness of Jesus' love more poignant than in its thoughtfulness. There was ever the individual touch which made word or deed perfect as it only could be perfect for the one person for whom it was intended ; and He gave always to each exactly as He knew the gift—whether of healing, comfort, or inspiration—could, and would, be best assimilated. Nowhere was the beauty of this thoughtfulness more conspicuous perhaps than after the raising of Jairus' daughter, when to bring the bewildered parents after their stress gently back to normal again, and to a realisation that all really was well with their child, He " commanded that something should be given her to eat ".

Jesus' love for Man was always in terms of—and synonymous with—holiness, because it was a ceaseless drawing upon that Divine Love which is Holiness. This love He exercised most potently and creatively through His changeless disposition of " For their sakes I sanctify Myself . . ." ; and through His unbroken resistance to temptation whereby He became for Man enslaved by the world, the flesh, and the devil, the one sanctuary where " the prince of this world . . . hath nothing ". He exercised it also by supplying Man's deficiency in love and obedience towards God in His perfect offering of ceaseless worship and penitence.

The perfection of our Lord's love was in large part constituted by the blending of elements which seem humanly antithetical. His boundless compassion was balanced by a tonic severity which is the indispensable complement to any compassion that is to be kept immune from sentimentality. His severity was not opposed to His compassion, but was its kernel. By reason of human weakness, all too often prone to be glad of a " soft and easy way out " wherever possible, compassion is more readily recognised as love than is severity. It is, therefore, well to trace here in some detail the element of severity in our Lord's love, not in order to try to explain—let alone explain away—justify, or water it down ; but in order to give it its full value as being the true gauge of the immensity of that love.

Any portrait of our Lord which omits to include a realist severity is altogether wanting in truth as well as in perspective. To gloss over the severity as incompatible with His tenderness, His patience, His inexhaustible forgivingness, is totally to misunderstand the real nature of that tenderness, patience, forgivingness, because it is to miss their underlying motive of which His severity was the index.

Our Lord's severity sprang from the nakedness of His sincerity in self-identification with holiness, and from His absolute refusal to hold any traffic whatsoever with sin. In His oneness with the Father His standards were super-human—" For My thoughts are not your thoughts, neither are your ways My ways, saith the Lord ". His love of holi-ness ; His detestation of sin : this was the ground of His severity. He could demand all because He gave all. He asked of others no more than He Himself had given ; and it was from sheer love that He could—and did—ask no less. He could not rest content with anything less for others than the perfect satisfaction of the Father's Will which was His own life, and joy, and peace, the *raison d'être*, the signific-ance, the consummation of all being. Holiness and death to self He knew to be absolutely impossible of attainment by sinful Man in his own strength which is no strength at all, but rather an abyss of weakness and folly. Yet He was inexorable in His demand upon sinners for this holiness and death to self, because He knew also that in Himself its im-possibility was done away, and that by union with Him in His self-donation for and to them their sin and selfishness could be annihilated, and His holiness and selflessness—through the generosity of the Father—be flooded in as their own.

The severity of Jesus showed itself very early in life. To His Mother's : " Son, why hast Thou thus dealt with us ? behold, Thy father and I sought Thee sorrowing ", He re-plied, though only twelve years old, without apology, and without any sop to human affection—unique in all the world as was the affection between such a Son and such a Mother—" How is it that ye sought Me ? Wist ye not that I must be in My Father's house ? " (Lk. ii. 48–49). Surely

" a hard saying " to any Mother less Spirit-possessed than she !

Jesus was not concerned to smooth things to easiness for people, but to develop them to the fulness of their spiritual stature ; and to this end He was ruthless in pruning as well as in demand. He made neither His teaching, nor daily life with Him, easy. In calling the disciples He cut relentlessly across the human security of their previous livelihoods, and across their home ties. His own were already cut across.

He refused to be satisfied with the moral and ethical standard conventionally attached to the Law by the professedly religious of His day. His re-interpretation of the Commandments imparts to them an infinitely more trenchant and exacting content. He pronounced mere outward conformity to rule utterly insufficient : everything is reduced to the test of inner motive. By His demands in the Sermon on the Mount He cuts clean across both the desires and the capabilities of " the natural man ", and sets forth His requirements as nothing short of perfection—perfection in supernatural love, purity, sincerity, and selflessness. He *forbids* anxiety with regard to the necessities of life, even for life itself. In no human circumstances whatsoever will He acquiesce in the excusableness of anxiety, being—as He shows it—both an insult to the Father All-loving, All-wise, and All-providing, and a hindrance to the furthering of the Kingdom.

" Not every one that saith unto Me, Lord, Lord, shall enter into the kingdom of heaven ; but he that doeth the Will of My Father which is in heaven. Many will say to Me in that day, Lord, Lord, did we not prophesy by Thy name, and by Thy name cast out devils, and by Thy name do many mighty works ? And then will I profess unto them, I never knew you : depart from Me, ye that work iniquity " [Gk. ἀνομίαν = lawlessness, lawless conduct. It is possible genuinely to believe that one is doing His work, and yet in actual fact to be working undisciplinedly outside the laws of the kingdom.] (Matt. vii. 21–23) ; " Strive to enter in by the narrow door : for many, I say unto you, shall seek to enter in, and shall not be able. When once the Master of the house is risen up, and hath shut to the door, and ye begin to stand without, and to knock at the door, saying, Lord, open to us ; and He shall answer and say to you, I know you not whence ye are ; then shall ye begin to say, We did eat and drink in Thy Presence, and Thou didst teach in our streets ; and He shall say, I tell you, I know not whence ye are ; depart from Me, all ye workers of iniquity " [Gk. ἀδικίας = wrong, offence, cause of displeasure, affront, injustice, or withholding of another's rights or dues. It is possible that even our Communions and our study of His teaching may be cause of displeasure and affront to Him] (Lk. xiii. 24–27).

These parallel passages are here given in full because they are all too frequently passed by as too terrible to bear dwelling upon. Yet they need the deepest meditation of which we are capable, as being the merciful " Lo, now speakest Thou plainly . . ." of our Judge, as to the precise touchstone upon which He has to make our Eternity depend. No longer is there any possibility of misapprehension as to what is required of us. Vocal prayer ; the spreading of spiritual truths ; successful ministry apparently like His own ; the act of communicating ; study of His teaching ; are not in themselves necessarily or unquestionably well-pleasing to Him, and may even be positively displeasing if lacking the " one thing . . . needful ", which is to be known of Him—that is to be abandoned to Him in such a way that there is no part of us from which He is excluded from abso-lute possession ; to be laid bare to Him in the unreserved self-donation of love in will, heart, and mind ; to be known exhaustively by identification of our whole being with His. The hearing of His words without response in obedience is the great fall.

" The sons of the kingdom shall be cast forth into the outer darkness " (Matt. viii. 12) ; " Many be called but few are chosen " (Matt. xxii. 14) ; Jesus shows the call as an opportunity, an invitation, but that it is the nature of our response to it—and not merely our having received and recognised it—which determines our eternal relationship with Him.

Our Lord throughout His parables and teachings emphasised the cost of Christian living. Never did He allow to be obscured the fact that it involves nothing less than complete renunciation and continuing death to self in every sphere.

Faced with the hungering multitude in the wilderness, He said to His disciples: " They have no need to go away ; give ye them to eat " (Matt. xiv. 16). He *expects* His disciples to co-operate effectually with the Father even under conditions which seem humanly insuperable.

When commissioning the Twelve and the Seventy (Matt. x. 5 ff. ; Mk. vi. 7 ff. ; Lk. x. 1 ff.), He permitted them no stock in hand of present necessities, let alone marginal precautions against the future.

It would seem as though He deliberately intended to identify Himself with the " austere man " of His parable of the Talents (Lk. xix. 22).

Our Lord's severity was the exercise of supernatural love at a cost to Himself in patience and human heartache— because liable to be misunderstood by those whose responsive love He so yearned to win—altogether beyond our power to plumb even in imagination, let alone in understanding. No matter what the risk of misunderstanding involved for Himself His love would not—for want of any warning within His power to give—permit Him to let us run any avoidable risk of misunderstanding the ultimate and eternal issues dependent upon the choices of our wills in time. His apparent severity was the precise measure of His love for Man, and of His desire—expressed to the Father in His high-priestly prayer (Jn. xvii)—for each and all eventually to be where He is ; to behold His glory ; to be infilled with the Father's love ; and to be eternally indwelt by Himself.

The Beloved Disciple records for us the faithfulness of

Jesus' love : " Having loved His own which were in the world He loved them unto the end " [R.V. or, to the uttermost. Gk. εἰς τέλος = the fulfilment or completion of anything ; its end or issue, not its cessation] (Jn. xiii. 1).

" This is My commandment, that ye love one another, even as I have loved you " (Jn. xv. 12) : this love for Man was shown both in life and death to be with fathomless patience ; for no human deserving ; with complete understanding, compassion, inexhaustible forgivingness, GENEROSITY and COURTESY ; in humility, in " heroic virtue ", i.e. sacrificial self-donation to the uttermost ; and all the time progressively freeing souls from enslavement to sin and self, so as to release within them the expression of the Father's original and eternal thought of them in Him.

16

PERFECT MAN

JESUS was a perfect man, sinless and mature; but He was more. As:

Word made flesh;

Risen and Ascended Lord;

Alpha and Omega;

the Holy Spirit has revealed Him—both in the New Testament, and in the hearts of worshippers all down the ages—as PERFECT MAN.

The Word made flesh was the revelation of Man not less than of God. Our Lord Himself said, with reference to a specific act on the eve of His death: " I have given you an example " (Jn. xiii. 15); and this applies equally to His whole life, incarnate, risen, and ascended. *He* was the true, the final, " pattern showed in the mount ". On the Mount of Transfiguration, in the Person of the Son of Man radiant in the *manifestation* of the glory wherein He was created and sustained by the Father, Man as God intended him to be was first shown to fallen men. This revelation was no mere " might-have-been ". It was the revelation of humanity in ultimate and eternal perfection as redeemed by God after the Fall. Early on in His public ministry, it was said of Jesus, at Cana of Galilee: " Thou hast kept the good wine until now " (Jn. ii. 10); and in these words there is enshrined an eternal truth—the truth of unfailing, ever-renewed perfection " as it was in the beginning, is now, and ever shall be . . . without end everlasting " in and through the Word made flesh.

The Word alone perfectly expresses the Father, and no less the Word made flesh alone perfectly expresses Man. Men falter prayers to God, entreaties, petitions, outpourings of fears, hopes, and desires, until at length in the hid silence of self perplexed, broken, and tired of self, there is heard—

in God's fulness of time for the individual soul—the Word eternally bespeaking the Father to Man. Listening to the Word the soul is gradually invaded by the sense of " nothing more to say " to God. All ' saying ' in prayer is suddenly recognised as self, and the Word made flesh is as suddenly known Himself—and not the soul—to be the Worshipper to Whom the dumb soul is oned and in Whom the whole being, body, mind, and spirit, is completely unified and utterly satisfied. The word is one only : Father. The Word eternally utters " Father " to Man ; and the Word made flesh, with His " Abba, Father ", eternally worships in Man. It is this perpetual " Abba, Father " of the Word within the soul which is Man's true life and only real self-expression.

Pilate's " Behold, the man ! " invited men to gaze upon a prisoner, derided, scathed in body, and on the verge of being sentenced to a criminal's death. God's " Behold, the man ! " is an invitation to gaze upon One gloriously free, Who can be holden neither by death, matter, space, nor time ; the Risen and Ascended Lord in Whom alone we can truly—needing all eternity to do it exhaustively—behold Man created in the image of God after His likeness (Gen. i. 26).

The Word made flesh deigned to take upon Himself a body subject to the physical limitations resultant upon the Fall, wherein Man laid himself open for all time to suffer from, and be dominated by, forces over which God had originally given him absolute control on sole condition of specific obedience to Himself. Our Lord rose in the spiritual body of Man as originally created by God *without physical limitation*. His Risen Body dominated matter—e.g. He could pass through closed doors (Jn. xx. 19)—and space. Yet for all His power of appearing and vanishing suddenly at will, and for all the subtle difference in outward form which time and again prevented His immediate recognition by closest friends and lovers, His Risen Body was no ethereal body having nothing in common with the ' natural body ' as we know it.

He Himself—the Truth—emphasised the tangibility of

His Risen Body : " See My hands and My feet, that it is I Myself : handle Me, and see ; for a spirit hath not flesh and bones, as ye behold Me having " (Lk. xxiv. 39). It was a body which could deal with food : " they gave Him a piece of broiled fish. And He took it ; and did eat before them " (Lk. xxiv. 42–43) ; and was capable of manual work with earthly materials, e.g. the Risen Lord laid and lit a fire, and cooked upon it (Jn. xxi. 9). The Risen Body of our Lord was, therefore, a body which could without let or hindrance deal perfectly with matter, and with the conditions of this world, so far as was necessary for the sake of others, but was in no way dependent upon or circumscribed by them as regarded Himself. It was a perfect medium for the limitless energising of Divine Love.

The Risen Body of our Lord was that of *a man*, Jesus of Nazareth, and had it remained upon earth, this ' spiritual body ' would have continued solely Jesus' own possession ; but by His Ascension in this Risen Body, that ' spiritual body ' which was the original gift of God to Man—i.e. to all men—was potentially restored to Man again. By the Ascension of Jesus this same ' spiritual body ' in which He rose, this perfect medium for the limitless energising of Divine Love, is gradually—by His ceaseless high-priestly intercession in the ' Heavenly Sanctuary ', and by His perpetual self-donation throughout time of His Body and Blood in the Blessed Sacrament of His own institution and bidding—built up within the ' natural body ' of all who will permit it.

" I am the Way, and the Truth, and the Life " (Jn. xiv. 6) declared the Word made flesh ; and this, as Ascended Lord eternally enthroned in the Majesty of the Father, He subsequently amplified by His : " I am Alpha and Omega, the beginning and the end, the first and the last " (Rev. xxii. 13). Comfortable words these, indeed ! the revelation of Man's source, goal, and all between, as Jesus and Jesus only, in His oneness with the Father and the Holy Spirit.

Behind the human heredity and environment of each and

every man is his untainted pre-existence in Jesus, just as for
the human Jesus there was His Pre-existent Glory with the
Father before the world was.   More deeply rooted in every
human being than any fallen tendency or self-created habit
is perfection : the basic perfection of God's original conception of them eternally safeguarded and fulfilled in the Mind
and Soul of Jesus.

Jesus, Son of God and Son of Man, is the Great Fulfiller.
In Him all types take their rise and are fulfilled : artist,
poet, architect, craftsman, philosopher, warrior, physician,
countryman, reformer, teacher, priest, or what you will.   In
Him all souls are fulfilled : every single vocation uniquely
vouchsafed by the Father is " hid with Christ in God ".
Every vocation is to specific and distinctive union with
Christ.   Eternally, before, during, and beyond time, Christ
maintains that distinctive union with the soul as conceived
by the Father, functioning for it—even, it may be said,
functioning *as* it—according to the Will of God, whatever the
soul itself may do.   The vocation is never less than perfectly fulfilled on His side, and in such a way that be the
erring soul's past what it may it can, at any time it chooses,
associate itself from its own side also with that fulfilment
without hiatus in its perfection.

To the disciples who had so signally and repeatedly failed
Him during His vigil in the Garden of Gethsemane, Jesus
immediately afterwards said : " Arise, let us be going . . ."
(Mk. xiv. 42).   He, sinless, the Victor in Whom the prince
of this world hath nothing, invited them to let drop their
failure there and then and to continue with Him in closest
companionship in the fulfilling of the Father's Will, just as
though there had not been any failure at all.   Full and free
was the fresh chance which—in the very act and state of
failure towards Him—He extended to them in their vocation
as His followers.   " Arise. let us be going . . ." is an eternal
disposition in the Son of Man, Who, Ascended, declared :
" Behold, I make [Gk. = continuously make] all things
new " [Gk. = new, primarily in reference to quality].

(Weymouth : " See, I am making everything new.—Rev. xxi. 5.) His continuing perfection without beginning and without end, itself the first and last and all between, is a perpetual and universal enablement for true fulfilment of vocation from the side of each and every soul who is ever willing at any given moment—as was the Penitent Thief—to close with Him in penitence and self-abandon. Be our failures beyond count, and altogether without excuse, yet still does the Word made flesh ever renew for the soul His " Arise, let us be going . . ." ; and in His own way and time He, our Omega as well as our Alpha and our Way, will somehow enable us to die to self so that we may rise with Him into that life destined by God for Man, and manifested and fulfilled in its perfection in Jesus alone.

JESUS AND EVERYMAN

THE Mediæval morality play " Everyman " concerns itself with the human common factor Death. But Life, as well as Death, holds for Everyman the common factor. Everyman at some time or another is subject to joy, sorrow, anxiety and fear, ignorance and doubt, conflict; material, physical, and spiritual need; aspirations, and self-despair. Just as in the play Good Deeds could alone avail Everyman in death; so now One alone can avail Everyman in all the common factors of Life—Jesus.

Jesus and Everyman : the perfect partnership for life. None of us can ever attain to a complete perception of Jesus. We are all too apt to try to make Him in our own image ; to conceive of Him only as He has revealed Himself in His personal dealings with ourselves. Such a Jesus can never be the Jesus of Everyman. The need of Everyman is for the Jesus of the Gospels Who met *all* needs : no lesser Jesus can ever fully satisfy him, or win his unreserved allegiance.

Jesus and joy. Wherever there was joy He was welcomed because He understood, entered into, and enhanced it ; and wherever there was not joy He created it. He it was Who was the life and soul of the marriage-feast in Cana, and those feasts which He so graciously and gaily attended in the houses of Levi and Zacchæus. He shared, heightened, and intensified the joy outpoured by the Seventy on their triumphant return from their missionary journey. He believed in the right and possibility of joy for every one : friend, follower, child, stranger, alien, outcast, pauper, and sinner alike. He made of joy a ministry and a sacrament.

Jesus and sorrow. Wherever there was sorrow He was welcomed because He understood, entered into, and dispelled it. His understanding of sorrow was so deep that no aspect of it ever left His compassion unstirred. He never

237

remained an onlooker in another's sorrow ; His love and power made Him always the deliverer. He penetrated to the root of sorrow ; transmuted it into joy, and glorified the Father in the process.

Jesus and anxiety and fear. He proved them both totally unnecessary, and that from several angles. He proved it by His revelation of the character of God as that of an infinitely loving and Almighty Father with a perfect purpose and concern for every single individual. He proved it by His revelation of the never-failing power of prayer to obtain from God anything and everything in accordance with His Will, which knows no anxiety or fear. He proved it by a life that dispelled every specific anxiety or fear that was ever brought to Him. Frequently He proved it by averting the catastrophe dreaded as humanly inevitable : condemnation, shipwreck, starvation, death. Time and again He proved it in clearing up human misconceptions. Martha need not have been " cumbered about much serving " had she rightly understood Jesus' desire for material simplicity and spiritual companionship. The father of the lunatic boy need not have despaired for his son at the foot of the Mount of Transfiguration had he brought the boy direct to Jesus, rather than have relied on imperfect human intermediaries. Peter would not have had to fear Jesus' prediction of His Passion in the way that he did had he realised it from God's point of view, instead of merely from his own. Finally, Jesus proved anxiety and fear unnecessary by His Ascension promise : " Lo, I am with you alway unto the end of the world " (Matt. xxviii. 20) : He Who promised, and is always present to help, is the same Who once and for all has conquered Evil, Ugliness, Pain, and Death.

Jesus and ignorance and doubt. He spent His life combating and dispelling it. He spared neither time nor energy that every one might know and understand the message of God's love in all its fulness. Simply and with authority He taught the masses. He clarified and rightly interpreted for them what they already knew imperfectly, and gave them

the further vision which they lacked. He met with infinite
patience all doubts as to His character and identity in
followers, critics, and those whom He had healed ; and went
to as great pains to enlighten an individual as a crowd. He
never left in darkness any who genuinely wanted spiritual
light and understanding.

Jesus and conflict. He destroyed interior, and conquered
exterior, conflict. He eliminated conflict of aim and desire ;
and brought peace and harmony to men torn—as was Legion
—between warring streaks of Self. He conquered exterior
conflict for men by making them spiritually indomitable.

Jesus and material need. He subordinated the material
to the spiritual ; He never ignored it, but always related it to
God. He proved men as safe with God materially as spiritually. He showed how little of the material—five loaves
and two fishes—is necessary with God for satisfaction ; and
how the spiritual can be mediated through the material.
He used the material as a bond with God : need of it for
dependence upon Him ; and satisfaction for thanksgiving.

Jesus and physical need. Jesus radiated liberating life
and peace to those in physical need. He revealed pain and
disease as an opportunity when " the works of God should
be made manifest ", and so took from them the sting of
futility. He utilised suffering ; and made its relief never an
end in itself, but always the turning of the sufferer from Self
to God.

Jesus and spiritual need. He always discerned and met
the need for forgiveness and enlightenment underlying
physical, moral, intellectual, or mental symptoms. He
penetrated further into people's spiritual needs than they
could do for themselves. He gratified spiritual longings
which they could not formulate, and were only conscious of as
a vague discontent or craving. He simplified the spiritual,
and delivered it from the complexities with which the Pharisees had overlaid it.

Jesus and aspirations. He fulfilled all aspirations. He
understood and made tangible all men's conscious and un-

formulated ideals.   His aspirations for men—as for Nathaniel praying under the fig-tree—far outran even the highest that they dreamed for themselves.   No aspiration but found its consummation in His : " Be ye therefore perfect, as your Father which is in heaven is perfect ".

Jesus and self-despair.   He turned self-despair to Christ-assurance.   He trusted those who—like Peter and the " woman which was a sinner "—dared no longer trust themselves ; and by His trust created in them a personality the very opposite of that which drove them to despair.

Jesus with Everyman

Jesus not only satisfied Everyman who recognised Him, but was with Everyman even unknown to him.   The unknown Jesus, equally with the Jesus Who was worshipped and petitioned, brought healing, light, and comfort as at the Pool of Bethesda and on the road to Emmaus.

Jesus in Everyman : transfiguring

His love and faith penetrated to the hearts of even the most careless or hardened sinners, and changed them completely.   Jesus in Everyman proved His redemptive and transforming power to the individual, not only in his own life, but in other lives around him.   John must have been not less amazed by the change that he could not help seeing Jesus had effected in Peter, than by the change which he was conscious Jesus had wrought in himself.   None were beyond the power of Jesus to transform.

The Spirit of this Jesus of the Gospels, this Perfect Son of Man, is to-day as potently at work as ever.   To-day we can have Jesus and Everyman (ourselves) : the perfect partnership for Life.   To-day we can have Jesus in Everyman (ourselves, those whom we love, and those whom we find it hardest to love and believe in) : transfiguring.   To-day, known or unknown, Jesus is with Everyman : helping, saving everywhere, and, where recognised, bringing joy and peace indescribable.

But there is yet another link between Jesus and Everyman —perhaps the most comforting of all.   Long ago Jesus said to one just like ourselves, unreliable until Christ-possessed and Christ-controlled : " I have prayed for thee lest thy faith fail " (Lk. xxii. 32)—*Jesus for Everyman* : making intercession.

" BEHOLD, THE MAN ! "

LET us each alone, in silence, in time, and for eternity, " Behold, the man ! " ; and may our contemplation issue in an ever-deepening self-abandonment to the Holy, Glorious, and Blessed Trinity in uttermost thanksgiving for the Redeeming Word made flesh for us in all the beauty of holiness.

LAMB OF GOD: REDEEMER OF THE WORLD

LAMB OF GOD: REDEEMER OF
THE WORLD

(See also pp. 10 ff.

For the Cost, pp. 124 ff.; 258 ff.

For the Mystery of Suffering, and for our Lord's dealing with sin, pp. 163 ff.)

TO " behold the Lamb of God " is to behold, not only " the Lamb that hath been slain from the foundation of the world " (Rev. xiii. 8), but is also to behold :

From what the Lamb has saved us.

At what a Cost the Lamb has saved us.

How the Lamb has saved us.

To what the Lamb has saved us.

It was through the Seer of " Revelation "—who is *par excellence* the Seer of the Lamb—that the Holy Spirit first articulated the revelation of " the Lamb . . . slain from the foundation of the world " ; but He had been gradually unfolding that revelation since the beginning of time, and throughout time and eternity He will continue to open up to Man deeper and deeper understanding of the inexhaustible content of glory in this Eternal Mystery. From the very beginning of time the Holy Spirit was at work preparing Man's heart eventually to receive—and to respond to— the revelation of the Lamb.

The study of anthropology and of comparative religions has revealed, beyond possibility of doubt, that the need to worship and the need to propitiate something—or someone— sensed as greater than himself are instincts innate in Man even at his most primitive. These instincts have existed in infinitely varied gradations of crudity and enlightenment : gradations determined in part by racial evolution, civilisation, and culture, and in part by purely personal factors in the individual. Thus worship and sacrifice have found similarly varied expression ranging from all that is mistaken, ugly, false, even basely-motived, immoral and cruel, to that which is the height of truth, beauty, reality, and holiness attainable by Man.

But these instincts have been the medium employed by the Holy Spirit to bring men to a gradual knowledge of the one true God alone to be worshipped, and of the one sacrifice alone perfect in motive and sufficient in efficacy. This progressive bringing of Man to the truth has been a ceaseless process exercised most concentratedly in the history of the Jews. The whole religious development of the Jews as recorded in the Old Testament may be said to be the Holy Spirit's preparation of Man for the Lamb of God : preparation to recognise his need of Him ; preparation to recognise Him Himself when " in the fulness of time " He was sent by the Father into the world.

The Lamb was first prophesied by the Holy Spirit through Abraham. Abraham, believing himself bidden of God to sacrifice Isaac his beloved only son as a burnt offering, accordingly made preparations, in the course of which Isaac said to him : " Behold the fire and the wood : but where is the lamb for a burnt offering ? " " My son, *God will provide Himself a lamb for a burnt offering* " (Gen. xxii. 7 f.) was Abraham's reply. But despite the fact that Abraham himself had in mind only God's " Take now thy son . . . and offer him . . . ", his words were the Holy Spirit's hailing of the Lamb, and also His sowing of a seed of human expectation for the coming of the Lamb, although neither Abraham nor his descendants for generations would in the least suspect that this Lamb of God's providing would prove to be *His* own Beloved Only Son—the Lamb of God indeed.

In the Passover, instituted and enacted in Egypt, and appointed " a feast to the Lord . . . by an ordinance for ever " (Ex. xii.), the Holy Spirit wondrously foreshadowed the mission of the Lamb. In the blood of a sacrificial lamb " without blemish ", as the God-appointed " token " [Septuagint has " sign "] to save the Israelites from death in the night when He willed to "execute judgment" in the land of their bondage, was symbolised the blood of the Sinless Lamb of God sacrificed to save all men from the spiritual death inherent in the sin which held them in bondage ; and in the memorial feast of the Passover was foreshadowed the Feast of His Most Blessed Body and Blood, and the worship of the Lamb throughout eternity.

The means by which the Holy Spirit first infused into the human consciousness of Jesus the supernatural knowledge that it was *He* Who was the Lamb of God's providing must ever remain for us, whilst still on earth, a worshipful mystery. But it is certain that it must—at some point or other—have been through the Scriptures that Jesus received the Holy Spirit's illumination as to what was involved in being Lamb of God. At the close of His Life our Lord, telling His disciples of the future coming of "the Spirit of truth", declared : "He will shew you *things to come*" (Jn. xvi. 13) ; and this surely must have been out of His own life-experience, peculiarly intense at that moment, of the Holy Spirit's *prophetic interpretation of vocation*, and particularly of His vocation in terms of the Lamb of God.

A "lamb . . . without blemish" (Ex. xii. 5) ; "a lamb as . . . oblation for a sin offering" (Lev. iv. 32), was the Holy Spirit's revelation to Him of the *perfect* penitential offering of love, worship, and sinlessness that alone "taketh away the sin of the world". The delineation of "the Suffering Servant" (Is. liii.) was the Holy Spirit's prediction to Jesus of the Passion of the Lamb—a 'prediction' which Jesus Himself eventually gave to the disciples in strikingly modified form (cf. Matt. xvi. 21 ; xvii. 12, 22–23 ; xx. 17–19), because His "I have yet many things to say unto you, but ye cannot bear them now" (Jn. xvi. 12) was true not once but always. To His disciples Jesus gave warning, as it were, of the *externals* of the Passion whose interior essence, as well as outward form, the Holy Spirit had laid bare to Him in the portrait of the Suffering Servant.

Our Lord before the disciples—and maybe even to Himself—was dumb as to all the "travail of soul", a soul "poured out . . . unto death", which the Holy Spirit foretold for Him.   To His consciousness of essential vocational identity with the Suffering Servant Jesus never gave explicit utterance but once, and that on the literal eve of His death when after the Last Supper He told the Eleven : ". . . that which is written must be fulfilled in Me, And He was reckoned with transgressors : for that which concerneth Me hath fulfilment " (Lk. xxii. 37).   He bore in silence His foreknowledge of all the inner anguish of spirit that must befall Him as the Lamb before He could " see of the travail of his soul . . . and be satisfied ".   In speech Jesus laid stress not upon the suffering of the Lamb, but upon " the joy that was set before Him " (Heb. xii. 2), i.e. the glorious liberation He was to consummate for sinners.   " For verily the Son of Man came not to be ministered unto, but to minister, and to give His life a ransom for many " (Mk. x. 45) ; and, " And I, if I be lifted up from the earth, will draw all men unto Me " (Jn. xii. 32), is Jesus' own verbal reference to His life and mission as Lamb of God.

None can ever plumb the profundity of that which underlies the angelic prophecy concerning Jesus : " He shall save His people from their sins " (Matt. i. 21).   But with the passing of the years few fail—through some deadly impasse brought about by themselves in their own individual lives, or corporately in family, social, economic, and international spheres—to realise in deadlock and bitterness of soul that " the burden of our sins is intolerable " is not the exaggerated and unreal statement it was once felt to be, but a humanly overwhelming and humanly inescapable truth, perhaps the most pervasive of all human truths.

Youth generally finds it hard, if not impossible, in any way to sense the burden of sin as " intolerable ".   Life seems more than tolerable ; it seems limitless in scope and in potentiality for enjoyment, adventure, and realisation of ambition and ideals.   There is a sense of dishonesty in having to affirm that " the burden of our sins is intolerable ";

it seems but a pious phrase grossly overstrong and out of
perspective. But, as life unfolds, experience teaches
differently even those whom it does not make cynics,
and to whom it leaves an abidingly keen perception of, and
belief in, the " so much good in the worst of us ". Gradually it comes to be realised that no words about sin are
' overstrong ', but that sin is, on the contrary, a horror for
which no words can ever be strong enough. It is only with
—and proportionate to—this realisation of something at
least of the true nature of sin that there comes, or can come,
the inwardly convincing recognition, knowledge, and
experience of " the Lamb that taketh away [Gk. = continuously taking away] the sin of the world ", and part-
understanding of the stupendous magnitude of what has
been, and is, involved in this process.

A Missing the Mark ;

A Canker ;

Slavery ;

Death ;

these are perhaps the most familiar among the many
descriptions of sin that have been attempted, but few perhaps realise a tithe of the reality implicit in such meta-
phorical language.

A ' mark ' is a ' thing aimed at ' ; ' an attainable point '.
The mark for each one is the soul's unique vocation designed
by the Father to be attainable in Jesus. To miss the mark
is as though a violin fashioned solely to transmit harmonies
of deathless beauty should refuse to utter aught but dis-
harmonies of torturing and outrageous ugliness. To miss
the mark is not a ' falling short ' of the ideal to be condoned
as inevitable, or to be dismissed as ' not serious ' since not a
sin of commission. To miss the mark is from God's side a
blasphemy (i.e. contempt or indignity offered to God) ; and
from Man's side both stark tragedy and a travesty of that
for which he was created. It is Man's self-forfeiting of
that which alone is perfectly satisfying to himself and
glorifying to God, and his substitution for an eternal bliss

of fulfilment—his for the cost of acceptance—of self-chosen, self-inflicted misery, futility, and worse.

'Canker' implies, not only corruption, rottenness, and destruction, but also *infection*.   One of the chief horrors of sin is its contagiousness.   None of us can sin to ourselves alone.   Each sin we commit comes as active temptation for at least one other person, probably for several, and possibly in some cases for many, e.g. our bad temper raises for others temptation to resentment and retaliation, perhaps to self-pity and to fear.   Our unkind gossip invites—almost seduces—others to drift into like uncharity.   Each sin of ours, besides raising for others concrete temptation which they may or may not be able to resist, intensifies the hardness of the moral and spiritual conflict with which they are already faced if they are not to be defeated by their own temptations.   Sin contaminates the whole atmosphere. Its influence transcends limits of time and space, passing from generation to generation all down the ages, and from individual to individual till families, classes, nations, and races are involved throughout the length and breadth of the world.   Nor is it only our " open and crying sins ", our sins of commission, but also our sins of omission and our every secretest tainted thought that spreads contagion to others. Our every sin of self-indulgence—whatever its nature or degree—is lowering, so inter-connected are we, the general resistance of all, both individually and corporately, to temptation.

A new perspective with regard to sin is needed by all who unthinkingly accept the conventional standard of 'grosser sins ' as incomparably the worst, and the rest as of altogether minor importance, if any. Some of the conventionally ' respectable ' sins—whose lesser manifestations are often regarded as the merest peccadilloes—are as certainly souldestroying as any of the ' grosser sins ', and far more dangerous by reason of their insidiousness and subtlety.

We all need to realise that there is no sin of which we ourselves as individuals are incapable, and perhaps none of

which we are completely innocent in its essence even if—
possibly solely from lack of temptation—we have stopped
short of it in its cruder forms.   Equally we need to realise
that there is no sin committed by any for which we are
totally immune from share of responsibility, by reason of our
own 'sin, our spinelessness in acute temptation, and by our
failures in intercession.   We may be inclined to doubt the
truth of anything so drastic as this, and indeed desirous of
so doing, but it is a truth that God can and does bring home
to us in many unexpected, strange, and inescapable ways,
as, for example, in such an instance as the following :

Some years ago there got into a bus a girl whose appearance was immediately arresting, because somehow conveying
a sense of great potentialities latent within her.   In a
moment or two the conductor came up to her.   It was at
once evident that they were no strangers to one another.
There ensued on the part of the girl an exhibition of brazen-
ness such as one could never have credited would, or could,
ever have been displayed in public.   The word ' exhibition '
is used advisedly.   The girl was as deliberately playing *at*
the other passengers as she was flagrantly playing *with* the
conductor, and was keenly on the alert watching the effect
upon each and all in turn.   The instantaneous reaction was
one of unutterable disgust.   Here was nothing less than the
whole essence and range of prostitution focused as in a
burning-glass.   Vast forces had been concentrated and let
loose.   The thing ceased to be purely personal to the girl.
She was less to be condemned than to be commiserated for
the misdirection of undoubted gifts and rare powers, which
rightly employed would have been singularly potent for
good.

Not knowing our Lord—as was patent—how *should* she
be able to resist such forces, when those recognising Him
and all they owe to Him, and professing to be His followers,
yielded to that which constituted their temptation, and so
weighed down the scale against her ?   Self-gratification, and
self-display : the same seeds in both cases.   What help had

ever been given her by *us* in our life or prayer ?   Had real
holiness, self-sacrifice, costly resistance to temptation, intercession been existent in our lives at all, and if so consistent
and such as to cover such as she whom we knew not personally ?   Such a question admitted of only one answer.   There
had been no such ministry.   Worship, penitence, moral
effort, faith, aspiration with intention for—and in sense of
identification with—others such as she had been lacking,
except possibly some faint effort in the case of one or two
known to us personally.   Why ?   It seemed He Himself
Who supplied the answer :   " Simply because you have not
cared about them.   Yet it was precisely such as these for
whom I, in the days of My flesh, cared and yearned ".   His
Mind had not been in us.

Words could not avail : neither, it seemed, did prayer.
No sudden-born desire to help, however genuine, could on the
instant call up effectual prayer.   It needed the prayer of a
saint, that is, His prayer freely pouring through a soul in
which consistently He is allowed " free course ".   Had that
girl but seen Him in the flesh, or seen the face of some praying saint of His transfigured by His indwelling, all her desires
would have been changed on the instant.   But as it was, they
continued in full play until she left the bus : her parting
words to the conductor appointing a meeting late that night.
Maybe God did intervene and prevent it : that is not known.
What was known was that her sin was literally ours, lying
at the door of a life imperfectly resisting its own temptations,
too self-enslaved to be able to intercede effectually even
when desiring to do so.

The personal responsibility of the professing Christian for
prostitutes—and for all whom the world would stigmatise
as criminals or outcasts—was brought home as an unquestionable reality challenging so-called Christian life and
thought to its very heart and innermost recesses.   It became abundantly plain that Man's desperate need to be
saved from sin was the need to be saved from it not merely
as misdoing, but primarily as the prostitution or desecration

of God's gifts—whether of body, mind, spirit, talents, or vocation—for the purposes of self as against the purposes of God, and His Kingdom.

Sin is insatiable. No sin but begets desire for more sin in ever-intensifying degree—desire which may or may not be resisted. Unresisted temptations eventually reduce a man to absolute slavery. Sin so disintegrates the personality that it becomes literally impossible for him *singly and with unified powers of body, mind, and spirit* even to *want* to break with established sinful habits. There is within him a vitiated desire which—as sharply distinguishable from the wish of his would-be "better self", that divine spark in every soul which can never be altogether quenched—is not himself, yet which progressively assumes an almost fatalistic dominance over all his actions, so that defeat is acquiesced in almost before temptation has actually made its assault. Even if such physical or mental wreckage ensues, such an agonising sense of thraldom and chaotic failure, that all *conscious* desire combines in wanting freedom, it is powerless to achieve it unaided.

In its final analysis the slavery of sin is neither more nor less than self-slavery. The self can become enslaved by anything and everything. The ultimate end of slavery to some things which in their milder forms appear merely "natural", and "harmless enough", is no less devastating and soul-destroying than slavery to that which is patently vicious at the start.

The love of ease is a "natural" thing, i.e. it is innate in everyone in varying degree. It is perfectly legitimate up to a point, but beyond that it becomes utterly corrupting. To-day this love of ease is manifesting itself in ways whose moral and spiritual nemesis is bound to be appalling. The widely prevalent attitude is the matter-of-course "cutting out", as far as ever possible, all suffering and hardship as such, regardless of the legitimacy or otherwise of the means necessary to this end. By the extensive practice of birth-control, and by the projected legalising of euthanasia (i.e. an

easy mode of death), Man is in a fair way blasphemously
to usurping the Divine prerogative to be sole arbiter of life
and death. The cumulative sin of the ages has left us heir
to a world in which life is for the majority a relentless
struggle, and the problem of bare existence a nightmare for
not a few.

But no problem, however intricate, is ever solved by sin.
The attempt at solution by way of sin merely creates fresh
and infinitely more serious problems ; and sin remains sin
despite expediency due to no matter what pressure of circumstances, and despite motives seemingly—or even genuinely—altruistic. So stupendous are the problems of life
under present-day conditions, and of suffering at any time,
that it is fatally easy for them to obscure eternal standards
and eternal issues even for those earnestly desiring to
attain to a Christianly sound moral judgment in all things,
birth-control and euthanasia included.

It is probably not far wide of the mark, at any rate as a
generalisation, to say that no one who has had to suffer very
prolonged and intense pain or weakness, but has once at
least—and probably far more frequently—had a craving to
be " done with it all ", be the motive longing for personal
easement, or longing for easement for those upon whom fall
the burden and expense of their illness. But no motive
whatsoever can ever justify Man—whether patient or doctor
—in breaking across the designs of God, Who leaves none
upon earth without a definite and creative purpose of love,
compassion, and potential fruitfulness. To forestall God's
invitation to the Other Side—no matter how pressing the
human inducement—can never be other than sin, since it is
neither more nor less than an act of self-will in defiance of
God, Who is of set purpose withholding His gift of death
awhile. Yet it is desired by some to legalise euthanasia—
with due medical and other safeguards—for those pronounced to be suffering from an incurable disease, who
themselves desire death.

The patient on a human, and therefore necessarily fallible,

verdict of 'incurable' would thereby be empowered—if so choosing—to " claim the absolute right to die ", despite the fact that the sole 'right' with regard to the issues of life and death is, and must ever be, God's alone.   To act upon such a basis is to rule out of count the fact that God may be desirous of intervening—as He has power to do at any moment—with " a miracle of healing " beyond all human and scientific expectation or present skill to achieve.

Any decision based solely upon love of ease, as such, must necessarily be unsound, and that altogether irrespective of whether it is ease for self or ease for others that is desired. In a world where there is no true gain, no way of fruitfulness, save the way of loving self-renunciation, sacrificial striving and travail, effort of will to persevere and to endure even where conquest seems on a human estimate impossible, any action motivated exclusively by love of ease must invariably and inevitably mean loss.   Such loss will be sustained, not only by the one who so acts, but by all connected with him ; in other words, the loss will be world-wide, even, it may be, infinitely wider than that and extending to those who have already passed on from this world to the next.

Literally God alone knows the degree and extent of the *loss*—as well as sin—involved in a single soul's forestalling death.   The time of " incurable disease " awaiting His appointed release—either into fuller life through death, or restoration of health here—may well prove eternally redemptive for the sufferer.   None can gauge, let alone limit, the sanctifying work of God in a soul, even if that soul be temporarily imprisoned in a pain-racked body, or even in so-called unconsciousness or in delirium.   A soul unable to respond to external human stimuli is yet susceptible to the secret working of the grace of God within.   Just as our Lord's active ministry was fructified for all eternity by His Passion, so such a time may serve—and indeed be absolutely necessary—to render abidingly fruitful all the sufferer's previous life and work.

For those to whom the sufferer accounted himself only a

grievous and sapping burden, and who indeed were bur-
dened and travailing with him, such a time may well beget
an eternity of bliss, and will do so if it evoke our Lord's own :
" Come, ye blessed of My Father, inherit the Kingdom
prepared for you. . . . Inasmuch as ye have done it unto
one of the least of these My brethren ye have done it unto
Me." What joy unsurpassable to have been privileged to
bear *His* burden ! What matter in eternity how heavy the
burden in time, except as cause for inexhaustible thanksgiving to have it end in union with Him, the Adorable
Beloved ! What deprivation unspeakable and irremediable
to be ' spared '—nay, rather, robbed of—that ' burden ' !
Such a time united to the Passion, Resurrection, and Ascension of Jesus, either by the sufferer himself, or by intercessors on his behalf, may well prove a channel of the
redemptive grace of the Lamb—Who is eternally Victor as
well as Victim—to other sufferers, and sinners, the world
over.

Do such glory and the humiliating, cruel, even maybe
sordid, details and apparent waste of " incurable disease "
seem utterly incompatible ? The Crucifixion was more
humiliating, more cruel, more sordid, apparently greater
waste than anything that has ever happened, or could happen again. *Such* a teacher silenced, such a healer cut off
in the prime of life ! Yet it was not waste, but the reclamation of all laid waste by sin. Nothing again—not even
" incurable disease "—*need* ever be waste. Nothing *can* be
waste that is done in conformity with the Will of God, or
suffered with intention to gain for all the grace of His more
abundant life, or endured patiently, trustingly, and lovingly
in the steadfast faith that " our times are in His Hand ".

Concentrate only upon the " incurable disease ", the
suffering and burden as such, and to " take painless poison
in a cup of tea " may appear justifiable. Sin looked at from
the level of that which prompts it seldom appears sin, but all
too easily passes itself off as " natural ", " excusable ", even
" necessary ". Sin in its own setting can never be exposed for

what it really is, but only in the setting of the perfect holiness
of Jesus. Contrast euthanasia with the Cross, not in externals only but in motive. Shudder at the blasphemy of the
bare thought of Jesus ever choosing " painless poison in a
cup of tea ". So may we come to some idea of the depths to
which love of ease can lead us, and thence to something of a
realisation of the nature of the slavery of sin in general, and
not merely in particular, with which the Lamb had to deal.
What love, what penitence, what thankoffering to Him,
could ever be adequate for making possible freedom from
perversion so enthralling, so degrading, so nauseatingly
ugly !

The death of sin is not ceasing to be—that were bliss
compared with the coming to be nothing but self, which
is the ultimate death consequent upon habitual persistence
in sin. The death of sin is self-chosen incarceration within
a self progressively experienced as unbearable even to itself,
and recognised as so leprous and repellent that no human
being penetrating it for what it was could possibly want
anything more to do with it. The death of sin is self-
centredness, with all that it implies of the isolation of wilfully
severed, or undeveloped, fellowship with God and Man.
The death of sin is the atrophy of will for moral effort for
whatsoever things are pure and lovely. Sooner or later the
non-exercise of moral effort must inevitably end in self-
disgust, the begetter of that cynicism with regard to God,
Man, and life, which is hell indeed. " God saw everything
that He had made, and behold, it was very good" (Gen. i. 31):
the death of sin is the self-distorted vision that sees only
rottenness and futility without and within, behind and
before.

" He shall save His people from their sins " : the
QUICKSAND in which Man of himself can never reach any
foundation which does not collapse beneath him time and
again—often when least expected or desired—sucking him
down and down to utter destruction, were it not that He has
given Himself as a Rock bridging the abyss of the death of

sin, and affording eternal standing-ground for each and all who choose to accept it and live by, and in, Him.

The Lamb of God has saved Man in his sin and in its consequent suffering, dereliction, cynicism, futility of existence, and despair. But not alone in its bitters, but also in its sweets has He had to save the world ; not only from the outcome of sin, but also from the false gods of glitter and pleasure, which are amongst its most potent stimuli, has He had to rescue Man, in order that he may " know to ... choose the good " which is true and endlessly enduring good, because it is the satisfaction of the whole being in its fulfilment in God, and not a misconceived " good " which can only, and inevitably, end in glutting and enslaving him to the point of mental and spiritual nausea.

The Trinity in Itself, apart from Creation, is an Eternal interaction of Love with Love in perfection of Holiness, Wisdom, Joy, and Satisfyingness : a timeless, changeless perfection never less than complete, and therefore incapable of expansion, development, or suffering.

In the Incarnation Love offered Himself for redemptive interaction with sin on earth and in time ; and for this He had to join to His Divine Nature, incapable of being touched by sin, a human nature capable of reacting to sin —and this reaction was suffering. None but the Father of the Lamb, the Spirit of the Lamb, the Lamb Himself, can ever attain—let alone sustain—plenary knowledge of the cost at which He has saved us. Yet we must, in bounden gratitude, try to realise as far as may be the immensity of our debt to the Lamb, in order that gradually and progressively we may come more nearly to worship, thank, and respond to Him as He deserves.

No more than bare suggestiveness is possible here : faint indications of some of the spheres and ways in which our redemption exacted from the Lamb a cost so unfathomable that words can in no wise convey it. Only a loving heart can even begin to penetrate anything of its sub-surface essence, and as—and in proportion as—it does so, it must perforce become dumb with the dumbness of penitence and worship, which is the offering up of the whole being in response to Him Whose love, generosity, holiness, and compassion it finds gradually more and more irresistible.   The cost to the Lamb of our redemption can never be learned second hand, but only at first hand by the soul fired with an intense initial attraction to, and loving sympathy with, the Jesus of the Gospels, and then subsequently having its own darkness supernaturally laid bare to it by His light, so that —to the utmost measure of its capacity to be sustained to endure it—it is itself brought into Gethsemane, and thence along the Via Dolorosa to Calvary.

The cost to the Lamb of our redemption was paid all through His life, unremittingly, all-pervasively, and in countless different ways.   It was sustained as :

Lifelong *kenosis* : He, the divinely unlimited, accepting and submitting to human limitations of body, mind, and spirit, and also of straitened circumstances in the fullest sense of the words—poverty, life in a ' backwater ' far from the world-centres of learning and culture, and seemingly greater opportunity.

Lifelong *effort* : unrelaxing exercise of His whole being at its highest—in self-abandonment to God in faith, in obedience, in sacrificial love, in discipline, in renunciation, in patience and perseverance ; and

Lifelong *suffering* : co-extensive with the entire range of mankind's capacity for suffering, this suffering assumed numberless forms.

During the ' hidden years ' Jesus must often have suffered from the longing to get out into " wider activity " for the exercise of His sin-saving ministry. During the public ministry He must often have suffered from the ceaseless encroachment upon His privacy, and upon His leisure for communion alone with the Father. He must have suffered bitterly from the realisation of the false values everywhere prevalent, and at the proud and hollow worldliness of "the kingdoms of this world". He suffered, not only on behalf of, and at the hands of, individuals ; but He suffered also on the wheel of the political and international situation of His own day. "If thou release this man, thou art not Cæsar's friend" (Jn. xix. 12) was the prevailing screw by which the Jews wrung out of Pilate the official sentence of death, which they desired to have passed upon Jesus. He suffered deeply and repeatedly from the false spirituality existing alike in the Temple and synagogue. Most bitterly of all He suffered from the contrast between eternal life as He experienced it Himself, and knew it to be possible for all who would consent to accept it, and the wilful sin-life of men ; the contrast between the glory of the Father's Will and the pitiable sordidness of human selfishness rampant on all hands. At least once—on His own showing —this almost universal failure to apprehend and act in accordance with basic truths came near to being intolerable : " O faithless generation, how long shall I be with you ? How long shall I bear with [Gk. = endure] you ? " (Mk. ix. 19).

The Lamb plumbed the depths of :
    Mystical suffering ;
    Physical suffering ;
    Moral suffering : in lifelong temptation, and in His
        saving identification with sinners.
    Loneliness, Misunderstanding, Criticism, and Rejection.
In relation to men He had to experience a life-time of spiritual loneliness through the inability of any human being to enter perfectly, as He Himself did, into the fulness of Truth as it is in the Being and Wisdom of the Father, or to apprehend the Vision Glorious with faith and under-standing like to His own. Even those who were most genuinely desirous of being one with Him in spirit failed time and again to bring their thought within spheres of His, as for instance after the Last Supper, when He said to the Eleven : " When I sent you forth without purse,

and wallet, and shoes, lacked ye anything ? And they said, Nothing. And He said unto them, But now, he that hath a purse, let him take it, and likewise a wallet : and he that hath none, let him sell his cloke, and buy a sword. For I say unto you, that this which is written must be fulfilled in Me. And He was reckoned with transgressors : for that which concerneth Me hath fulfilment " (Lk xxii. 35–37).

To Him, with His heart overflowing with, and immersed in, the profundity of all that the Holy Spirit had—through the prophecy of the Suffering Servant—revealed to Him concerning Himself as the Lamb, all that the disciples were capable of responding was : " Lord, behold, here are two swords ". Surely His reply, " It is enough," marks a depth of unsurpassable human loneliness of spirit. He, travailing with His whole being for the redemption of mankind, wrestling in the moral and spiritual arena of all time ; His disciples unable to " catch on " to anything more than a material detail, which had been brought up by Him only to try, by way of loving and patiently humoured irony, to open their eyes to the true state of affairs and the response which these demanded.

He was exposed to misunderstanding and criticism alike from relatives, neighbours, disciples, the professedly ' religious ', and from ' the multitude '. Much of the criticism had concealed in it the poisoned barb of jealousy and wilful self-motivated antagonism, and deliberately aimed at wounding Him in precisely those areas where criticism stabs most bitterly : the areas of personal behaviour, personal religion and relationship to God, human relationships, personal teaching (i.e. the convictions for which the whole life stands, and aims at realising in being and action) and its credentials.

Misunderstanding of His teaching on the part of His disciples was often but little less as such—though mercifully free from any admixture of wilfulness or intent to wound—than was that of His acknowledged opponents. Even the inner, as well as the outer, ring of His disciples placed material interpretations upon the spiritual truths which He

expounded to them, and failed, more or less completely at
times, rightly to understand His teaching even upon such
fundamentals as the true Nature of His own Person ; and
what was involved—both as to the way and as to the ultimate goal—in following Him ; the nature and *power* of His
protection ; the sacramental and costly nature of His
ministry ; the true nature of that which He had primarily
come to offer to Man, and the method by which it must be
fulfilled ; the nature and necessity of re-birth for all.

The suffering of Holy Week was but the culmination of
a life-time of suffering steadily converging towards it.

In the past there has often been an undue stressing of the
physical aspect of the Passion at the expense of the mental
and spiritual, with the result that reaction has now swung
almost to dismissing it as comparatively nothing.   But the
physical suffering, though the least part of the Passion, was
nevertheless a very real and costly part of it, both as sheer
pain and sheer exhaustion as such, and still more as a state
inevitably tending at one and the same time to sap resistance
to such mental and spiritual suffering as already existed
independently, and to heighten it by contributing fresh
elements solely of its own origination.   It is fatally easy to
find ourselves so accustomed to the story of the Passion
that it fails to come home to us as actually having happened
to Someone not only as sensitive to suffering as our own
selves, but infinitely more so.   Only if we try to imagine
what it would mean to ourselves on the physical side alone
—even in its apparently ' lesser details ', such as the inability
to move even a fraction of an inch to gain relief from racking
muscular strain and cramp by change of position—can we
have any faintest idea of what the Lamb underwent for us
physically.   Assuredly physical martyrdom, though a light
thing in comparison with mental or spiritual martyrdom—
in so far as they can ever be separable—is something which
cannot be minimised as less than martyrdom in its sense of
' torment generally '.

There is no physical pain, exhaustion, discomfort, humiliation, ever experienced by any sufferer but is understood by the Lamb *from the inside*, from the furnace of physical suffering in which His Passion plunged Him in such wise that no atom of His body remained untouched.

The suffering of the Lamb amassed itself cumulatively in Holy Week, which was the refinement of simultaneous torture of body, mind, and spirit. But even in this general plethora of suffering, certain things, certain cruelties—each in itself more than humanly sufficient to prove a " last straw "—glare out with peculiar poignancy :

The temptation of knowing that He *could* escape and yet *must* not, in contrast to our frequent endurance of things simply and solely from sheer inability to escape.

The human injustice throughout.

The æsthetic suffering in addition to all the rest. " They were instant with loud voices, asking that He might be crucified " (Lk. xxiii. 23) : an outrage of *ugliness*, this bloodthirsty clamour.

The swift giving-place of the acclamations of Palm Sunday to the execrations of Good Friday.

The deliberate and repeated attempts to entrap Him by spurious questioning.

The presence at the Last Supper—His love's supreme self-giving—of *not one* but that was within less than twelve hours either to betray, deny, or forsake Him through being " offended " in Him, or frightened for their own skins. The Last Supper : His giving of that which was holy ; His giving of the Pearl of unique price ; His Very Being, Life, and Death, only to have those to whom He gave it " turn and rend " His very soul, only to be " wounded in the house of His friends ", that most bitter anguish which can be sustained by the human affections—and none ever so human in His affections as the God-man Jesus.

The Gethsemane martyrdom of sense of identification with the sins of the world, i.e. *Our sins made Him feel Himself to be* :

A deliberate lover and chooser of self rather than of God.

18

Impure.

Hypocritical.

Uncharitable.

Hemmed in, overclouded, engulfed, and enslaved by a leprous self.

Lost in a maze of complexity without hope of solution.

Sinking in a quicksand steadily sucking down everything to final destruction.

If at times it is literal hell even to us to realise that it is this with which we ourselves—apart from Him—are self-identified, *what* must it have been to Him Who all His life had consistently abhorred sin with every fibre of His being and renounced self to the uttermost! An agony this, of which Man is altogether incapable of attaining even an approximate conception.

The intensifying of this Agony in the Garden through the human loneliness of having even Peter, James, and the Beloved Disciple fall asleep each several time He craved their companioning vigil of prayer in His soul's abyss of need.

The bitter disappointingness of having Peter, even on the very eve of His death, so far fail to assimilate His teaching, to understand His Mind, purposes, and Will, as to cut off Malchus' ear.

The added horror of the Agony, and ' arrest '—which He Himself had to enable His would-be captors to put into effect —taking place at night, and a bitterly cold one at that.

The incalculable additional strain for body, mind, and spirit, involved in having to undergo Good Friday on top of an entirely sleepless night ; and having to have as the immediate prelude to the final stages of the Passion, such a draining of vitality as was necessarily inseparable from the whole gamut of emotions and sacrificial intentions intensively experienced, and exercised, by Jesus in His swift passage from Love's pinnacle in the Last Supper to Love's nadir in the Agony, betrayal, forsaking, and denial.

He, the Sinless One, to be seized and bound, and taken

hither and thither at the malicious will of sinners for whom
He was even then in process of laying down His life.

The mockery of His trials, and the *number* of them.

The sacrilege of having His Messiahship called in question
by—of all people—Caiaphas, *the high priest* (who ought to
have been, and might have been expected to be, the Prophet
and Acclaimer of the Messiah), solely with a self-interested
view and determination of having Him put to death by fair
means or foul.

The bitterness of being rejected *in favour of a murderer* by
His own people, amongst whom He had gone about doing
only good.

The *immensity* of personal outrage against Himself to be
forgiven upon the Cross ; and the literally countless number
of those contributing towards that outrage—not only those
who actually crucified Him by nailing Him to the Cross, but
also the intimate friend (Judas) traitorously betraying Him ;
the yet more intimate friends who failed to keep vigil with
Him in His Agony in Gethsemane ; the friend who broke
His law of love by resorting to violence (Peter against
Malchus) ; the friends whose fear for themselves led to their
precipitate desertion of Him in face of danger ; the friend
who in panic repudiated all connection with Him to whom
he owed everything ; the officer who struck Him after a
perfectly civil answer to the high priest ; the many who—
from various motives of greed, fear, jealousy, false religious
zeal, desire to curry favour with those in authority, or
merely to " have a finger in the pie "—bore false witness
against Him ; those who ridiculed, insulted, and humiliated
Him, and brutally and despicably took advantage of external circumstances to taunt One against Whom things
looked black ; Annas, Caiaphas, Herod, and Pilate all de-
frauding Him of justice *as they very well knew* in order to
serve their own ends.

Those who deliberately lied about Him and His teaching ;
the undiscriminating multitude ready to clamour for
Barabbas' release rather than His ; those who scourged

Him and crowned Him with thorns ; those who wantonly cut Him off in the prime of life from Beauty and joy and just sheer human life as such, who tore Him away from His Mother, friends, converts, and those whom He still longed to help and establish ; those who failed to keep faithful to a vision they certainly had *seen* ; the fickle Palm Sunday crowd ; the bigoted religionists of the day who deliberately cast out truth ; those who confused the real issue ; those who railed on Him upon the Cross, and tempted Him by challenging Him to come down ; His " acquaintance " who dared do no more than stand " afar off " whilst He was being crucified ; and not these only, but every sinner before, during, or since the " days of His flesh " in Galilee.

The abyss of dereliction when He *believed* Himself to be abandoned by the Father.   May it be that that desolating : " My God, My God, WHY hast Thou forsaken Me ? " was wrung out of him by torturing remembrance of the Scriptural pronouncement that " he that is hanged is accursed of God " (Deut. xxi. 23), and that in taking away the sin of the world He did actually feel as though literally " accursed of God " ?   Beneath His lifelong " I can of Mine own self do nothing ", there had been as a mine of conscious assurance His dependence upon the Father, infallible, ever hearing, directing, and enabling Him.   But in the dereliction He no longer sensed with mind, or even with spirit, the Father operating through Him.   None can ever know more than a fragment of what the dereliction involved for Jesus, but this at least is certain—it must have meant *a cessation of consciousness of the Father's act of atonement being wrought out through Him.*   What an agonising test of faith !   What temptation to believe that He had utterly failed in His vocation—than which there could be no sorrow more bitter —and that despite the Divine *promise* that " He shall save His people from their sins " both they and He were perished together.

Once in a life-time it is possible for some souls to experience in a few moments of time the diffused suffering of the whole of their own time-span ahead. That experience came to Jesus on the Cross, and because of His uniquely perfect love-identification with every soul in creation, past, present, or future, it was a unique experience of infinitely detailed suffering of the whole time-span of all Creation. In the dereliction was comprehended, not only all His own direct incarnate suffering, but also all His future suffering in His Body the Church on earth ; in " the least of these " outraged and untended ; in the Blessed Sacrament insulted and neglected. Love in that dereliction ran the whole gamut of every sin throughout time, and reacted to it with *a suffering which was finally exhaustive as suffering in His own Person.*

To dwell upon the cost to the Lamb of our redemption is to dwell upon a cost paid by Him ; but we must never lose sight of the obverse fact that it is a cost to which each of us individually has actively contributed. Such a cost is not something extraneous to us ; but something in which we *personally* have involved the Lamb. It is *our* sins precisely that crucified Him. Their occurrence in time—whether prior to, contemporaneous with, or subsequent to the actual Crucifixion—is completely irrelevant, since time with God is not. The Crucifixion took place at a specific point in history, but *in essence eternal* it was determined by the whole time-sequence of creation, and not merely by that fragment of it which coincided historically. Our present sin cannot crucify Him now in time, except in so far as it crucifies Him afresh in our own soul or in the souls of our fellow-men ; but for all that it is none the less really part-cause and part-content of the historic Crucifixion, because in essence we must either be utterly and completely identified with the Crucified or else with the crucifiers. There is absolutely no alternative to this stark fact ; altogether irrespective of whether we ourselves acknowledge—or even recognise—it, it just is so.

Utterly and completely identified with the Crucified in selfless love we know only too well we are not—but neither, surely, utterly and completely identified with the crucifiers ?

We recoil in horror at the mere thought of the nails, let alone hammering them in ; and we begin to comfort ourselves. But no, there is a vision which sweeps on remorselessly. We see the crucifiers, not as brutal men with nails and hammer, but as men and women caught up in a whirl of mob emotion ; men and women carried away by sheer craving for excitement and heedless of the consequences of their clamant action ; men and women less gloatingly cruel than ununderstandingly thoughtless or fear-driven by a " something " beyond their normal comprehension ; men and women agog with self, hurting One Who interfered with their interests or desires—hurting Him both actively by torture and passively by lack of response to His selfless and compassionate love. We know that we are one with these. But the vision ends not in despair : it goes on unfolding, and it is full of hope.

The Crucifixion amid those on Calvary is unveiled, not as an incident in point of time so much as an eternal and abiding reality ; not as an incident in which our parts are irrevocably and basely played and finished, but for us still in time as an issue in the present and future as well as in the past. And so there comes a passionate longing and determination, that not only we ourselves, but also all our companion-crucifiers should one and all of us awaken out of our blindness, calm down from our frenzy of fear and self, lose our morbid craving for excitement and gratification, and become utterly and completely identified with Him amongst Whose crucifiers—whether wantonly, carelessly, or half-unknowingly—we at present rank.

All down the Christian era men have been wrestling—both spiritually and intellectually—with the doctrine of the Atonement ; in other words, with *how the Lamb has saved us,* and why that particular ' how ' was necessary.

All individual approaches to the Atonement must of necessity be altogether inadequate and incomplete, since such is even the cumulative and corporate approach of diverse ages, schools of thought, and tempers of personal religion. But all honest approaches—even in those cases where resultant theories have later been more or less discredited or superseded by others—contribute in some measure to define the extent, profundity, and inexhaustible glory, if not to elucidate the rationale, of a mystery which in its fulness must ever remain beyond Man's intellectual grasp on earth, even whilst meeting the exigencies of his life and being as absolutely nothing else can do.

It is the Lamb—Who is also the Word—Who Himself has given us the clue as to how we are saved by Him. Three sayings of His in particular illuminate the Cross:

" I can of Myself do nothing " (Jn. v. 30).

" . . . the Father that dwelleth in Me, He doeth the works " (Jn. xiv. 10).

" I, if I be lifted up, will draw all men unto Me " (Jn. xii. 32).

The availingness of the Cross in no wise lay in anything humanly suffered, sacrificed, or effected by Jesus. There was no merit in Jesus' physical suffering as such, but only in so far as voluntary submission to it was *the sacrament of nothing withheld* from Love's vicarious self-oblation in penitence for the sin of the world. The Cross availed as the medium of the declaration and operation of the Father's Will for the reconciling of the world to Himself. Its avail was not even as a *divine* assumption of temporal human suffering, but as a sacrament of the sanctifying Will of the Father Uncreate Who is Holy Love. Holy Love, and not the incarnate suffering *even of God*—let alone suffering as suffering—was, and is, the effectual redemptive essence of the Cross : Holy Love so infinite and inexhaustible that nothing but Itself can ultimately endure. Jesus' love—proved literally without limit in His willingness and power to let no extremity of suffering deflect, wither, or diminish it—was the sacramental declaration, expression, exertion, and mediation of the invincible, inalienable love of the Father willing, and thereby making possible, the reconciliation of all creatures, all Creation to Himself.

It was not suffering as such that Jesus in His Passion offered to the Father, but that which His senses, His physical brain, His spiritual consciousness *felt* as agony His faith offered *as love,* as worship of God's Holiness and of His eternally Immutable Being. The peace that came upon Him after the prayer of the Agony in the Garden, all the serenity, spiritual majesty, and triumph of the rest of the Passion from that moment forward was due to the fact that, although suffering was never more keenly felt as suffering, it ceased thenceforth to be offered as itself. What impinged upon and lacerated body, mind, and spirit as suffering and travail His *will*—surrendered to and empowered by the Holy Spirit—gave back to the Father as love. Hence His Passion, despite agony of body, mind, and spirit, was also in a true sense a passion of joy—the joy of Love's offering the very agony and darkness *to be love* and *to energise as love*—although, whilst the suffering was sensible, the joy was hidden in the innermost citadel of the spirit beyond sense and thought.

Love. There is the whole key to the Atonement. Love is the Lamb's ' how ', because Love is the Father's Being and Will with which He is eternally one. The love of the Lamb is love that is perfect (i.e. unreserved and eternal) identification with the Beloved. It is the conjoining in the Person of the Lamb of that co-existent identification with the Father and with fallen—yet none the less still well-beloved—Man, which makes for that reconciliatory identification between mankind and the Father which is Atonement (at-one-ment). The Lamb is the oneness of the Father with men ; He is also the oneness of men with the Father : and this in—and by the operation of—the Holy Spirit.

The Lamb's ' how ' of Love had to assume the particular form it did—the Incarnation culminating in the death on the Cross—because it is a property of Love to save by way of identification ; and because Love Omnipotent, choosing to respect the free will It had given to Man, could only draw him to voluntary identification with Love *from his side* by a revelation of Love in the only terms in which he, because sinning and sinful, could receive It so as to recognise It for something at least of what It is, to desire and be enabled to respond to It. These terms were Love's Will to suffer limitlessly in the Person of the Lamb the consequences of Man's sin—i.e. all the sins of all men—so that His redemptive Self-donation might be, and might be realised to be, without any limit whatsoever.

The " Wrath of the Lamb "—apprehended by the Seer of " Revelation "—is the Divine Compassion of the Lamb's ' how ' of Love redemptively exercised at its intensest. The wrath of the Lamb is the Holiness and inescapable Reality of this Love in Whose recognised Presence self and unreality cannot live. It is not anger nor condemnation, although sinful Man subjectively reacts to it as though it were ; but it is rather God's supreme presentation of what is eternally involved in the choice or rejection of self-abandonment to Love. It is Light laying bare the bliss of Love, and the hell of separation from Love by identification with self. It is that Love's supreme warning and appeal to the soul through mind, will, and senses, to break at any cost—even that of seeming annihilation—with its insane, suicidal self-love, and to accept peace and life in the Beloved. Its essence is the absolute incompatibility between holiness and sin. HOLI-NESS is the heart of the wrath of the Lamb, since Holiness and Love are one and the same thing. It is wrath of *the Lamb*, that is, wrath of the spotless, sinless Victim without blemish.

This wrath penetrates to the depth of the individual soul. It is experienced not as frenzy, nor vituperation, nor even as explicit accusation ; but in supernatural *stillness* in which Love and the soul are Face to face, Heart to heart, Being to being, in naked aloneness. Intensely, frighteningly simple, almost to the literal parting asunder of soul and body, it is *whippingly cold*, just as water beyond a certain pitch of burning heat feels icy. This Holiness that is Love, this Love that is Holiness, is *ruthless* towards sin, and therefore to all that is identified with sin.   But it is also *magnetic* to deliver from the clutches of sin, and to draw to Itself anything that wishes—however faintly—to repudiate sin and self and become altogether other than it is.   It is this magnetism of Holiness that is Love and Love that is Holiness—the fulfilment of His promise : " I, if I be lifted up, will draw all men unto Myself "—which is the saving power of the Lamb.

The Lamb in drawing men to Himself is drawing them into oneness with His sharing of the Father's Being, and of His unassailable knowledge of the Father's Will and power to redeem every single soul whatsoever.   He is drawing them to prove in their own experience of salvation—despite all recognised deserts to the contrary—that " it is not the Will of your Father which is in heaven, that one of these little ones should perish " (Matt. xviii. 14).   Identification with the Crucified—Who is the Lamb slain from the foundation of the world, and after the Crucifixion Risen and Ascended—*is* Man's salvation, and the only salvation there is.

An instantaneous revelation of the full implication of utter and complete identification with the Crucified is mercifully—for its overwhelmingness—withheld from us by God, Who spreads its gradual unfolding throughout life.   But progressively there comes the revelation of at least something of that implication.   All that He is, we in His power must be.   His compassionate and yearning love for all the world—the repulsive, the proud, the unthankful, the traitorous, the violent, the hypocritical, the foolish, the self-seeking, equally with the easily-lovable—a love which, absolutely self-mastering as it was, had yet ample time, graciousness, and vitality to spend itself individually, and in all-inclusiveness forgot neither its nearest and dearest, nor its neighbour : this love must be ours.

His courage in facing the extremest issue with a clear brain must be ours : never more can a cowardly refuge be taken in hiding facts out of sight as though they did not exist.   His willingness to face the dereliction where temporarily He loses conscious sense of God must be ours also, if by it we can reach someone else in dereliction. Identification with the Crucified is identification with all and every sort of humanity, congenial and uncongenial; but it is more than this. It is His identification with the Father in His beauteous, unfolding, and redemptive purpose for the world; it is absolute and unreserved co-operation with Him in the fashioning of His dreams.

The Crucifixion is an abiding and eternal spiritual reality, and so must be our identification with the Crucified; it cannot be a momentary wish or act, it must be an unbroken and consistent life. Easter, no less than the Crucifixion, is an abiding and eternal spiritual reality. The real Easter is not merely an historical incident of a morning two thousand years old, but the triumph in continuance and perpetuity of the Selfless Spirit of the Crucified, as against the apparent might of Self run riot in the crucifiers. Our Easter is not merely an early morning service—however wonderful and beautiful—but the triumph of continuance in us, through His grace, of that Selfless Spirit of Him with Whom we are ever striving to grow more and more closely identified.

The Lamb made possible for Man a renewal of that original at-one-ment with God, which—once having wilfully violated it—he himself was for ever powerless to restore from his side. But although Christ wrought for us what we could never have done for ourselves, offered vicariously that perfect penitence of which no sinner is capable, and filled up that which was so flagrantly lacking in our bounden duty of worship and obedience to the Father; it was yet *in no sense substitutionary*. The Cross—together with the Resurrection and the Ascension which are integral parts of the Mystery of the Cross in its entirety—was the Lamb's consummation of redemption as a universal potentiality. The Lamb, through the operation of the Holy Spirit and as the agent of the Father, in this Mystery effected all-sufficingly once for all that which was indispensable for Man's salvation, and that which alone could bring it about. The Cross is all—and amply all—that is requisite for redemption. But although in the Lamb there has been wrought out the Divine *fait accompli* of potential universal atonement, the Cross is none the less fraught for each individual soul with the eternal issue—to be determined solely by its own free and considered choice—as to whether or not *in it* that potential redemption is to become actualised.

Never does the redemption of the Cross operate automatically in any soul, apart from that soul's appropriation of it in sustained faith and deliberate embrace of will. Potential redemption can only become actualised in the soul by its mystical death and resurrection in union with the Passion, Resurrection, and Ascension of Jesus Christ. This mystical death and resurrection is essentially the same in all souls, in that it is death to self and life eternal in Him ; but it nevertheless finds different expression, both interior and exterior, in different souls. It is not merely ' experience ', 'emotion', 'illumination', or 'mental consciousness', as such—though all these are included—but a process, a reality involving, transforming, liberating, expanding the whole being. Potential redemption is an act wrought for the soul objectively by the Lamb as the agent of the Father. Actualised redemption is an act—or series of acts—wherein the Holy Spirit enables the soul subjectively to mate itself with this objective act.

The Cross is the Lamb's " What wilt thou that I should do unto thee ? "—proffered with all the limitless yearning of the Sacred Heart of Love—to each separate soul. It is the testimony—sealed in His heart's blood—that there is nothing too great for Him to do for the soul ; nothing, *however vile*, in that soul that can ever alienate His love or readiness to do for it, at its barest wish, beyond all that it can ask, or even imagine, in the matter of purifying and transforming it, making it literally " a new creation " in Himself. What a miracle of glory and wonder is this re-creation ! Our original creation being from nothing

offered neither obstacle nor opposition to God.   But in our
re-creation He has to deal with something already in existence which presents both obstacle and opposition.   He has
to deal with what we have mis-made ourselves, and transmute it whilst still having respect to that gift of free-will
originally and enduringly bestowed upon us by Him.

"What wilt thou . . . ?"   Does the soul wish that in it He
should "see of the travail of His soul and . . . be satisfied"?
Does it wish Him so to exert upon it that magnetic drawing
to Himself, which He promised through the Cross, that it
shall verily become one with Him and so also with the
Father with Whom He is ever one and at one?   If so, then
for that soul there must inevitably come—be it how it may
—the utmost participation in Christ's "making cost" of
atonement of which it is capable.

Self-exposure in the light of the vision of Jesus, and the
travail to assemble the sin-enslaved and sin-disintegrated
personality to single desire to abandon selfhood, must always
involve crucifixion of every sense and faculty of body, mind,
and spirit, in the process.   There is no punishment exacted
by God as "dues", nor does punishment lie in anything imposed by Him as "discipline" or "warning"; but it is
found as the bitterness of total and inevitable inability to
pass swiftly from self-love to true and single love for Him,
even when there has come *desire* to respond to His love, and to
love even as we recognise He has loved us—a bitterness beside which anything else that could be exacted or imposed
would be as nothing in comparison.   And even this self-
generated "punishment", the Lamb mitigates for us, so far
as ever we will allow Him to do so, i.e. He infuses into us
supernatural love to the utmost degree to which we will
empty ourselves to receive it.

The Lamb's offering for us was, as has been said, in no
sense substitutionary.   The soul must unite with that offering.   It endeavours to offer such penitence, such worship,
such love, such obedience, as it can.   But the day eventually
comes when the soul is caught up into the paradox of the

Lamb, Who offered not instead of us, but Who yet is all our offering. The soul recognises that no longer is it—nor can it be—a case of itself trying to offer anything, because self is incapable of pure offering. Instead, the soul finds *itself* being offered up by the Lamb, absorbed into *His* offering, in such wise that in place of anything of its own the soul is now offering to the Father the Lamb and Him alone. It knows suddenly as its most profound conviction that " the help that is done upon earth He doeth it Himself " ; and inwardly it knows that there is " in the midst a Lamb as it had been slain ", and gazing upon Him it experiences peace and the forgiveness of sins flooding it through and through with life which swallows up all that is past.

Then the soul learns that, to unite with the offering of the Lamb, is to adore the Lamb in the midst—in the midst of time as well as of Eternity ; in the midst of men and nations ; in the midst of human poverty, suffering, and wreckage ; in the midst of sin's strongholds ; in the mid-depth of each and every soul—is by faith to endure steadfast in hope and confidence for all the world, including even its own self, and to live in the belief that in spite of any and every appearance to the contrary the Lamb, Who is even now and always in the midst redeeming, will perfect all things in the Father's time and to the Father's glory. To this end the soul comes gradually more and more to abandon itself, and all souls, to the Lamb as an arena in which He may have " free course " to exercise and establish to the full—by perpetuating His incarnate resistance to temptation—His victorious power over sin and death and all their train.

The Holy Mystery of the Cross is the substantiation of Jesus' stupendous, supernatural claim Himself to be both Light and Life. It is the Lamb's supreme self-donation as " the light of the world " (Jn. viii. 12), and also as " the life of the world " (Jn. vi. 51) which He openly declared Himself to be. The Mystery of the Cross *is* light, i.e. the Revelation of Truth ; and it *is* life.

The Cross is the revelation of the Eternal God and Father,

in such wise as to give sinful Man at one and the same time a realisation of all that is due to Him in penitence, worship, obedience, and love ; and also the confidence to re-approach Him in His infinite loving compassion. It is the revelation— in the Lamb—of Man in his original God-created perfection as contrasted with his own subsequent self-perversion. But the Cross is revelation, not only in terms of God and of Man, but in terms of God's vocation for Man. It reiterates God's call to holiness, and to love. It reveals the limitless corre- spondence to grace which the Holy Spirit can infuse into the soul truly abandoned to Him. The Cross is *the* stilling Peace and Reality, transmuting both suffering and worldliness : the exposure of worldliness for the transient, perishable, and wholly unsatisfying thing it is ; as well as the revelation of suffering for what it can, and may, be as the instrument of Love.

The Holy Mystery of the Cross is a source of life in that it is the Lamb's annulling of sin and death by the exhaustive triumph of Love and Holiness. But it is also a perpetual source of life, in that it is *essentially*, although not *modally*, identical with the Sacrament of His Most Blessed Body and Blood—a body broken ; blood outpoured—which is His continuously renewed imparting to us of Himself (i.e. Life) throughout time.

In the Sacrament of Holy Communion the Lamb gives Himself to be the life of the soul, drawing the soul voluntarily to lose itself in Him whilst deliberately seeking and accepting His substitution of Himself, and all He is and wills, for itself, and all it has been and desired. In that Sacrament He fills the soul with His own Spirit of oneness with the Father, and with His own prayer which is life in its intensest form as infinite worship and all-embracing, sacrificial love. In it also He catches up the soul into Himself, into Eternity, into the bosom of the Trinity, into the Communion of Saints. He imparts to it life as renewal of the whole being, though this is not always—or even perhaps frequently—sensibly felt as such at the moment of reception, but only so experienced in

increased ability to meet the subsequent requirements of
daily life, be they what they may.   He imparts to it His
Mind, bringing it gradually into a progressive perception of
an altogether new standard of moral and spiritual obligations,
desire for holiness, and abhorrence of any and all sin whatsoever ;   and also bringing it gradually out of its own self-
centred and petty concerns into the limitlessness of His
passion of universal love for all creatures.   He imparts to it
life as reinforcement of power—the enabling power of the
Victor Lamb—both to will and to persevere in trying to do
that which, through knowledge infused by the Holy Spirit,
it knows with ever-strengthening and simplifying conviction
to be right.

Our Lord in Holy Communion imparts to the soul life, not
only in Himself and in the Blessed Trinity, but also in the
whole family in heaven and earth ; so that the soul comes
consciously to experience the Communion of Saints as it
finds itself upborne by their prayer and by the holiness to
which the Lamb has sanctified them, and not only the Communion of Saints, but also the Communion of the Quick and
the Dead, the Communion of Sinners, and even at times the
Communion of Angels and Archangels when their worship of
the Lamb breaks in upon it.

In the Sacrament of His Body and Blood—given for all
souls without distinction—the soul, slowly, grows into a vivid
realisation of its oneness with all other souls, none excepted,
be they never so saintly or never so sinful.   This realisation
affords the soul, in times of darkness, the unspeakable
comfort of knowing that, no matter what its own individual
deserts to be abandoned for its infidelity, it never will be so
abandoned by God, because for Him to abandon one soul
would be to abandon all souls, with whom it is but one body ;
and the soul, even in its darkest hours, knows unshakably
that this is unthinkable, impossible.   The life of all depends
upon the life of each as surely as the life of each depends
upon the life of all.

In this Sacrament of Life the soul finds communion

within the Heart of Jesus with those who have passed to the
Other Side ahead of it. Gradually it readjusts, through
this Sacrament, to a new and altogether deepened oneness
with those whom it loved most dearly in the flesh, and who
have already received their invitation into His Unveiled
Presence. It even finds a living friendship with souls on the
Other Side whom it has never known in the flesh, and who,
it may be, lived in an altogether different age and country.
It is He, Jesus, the Lord, the Lamb—not nearness on earth
or in time, not sameness of human interests, environment, or
occupation—that is the living bond 'twixt soul and soul.
Two who meet in Him are one indeed, be they earth's poles
apart. Two even of the same family, household, calling,
country, can never be truly one except it be realised in Him.

Truly a sacrament of *Life* is Holy Communion. It is the
life of God infused into Man ; the life of the God-Man laid
down for Man ; the life of God drawing the life of Man ;
Man's responding to that drawing by a lifting up, and would-
be laying down, of his life both for God and Man. In it Man
receives life through the never-ceasing prayer of the Lamb
Who ever lives as High Priest to intercede for us. But the
glory of glories in this life of the Blessed Sacrament is that,
although it is the soul's all-in-all with the Beloved, it is yet
a receiving Life, an offering life, not for itself alone but for all
souls. Coming to Jesus in Communion is the soul's response
in penitence, faith, and love to that " Come unto Me " of
His which it finds irresistible for itself.

But it knows itself privileged—despite utter unworthiness
—to come, not for itself alone, but for whomsoever it will.
Come to offer itself to Him, come to seek Him for itself, it
may also offer to Him and seek Him on behalf of all who
would fain be there at Communion themselves, but are
prevented by illness or duty ; all lapsed communicants ; all
who know Him not to yearn for Him as their hearts' desire ;
all who suffer in body, mind, or spirit ; all who are tempted ;
all who are enmeshed in sin ; all human wreckage ; all who
languish in slum or prison ; all who are perplexed, fearful,

despairing, weary, poverty-stricken ; all who are labouring valiantly ; all priests, religious, doctors, nurses, missionaries, and others bearing the burdens of others ; all children ; all mothers and fathers ; all souls who beyond death are yet seeking help from the prayers of those still on earth ; and this it can do in the certain knowledge that these all are brought to the very sluice-gates of Life, where the surging tide of Love, Compassion, and Holiness, floods out in sustaining and renewal to each and all, though some like Ephraim— " I taught Ephraim also to go, taking them by their arms, but they knew not that *I* healed them " (Hos. xi. 3)—may not as yet know whence or why their refreshment has come.

Man, in order to be wholly redeemed, must undergo a radical moral change. This moral change may be initiated, but can never—normally—be entirely wrought out by appeal to the natural love, let alone fear, that is in him. It is largely wrought out as a gradual—probably almost imperceptible—process consummated by the progressive infusion into the soul, through regular and frequent participation in the Blessed Sacrament, of the perfect dispositions of Jesus' mind and spirit underlying His Body broken and His Blood outpoured. It is timelessly true : " Except ye eat the flesh of the Son of Man, and drink His blood, ye have no life in you. Whoso eateth My flesh, and drinketh My blood, hath eternal life " (Jn. vi. 53–54) ; life which is Love's passion of self-immolation to the glory of the Father and the redemption of all souls—self-immolation which nothing can stem, not even a Cross which but becomes the triumphant and exhaustless source of freshly flowing and fructifying Love.

Our Lord is never confined to any particular mode or modes in His Self-donation to the soul. He is omnipresent, and can impart to the soul the knowledge of His Presence, both within it and without, in any way He pleases ; and He is pleased to do so by means the most varied, differing with different souls, and even with the same soul at different times. But though He from His side is absolutely unconfined, and can never be more nor less than His infinite and Eternal Self in any form of Self-donation He may choose to adopt, there are yet certain channels of His Self-imparting as Life which Man *as being himself more receptive to Him in them* especially cannot afford to neglect ; and these channels are those in which the Lamb gives His Body broken and His Blood outpoured. This He does, not only through His priests in the Sacrament of the Altar ; but also direct through His own High Priesthood, and without the outward and visible sign of bread and wine, in spiritual communion, simply that He may never be inaccessible to any soul desirous of receiving Him in the totality of His Being, even although it be prevented by sickness, work, or obligations of charity, from doing so sacramentally. Such is His generosity, that He will communicate Himself spiritually as life to the genuinely hungering, thirsting soul any moment of the day or night it so desires.

But over and above all this there is yet another channel of the Lamb's Self-donation of His Body and Blood, and that is, in and through the Reserved Sacrament : *the blessed and glorious, unearthly Mystery of Jesus in the Tabernacle.*

The Mystery of Jesus in the Tabernacle is one over which there has been—and still is—much controversy and misunderstanding. Not a few professing Christians feel that Reservation is only justifiable solely in order that the sick may be communicated, and that on any and every other ground it is to be eschewed as "dangerous". The tacit fear is that of idolatry or sentimentality. There is no denying that Reservation is dangerous, in that it may be abused ; but then so may be—and, alas! *is* by someone or other—every means of grace. There may be, and are, broken Confirmation vows, dishonest Confessions, sacrilegious Communions ; but the Sacraments of Confirmation, Penance, and Holy Communion are not—and cannot be—discontinued on that account. It has, moreover, to be realised that to *neglect* any means of grace, is no less an abuse than to misuse it.

The Mystery of Jesus Present in the Tabernacle is not a

matter of theory, prejudice, or of argument ; it is a fact. It is not necessary for the average person to understand the how and why of electricity in order to switch on an electric light.   So neither is it necessary to be a theologian, nor to understand intellectually the how and why of the Mystery, in order before the Tabernacle to tap Life, Light, and Peace at its Source in Jesus ever one with the Father and the Holy Spirit.

The power of electricity is experienced *in its effects* even by those ignorant of its laws.   So whatever *in theory* a soul may or may not understand about the Presence of Jesus in the Tabernacle—whatever its preconceived prejudices against any special indwelling there—if once in actual fact it eventually finds itself before the Tabernacle, then it *knows* His Presence there by experiencing It in Peace, and a descent of the Eternal upon the temporal in such a way as is seldom, perhaps, so experienced any other how.

As surely as—when in the days of His flesh "many of His disciples went back, and walked no more with Him "—He appealed to the Twelve : " Would ye also go away ? " (Jn. vi. 66–67), so in the Tabernacle He makes identical appeal to His lovers throughout the agelong falling away of so many who professing Him, yet find His words " hard saying".   There in the Tabernacle He both makes the appeal, and infuses the grace of determination to cleave to Him at all costs, and that for His sake, for love of Him, and not from motives of self-interest.

There is always a consciousness of His special Presence in the Tabernacle, or rather there is always a special consciousness of It there, though this more often than not is the knowledge of faith rather than of the senses.   Prayer before the Tabernacle is not—as is sometimes supposed by those who have not attempted and persevered in it—an indulgence of the senses of the soul, let alone an orgy of sentimentalism, but is for the most part dry, the soul's supreme and costly effort to worship the Blessed Trinity, the supreme unveiling to the soul of its own darkness, the reality of will to become united with and conformed to Jesus. " Be ye transformed by the renewing of your mind " (Rom. xii. 2) ; *this* is the " moral change " in Man, when " the Mind ... which was ... in Christ Jesus " becomes his ; and it is eminently in regular and prolonged worship of Jesus Present in the Tabernacle, and in the operation of the Holy Spirit of Jesus dwelling therein, that this is effected, not by any conscious process of thought, nor by any sensible emotion, but by the interpenetration of Soul with soul, Heart with heart, Mind with mind.

To be specially conscious of Jesus Present in the Tabernacle is not to confine Him there, nor to be satisfied with trying to worship Him there alone. The dry worship before the Tabernacle of Jesus, the Lamb of God, Redeemer of the World, increases the soul's hunger and thirst to receive Him in sacramental or spiritual communion, and it increases the soul's recollectedness—and so its consciousness of His Presence—at all times and in all places. To come into the Presence of Jesus in the Tabernacle is to be STILLED—albeit sometimes only after an appreciable time—from turmoil of anxiety, fear, sorrow, preoccupations of earth, time, self, and sense. From the Tabernacle Jesus unfailingly fulfils His : " My Peace I give unto you : not as the world giveth, give I unto you " ; He there gives peace which is life. This stilling of the whole being before the Tabernacle is not effortless substitute for other prayer, but the deliberate and costly self-abandonment giving to Jesus that " free course " within the soul, which gradually enables Him to pray in it without ceasing His prayer for the glorifying of God's name and the redemption of souls.

It is because Jesus is present in the Tabernacle both as Very God and Very Man that uninterruptedly there ever flows from thence an all-embracing stream of Love, Compassion, Light, Life, and transfiguring renewal of mind and spirit, and ofttimes even of body as well.

" Look on Me, and be ye saved " is the perpetual invitation of the Hidden Jesus of the Tabernacle. The Lamb of

God Who laid down His life for Man calls to the soul to look on Him in the Tabernacle *by faith*, and so to receive there the flood of redemptive grace eternally flowing from the Cross— and to receive it not for itself alone, but on behalf of all men everywhere.

The Holy Mystery of the Cross is also a source of life in that it is the solvent of the practical problem of living, and the only real solvent there is. All the basic problems of life— both individual and corporate—are in the last resort insoluble except in and through the Cross. It is the Lamb alone Who can make " all things work together for good " (i.e. issue in the progressive losing of self in the more abundant life of Love), and Who can—in spite of all it contains of sin, suffering, heart-gnawing mystery, and seeming injustice—resolve human life in enduring terms of Divine Glory, purposefulness, and ultimate human bliss in re-creation.

The Cross is the solvent of life, both as the perfect example of how to live and to deal with all that life can ever present, and as being—for each and all who desire and will appropriate it—the source of inexhaustible enablement so to live. It is precisely the same raw material of life in a fallen world with which, incarnate, the Lamb had—as we have—to deal. The only difference being that He sampled it in a degree of taxingness which has never fallen to any other, or ever could. His Cross-overcoming of evil with good overcame it in His own Incarnate Person ; but it is, moreover, in perpetuity an overcoming also in the persons of each and all who by faith, and a deliberate, continuing act of will, unite themselves mystically with Him for the resisting of temptation, the denial of self, the overthrowing of the powers of darkness. Life presents to us opportunity identical with that which it presented to the Lamb—the opportunity to live and die in and for Love : the only difference lies in the reaction offered to it.

Sin, suffering, mystery, death : these are the humanly stone-wall problems Man is ever up against practically ; and

each yields only to the Lamb and His Cross, Resurrection
and Ascension, that is to the divine economy of the Holy,
Blessed, and Glorious Trinity.

There is no sinner upon earth, however seemingly debased,
who does not once at least desire to break with his sin if he
but 'knew how, and believed it possible.   Thousands suffer
torturing remorse on account of their own individual sins ;
and many suffer even more deeply—because more unselfishly
—at the thought of the sins of the world, and the wreckage
of souls, both known to them and unknown.   Alas, not all
who agonise over their sins know—and even of those who
know theoretically, not all believe in its practicality in the
realm of here and now, and in the circumstances of sense and
time—that " If any man sin, we have an advocate [Παράκλη-
τον = strengthener] with the Father [πρὸς τὸν Πατέρα—the
Gk. has the connotation "of close proximity"], Jesus Christ
the righteous: and He is the propitiation for our sins; and not
for ours only, but also for the sins of the whole world"
(1 Jn. ii. 1–2).

Sinners, we have, then, in the Lamb a more than sufficient
Saviour ; not One Who pleads for us with a Father less
mercifully disposed towards us than Himself, but One Who
is in close proximity to the Father, Who is Himself the
Source of all mercy, and One Who is our Strengthener in
Holiness because He is in close proximity—proximity so
close that it is absolute identification—with the Father Who
is the Source of all Holiness and Whose Spirit is the Source
of all sanctification.

The Cross is the Lamb's practical solution of the appalling,
universal problem of sin offered in terms—and by means—of
Love's Divine Will for Holiness, omnipotent, and generous
beyond human conception.   Our hope as sinners is with the
Lamb, Who instituted the Saving Sacrament of His Body
and Blood " *in the same night that He was betrayed* ", so
covering us actually *as* we betray Him by sin—for never is
there any moment of the day or night in which we may sin
but, somewhere in the world, at that very instant He is

immolating Himself for sinners, *for us*, in the Blessed Sacrament—and even forestalling with this redemptive grace sin
that would otherwise have been committed ; and it is also
His medium of restoration for the sinner who has fallen.
Especially does the Lamb apply all the saving and re-
creative merits of His Cross to the soul who humbly, con-
tritely, and yet confidingly, in all honesty but without over-
scrupulosity, in the Sacrament of Penance bares to Him its
sins with sincere desire and intention completely to cease
from them in His power, and for His sake.   There then His
Love as a Fire consumes what is evil ; restores atrophied
and misused powers to be used aright and energetically in
Love's service for God and Man ; and floods in peace as the
soul experiences His effectual response to its desire again to
be cleansed, and oned with Him in His Selfless way of Life,
Truth, and Holiness.

   In Jesus, the Lamb, prodigal Man comes to himself, and
by faith, and in penitence, offers sin as a holocaust to God,
affirming—despite its tyranny, sacrilege, degradation, and
perversity, cumulatively and exhaustively exposed on
Calvary—the absolute unthinkableness that it should, or
could, continue to endure endless in face of Love, Holiness,
and Truth alone worthy to be eternal.   The Cross was the
most profound obeisance of the strong man bound to the
Stronger than he ; it was Perfect Man prostrating sinbound
mankind before the Sinless One, Whom alone nothing can
ever bind save Love.   The problem of sinbound mankind
was how the multiplicity of fallen Man's ever fluctuating,
and often vitiated, desires could be singled to one steadfast
pure desire, solely for God and His Holy Will.   The only
solution lay—and lies—in the Cross, that most dynamic
energising of God's desire for Holiness to prevail and for all
men to be one in Love, which gradually influences the desires
of men until they are *voluntarily* changed.   When even
disinterested human desire for our good can often draw us
forcibly, how much more so, then, the Divine !

   Suffering sooner or later forces itself upon every thinking

person as a problem so clamant that *some* sort of solution must be found for it. In the last resort the problem is always felt at its most bitter when it comes to a head in the concrete sufferings of others, particularly perhaps those of children (who can in no way be felt to deserve them), or animals (who cannot understand or utilise them for the general welfare). A common reaction in face of such suffering as is only too patently widespread in manifold and terrible forms—injustice, oppression, unemployment, torture of body and of mind, extreme poverty, bad housing, to instance but a few—is to feel that either there is no God, or that if a God exists and allows such things He cannot possibly be a God of Love. But this is no solution of suffering. It neither does away with suffering, nor does it offer any creative help in dealing with it as it undeniably exists. It merely adds to suffering by leaving it in chaotic and malignant possession of the field. Suffering separated from God is a nightmare of unmeaning, and of wanton cruelty. Only as suffering is interpreted by the Cross is there any practical solution of it in terms of daily life and circumstance triumphantly met, and vindicated in glorious purposefulness.

The lives of victims of the passion, greed, brutality, selfishness, callousness, or folly, of others, *looked at humanly*, are nothing less than abominations which do not bear thinking about ; and yet they have to be endured, lived out, day in day out, maybe year in year out over a long life, by these same victims, some of whom may quite literally have had their lives blighted even before they were born. *There is no escape by way of the ostrich in the sand.* Humanly it seems diabolically cruel ; waste ; a crying injustice ; and humanly there seems no solution and no point, which last is the most bitter sting of all. But anything as negative as this is not life, but death in life. Only in the light and life of the Cross is there solution for such things, *as they are seen to be absolutely and eminently consonant with Love.*

The victims of others' sin are *in fact* identified with Jesus

the Victim of the sin of the whole world.   God the Father
" sent " the Lamb into the world in the complete foreknowledge of all the suffering that would be involved for Him ;
but He did it *deliberately for the purposes of Love*—Love that
is bliss of eternity, eternity of bliss—and set over against the
limitless suffering an inexhaustible treasury of grace to help
Him in His vocation of saving by love a fallen world.   So,
too, for human ' victims '.

God has complete foreknowledge of the whole life circumstances and travail of each ' victim ' brought by Him to
birth.   His gift to them of life is for the purposes of Love ;
and in order that Glory, and Holiness, and Bliss may be their
eternity with Him.   In myriad cases the identification of
sufferers with Jesus extends only to this fact of *suffering* as
victims of the sin of the world ; but in faith and vision from
the Holy Spirit it can be taken on further to conscious and
voluntary identification with the whole divine purpose of
the Atonement.   Then, what was humanly an abomination
becomes a blessed, privileged, and glorious vocation holding
much of joy as well as infinite purpose.

Here is solution indeed of lives that otherwise would, and
could, only be wreckage.   It is not necessary to associate
with the ' victim life and vocation ' the sensational elements
sometimes falsely attached to it.   Daily life, altogether
apart from extraordinary calamities and trials, constitutes
quite a real ' victimisation ' for many.   But their comfort,
their abundant life, resides in the fact that they are born,
where and what they are, in order to become one with the
Lamb in His one " full, perfect, and sufficient sacrifice,
oblation, and satisfaction, for the sins of the whole world " ;
and their daily lives are solved in the offering of their concrete suffering and limitation as penitence and love to God
and on behalf of all men.   To them the Lamb's " Take up
thy cross " is not a counsel of mere resignation to, or endurance of, the inescapable, as such ; but His invitation to
them to overcome the world even as He Himself did, and
instead of letting it crush them, and break them in self-pity,

to let it break them sacrificially to the finding of life and joy for themselves and the mediating of it to others.

The ' victim's ' offering of daily life begins as the offering of pain in union with our Lord's *suffering* in the Passion ; but it cannot end there, else the whole stress remains solely upon pain, which is only effort towards readjustment, not readjustment itself, a fiery way to the goal, but not the goal, neither an ultimate end in itself, nor of any intrinsic merit whatsoever merely as pain. This offering of suffering gradually changes to an offering of pain, not as pain, but as love and penitence, in adoration of—and union with—Jesus the Transfigured and Transfiguring, Who in the Passion transmuted pain, anguish, and sin, to love, peace, and holiness in the invincible, indissoluble, and indivisible Love wherefrom, wherein, and wherefore God created Man for Himself. Such offering of suffering as love and as penitence, in union with the offering of the Lamb, releases the stream of life continuously flowing from His Cross to counteract Man's perpetual self-maiming and suicidal sinfulness.

So the offering of pain with generous intent for the Lamb's restoration of universal wholeness and vigour frees the sufferer from morbidity and self-preoccupation in suffering ; and results in a practical solution of life which consists not in escape from suffering, *but in freeing to suffer unselfregardingly*, for love of God and Man, what must be suffered until that final and eternal consummation of Love, when " God shall wipe away all tears . . . and there shall be no more death ; neither sorrow, nor crying, neither shall there be any more pain : for the former things are passed away ".

The passing of years brings experience and knowledge of many things. But the knowledge which it brings perhaps most inescapably to those who really ponder life is that of its essential, humanly unfathomable mystery. Youth that is really alive wants to know and understand all life, and unfalteringly imagines that there exists for the discovery— which it expects itself to light upon—some philosophy which, quite simply, shall cover and account for everything, some infallible formula of life in terms of such cause such effect, such effect such cause, such happening or state such intrinsic significance. But the facts of life, as they unfold, prove obstinately irreducible to any such formula ; and there is discoverable no humanly explanatory system which will hold good in all circumstances. Facts sooner or later cut across every theory, and result in a *reductio ad absurdum* in some instance or other. " Reading without tears " there may be for books, but not for life. Understanding of life without travail of the whole being there cannot be ; and deepest understanding acknowledges deepest mystery. Even theories forged on experience suddenly break down, when further experience introduces some new and unforeseen element. Happenings occur which baffle understanding, and seem only to make nonsense of everything ; and things in retrospect more often than not prove quite other than they seemed originally.

The mystery of events can be grievously bewildering, but it is as nothing in comparison with the mystery of personality. It sometimes occurs that human personalities thought to have been intimately known and accurately gauged—over a long period it may be—suddenly seem to contradict every characteristic previously and intrinsically associated with them, inflicting a humanly devastating sense of insecurity. But it is in the self that the mystery of personality is experienced at its most torturing.

The ego is liable unexpectedly to come on phases when it is totally unintelligible to itself, when in it streak mocks streak, when there is conflict over it knows not what, an agonising sense of complexity which it feels in some way peculiar to itself—and must be due solely to evil in it—complexity unshared by others who must undoubtedly in themselves be simpler, more straightforward, more of a piece than its wretched self, which would fain be anything other than it is. It is persistently haunted by the consciousness of harbouring within itself some mystery, which, wrestle as it may, it can in no wise either penetrate or escape, but which—almost fatalistically—it feels to be undermining everything.

No longer does all that by, and for, which—at its best—it has previously lived seem either an anchor or a goal. Everything is reduced to impenetrable confusion ; and whilst the senses afford nothing but deep dissatisfaction, things spiritual seem a mockery hollow precisely in proportion to their former reality. The unwilling sense that God Himself is failing it brings to the soul a torturing sense of blasphemy, and the conviction that within it must be abysses of wickedness which can never be exorcised. All is in some way linked up with a seemingly ineradicable past both exterior and interior. Anguish is unspeakably heightened by some inextinguishable good-will still feebly struggling—despite every oppression and distortion—to pursue earlier lights. Desperate appeal to our Lord seems to bring no answer but His : " What I do thou knowest not now, but thou shalt know hereafter "—and even this " shalt know hereafter " seems humanly incredible.

There is only one solution of the mystery of life as it assaults us personally in the depths of our being, and that is, the solution of the Lamb's :

" My God, My God, WHY . . . ? "

answering itself in His :

" Father, into Thy hands I commend My spirit ".

The Cross is the revelation—and the enabling means—of the only way in which life in its most piercing and perplexing need can be met : the way of total self-abandonment to God without understanding ; content to be united to Him in the dark if needs be ; willing to accept the mystery of self and of life and of death once and for all, in order to entrust and leave it finally and peacefully with Him, and forgetting self to let Love alone suffice. To let Love suffice to live by, and to live for, this and this alone—be circumstances what they may without or within—can, and does, solve life so practically and satisfyingly that present ununderstanding is more than able and content to wait for its enlightenment until " hereafter ".

> The sufficing of Love is how the Lamb has saved us ;
> the sufficing of Love is all the ' how ' of the Atonement.

Humbly, worshippingly, lovingly, and with profound thankfulness, to contemplate from what, and how, the Lamb has saved us is to apprehend stupendous truths of ineffable wonder, but even wonders so inexhaustible as these pale before the Spirit's revelation and " earnest " [Gk. ἀρραβών = part payment in advance for security, a first instalment] of all *to which* we are saved by the Lamb. This revelation is unveiled for us perhaps most luminously—certainly most specifically—through " the Seer of the Lamb " in " The Revelation " attributed to St. John the Divine ; and the " earnest " is experienced in every victory great or small won, through Christ, by any member of His Church Militant over sin, self, evil, pain, or death.

The Lamb's saving of us is not a bare rescue from the human deadlock of sin, suffering, and death ; but is a saving into freedom purposeful as it is limitless—as is implied by the poet Robert Norwood in his inspired and unforgettable :

> " Since I saw You crucified
> All the doors are opened wide."

Boundlessly true it is that, through the Passion of our Lord, all the doors are opened wide : the doors of life and death, of pain and hope and joy.

Pain as a stranger strikes initial dread, and fires the longing to escape. Pain become a frequent companion is the *open sesame* to treasure inexhaustible.

Pain is no foe, but an insistent friend when once it fastens on a body, mind, or heart. At first repellent, seeming altogether bad, it later, through its inescapable darkness, lightens everything to life and freedom such as ease can never know.

Pain long-continuing forces the whole being sooner or

later—perhaps many times—to echo that derelict cry: "My God, My God, WHY . . . ?" It shatters the merely superficial, and strips off all that is not stark reality—in itself most blessed gift. It narrows time to the one moment present, thus freeing the soul into Eternity.

Pain first isolates, then unites. By the compelling overshadowing of its mystery it isolates the essential self from all created things, so that realising its absolute aloneness—notwithstanding any ministry of human succour—it *seeks* Truth, and so finds and is found of God. Through pain's interpretation and illumination of the suffering and Passion of Jesus, there comes the baptism of progressive understanding—however faint—of God as LOVE. Then comes experiential union with Him as furnace-Companion, Himself bearing all pain's *sting*, transfiguring it to Peace and Joy, transmuting it—till its removal—from waste to golden opportunity of further love poured out and gathered in again.

Experience of His glorious, never-failing sufficiency for the depths of personal need—of His love miraculously beautiful, sanctifying and satisfying precisely in proportion to the depths it plumbs in rescue—creates an unshakable faith in His all-sufficingness for each need of every man, woman, and child, be the suffering as humanly intolerable as it may. Then pain, having united the inner self to Him, next unites it in love and compassion to all other of the Father's children. Then does pain, whilst still pain, yet become naught but faith and love : faith in the Blessed Trinity all adorable ; faith in the Divine Will and power to transmute all pain to life and wholeness according to the designs of the Father ; and love of His lovableness, love of His lovingness, love of all His creatures in Him.

Pain, initial tyrant, gradually becomes the compassionate interpreter of Love ; and the mould into which the love therein consciously received from God is offered back to Him in glad spontaneity. Pain becomes itself a pæan of trust and worship : trust that while the pain remains He, by uniting it to the Passion of Jesus, will use it creatively for a further outpouring of redemptive love into other needy hearts : worship of Love to Whom pain and painlessness equally are raw material for sacrificial self-donation.

Pain is the door to Love, in Whom alone all doors are open wide. O wondrous, yet most actual, mystery bespeaking the invincibleness of Love that God can, and does, make of pain—the fruit of Man's sin—a sacrament sanctifying and unifying Man to Himself. So the Father, through the Lamb, redeems pain from waste, futility, and frustration. Love, illimitable save for the bounds of holiness, trusted and honoured the Lamb with the one *measureless* cup of suffering that by His love-acceptance of it sin—the source of suffering —might be slain at its root, and all subsequent human suffering be rendered potentially creative instead of destructive. Even so the Father allows us to share with the Lamb in Love's redemptive treasure and privilege of pain.

It is to union with Him in every phase of His eternal life, vocation, and oneness with the Father and the Holy Spirit, that we are saved by the Lamb. We are saved to union with Him in the extension of His incarnate life in us—" as the Father hath sent Me, even so send I you " (Jn. xx. 21) ; sacrificially to live and love, toil, minister, suffer, and above all to pray that all men may be saved according to the will of the Father. We are saved to ultimate union with Him in His triumphant Risen and Ascended Life : " the Lamb shall overcome . . . for He is Lord of lords, and King of kings : and they also shall overcome that are with Him " (Rev. xvii. 14). We are saved to union with Him in His High Priesthood: " . . . Thou wast slain, and hast redeemed us to God by Thy blood . . . and hast made us unto our God kings and priests " (Rev. v. 9–10). We are saved to union with Him in " the Marriage of the Lamb " (see below under " The Mystical Body: and Communion of Saints ", pp. 342 ff.).

" The Lamb shall overcome . . . and they also shall overcome that are with Him " ; here in this " overcome " is the whole key to that to which the Lamb saves us. The death of the Lamb *per se* was not redemptive.   It was, rather, the apparently plenary triumph of sin, selfishness, and the powers of darkness annihilating love and light uniquely manifested in their very essence.   The incarnate life of the Lamb, " a prophet mighty in deed and word before God and all the people ", had aroused limitless hopes.   His death occasioned despair of an intensity none the less absolute for the utter quietness with which it was voiced by Cleopas : " . . . and our rulers delivered Him to be condemned to death, and have crucified Him.   But we trusted that it had been He which should have redeemed Israel : and beside all this, to day is the third day since these things were done " (Lk. xxiv. 20–21).   The death of the Lamb shattered the hopes raised by His life and teaching until both—and with them the character of God, and the invincibility of Love, Light, and Holiness—were vindicated by His rising from the dead.

Redemption lay, not in the Lamb's death—which was, however, an indispensable factor of it—but in His victorious incarnate reversal of every consequence, death included, inherent in Man's wilful sundering of union with God.   Man, by the false choices of a free will, had delivered himself beyond possibility of self-extrication into the bondage of sin, with its train of suffering and slavery to sense and self, terminating in death physical and spiritual.   Jesus by a lifelong, perfect union of His will with the Will of the Father achieved —incarnate—exhaustive immunity from every form of bondage to which all mankind was inescapably subject save He, " Whom God hath raised up, having loosed the pains of death : *because it was not possible that He should be holden of it* " (Acts ii. 24).

The " Seer " of " Revelation " received for us from the Lamb His promise : " He that overcometh shall inherit all things ; and I will be his God, and he shall be My son " (Rev. xxi. 7)—a promise born of His own experience and consummation of victory.   To be sons of God : this it is, and nothing less, to which the Lamb, in the light—and by virtue

20

—of His own unique and perfect Sonship saves us, in so far as we are willing to yield ourselves to be mystically united with Him in His Death, Resurrection, and Ascension wherein He lifts humanity into His own incarnate immunity from any and every bondage constituting a check to the soul's limitless energising of love in the eternal union of Father, Son, and Holy Spirit.   This overcoming is the heart of the Peace of the Lamb.   His Peace, given not as the world gives peace, is not only peace in spite of those things which cross human ease and satisfaction, and test human endurance to the uttermost.   It is peace in a progressive process of deliberate and steadfastly willed self-abandonment in union with, and unassailable faith in, the initial and all-covering victory of the Lamb for the moral and spiritual overcoming of all evil with which the soul is confronted within or without itself.

Our redemption has for its consummation the limitless indwelling of the Holy, Blessed, and Glorious Trinity within the depths of the soul ; and the anchorage of the soul, in pure self-donation of love, within the depths of the Trinity : a consummation intensely personal, but essentially corporate as being realisable only in the Communion of Saints inherently complementary to the union between God and the individual soul.   The Lamb, pouring out His Heart's desire to the Father on the eve of His immolation of Himself for the salvation of the world, prayed : " Father, that which Thou hast given Me, I will that, where I am, they also may be with Me ; that they may behold [Gk. θεωρῶσιν.   Abbott-Smith : Hebraistically = to experience, partake of] My glory, which Thou hast given Me . . ." (Jn. xvii. 24) ; and so let it be known beyond shadow of doubt—humanly incredible as it seems for sinners like us—that it is to share with Him, in the Holy Spirit, His being ever " in the bosom of the Father " to glorify Him, and to be fulfilled and satisfied by His glory : the glory of His own Immutable Being and Self.

HIGH PRIEST

IN "all . . . things concerning Himself", Jesus, it is mystery of Glory ever opening upon fresh mystery of Glory : each mystery inexhaustible and distinct, yet attaining its consummation of glory, significance, and power in virtue of its enshrining within itself the sum and essence of *all* the mysteries of His Person and Life. All these mysteries are inextricably one. Vastly daring, it might almost be said—as true *au fond* if not *ab extra*—that they are interchangeable. Each mystery of our Lord's Being illuminates, interprets, fulfils all the rest. So it is pre-eminently with His High Priesthood, which is the sum, essence, and exercise of His Divine Sonship, Kingship, and Saviourhood, and the heart of His " authority to execute judgment also " (Jn. v. 27).

The High Priesthood of Jesus is a mystery which none but the Holy Spirit of Jesus Himself can make known to the individual soul—as to that first love-fired Seer of the High Priest who wrote the Epistle to the Hebrews—as " the hope . . . which . . we have as an anchor of the soul both sure and stedfast " (Heb. vi. 18–19). But in and through the warp and woof of daily life itself, the Holy Spirit will gradually draw all who will allow it to anchor more and more in Jesus as High Priest, the Supreme—and only—Hope, not for themselves alone, but for the whole world. To try perfectly to respond to the Holy Spirit's drawing to union with Jesus as High Priest might well suffice the soul as its sole prayer for time and eternity, because it is an all-embracing prayer which must gradually become ceaseless worship of Father, Son, and Holy Spirit, and a ceaseless sacrificial self-immolation for sheer love of God in His Glory and all souls in His holy Will and glorious purposes. To contemplate Jesus as High Priest is gradually to learn in the heart of hearts—and perforce adore—Him as all, and in all, and for all.

"Called of God an high priest " (Heb. v. 10) ; " a great high priest . . . Jesus the Son of God " (Heb. iv. 14) : here is the heart, essence, sole source, and basis of the mystery of Jesus' High Priesthood ; vocation inherent in His Divine Sonship.

Vocation is the Father's eternal design for the soul's abandonment to, and union with, Love in a love-life finding such unique interior and exterior expression as shall be the necessary complement to that designed for all other souls. Hence in essence a soul's vocation remains identical in time and in eternity, and differs only in expression. Jesus' vocation as " high priest for ever " (Heb. v. 6) is, therefore, an eternal vocation whose " for ever " is as much without beginning as without end. Timeless, the High Priesthood of Jesus is before time, throughout time, and beyond time. Inherent in His Divine Sonship it is immutable in its essential perfect self-oblation " through the eternal Spirit " to the Being and Will of the Father. An eternal offering to the Father of His Very Self " with intention " for the Father's " intentions " for all souls—that is " with intention " for the vocation of each and every soul to be fulfilled to the glory of the Father, and to her own eternal joy and peace in the Communion of Saints—this high-priestly offering of Jesus has its distinctive modes appropriate to His Pre-existent Glory, His Incarnation, and His post-Ascension " Heavenly Session ".

The high-priestly offering of the Pre-existent Jesus was the perfect self-oblation to the Father—in love and oneness of purpose—of Himself as " the Lamb slain from the foundation of the world ". The high-priestly offering of the Incarnate Jesus was His " I lay down My life " ; the hourly laying down of life in sacrificial love year in year out, moment by moment in daily life, and issuing in the consummatory laying down of life in death. The high-priestly offering of the Risen and Ascended Jesus in His " Heavenly Session "

is the offering of His " I lay down My life, that I may take it
again " (Jn. x. 17) : the eternal, all-inclusive, consummate
offering of the life laid down in life and death as the one " full,
perfect, and sufficient sacrifice, oblation, and satisfaction, for
the sins of the whole world ", and taken again for all eternity—
and on behalf of all men—in God's raising Him from the dead
in virtue of His own invincible and indestructible life.
Jesus Himself has told us, " For as the Father hath life in
Himself ; so hath He given to the Son to have life in Himself " (Jn. v. 26). It is this " life in Himself " expended in
ceaseless offering to the Father, and for love of Him on
behalf of all souls, which is the eternal high-priestly
offering of Jesus before time, throughout time, and beyond
time.

The " Fiat "—the " So let it be "—of the Pre-existent and
Omniscient Son of God for His Incarnation was the perfect
high-priestly offering of sacrificial self-oblation to Love and
Holiness for the purposes of Redemption : perfect in the
sense of being exhaustively complete in will and desire, and
one to the uttermost with the Will of the Father in Whom
the end is eternally fulfilled in the beginning. This " Fiat "
of One taking full stock of all that was involved, foreknowing
the price and being willing to pay it in its entirety, was of
such potency as necessarily to constitute that whole incarnate life intrinsically—at large, and in detail from the very
moment of birth—a high-priestly offering altogether irrespective of, and prior to, His human recognition of His vocation
as " high priest for ever ".

But that human recognition of His inherent, eternal High
Priesthood necessarily dawned and developed in time.
Upon its first dawning none can dare speculate. Neither
can any doubt that its full development must have involved
infinite travail of mind and spirit for Jesus of Nazareth, Who
had steeped in the Scriptures and was saturated with the
conceptions and historical knowledge of the Jewish priesthood as it had emerged down the centuries, until in His own
day it was hedged about with apparently infrangible laws

absolutely precluding His eligibility to the priesthood as not
being descended from the priestly tribe of Aaron.

Sensing irresistibly His own priestly vocation, our Lord's
non-eligibility for the Aaronic priesthood—the sole Jewish
priesthood of His day—must have constituted a real problem
for Him until, by the illumination of the Holy Spirit, He
penetrated to the heart of His own eternal High Priesthood.
His fulfilment of His Messianic vocation ran clean counter
to every previous Messianic conception enshrined in the
traditional expectation of the Jews. His fulfilment of His
high-priestly vocation ran no less counter to every Jewish
conception and tradition historically rooted in the nation's
past. For the National Deliverer of Messianic expectation,
who should usher in a golden age, was substituted the
Suffering Servant. For the priests, anointed and regarded
of men, whose ' sacrifices ' external to themselves were in
large measure their livelihood and were misused to minister
to their own ends, was substituted the High Priest, anointed
of God, unrecognised and disallowed of men until after His
Ascension, Whose sacrifice was His Very Self and own
Heart's Blood. The earthly anointing as priest which could
not be His would have confined His priesthood to the single
Church within which it had to be received ; a Divine
anointing would leave Him free to be the priest of all
humanity instead only of one race or sect.

In the Father's " Thou art My Son . . ." at His Baptism,
there came to Jesus the human consciousness of His unique
Sonship as itself a Divine anointing so tangible, that very
shortly after His return from His post-baptismal Tempta-
tion in the Wilderness, He gave—in the Synagogue at
Nazareth—explicit utterance to His recognition of it as
something definitely and objectively received : " ' The
Spirit of the Lord is upon Me, because He hath anointed
Me. . . .' To-day is this scripture fulfilled in your ears "
(Lk. iv. 18 ff.).

Nowhere in the Gospels is our Lord recorded as having
explicitly proclaimed Himself as High Priest. (Perhaps

because hiddenness was of the essence of His deepest sacrificial offering, known only in its interior fulness and intensity to the Father alone, although in its redemptive fruits overflowing for all men.) But that He Himself had recognised His Divine anointing specifically as anointing as High Priest for all souls living and departed, our Lord left no possible shadow of doubt on the Tuesday of Holy Week, when before the Pharisees He appropriated to Himself the Messianic Psalm (Ps. cx.) beginning : " The Lord said unto my Lord, sit Thou on My right hand, till I put Thine enemies underneath Thy feet ". He must needs have appropriated to Himself the whole psalm in its entirety, and therefore the Father's appointment to an eternal priesthood which it prophetically enshrines : " The Lord hath sworn and will not repent, Thou art a priest for ever after the order of Melchizedek " (Ps. cx. 4).

The ' high-priestly prayer ' of our Lord's, recorded in Jn. xvii., lays bare the conspectus of His incarnate exercise of His High Priesthood as being :

First and foremost *Sacrificial* : " Father, the hour is come . . ." : the hour in which He was to consummate His lifelong offering of vicarious penitence and reparation (see pp. 113 ff.) by the offering up of the supreme sacrifice of laying down His life ;

Then *Intercessory* : " Father, glorify Thy Name . . . the men whom Thou gavest Me out of the world . . . I pray for them. . . . And for their sakes I sanctify Myself, that they themselves also may be sanctified in truth " ;

Prophetic (i.e. revelatory and interpretative): " I manifested Thy Name unto the men whom Thou gavest Me out of the world . . . the words which Thou gavest Me I have given unto them . . . I made known unto them Thy Name " ;

Pastoral : " I kept them in Thy Name which Thou hast given Me, and I guarded them, and not one of them perished. . . ."

The sacrificial system was at the heart of Jewish worship, rooted in the far past, its innumerable regulations minutely recorded in the Scriptures. But it was a merely symbolic system utterly failing to approximate, either in reality or effectuality, to that which it purported to signify. An explicit acknowledgment of Man's profound recognition of the fact that his sin absolutely necessitated sacrifice, it yet failed completely to recognise the true nature of sin, let alone to provide any adequate sacrifice. Self-admittedly it did not profess or even attempt to cover what was regarded as " sin with a high hand "—i.e. wilful moral guilt of any kind whatsoever—but only the ceremonial uncleanness resulting from accidental, morbid, or hygienic causes. There was, moreover, profound hopelessness implicit in the very fact of these sacrifices being offered in perpetuity, as without any expectation of permanent eradication of the sin for which they were offered.

There was futility in the fact that these sacrifices were never truly sacrificial because ever remaining external to the sacrificer. Deficient alike in moral objective and in moral content, the Jewish sacrificial system left utterly untouched that most crying need of Man—beside which all his other needs are as next to nothing—the need to be morally cleansed " from within ".

That " from within " is our Lord's own. He alone it was Who penetrated to the core of sacrifice, both as to what it must effect, and how. " That which proceedeth out of the man, that defileth the man. From within, out of the heart of men, evil thoughts proceed, fornications, thefts, murders, adulteries, covetings, wickednesses, deceit, lasciviousness, an evil eye, railing, pride, foolishness : all these evil things proceed from within, and defile the man " (Mk. vii. 20–23) . . . " But to eat with unwashen hands defileth not the man " (Matt. xv. 20) : by this He once for all exposed the Jewish sacrificial system as utterly beside the mark, and totally misdirected in its aim. He revealed the sin " from within "—which is the " sin with a high hand "—as the true matter of sacrifice. He revealed, moreover, *by offering it*, that there is a sacrifice which can avail for the sin " from within ", and one sacrifice only, the perfect and exhaustive sacrifice " from within " (i.e. the sacrifice of self in the very essence and sum of its whole being), which neither needs nor brooks repetition, since fully sufficient in itself for the ultimate annihilation of all sin by the substitution of holiness.

" . . . But now once . . . hath He appeared to put away [Gk. = annul, make of no effect] sin by the sacrifice of Himself " (Heb. ix. 26), " Who His own self bare [the Gk. bears both the meaning of " offering up as a sacrifice ", and " taking upon one "] our sins in His own body on the tree, that we, being dead to sins, should live unto righteousness . . ." (1 Pet. ii. 24).

(For our Lord's incarnate intercessory ministry, see pp. 106 ff.)

" For the priest's lips should keep [the verb in the Septuagint implies " custody and protection "] knowledge, and they should seek the law at his mouth : for he is the messenger of the Lord of hosts " (Mal. ii. 7) ; how long and deeply must our Lord have meditated upon this before He publicly endorsed it in His Sermon on the Mount : " Think not that I am come to destroy the law . . . I am not come to destroy but to fulfil " (Matt. v. 17). Custodian of the ' knowledge ' that is the sum of all Truth and Wisdom, He guarded it intact in the purity of His own Being and life, and kept it undiluted as well as unpolluted. Only as the Messenger of the Lord of hosts did He ever speak, as He Himself openly declared towards the very end of His public ministry : " For I have not spoken of Myself, but the Father which sent Me, He gave Me a commandment, what I should say, and what I should speak. And I know that His commandment is life everlasting : whatsoever I speak therefore, even as the Father said unto Me, so I speak " (Jn. xii. 49–50). He was the ever faithful transmitter of the message of the Father ; but more than that He was the Glorious Interpreter of the Father's Self that sent to the world His message of " the gospel of the kingdom of God ".

' Father ' : it was thus He interpreted God, Jahweh, " I

am that I am ", the Lord of Hosts, the Holy One of Israel. The Father He interpreted in the likeness of Himself—" He that hath seen Me hath seen the Father " (Jn. xiv. 9)—bent not on judging and condemning, but on saving, and finding good (" She hath done what she could ") ; overflowing with compassion for the guilty and innocent alike ; mighty to deliver the distressed in body, mind, and soul ; matchless in gracious courtesy of manner, and in intuitive understanding of the hopes, fears, aspirations, joys, and sorrows of each and every heart and mind ; inexhaustible alike in generosity and patience ; the friend of sinners, and of " the common people ", of rich and poor, ignorant and learned, men, women, and children ; drawing to Himself—and commissioning in His service—men and women of utterly varying temperaments, gifts, and backgrounds. Loving all with a love as boundless and uninterrupted as if each was the sole object of His love, and because of this love ruthlessly opposed to the death to all that savours of sin and self : as such did Jesus manifest our Father in heaven.

Jesus interpreted God, the All-Knowing and Infinite, in terms potentially intelligible to all be they never so unlearned, because He interpreted Him in terms which for their intelligibility need no more than good-will brought to bear upon them. He interpreted Him as One Who delights Himself in little children, and in beauty ; as One Who has not it in Him to despise any man or woman ; as One Who desires to share all Eternity's riches of holiness and joy even with sinners as ' notorious ' as a woman who has " lived in sin " over a long period of time, or a man who has come to forfeiting his life for robbery with violence ; as One so inwardly aflame with love as to be unable to refrain from washing soiled feet, touching a leper, or talking with a raving maniac ; as One easy to be intreated, indeed eternally proffering to each and all His : " What wilt thou that I should do unto thee ? "

Every truly priestly function and attribute ever in any way—however imperfectly—apprehended, typified, or exercised in the Aaronic priesthood, was perfectly fulfilled by our Lord during His incarnate life. He was *par excellence* the Sacrificer ; the Intercessor (and oh, the quality of His worship and of His pleading !) ; the Teacher and Interpreter. But over and above all this He apprehended that which had never before, but has ever since, been regarded as integral to the priestly vocation—namely, its pastoral element. The pastoral element has now for so long been regarded as a *sine qua non* in true priesthood, that it is not always realised that there was absolutely no pastoral conception of priesthood at all until it was introduced by our Incarnate Lord.

It was as "that great shepherd of the sheep" (Heb. xiii. 20) that the Seer of the High Priest summed up all his life's vision of Him, and it was primarily as "that great shepherd of the sheep" that the High Priest captivated his worshipping mind and heart—captivated it to the point of silence. Nowhere does the Seer of the High Priest elaborate his perception of Him as Shepherd, because—for the very worship and love that at their most intense must ever elude all words—he cannot.

None can unfold to another the unutterable wonder of Jesus' Shepherd-love and Shepherd-lovableness. The Shepherd alone can reveal it to the individual soul, and does so either in some personal exigency of its own, or, still more probably, in meeting some need of one whom it loves more than itself.

Priests as sacrificers (of sorts) and priests as teachers (of sorts) there had been before our Lord ; but priests as shepherds there had been none. " All that ever came before Me are thieves and robbers : but the sheep did not hear them " (Jn. x. 8) : a self-seeking priesthood living *on*, and not *for*, the people, caring nothing for them. What a contrast to the Shepherd of the sheep ! " . . . He calleth his own sheep by name, and leadeth them out " (Jn. x. 3) : the passionate individual caring for—and intimate knowledge of—each one.

What a contrast to the shepherd our Lord revealed Himself to be ! Jesus Himself—that all men in all necessities might have wherewith to comfort themselves—told us that He is " the good shepherd " ; and for our further comfort He further unbared His Shepherd-Heart : " the good shepherd layeth down his life for the sheep . . . I am the good shepherd ; and I know Mine own, and Mine own know Me. . . . And other sheep I have, which are not of this fold : them also I must bring, and they shall hear My voice ; and they shall become one flock, one shepherd " (Jn. x. 14–16).

" The Good Shepherd " : here indeed are " comfortable words " ! Here, offered to us in uttermost simplicity and with irresistible appeal, we have the Self-portraiture of the Word, the Truth, in His Wisdom disclosing His—and so also the Father's—eternal disposition towards Man in terms of Shepherd-love. What this means the Holy Spirit in part reveals in and through the Gospels, each and all redolent with the Shepherd-love of Jesus, and in part in our experience of life in time and in a fallen world ; but fully to glorify Jesus as " Good Shepherd " He will need all eternity, for only then can the profundities of His goodness towards us be exhaustively revealed.

But even part-realisation of the meaning of His Shepherd-love fills the whole being with joy and hope—of which we all stand in such constant need of renewal—for it brings recognition of *how* " His mercy is over all His works ". It is the unspeakable, unquenchable mercy that the love He has set upon us His creatures is Shepherd-love : the love that takes full cognisance of the stupidity and defencelessness of the sheep, and is thereby stirred only to compassionate them and itself do for them all that is necessary—ministering to all their day to day wants ; leading them forth ; protecting ; battling for them ; above all rescuing them in any emergency or disaster that may overtake them, whether from without, or by reason of their own folly.

The Shepherd-love for the sinner—fount of the Incarnation—must surely remain for time and eternity the glorious

mystery of mysteries, revealing, not only Love Who cannot
but love, but Love Who, whilst loving all incessantly, must
needs *most* outpour His love, Himself, His gracious, tender,
wooing, rescuing, bracing, redeeming energy of re-creative
compassion precisely upon, and around, the souls self-
reduced to direst extremities by reason of their own folly,
selfishness, or wilfully chosen sin. Is any soul wrecked in
body, mind, or spirit, or shattered in its external circumstances and relationships with others, by its own grievous
fault ? Then upon that soul in its present wreckage the
totality of Jesus' rescuing Shepherd-love—without ever any
neglect of any other soul—is concentrated so that, despite
all human impossibility, it may by His high-priestly inter-
vention be brought enduringly to accept its reinstatement
in the holiness, peace, and joy, in which the Father created
and willed eternally to perpetuate its life and being.

" The good shepherd layeth down his life for the sheep "—
that is not merely to die for them, but purposefully to live
for them as well. Every action of our Lord's was perfect
in itself, but it was never an end in itself, being offered always
" with intention " for the glory of God (i.e. as priestly worship), and directed " with intention " for others " that where
I am they may be also ", i.e. come to share with Him in His
oneness with the Father in love and holiness.

Jesus as Good Shepherd made concrete and specific
offering for other souls of all the events and states in His own
life and soul, e.g. His weariness at the well for others wearied
in the journey of life (and then the refreshment which came
to the Woman of Samaria and all in her village !) ; every
hardship or human uncertainty (" the Son of Man hath not
where to lay His head ") ; every suffering, sorrow, or effort-
ful travail, for others in like case, yes, and every joy and all
delight in beauty and simplicity, that they—like Himself—
might be enabled to accept in perfect union with the Father
all things whatsoever. So did He render limitless in
potentiality His laying-down of His life both for His sheep
individually and as a flock.

But the laying down of life appertains essentially to war, and so it was, not as a gesture, but in the grim reality of relentless and unceasing warfare with sin, and all its train of suffering and death, that Jesus laid down His life : on behalf of the sheep meeting and victoriously resisting in His own Person the uttermost pressure of evil, which they themselves were absolutely powerless to combat with any success.

Perhaps it may not untruly be said that one of the outstanding preoccupations of the Gospels is with our Lord's incarnate exercise of His pastoral ministry, of which they give so rich a selective record. His pastoral ministry to the sick, to the poor, to the bereaved, to the ignorant, to the outcast, to the sinner, is there cumulatively mirrored in such a way that none—doubt what else they may—can question His essential priestliness. " Thou art a priest for ever ...." : so Jesus livingly emerges from the Gospels—the ' born ' priest, who cannot think or live other than priestly, i.e. sacrificially to offer Man to God and God to Man.

The Gospels reveal a quite definite development in our Lord's incarnate exercise of His pastoral ministry, and nowhere more clearly than in His exercise of the priestly function of absolution. This development of His exercise of absolution traced in detail shows—perhaps more vividly than anything else could do—the never-failingness of His Shepherd-Heart to pass from need to need of His sheep, meeting each ever more deeply and widely.

Early in His public ministry, to Peter's : " Depart from me ; for I am a sinful man, O Lord ", He only replied : " Fear not ; from henceforth thou shalt catch men " (Lk. v. 8–10), and pronounced no specific absolution (perhaps because He had not yet come to the interior knowledge of His power on earth to forgive sins ?) Later, to the woman in the house of Simon the Pharisee, He did give specific absolution : " Thy sins are forgiven " (Lk. vii. 48). Surely, this was the deliberate outcome of prayer evoked by His whole interior response to the stimulus of Peter's articulated sense of sinfulness, and His realisation that more

than vision and encouragement are needed for the penitent
even where these *presuppose* absolvedness. It was after
this [see Ponsonby's *Life of our Lord* " arranged chronologically "] that there came—in the case of the man sick
of the palsy—His : " . . . that ye may know that the Son
of Man hath power on earth to forgive sins " (Mk. ii. 10) :
His exercise of the priestly function of absolution for the
penitent woman, in her love's contrition, having proved to
Him Himself His power to exercise it at large for all other
penitent souls as well.

Taking the development of His exercise of this priestly
function of absolution beyond His incarnate life, we find the
Risen Lord acting on behalf of all sinners for all time, and,
in the recognition of His power to transmit to others His
Absolving Spirit, saying to the disciples in the Upper Room :
" Receive ye the Holy Ghost : whose soever sins ye forgive,
they are forgiven unto them ; whose soever sins ye retain,
they are retained " (Jn. xx. 22 f.). Ascended, He perpetuates,
to His priests all down the ages, this transmission of His
power to absolve sinners, so that none but can—at will—
have their extremity met by Him to the uttermost.

The Gospels likewise reveal a quite definite development
as to range in our Lord's incarnate exercise of His pastoral
ministry. Initially He recognised only a limited call, as He
Himself explicitly declared to the Syrophœnician woman
craving His help : " I was not sent but unto the lost sheep
of the house of Israel " (Matt. xv. 24). But, through this
outside siege upon His Shepherd-love, He was drawn on to
recognition of a universal call, which He as explicitly, and
publicly, declared : " . . . other sheep I have, which are
not of this fold ; them also I must bring, and they shall hear
My voice ; and they shall become one flock, one shepherd "
(Jn. x. 16).

So did our Lord leave nothing unsaid, nothing undone, to
try to make us realise both the all-embracingness and all-
sufficingness of His pastoral ministry. " Such is the
Shepherd and Bishop of your souls " : the High Priest

21

beyond the pale of Whose love and passionate concern no
sinner can ever pass ; the High Priest having power wholly
to sanctify even the most abandoned of sinners once giving
Him heart-entrance by but a spark of contrition, an ache of
would-be-otherness ; the High Priest ceaselessly wooing
sinners to become sons of God, such sons as He is Perfect
Son, sons in His own Sonship.

Risen and Ascended, our Lord not only exercises His high-
priestly ministry from within " the Heavenly Sanctuary "
by the intercession of His eternal Self-presentation to the
Father as the one " full, perfect, and sufficient sacrifice,
oblation, and satisfaction, for the sins of the whole world " ;
but also by mystically perpetuating its incarnate exercise,
and that in twofold mode, i.e. through the ministry of
" another Comforter " (Jn. xiv. 16), and in and through His
Mystic Body (see pp. 333 ff.). All that the Gospels record of
the gracious tenderness, the beauteous, strong compassion,
the never-failing rescuing, liberating, and sanctifying
efficacy of the incarnate exercise of His pastoral ministry is
as true—only with a heightened intimacy—of its post-
Ascension exercise, in the fulfilment of His promised : " I
will pray the Father, and He shall give you another Comforter that He may abide with you for ever ". The Comforter perpetuates Jesus' pastoral ministry *within the soul*, as
the members of His Mystic Body perpetuate it exteriorly ;
and between the Comforter and the members of His Mystic
Body is fruitful union and co-operation in that pastoral
ministry in which interior and exterior are interwoven.

" My grace is sufficient for thee " (2 Cor. xii. 9) : this life-
steadying, life-bracing revelation, originally vouchsafed by
the Risen and Ascended Lord to St. Paul in his need, was also
—as St. Paul knew when he brought himself to lay bare to
others his Lord's secret converse with his own soul—a revelation intended equally for all souls in any need whatsoever.
This Risen and Ascended mediation of His grace—the
grace of His Spirit, Who is the Heroic, as well as the Holy,
Spirit—is the climax and fruit of our Lord's consistent high-

priestly building-up of His incarnate life self-denial by self-denial, flawless act of worship by flawless act of worship, intercessory prayer by intercessory prayer, and above all resistance by resistance to temptation ; perfect detail by perfect detail gradually creating and achieving the perfect whole, which can for ever inexhaustibly and effectually be drawn upon by all desiring souls in need.

" We are . . . the sheep of His hand " (Ps. xcv. 7) says—or sings—the Church daily. Do those of us who are familiar—perhaps over-familiar—with it merely acquiesce in this assertion as a poetic figure of speech ; or do we act upon it as the basic determinant of our whole way of practical thought and living ? Is the so generally favourite Twenty-Third Psalm æsthetically delighted in for its exquisite imagery, or cherished because it provides the soul with a pæan of thanksgiving expressive of her own relationship with Jesus—the one only Jesus Who is increasingly all in all to her—as High Priest ? " The Lord is my Shepherd " (Ps. xxiii. 1) [Septuagint : " tends me as a shepherd ". In the Greek this " tends . . . as a shepherd " is a single verb including oversight as well as feeding] : is this allegory or creed for our soul ? Is it picture-language, or profoundest homage ? Is it external to the soul, or is it the soul's self-confessed way of life as the way of continually betaking herself to Jesus as High Priest ?

The soul betaking herself to Jesus as High Priest finds everything in Him, everything of Him, everything for herself, everything for others. To come to Jesus as High Priest is to find the Son of God, the King, the Judge ; it is also to find the Son of Man, the Saviour : all this we find as " we fall down before His footstool " (Ps. xcix. 5) and quite literally prostrate body, and—as far as may be—mind, and spirit, before Him as He is " set on the right hand of the throne of the Majesty in the heavens " (Heb. viii. 1), i.e. place ourselves imaginatively and mystically before Him as Priest, as a Confirmation candidate kneels before the bishop. He is the Priest Who is to hear the soul's confession, not because He exacts it, but because she—in the light of His Presence—becomes herself a wordless confession, the recognised, repented, unlikeness to His revealed holiness, love, beauty, and truth.

There is no need for words to Him Who understands her as none other—even herself—can. There is relief in the very absence of need to try to explain anything. The naked " I " cries to Him in the silence of dumb self-accusation. Immediately there comes His: " Fear not ", as He unfolds the true nature of Himself as Judge, desirous not to condemn, but to reward and sanctify. " For as the Father hath life in Himself ; so hath He given to the Son to have life in Himself ; and hath given Him authority to execute judgment also, *because He is the Son of Man.* . . . I can of Mine own self do nothing : as I hear, I judge : and My judgment is just ; because I seek not Mine own will, but the will of the Father which hath sent Me " (Jn. v. 26–30) ; and " it is not ", He says, " the will of your Father, which is in heaven, that one of these little ones should perish " (Matt. xviii. 14).

So He reveals Himself appointed our Judge solely by merciful reason of His Incarnation having given Him, eternally, the power to understand everything human from within, from personal experience of temptation and travail, and from exhaustive measuring of the assailant forces of evil ; and beyond the power to understand, the power—by virtue of His complete victory over sin and death—also to sanctify. Our Hope is in Him as High Priest, because as High Priest He is the Judge applying His Saviourhood ; the Shepherd turning our souls back to God. To reach His high-priestly footstool is to receive the benediction of benedictions : His Absolution—and then to be led on.

The High Priest does not absolve, and then leave us to go on our way undirected. He illumines us to peace by His Spirit, the ultimate Director of all souls, at one time it may be by clarifying what we have next to do, at another—without word, emotion, or even thought—simply by filling our whole being with Himself. But glory of glories, the

High Priest Who is ever ready to prove to us in our own lives that He is " able to save them to the uttermost that come unto God by Him " (Heb. vii. 25), saves us—after absolution—by uniting us with Him in this intercession. He sanctifies us by the infusing of His priestly Spirit towards God' and towards others ; and saves us in the voluntary losing of our lives in His high-priestly " intentions." This it is to be " the sheep of His hand " : to be absolved, and directed by Him, and then enabled to co-operate with Him in His shepherding of others, until we all become " one flock, one shepherd " because He " hath made us . . . priests unto God and His Father " (Rev. i. 6).

" . . . seeing He ever liveth to make intercession . . ." : here is the soul's anchor, not for herself alone, but for the whole world. Here—and here alone—is comfort, and justification for invincible hope, for those whose hearts must otherwise break at the world's self-inflicted plight to-day, who grieve over the sorrows of others, whether known or unknown, individuals or nations, as their own ; and know themselves impotent in the last resort really to help at all, because recognising that financial, economic, international, and racial chaos are but symptoms of basically unregenerate wills and minds in men and women the world over. However much they may yearn that it were otherwise, they realise the truth that " no man may deliver his brother : nor make agreement unto God for him ; for it cost more to redeem their souls : so that he must let that alone for ever " (Ps. xlix. 7–8).

Man can do nothing now, or ever, except anchor in contrition and faith upon the eternal truth : " the help that is done upon earth, He doeth it Himself "—by His ever living to make intercession for all souls. We cannot even pray aright for the world except by striving to abandon ourselves to Him in union with His high-priestly prayer (which prayer is Himself, Pre-Existent, Incarnate, Risen, Ascended, and Glorified), and by striving sacrificially to unite ourselves with Him in His offering upon our behalf—simply by its fulness eternally in His own Being—that which we lack in worship, and penitence, and genuine desire for God's Will.

The ' high-priestly ' prayer of Jn. xvii. once for all revealed the heart of our Lord's High Priesthood as love ; and His high-priestly " intention " as directed to bring all souls to the unitive knowledge of God as Love, and in so doing to perfect the circuit of Love between all men. This remains the eternal " intention " of that intercession which Risen and Ascended " He ever liveth to make. . . ". This intercession—His eternal Self-presentation to the Father as Lamb of God, Redeemer of the world—is a high-priestly prayer pardoning, healing, redeeming, transfiguring all souls living and departed. It is as High Priest that Jesus of Nazareth, " the man of sorrows, acquainted with grief "—the Radiant One Whose love plunged Him into the heart of our sorrow and our grief—fulfils His incarnate promise : ". . . your sorrow shall be turned into joy " (Jn. xvi. 20).

His high-priestly intercession is ever in process of transmuting all things : sin to holiness ; selfishness to sacrificial love ; disease to wholeness ; death to life ; disaster to opportunity. He, as High Priest, does not simply take away sorrow and evil, but actually converts it into joy and good. That which was formerly matter for tears—even, it may be, despair—He, by His intercession, makes to become eternal cause for worship and wonder-filled thanksgiving ; and this not only in Eternity, but ever and again even here also in Time : pledge in miniature of Eternity's all-embracing consummation in Bliss and Perfection.

May He increase our faith, and so bring us practically to know and believe in the efficacy of His high-priestly intercession, that we may never despair for any, but ever bring our own and all souls to Him as the Priest Who absolves, and sanctifies, and then bestows upon the soul the eternal life of progressive self-abandonment to union with Him in His high-priestly prayer, wherein is ever fresh glory, worship, love, peace, truth, joy, beauty, and enduring fruitfulness.

THE MYSTICAL BODY: AND COMMUNION
OF SAINTS

THE MYSTICAL BODY: AND COMMUNION OF SAINTS

THE *infinity* of Jesus Christ: this it is which sooner or later invades, engulfs, and as it were overwhelms the minds and hearts—whilst kindling to fresh life the spirits —of all who ponder long and deeply concerning Himself. The writer of the Epilogue to the Fourth Gospel was inundated with this consciousness of inexhaustibleness even with regard to the earthly actions of Jesus of Nazareth: " And there are also many other things which Jesus did, the which if they should be written every one, I suppose that even the world itself could not contain the books that should be written " (Jn. xxi. 25). Whilst for St. Paul this consciousness was focused in " the unsearchable [Gk. = lit. that cannot be traced out, inexplorable] riches " [Moffatt: " the fathomless wealth "; Weymouth: " the exhaustless wealth "] (Eph. iii. 8) of the Redeeming Christ, the Messiah.

We may—and in proportion to our recognition must— worship Jesus as :

Son of God.

Son of Man : Lamb, Saviour, and Redeemer.

High Priest.

Risen, Ascended, Glorified Lord " set on the right hand of the throne of the Majesty in the heavens " (Heb. viii. 1).

But no one, nor even the sum total, of these aspects exhaust either His nature or office, as St. Paul not only apprehended but with glorious boldness articulated, when writing of the Church: " . . . the Church, which is His body, the fulness of Him that filleth all in all " [or rather : " . . . Who is thereby all-in-all fulfilled ", being—according to Westcott, Armitage Robinson, and Dr. S. C. Carpenter— the correct translation] (Eph. i. 22–23).

Professing Christians affirm—or at least assent to—belief

in " one Holy Catholic and Apostolic Church ". But what precisely is meant—individually and corporately—by this ? Do we really share St. Paul's passionate conviction in a Church which is the Body of Christ, " the fulness of Him Who is thereby all-in-all fulfilled " ?   And if so, do we believe She exists in actuality, or only as an ideal in the Mind of God—an ideal as yet unrealised among men ?   If we believe in Her already realised existence, how all-embracing is that belief ?   Does it extend beyond a particular branch of the Church on earth to include all branches and sects, yes, and all souls in " the whole family in heaven and earth " ? " I believe in . . . one Holy Catholic and Apostolic Church " : is this for the majority an affirmation made only with reservations, or with specialised interpretation ?   By the very acuteness of the present-day " problem of the Reunion of the Churches " it would seem so, and that the predominant sense is one of divisiveness rather than of unity, of a Church lost in the Churches, of unity precluded by multiformity—multiformity of religious thought and practice.

In the days of His flesh it is recorded of our Lord that " there was a division among the people because of Him " (Jn. vii. 43)—and so it has continued ever since.   The division has intensified, and extended beyond His Incarnate Personality to the nature and office of His Mystical Body ; and the grounds of this division with regard to His Mystical Body have remained constant, resting—as they have always done—upon the perennially vexed questions as to :

Who constitutes the " true Church " which is His Body ;
How this Church is intended to function ; and
What She is intended to teach.

The follies, the blindnesses, the wilfulnesses, and obstinacies of mankind remain essentially the same down the ages, however great the difference which may creep, or sweep, into their outward expression.   " There is no new thing under the sun " (Ecc. i. 9) is as true of " Church problems " as of anything else.   We are apt to overlook the fact that all which constitutes for us a basic stumbling-block in the " problem of the Church " to-day was already a stumbling-block to the Apostles. Overlooking this, we overlook also the fact that the solution of our " Church problem " is not to be discovered in ever-renewed Conferences and discussions. The ' solution ' has already been vouchsafed centuries ago, being identical with that which the Apostles received direct from our Lord and His Holy Spirit : a timeless ' solution ' because the Eternal Word operates in terms of abiding principle, penetrating beyond the ephemeral and incidental in any given difficulty to the underlying causative human characteristics ever creating and perpetuating difficulties of like nature.

Man has so complicated the " Church problem " as to render it beyond possibility of human unravelling. To the majority who seriously concern themselves with " the problem of Reunion " it seems that there are a number of principles involved—principles of doctrine and of ritual—all of which ought to, and must, be contended for as fundamental and of unrelinquishable obligation. To the Holy God, with Whom can be no complexity, only profound simplicity, the ' problem ' must surely be single, and not multiform as we construe it to be : a problem in the realm, not of dogma or of ceremonial, but of love—insufficient love of God, and hence insufficient love of fellow-man.

It is the spirit of Man's exclusiveness which throughout has been—and continues to be—the disruptive bane of the Church. A spirit utterly opposed to the all-embracing Spirit of Christ, this exclusiveness—whether consciously or otherwise—is based on pride, self-will, and determination to impose upon others personal beliefs, opinions, practices, tastes, etc. " . . . we are they that ought to speak, who is lord over us ? " (Ps. xii. 4) is all too often the attitude taken by individual members or branches of the Church. " We are they . . ." : we, and we only, are the " true Church " ; we see and hold the truth in trust, we and none other in any real or vital degree. So it has been from the beginning.

Even the Apostles felt precisely this ; but they had—painfully—to learn differently from the Spirit of Jesus.

We feel it to-day : Romans, Anglicans, Orthodox, High Church, Low Church, Nonconformists. There is little, if anything, to choose between us in the matter of our own self-righteous exclusiveness, which we term " standing up for principle ", and our dislike of the exclusiveness of others, which we term " intolerance ". With exceptions among individual members, but probably without any corporate exception at all, each branch or sect of the Church to-day feels : " We are they . . ." ; and we have all failed as yet really to learn differently, to learn what was unmistakably revealed to the Apostles as the abiding truth concerning the Church, viz. that no one branch or sect exclusively comprises the " true Church " in its entirety.

This problem of spiritual exclusiveness is integral to the problem of Church unity ; and it was specifically and fundamentally resolved by our Lord in the days of His flesh, by His explicitly discountenancing any exclusiveness whatsoever amongst those who, however differently, believed on, and acted in, His name. " And John answered Him, saying, Master, we saw one casting out devils in Thy name, and he followeth [Gk. = also, to accompany, be in conformity with] not us : and we forbad [Gk. = lit. cut short ; prevented ; hindered] him, because he followeth not us. But Jesus said : Forbid him not : for there is no man which shall do a miracle in My name, that can lightly speak evil of Me. For he that is not against us is on our part . . ." (Mk. ix. 38–40). John's grievance—" he followeth not *us*," and not " he followeth not *Thee*"—has rankled in every phase and area of the Church's life all down the ages. This grievance has been rampant between Jew and Gentile, between classes, sects, races, and colours : a canker steadily sapping the life of the Body as a whole. It remains a crying disgrace amongst professing Christians that all too often unbelief in Christ is tolerated with the equanimity of indifference, whilst envenomed antagonism is immediately evoked by any dissimilarity of belief in Him, any dissimilar conception of the best method of worshipping, following, and serving Him.

Spiritual exclusiveness is not only forbidden, but mistaken. For the " true Church ", as St. Paul long since apprehended in the Spirit, there can be no " we are they " which is less than universal : " For as the body is one, and hath many members, and all the members of that one body, being many, are one body : so also is Christ. For by one Spirit are we all baptised into one body, whether we be Jews or Gentiles, whether we be bond or free ; and have been all made to drink into one Spirit. For the body is not one member, but many. . . . And if they were all one member, where were the body ? But now are they many members, yet but one body " (1 Cor. xii. 12 ff.). It is mankind in its totality which God, in His eternal thought, has destined to be the Body and Bride of Christ.

This human restrictiveness in the Church has not confined itself merely to personnel, but has also insinuated itself into both individual and corporate conceptions of how She ought to function, and what She ought to teach. There has always been a tendency for those who recognise the obligation or utility of certain aspects of Church worship, life, or activity, to want to impose them on all others—in complete ignorance and disregard of what may be their God-given *attraits*—and to discount the value, as well as necessity, of those aspects which lack personal appeal for themselves. This it is which has given rise to false distinctions, stresses, and comparisons, between one and another form of worship or of service—or even between prayer and service—when in reality it is no case of " either or ", since all forms are necessary and complementary, and none so perfect as to be exempt from need for further purifying.

Similarly with teaching : wherever there has been keen perception of any particular aspect of the truth, it has tended to obscure other aspects equally true and equally vital. The teaching of any specific branch of the Church is never entirely in focus at all points.   So the true centre of gravity is upset, and secondary things usurp the place of primary. No one branch of the Church perceives—let alone retains in perfect perspective—the sum total of truth apprehended by the aggregate of Churches and sects, each of which has its own distinctive perception to contribute to the whole. Men in all branches of the Church have tended again and again, at widely different stages in Her life, to expand and try to supplement " the faith which was once for all delivered unto the saints " (Jude 3).   Such accretions have proved very real stumbling-blocks time and again to many souls, when ' authority ' has sought to lay down as " of faith " some newly formulated doctrine—or some development of ancient doctrine totally beyond its original and legitimate scope—having no " warrant of Scripture " ;   or else has sought to impose as obligatory some fresh practice or devotion, having no title whatsoever to rank as " generally necessary to salvation ", and at best only helpful to some souls on some occasions.

Eternity certainly does not depend upon what we think of such matters—important though they may be—as, for instance, the Infallibility of the Pope ;   the Immaculate Conception ;   the invocation of Saints ;   prayer for the Departed ;   or even the Sacraments as such ;   because in the last resort it does not even depend upon what we *think* of Jesus Himself. No Christian would dare to make this quasi-blasphemous assertion, were it not that our Lord Himself voiced it to the Pharisees : " Whosoever shall speak a word against the Son of Man, it shall be forgiven him . . ." (Matt. xii. 32).   He knew well enough that what we think of Him is all too often thought of what we *think* He is—a very different matter from pure thought of Him *as He is*, to which He knows our finite minds cannot attain here in Time.

One of the world's starkest tragedies is the perversion of thought about the All-Loving, All-Lovable, and All-Lovely Jesus due to the un-Christlike lives of so many of His most

loud-professing followers. Far from ' commending ' Him
to those who as yet know Him not, the self in us all too often
obscures Him for them either in part or in entirety ; so that
they " have no use ", and no respect, for the Christ they
misconceive from our false representation of Him, Whose
True Self once recognised would be their soul's delight.
Eternity depends upon personal response to the supreme
test of sacrificial love which Jesus Himself has disclosed, in
His description of " the Last Judgment " (Matt. xxv.
31 ff.), as the sole determinant of life hereafter.

True thought about Jesus, some recognition of Him as He
really is—God of God, Light of Light, Very God of Very God,
Who is LOVE and with Whom all things in the way of redemption and sanctification are possible—is of vital importance, in that to catch even a glimpse of Perfect Love must
needs be to fall in love with Love, and progressively to want
to abandon self to live for Love, by Love, and in Love.
" For the love of Christ constraineth us " [Moffatt : " . . .
controlled by the love of Christ " ; Weymouth : " the love
of Christ overmasters us "] (2 Cor. v. 14) : this recognition of
the Love of Christ and reciprocal love for Him—admitted
by St. Paul as the master-motive and dynamic of his own
life—has engendered countless deeds and lives of sacrificial
love. Love for Jesus, combining with the Love of Jesus,
can scale heights of self-abnegating love, performing meanest
tasks, enduring vicarious suffering, such as literally no other
motive or power on earth could nerve to achieve or endure.

But thought about Christ can never unite the Churches,
because no thought of Him but is incomplete and fraught
with some element of human distortion. Human thought
about Christ must, necessarily, beyond a certain point remain separative rather than unifying, because ever taking
on and retaining something of the disparate selves, temperaments, casts of mind, embracing it. Never can the
Churches be united save as their members, individually and
corporately, become wholly abandoned to, possessed and
indwelt by, Him Who is Love. He as He is, His Very Self

and Being—and not our thought about Him—is our only *unifying* " common bond ".

All human effort to solve the " problem of Reunion " defeats itself because there is, at bottom, no problem to solve. The Churches are divided, and so to some it appears that the Church Herself is divided. Any body cut in pieces would cease itself to live, let alone be a perennial source of life, as is the Mystical Body in which all life both inheres and coheres. The self-evident impossibility of fundamental disunion rings down the centuries in that glorious " Is Christ divided ? " (I Cor. i. 13), which St. Paul found it absolutely unnecessary to answer as he ranged it alongside the queries : " Was Paul crucified for you ? or were ye baptised in the name of Paul ? ". It is as unthinkable, as untrue, that Christ is or ever could be divided, as that Paul was or could ever be a Crucified Redeemer into whose name men and women could be baptised as into life. The Mystical Body is the Body of Christ. " Is Christ divided ? " applies equally to His Body as to His entire Personality and life as such, and it is in realising this that we approach the fringe of the " great mystery " of His Mystical Body.

This Mystery must remain unfathomable upon earth, yet to receive any faintest glimmer of its light is to receive light outshining all things human ; and also to receive a confident hope for all mankind outsoaring any and every previous experience of good or ill, carrying the soul into the peace of the knowledge of the truth that with God all things are eternally being made new, and that in Him is Life, our life, and life for all. One such glimmer floods through His own Last Supper words : " This is My body " [or, according to scholars, simply " This My body " in the Aramaic in which these words would originally have been spoken] (Mk. xiv. 22).

" This is My body which is broken for you " are words so embedded in the consciousness of all Communicants that the realisation that this " which is broken for you " does not occur in any of the Gospel accounts of our Lord's Institution of the Last Supper, nor in the Communion Office, but only in the A.V. and R.V. margin of 1 Cor. xi. 24 [the R.V. itself having simply : " This is My body, which is for you," whilst the margin adds : " Many ancient authorities read ' is broken for you ' "] is liable to come as a startling shock immediately firing a train of fresh thought about the Blessed Sacrament.

The human intellect finds it easier to apprehend and concentrate upon that which presents itself within the limits of sense and time, rather than upon that which exists invisibly and eternally, infinite and transcendent. The external aspect of the physical and historic Passion on Calvary more readily grips the mind than does—at any rate at first—its interior and eternal significance. It is not difficult imaginatively to reconstruct the successive details in that series of physical indignities and tortures whereby the body of Jesus was—by His own permission and consent—finally " broken " upon the Cross, and taken down thence a corpse for burial. But the Gospel narratives of the Institution of the Last Supper are, surely, challengingly significant in this connection. It is to be noted that the words spoken by our Lord in regard to the bread which He blessed, and brake, and gave to His disciples, are respectively recorded by St. Mark, St. Matthew, and St. Luke, as :

" Take ye : this is My body " (Mk. xiv. 22) ;

" Take, eat ; this is My body " (Matt. xxvi. 26) ;

" This is My body which is given for you : this do in remembrance of Me " (Lk. xxii. 19 A.V. and R.V. ; but R.V. margin adds : " Some ancient authorities omit ' which is given for you ' ").

This being so, one conclusion is inescapable : that the whole stress of the Spirit of Jesus is designedly upon His Body purely as such, and not exclusively—nor even primarily—upon its physical " breaking " upon Calvary. Even the " remembrance ", the commemoration, is commanded to be a commemoration of *Him*, and not of His death specifically, although naturally—and inevitably—any commemoration

22

of Him must centrally include His death. The implications
of this are deep, far-reaching, and very creative. The Holy
Spirit does not desire us to concentrate upon Calvary as an
end in itself. It is not death as such—not even the death
of Jesus—where He would have us halt, but Life : the Life
which, after Man's sin, could only be reborn of, released
through, and imparted by, His death.

It is not His corpse, but His living Body which Jesus
communicates to whomsoever will receive Him : and this
living Body—a mystery which the mind cannot rationalise,
and dare not even if it could—is His Incarnate Body (that
body which lived and laboured and was " broken " in
Palestine) ; is His Risen Body (" See My hands and My feet,
that it is I Myself " (Lk. xxiv. 39)) ; is His Mystical Body
(comprising all created souls) ; inseparably one Body. It is
this Body which is " given " [διδόμενον] (Lk. xxii. 19) : and
there is a continuity in the " givenness " which is not exhausted by the temporal act of humanly exhaustive self-
oblation and self-donation on Calvary. The " givenness "
of the body " broken " on Calvary is not only a " givenness " to God on our behalf, and a giving of life to—as well
as for —us, but it is also the consummation and perpetuation
for eternity of a " givenness " synonymous with the generation of the Only-Begotten of the Father, i.e. a " givenness "
inseparable from the Father's Self-Communication of His
own Essential Nature.

Human words fail utterly before a Mystery so transcendent
as that of the Mystical Body of Christ, but so far as words
can go, may it not, then, be said that the Mystical Body
is the infinite projection of Uncreate Love of which It is
the expression, reflection, and consummation. " In Him
dwelleth all the fulness of the Godhead [the Gk. connotes
essence rather than qualities or attributes] bodily " [Moffatt :
" It is in Christ that the entire Fulness of deity has settled
bodily " ; Weymouth : " For it is in Christ that the fulness
of God's nature dwells embodied "] (Col. ii. 9). So it is
Love—not as humanly conceived, but as eternally begotten

of, and abandoned to, Uncreate Love—and Love alone, which is both the Nature and the Office of the Mystical Body of Christ.

" Ye are Christ's ; and Christ is God's " (1 Cor. iii. 23) : this is the ineffable *unitive* Mystery of the Mystical Body of Christ into which God, of His infinite love, condescension, and generosity, creates each and every soul a member incorporate.

The gift of the Body of our Lord Jesus Christ is a gift infinite in content : the gift of all in heaven and earth ; in Deity and Humanity ; in time and in eternity. Infinite, moreover, is the Divine desire that all souls—both individually and corporately—may consciously receive, i.e. welcome and accept this Gift of Gifts. But all too often, and with all too many of us—even regular Communicants—it is a case of " not discerning the Lord's body " [Moffatt : " without a proper sense of the Body " ; Weymouth : " fails to understand the body "] (1 Cor. xi. 29). " If thou knewest [Gk. = to know by reflection] the gift of God . . . .thou wouldest have asked of Him . . . and He would have given thee " (Jn. iv. 10).

How often we limit Him in His giving ! We either will not ask at all ; or else we ask according to our own wishes, needs, or intellectual conceptions of what must or ought to be. He in His humility never forces Himself upon us. He comes to us *as we want Him* ; and as He knows us to be able to bear His coming. Thus—out of His Heart's love, compassion, and patience of faith for us—does He adapt to our weakness of body, mind, and spirit, His giving to us of His Body. So, at one time we shall be most conscious of, and comforted by, His Perfect Humanity as received through the gift of His Incarnate Body. All our drawing will be to Jesus of Nazareth ; all our strength be derived from the companionship of the adorable Jesus of the Gospels ; and our longing be, as far as possible, to imitate Him in His going about " doing good ". At another time we shall be supremely conscious of the gift of His Body as the gift of

His Risen Body : the seed of Love's victoriousness over sin and death implanted within the very soul as its own essential and expanding life.

Yet again, even more comforting than the comfort of the human Jesus " tempted at all points *like as we* are, yet without sin "—which comfort it was fully, and for long, believed no other comfort could ever equal, let alone excel—comes the sudden all-surpassing comfort of the OTHERNESS of God in some way consciously apprehended within and through the Mystical Body : an Otherness in which we are lost and found, both individually and corporately, in the oneing of all souls in the Holy, Blessed, and Glorious Trinity. In the gift of His Incarnate Body we have Christ alongside : the Divine ' without '. In the gift of His Risen Body we have Christ indwelling : the Divine ' within '. In the Otherness of His Mystical Body we have both ' the without ' and ' the within ', inextricably one : an all-engulfing, all-pervasive emanation of love : the ebb and flow of the Tide of Uncreate Love.

Whilst *in essence* there is no " problem of Reunion ", since Christ is not—and never can be—divided, yet in human thought and feeling the surface-divisions between the Churches do constitute a bitter problem. These divisions are a veritable sword-pierce to innumerable Christians in all denominations, and a seemingly insurmountable stumbling-block to thousands both within and ' without ' the Church. All down the ages this problem has been thought and talked about. There has been much would-be constructive discussion, and even more negative criticism : discussion and criticism arising both in and out of the Churches. But all this human thought and talk has for the most part been either defeatist or erroneous. Many conclude that these divisions are insoluble, and inevitable so long as time shall last ; and others believe that some human solvent must exist if only it could be lighted upon : yet neither is true.

Surely we all need to pause, " lest haply " in our efforts

towards Reunion we " be found to fight against God ". It is
God and not Man to whom we must listen in this matter ;
and listening, surely we shall have borne in upon us with a
burning conviction of truth His : " For My thoughts are not
your thoughts, neither are your ways My ways, saith the
Lord. For as the heavens are higher than the earth, so are
My ways higher than your ways, and My thoughts than your
thoughts " [Septuagint : " . . . But as the heaven is
distant from the earth, so is My way distant from your ways,
and your thoughts from My mind "] (Is. lv. 8 f.).

Is not this the crux : that our thought of unity differs
from God's ? However we may profess not to, at bottom
we all tend to confound unity with uniformity—or at least
to desire others to " come into line " with our own conceptions and tastes—forgetting that " diversity " is of the
essence of the gifts, administrations, and operations of the
Holy Spirit incarnate in the Mystical Body [see 1 Cor. xii.
passim], and that it is designedly so, and because diversity
is a root-principle in the economy of God, a necessary
property of the Divine Nature.

Striving for uniformity we are striving for the impossible ;
we are striving for the undesirable ; and we are, moreover,
striving dead against that for which we were created in the
image of God. Uncreate Love is ever the same *in essence*,
and yet, of necessity, requires infinity of form for the expression of infinity of perfection. To this all creation bears
witness. There is no reduplication of souls ; neither are any
two animals, trees, or flowers, even of the same species,
identical. Each of Love's myriad creations is unique and
without repetition, for infinite variety alone can reflect and
express Love's inexhaustible Beauty and energy ; but the
perfection of these myriad creations is only fully manifest in
the high relief into which each is thrown by its relatedness to
all the rest. This applies equally in Nature and in humanity ;
in sunrise combinations and contrasts of ever-varying lights
and darkness ; or in the interplay of diverse temperaments
and mentalities.

Difference, in the sense of variation, can never be eliminated, because variety is not only intrinsic to creation but integral to the purpose of God, else would it not exist. Each innate differentiation of form, whether in form of matter, mind, or spirit, is a differentiation Divinely directed towards a differentiation of function in the individual to combine and harmonise with all else in the universe for the perfection of Love's functioning as a whole. Differences between the Churches are to be deplored in so far as they are differences in the sense of antagonisms and antipathies.

But variety in the Churches, rightly understood in relation to God and His purpose, and in relation to the true Nature and Office of the Mystical Body, is essentially matter for rejoicing : a potential medium for a fuller revelation of Christ to the world than could ever be possible without it. Truly to realise this Divinely designed differentiation of function within Love's essential oneness is to receive Divine healing of the aching sense of division at human level, with its sometimes almost tortured longing—analogous to homesickness—for all the Churches consciously and visibly to be oned. " If the foot shall say, Because I am not the hand, I am not of the body : is it therefore not of the body ? And if the ear shall say, Because I am not the eye, I am not of the body ; is it therefore not of the body ? If the whole body were an eye, where were the hearing ? If the whole were hearing, where were the smelling ? But now hath God set the members every one of them in the body, as it hath pleased Him. And if they were all one member, where were the body ? But *now* are they many members, yet but one body " (1 Cor. xii. 15 ff.).

The life of the Mystical Body in time is one in essence— though differing in form and expression—with the life of the Mystical Body in eternity. It is the ceaseless, unquenchable, and indestructible life whose Source and Goal is God Himself : a love-life consciously deriving from, and ever tending towards, the Father, and motivated throughout by Jesus' eternal " knowing that the Father had given all things

into His hands, and that He came forth from God, and goeth
unto God " (Jn. xiii. 3).   The life of the Mystical Body in
time blent with the life of the Mystical Body in eternity is
the sole plenary revelation, expression, and consummation
of Jesus as Perfect God and Perfect Man.   It is, moreover,
the response of His whole Being, in absolute and exhaustive
singleness of will, to the Unitive Will of the Father in
Creation : the means whereby He is ever satisfying to the
uttermost—both in Himself and in all souls given Him by the
Father—that Divine necessity of Uncreate Love to beget
Love *ad infinitum.*

The Divinely designed function of the Mystical Body here
upon earth and in time is " the extension of the Incarnation " ; and this extension is more than a copy of " the days
of His flesh ".   It is more even than that true " extension of
the Incarnation " by priestly consecration of the elements
of bread and wine in the Blessed Sacrament, and their
reception by " the faithful " (i.e. sinners consciously drawn
to Jesus) ; being nothing less than an ever-fresh perpetuation of the eternal truth that " in Him dwelleth all the fulness of the Godhead bodily ".   So ravishingly beautiful and
full of wonder is this vocation that its potential glory is
literally inexhaustible.

This " extension of the Incarnation " in the Mystical Body
upon earth includes the continuation of the fulfilment of the
purposes of the Incarnation—i.e. the true revelation of God
and Man in Christ Jesus, and the Father's reconciliation of
men to Himself in Jesus Saviour from sin, Quickener of
Holiness—and the perpetuation of the prayer and activities
of the Incarnate Jesus.   It necessarily involves, and is only
realised in and through, reproduction of all the Mysteries of
the Incarnate Life both in the souls of individual members of
the Body, and corporately in the Body as a whole : such
reproduction being always reproduction by identification—
love's would-bè identification with Love.   Plenarily to
perpetuate the prayer and activities of Jesus must mean
infinitely more than our finite minds can ever comprehend in

time, but this much at least it certainly means : in each soul separately, and in all souls conjointly, must eventually be mystically re-enacted Jesus' unceasing "Fiat" to the Father's Will ; His Birth ; His spirit's preparation in hiddenness, obedience, meditation, worship, and labour ; the Baptism of the Spirit ; temptation ; sacrificial ministry to Man ; the transfiguration of the natural into the supernatural ; rejection ; betrayal ; Agony ; Passion and Death ; Resurrection, and Ascension to the Father.

The individual soul, and the Church alike, must be stripped and die to self that the life of the Sinless Jesus—sinless not through absence of temptation, but by Love's overcoming of it—may rise in the Mystical Body, as sap in the tree, vigorous and abundant. " Once, only once, and once for all ", the Incarnate Jesus died and rose on behalf of all humanity ; but in His Mystical Body He perpetuates this Death and Resurrection throughout time. There is no second of time in which there is not some soul in identification with Him undergoing that mystic annihilation of self following upon agony and stripping. Likewise there is no second of time in which there is not some soul in identification with Him mystically rising out of that seemingly final extinction of self-annihilation into the life that is hidden with Christ in God, the life in which all things are new, and in which Love surmounts all barriers.

So with the Church in her individual members : at one time it is mystic death in one specific Church or sect, at another time mystic resurrection in another ; and all in identification with Jesus, with vital connection between the mystic death in one soul or member, and the mystic resurrection in another. To the soul in mystic process of crucifixion it seems as though all is irretrievably lost ; but for all that, the life of the Body is indestructible, and continues, not only irrespective of the soul's own consciousness or lack of consciousness of it in herself or elsewhere, but actually augmented by this very death of hers. To the soul mystically risen in Christ, and abounding in His life, that life wells up in her not as hers, but back to Him as His for whomsoever He will, and thus again is augmented the life of the whole Body. Whether by death or by life, all issues in Life in Jesus, and in Life ever more and more abundant.

Infinite are the prayers and activities of the Incarnate Jesus, because those of the Infinite Word of Love : the prayer and activities of One in Whom self was continually annihilated that God might be in Man and Man in God to the heart's content of both. The vocation plenarily to per-petuate this prayer and these activities, what else does it mean ? The perpetuation of all the FULNESS of the prayer of Jesus of Nazareth ; the perpetuation of that unbroken, and limitlessly redemptive, energising of love, patience, courtesy, compassion, and illumination—energising never dissipated or suspended by self—which was the essence of all His activities, however varied their form. " Who is suffi-cient for these things ? " Who indeed ! No single person, no single group of people, no single sect or Church. It needs the whole vast Communion of Saints, the " great multitude . . . of all nations, and kindreds, and peoples, and tongues ", inspired and infilled, reclaimed from sin, sanctified and re-deemed, by the Holy Spirit to perceive and reflect—each soul perceiving and reflecting only a minute, but unique fragment of the whole—the sum of all that was included in the prayer and activity of Jesus of Nazareth.

It could not be other than that myriad upon myriad of souls are needed to perpetuate the FULNESS of Jesus' prayer, to perpetuate it in its vocal and corporate aspect and in all its interior methods (see pp. 44 ff.), each single one of which is infinite in content and potentiality ; and to perpetuate all those as spiritually infinite pastoral, healing, and teaching, activities comprised in His incarnate high-priestly ministry.

This perpetuation of Jesus' incarnate prayer and activity is both a matter of limitless detail in individual souls, and a corporate harmony in the Communion of Saints as a whole. It is something co-extensive with all life : so immense that it defies any reduction to words, or ordered sequence, let alone exhaustiveness, since it involves the history of all souls in all nations ; the secret and public prayer of all souls and all Churches ; every atom of every work whatsoever—be it domestic, social, philanthropic, political, educational, medical, surgical, industrial, commercial, artistic, literary, or what it may—ever undertaken for the common weal. It is all part of " the glory that shall be revealed in us " hereafter : glory no book can begin truly to chronicle save that one which shall contain and unfold it in its entirety—the Lamb's Book of Life. Yet though we cannot yet apprehend this " exceeding and eternal weight of glory ", it is given us even on earth to experience the " earnest of our inheritance " in the Communion of Saints incorporate in the Mystical Body of Christ.

Each article of the Creed should for the professing Christian be a governing truth, as determinant of his whole manner of life as those material axioms upon which he so unquestioningly stakes as consistently to regulate his action. Conduct should be at least as potently influenced by each and all of the truths set forth in the Creed as by knowledge that man must eat to live ; that money is indispensable for food and clothing ; or that fire burns. But how far is this the case ? Is the profession to " believe in . . . the Communion of Saints " merely lip-assent unbacked by any clear thought or experimental knowledge of what is involved ; or is it the joyous, thankful witness of the whole being to something which permeates daily life at all points as an intensely practical factor decisively influencing choice of action ?

The Communion of Saints : surely this is " a joyful mystery " if ever there was one ! It is the Fellowship not of souls born naturally good or holy without effort—for no such have ever existed, even the holiness of Jesus had to be achieved through moral struggle—but the Fellowship of sinners, who have so genuinely fallen in love with Jesus that they have set and kept themselves to endure the whole self-crucifying process of His reclamation of them from just

such sins as ours to holiness such as His own ; sinners who
have refused to allow any self-despair, cowardice, temptation, bewilderment, suffering of body, mind, or spirit, to
prevent His gradually and progressively obtaining His
perfect way with them. The Communion of Saints is the
Fellowship of those who—undeterred by the cumulative
attack of the world, the flesh, and the devil both from
without and within—have set themselves to become par-
takers of the life of Jesus, and fellow-workers with Him
in His Holy Spirit's fulfilling of the Father's Will.

The Saints are the mirror and flowering of " the unsearchable riches of Christ " ; each perceiving and reflecting a
different, and unique, aspect of His infinite Personality.
The Christ of St. Peter ; the Christ of St. John ; the Christ
of St. Paul : it is one and the same Christ ; and yet how
vastly different their perception of Him ! But for all their
difference these perceptions are complementary and not
contradictory.   Here on earth we can each at best apprehend
only an infinitesimal fragment of His Infinity ; but in
eternity, when words cease to obscure vision, surely souls
will luminously interchange personal perceptions of Him,
each perception being supplemented by all the rest into an
ever-extending individual and corporate knowledge of Him
in all His " fulness ".   What thrilling, endless joy when
each soul comes to know the Christ of, and in, all other
souls !

It is the Communion of Saints which is the Mystical
Body's rounded extension of the Incarnation : an extension
begun in time and perpetuated and consummated in eternity.
" The Word was made flesh and dwelt among us, and we
beheld His glory, the glory as of the Only Begotten of the
Father, full of grace and truth " (Jn. i. 14) : as in Jesus of
Nazareth in unique and plenary degree, so again in lesser
degree in each and all the Saints " the Word . . . made
flesh " so dwells in our midst as to reveal something of the
glory of the Father's *Alter Ego*. Jesus of Nazareth *was*
Perfect Man ; but by the very nature of the Incarnation,

with its inherent limitation, His revelation of Himself as such, though infinite in its suggestiveness, was not—and could not be—exhaustive in detailed expression.   Prolonged steeping in the Gospels confirms them as the "treatise [Gk. = narrative] . . . of all that Jesus *began* both to do and teach . . . " (Acts i. 1), as there follows upon intimate familiarity with their episodic detail the Holy Spirit's drawing to what He has written "between the lines ", His drawing from the outward to the inward, from happening to being, and His revelation that each of our Lord's words, actions, and activities, though fully perfect in itself, is in no way exhaustive, being but a ' squint ' opening upon vista upon vista of a Personality Whose depths can never be plumbed.

The Gospels etch in our Lord as countryman, and carpenter, and son in the home ; as healer, teacher, prophet, poet, servant—and " *Suffering* Servant "—in the midst, they portray Him far more fully ; and fullest of all, though without any specific ascription of the title, as priest in worship, sacrifice, and ministry.   Yet not even as healer, teacher, prophet, poet, servant, sufferer, or priest, was He exhaustively Self-expressed "in the days of His flesh ",when, though He poured Himself out to the full, there none the less remained in Him profundities of prayer, priestliness, self-immolating love, prophetic truth, and healing effluence, which could find no expression without violating the essential limitations to which His "Fiat" for the Incarnation pledged Him.   It is all these profundities—as well as " that which is lacking of the afflictions of Christ " (Col. i. 24)—which the Communion of Saints has to " fill up " ; and as it does so there emerges a literally never-ending revelation of Jesus extending beyond even the revelation of " the days of His flesh ", and the record of Gospels and Epistles, but all of a-piece with them.

Each of the Saints reveals—and affords expression for—some essential spark of Jesus' innermost Being never before revealed or expressed.   The Communion of Saints is the Holy Spirit's continuation of all that Jesus began, and

might in a true and fitting sense be called " The Last
Gospel ". What a vocation, both glorious and dread ! Each
priest called to reveal and express some spark of Jesus'
priestliness never before revealed or expressed : the glory if
he does so—the inestimable tragedy and loss if he fails.
Each healer—whether doctor, surgeon, nurse, or " spiritual
healer "—called to reveal and express some spark of Jesus
the Healer. Each teacher—parents surely specially so—
called to reveal and express some spark of Jesus the Teacher.
All souls in some measure called to reveal and express the
Praying Jesus, whether in hidden or public worship, meditation, contemplation, thanksgiving, ecstasy, dryness, darkness, joy, sorrow, suffering, temptation, interior martyrdom,
intercession, or otherhow. All souls called to reveal and
express His daily self-denial for love of God and man.

In the Communion of Saints we truly " behold, the
Man ! " To take every opportunity to try to get to know
the Saints—as many, and as well, as possible—is to widen
and deepen and heighten our knowledge of Jesus, as we are
drawn clean through them, to Him not only in them but as
He is in Himself. They may be Saints still on earth with
whom we are privileged to come into personal contact ; or
they may be Saints throughout the whole gamut of time and
space whom we come to know only through books about them
—but what a knowing it can be, often more intimate and
precious by far than friendships made " in the flesh ".

Sometimes there are God-given *attraits* when, with a
supernatural intensity and unabating persistence, the soul
is drawn to some special Saint or Saints for purposes of His
own. This attraction may possibly be felt to Saints of
utterly divergent temperaments, widely separated in time
and circumstance, yet having for the individual soul that
spark of Jesus which He knows her to need for growth in her
vocation in Him. The soul is always helped in an intensely
practical way by the Saints for whom such an *attrait* is felt.
It may be at one time by the inspiration of their life and
example ; at another time by the remembrance of some

word or teaching of theirs ; time and again by their prayer ; sometimes perhaps even by a supernaturally stilling sense of their actual, though invisible, presence withholding the soul from yielding in time of temptation, or enabling her to seal for love of Him some sacrifice or self-oblation.

" And the multitude of them that believed were of one heart and of one soul : neither said any of them that ought of the things which he possessed was his own ; but they had all things common.   And with great power gave the apostles witness of the Resurrection of the Lord Jesus : and great grace was upon them all . . . and distribution was made unto every man according as he had need " (Acts iv. 32 ff.) : this record of the life of the Christian Church in her infancy is none the less true a spiritual record of the ever-maturing life of the Communion of Saints.   The Communion of Saints is itself the enduring witness of the reality of Jesus' Resurrection, and—to an extent for the most part insufficiently realised—truly a common life in which distribution is made according to the need of each.   It is the life with common Source and Goal : the unitive life of Triune Love.   It is the life with common Way : the coming after, and in, Jesus— by daily self-denial and taking up the cross—to where He is in the bosom of the Father.   It is the life of common experience : the life of sinners experiencing, at self-crucifying cost, redemption in the blood of the Lamb, i.e. being drawn into union with the " laid down " life of Jesus " taken again " for all eternity.   It is a life of common entry through suffering into glory ; and a life of common offering for love of God and Man—a life in which all rise or fall together.

It is the common storehouse of all the atoning merits, and would-be redemptive yearnings, of Jesus Christ available for application in all their totality for each and every sinner desirous of turning to Him in need.   It is the life of common resistance to temptation, and common abandonment to Holiness : the common yet infinitely diverse life of love in and for Love.   It is the common life of Church Militant and Church Triumphant : the life of Jesus one, indivisible, and

almost it may be said interchangeable—the life of the Church
Militant being not without its earnest of triumph in Christ,
and the unitive life of the Church Triumphant an infinitely
more potent factor in the warfare of the Church Militant
than all her own none the less indispensable efforts.

The practical import of this common life of the Saints is
incalculable for each individual soul in the Church Militant,
when the fight seems often so lonely an affair in face of
oppressive sense of the powers that be against her. The
Communion of Saints, with its " so great a cloud of witnesses " (Heb. xii. 1) both in the Church Triumphant and in
the Church Militant of our own as of every previous day, not
only substantiates the truth that " they that be with us are
more than they that be with them " [i.e. the enemy] (2 Kings
vi. 16), but makes of that " with us " far more than mere
companioning in the fight, makes of it an actual identification because " the love of Christ constraineth ". The life of
the Communion of Saints is not only alongside every single
soul, but actually at her disposal for appropriation as her
own whensoever she may choose.

The temptation and suffering of each Christian soul are,
then, not so much her own raw material which she may try,
or fail, to offer to Christ as love, but HIS raw material
through which to achieve afresh the victory of His love—
invincible alike before temptation, sin, suffering, and death
—not only in her, but also to the quickening and enriching
of the whole life of the Communion of Saints incorporate in
His Mystical Body. Never can the temptation or suffering
of the individual be spiritually isolated, however exteriorly
or even interiorly alone she may seem to be. " And
whether one member suffer, all the members suffer with it ;
or one member be honoured [Gk. = glorified], all the
members rejoice with it " (1 Cor. xii. 26) : the togetherness
not only in suffering, but also in opportunity for the extension and perpetuation of the victory of the Glorified Christ,
Whom it " behoved . . . to suffer . . . and to enter into
His glory " (Lk. xxiv. 26).

The Saints are those who refuse to allow their own temptations or sufferings to defraud Jesus of His victory in them ;
but more than this, they are those who equally refuse—so far
as ever it is in the power of their sacrificial union with Him—
to acquiesce in the defeat of any other soul in her temptation
or suffering.   Theirs is that pure love of Christ which not
only enables Him to sanctify them, but also braces other
souls—infinitely more costly even than bracing themselves—
to will to endure to the end that process of self-crucifixion
which alone can give birth to " the glorious liberty of the
children of God " (Rom. viii. 21).   The Communion of
Saints is the age-long " filling up " of the heroic love of
Christ for souls—that love which first immolates itself for
sinners, and then ceaselessly woos them to accept their
redemption in Him—a " filling up " to which our own cen-
tury has contributed, and is contributing, as gloriously
as any.

The Communion of Saints is the Fellowship of Souls individually spiritually wed to Christ : the earnest of the
" Marriage of the Lamb " in which Humanity is wed to
Deity.   Such a Mystery as the Marriage of the Lamb could
only have originated in the Mind of God, in the furnace of
Uncreate Love, for no human brain could ever have conceived so transcendent a prodigality of Love.   Such a
stooping of such a King of Kings to so soiled and ragged a
beggarmaid as Fallen Humanity would be humanly incredible, were it not that the revelation of its eternal reality is
vouchsafed us by Jesus, Who is the Truth, and by His Spirit
Whom He promised should lead us into all truth.

The Incarnate Jesus virtually declared Himself as Bridegroom early in His public ministry (Mk. ii. 19) ; and His
parables of the Great Supper (Lk. xiv. 16 ff.) and of the
Marriage of the King's Son (Matt. xxii. 1 ff.) delivered
towards the close of it were His Bridegroom's proposal to
His Bride—although this has been most tragically obscured
by later additions due to misunderstanding of our Lord's
teaching by Jewish minds soaked in, and prejudiced by,

apocalyptic ideas. (It is impossible in this connection to overstress the value of Percy Dearmer's *The Legend of Hell* throughout.)

Jesus' stress was upon the all-embracing extension of the invitation to the Marriage-Feast, and upon the fact—so won'drous when pondered—that " all things are now ready ", because divinely " prepared ", for it. But this stressing by Jesus of the exultant " good news " of the now ready Marriage-Feast is somewhat eclipsed in the parables as they now stand by the further stress laid upon the terrible idea of exclusion from it *from the Godward-side*. But it is precisely this exclusion from the Godward-side which is accretion, and not His Who has disclosed Himself as the Good Shepherd Who will " go after that which is lost *until he find it* " (Lk. xv. 4). Jesus certainly stressed instances of Man's self-exclusion from this Marriage-Feast, yet surely it was just on this account that He gave the parable of the Two Sons (Matt. xxi. 28 ff.) to show that a son's " I will not " to his Father's bidding is *not final*, for " afterward he repented [Gk. = also to rue, regret, to change one's purpose or line of conduct] and went."

Both the parables of the Marriage of the King's Son, and of the Great Supper, bear stress, which is Jesus', that it is for God's sake altogether apart from Man's that there can be no absenteeism from the Marriage-Feast, which cannot proceed while " yet there is room " [Gk. = " a portion of space in reference to its occupancy or as appointed to a thing "]. Not until the King's universal invitation has been accepted by each and every soul, not until the Father's House is filled completely, can the Feast proceed ; for only then, and never until then, has the Bride affianced herself *in the totality of her being* to her Bridegroom in the totality of His. Only when the Bride is as wholly and unreservedly given to her Bridegroom as He to her can there be consummated, in the absolute satiety of an eternal insatiety, the perfect Love-begotten love-begetting interchange of Love with love.

The preparation for the Marriage of the Lamb is itself a

23

wondrous and glorious twofold Mystery : both unutterably humbling and exhilarating in the well-nigh overwhelming Generosity of God, which crowns itself by giving us opportunity to meet Generosity with generosity if we will. It is the twofold Mystery merging in one " the help that is done upon earth He doeth it Himself " with that truth revealed by the Holy Spirit to the Seer of " Revelation " in his vision of the Church Triumphant: " his wife hath made herself ready. And it was given unto her that she should array herself in fine linen, bright and pure : for the fine linen is the righteous acts of the saints " (Rev. xix. 7–8).

" All things are now ready " for the Marriage-Feast because Jesus, by the mutual Will of Father and Son, has in His Incarnation come as Divine Lover to woo His Beloved. Jesus' incarnate self-immolation in love and penitence has made possible the otherwise impossible. He has thus enabled the soiled and ragged Beggarmaid of Fallen Humanity to respond to His love in purity—His purity—and to be raised by, and in, Him to that affinity of spirit essential to true marriage. The fundamental preparation for the Marriage is entirely His ; but by giving to every individual soul the opportunity to act in and for love if and when she will, He has—in the Communion of Saints—put it within the power of His Bride and Wife-to-be to add to her preparedness by ' making herself ready ' in the practice of love.

This ' making ready ', although a twofold Mystery, is also unitive. It is unitive in the Person of the Lamb, Who Himself both woos as God, and Himself responds as Man. It is unitive also in that we are " labourers together with God " (1 Cor. iii. 9) : by love growing up into Him as the stalagmite imperceptibly grows into one complete column with the pendent stalactite, from whose slow, but steady, dripping from far above it, it has its sole origin and growth. Jesus—and His sanctification of His Bride—is the sole foundation for the Marriage of the Lamb : but " if any man build upon this foundation gold, silver, precious stones, wood, hay, stubble ; every man's work shall be made manifest : for the day shall declare it, because it shall be revealed by fire ; and the fire shall try every man's work of what sort it is. If any man's work abide which he hath built thereupon, he shall receive a reward. If any man's work shall be burned, he shall suffer loss : but he himself shall be saved ; yet so as by fire " (1 Cor. iii. 12 ff.).

The Marriage-Feast is the Furnace of Love which will declare the works of all souls. How will all lost opportunities of love then fire the soul with aching contrition ! Happy indeed those souls who then have some abiding gift —how trifling at best in comparison with His gifts—some love-offering to bring to the Bridegroom from Whom *all* has been, and ever will be, received.

When questioned by the disciples of John and of the Pharisees as to why His disciples fasted not, Jesus replied : " Can the children of the bride-chamber fast, while the bridegroom is with them ? as long as they have the bridegroom with them they cannot fast. But the days will come, when the bridegroom shall be taken away from them, and then shall they fast in those days " (Mk. ii. 19–20). Then on the very eve of that ' taking away ' He explained to His disciples . " I go to prepare a place for you. And if I go and prepare a place for you, I will come again, and receive you unto Myself ; that where I am, there ye may be also . . . I will not leave you comfortless : I will come to you . . . I go away and come again unto you " (Jn. xiv. 2 ff.)—His Coming Again : the Return of the Bridegroom to receive to Himself His Bride. Very shortly before this our Lord had also given them other teaching concerning His Coming Again (Mk. xiii. 1 ff. ; Matt. xxiv. 1 ff. ; Lk. xxi. 5 ff.). Since He always presented truth in terms familiar to His hearers' own innate habit of thought, He clothed this teaching in the current apocalyptic imagery then influencing— both intensively and extensively—all Jewish thought and expectation.

So literal and materialistic, however, was the disciples' interpretation of the apocalyptic imagery employed by our

Lord, that it led eventually to the essence of His teaching about the Second Coming being most disastrously overlaid and confused in the Gospels, owing to the interpolation of further apocalyptic elements now generally accepted as not originally deriving from our Lord Himself at all. The disaster lies in the human shifting of emphasis from where it was laid by our Lord, to other elements which He recognised as necessarily involved in, but not constituting the essence of, a Mystery as dynamic, far-reaching, and many-sided as the Mystery of the Second Coming.

Our Lord's emphasis was upon the renewed Presence of the Bridegroom as the essence of His Coming Again [παρουσία = both " an advent ", and " presence ", an unveiling of a presence] : the Bridegroom come again to woo His Bride until He gain her entirely. The human emphasis has tended to be infinitely more upon the *how* and the *when* of the Return, rather than upon the Person, Nature, and Purpose of the One returning. The Divine interpretation of this Glorious Event is an interpretation in terms of Love eternally Victorious. The human misinterpretation is one in terms of FEAR (the antithesis of Love), and time (which has no real existence in Eternity : a misinterpretation— whose danger can never be overestimated, least of all in a time as disturbed as our own—tending to fix the mind upon human terrors, rather than upon the Bridegroom Deliverer. It may be true that it is darkest just before the dawn ; but for all that the darkness is not the dawn, but dawn the displacement of the darkness by light.

There is to-day a very widespread feeling that we are on the verge of " the end of the world ". It is nothing new. Twenty years ago towns were placarded with flaming posters : " Millions now living will never die ". This sense, which was at its most practically expectant with the Apostles and in the Infant Church, has recurred persistently all down the ages ; and usually most strongly precisely with the most spiritually minded to whom the Other World is more real than this, and who—living much in Eternity already—

tend to telescope time. No age is altogether exempt from outstanding horrors ; and these horrors always seem to it out of all proportion worse than those of any previous age. So it is that each age tends to interpret its own horrors as the cataclysm apocalyptically believed to be the inevitable prelude to the end of the world at our Lord's Second Coming ; and so it is that there is among us to-day such a preoccupation with world events *as a " sign " of the end.*

But in the light of two indisputably authentic sayings of our Lord's, this preoccupation is both futile and misplaced. To the disciples He said : " But of that day and that hour knoweth no man, no, not the angels which are in heaven, neither the Son, but the Father " (Mk. xiii. 32) ; and also " It is not for you to know the times or the seasons, which the Father hath put in His own power " (Acts i. 7)—and this still applies equally to-day. It is enough for us to know that in His own time, which He has of set purpose hidden from us, Love will come wholly into His own.

The cataclysmic element in His Coming Again was definitely, and deliberately, introduced by our Lord in foretelling to His disciples, as He undoubtedly did, the Fall of Jerusalem, which took place roughly forty years after His death. This element they threw into such high relief as to make it appear almost the whole, which was clean contrary to our Lord's own teaching—emphasising the gradual and continuous in His Coming Again quite as strongly as the cataclysmic—and also clean contrary to all the facts of experience, which abundantly go to prove that cataclysms are never spontaneous, but always the outcome of hidden causes gradually fermenting over a long period. His Coming Again—whether for the individual soul, or for Humanity at large—is a continuous process. As Bridegroom seeking His Bride He came again in His Resurrection and Resurrection appearances ; His Ascension ; and Pentecost ; and so He has continued to come in all the unfolding life of the Church ; in the Communion of Saints ; in each and all the crises of history ; in each and every event—joyous or tragic—of

each and every individual human life ; and not less in stillness, and apparent uneventfulness. Alike through all that
happens, and through all that does not happen, He woos
unbrokenly. Even through the very storms, tragedies, and
horrors we bring upon ourselves He ceases not to woo us,
breathing through our shattered complacency and self-
sufficiency His " Come ".

His Coming Again is always, and rightly so, connected
with judgment ; but here again human emphasis—in tending towards fear rather than Love—has differed from His.
Judgment is, for many, synonymous only with condemnation and punishment ; and His Coming Again " to judge "
associated with a dread Day of Judgment, following upon
the end of the world, in which He will search exhaustively in
every soul for that which is culpable. But Jesus openly
declared : " I judge no man " (Jn. viii. 15) " . . . for I came
not to judge the world, but to save the world " (Jn. xii. 47).
He totally repudiated the rôle of Criminal Referee ; yet
elsewhere He as explicitly declared that " the Father hath
committed all judgment unto the Son " (Jn. v. 22) ; and on
Palm Sunday proclaimed : " Now is the judgment of this
world . . ." (Jn. xii. 31).

God the Father has chosen to repose all destiny in His
Son : and every moment of time—since time is " the valley
of decision "—is the judgment of this world, and of the
individual soul, not in external condemnation, but in self-
chosen relationship to Him Who is Love. His continuous
Coming Again is a continuous judgment, in its fundamental
sense of ' crisis ' : the point or time for deciding anything ;
the decisive moment or turning-point. Every moment,
with its fresh coming of the Bridegroom forces upon us,
consciously or unconsciously, whether we will or no, the
inevitable choice, sometimes clearly defined, sometimes
subtly confused : " Whether of the twain will ye that I
release . . . ? "—self or Christ ? This choice may, and
will, present itself in myriad different guises, but basically
it is always the same : an inescapable choice between selfish-

ness and Love.   As we make choice on occasion, so we come
to choose habitually ;   and this habitual choice is the self-
appointed, and only, " judgment " determining our eternal
relation with Love, with Son, with Father, with Holy Spirit,
and with all souls incorporate in the Mystical Body of
Christ.

   " Behold, He cometh . . . and every eye shall see Him "
(Rev. i. 7) ; this is the climax of His Coming Again : a final
unveiling of Himself so that recognition of Him becomes
universal, and each and every soul without exception knows
Him at last as Saviour, Lover, Bridegroom, Perfect Man,
and Very God of Very God.   How greatly is this Coming
Again to be desired, and prayed for with heartfelt urgency
of love !   He Himself promised :   " I will see [Gk. =
visit] you again, and your heart shall rejoice, and your
joy no man taketh from you.   And in that day ye shall ask
[Gk. = question] Me nothing " (Jn. xvi. 22 f.).   His Final
Coming will bring to all souls the unveiling of—

> The Light that is Life ;
> The Life that is Light ;

the unveiling which leaves nothing more to question of Him,
let alone of any human being ; because all is known—seen
and understood—with the Mind of Christ, and accepted in
adoration and thankfulness as Love's transcendent Mystery
of Beauty and Joy for all eternity.   " Till we all come
[Gk. = reach one's destination] in the unity [Gk. = unanim-
ity, state of being of one mind, agreeing in will, done with
the agreement of all] of the faith, and of the knowledge
[Gk. = acquaintance, discernment, recognition] of the Son
of God, unto a perfect [Gk. = full grown, mature, complete,
having reached its utmost development] man, unto the
measure of the stature of the fulness of Christ " (Eph. iv. 13),
there must needs remain mysteries of suffering and darkness
which are beyond human unravelling, save as safe in His
keeping and certain of ultimate solution in Himself.   But
in that day of Eternity, that day of His Final Coming, when

we have all come to possess, and be possessed by, the **Mind of Him** Who is " the Head of the body, the Church " (Col. i. 18), then—in this single consciousness embracing all—all will be stilled and resolved in Love's perfect and eternal satisfaction.

The Coming Again of Jesus is in process now, and even now tending—and tending rapidly—towards this eternal consummation of Love : " And the Spirit and the bride say, Come.   And let him that heareth say, Come . . . Surely I come   quickly.   Amen.   Even   so,   come,   Lord   Jesus " (Rev. xxii. 17 ff.).

VERY GOD OF VERY GOD

VERY GOD OF VERY GOD

" NOW on the last day, the great day of the Feast [of
Tabernacles], Jesus stood and cried, saying, If any
man thirst, let him come unto Me, and drink. He that
believeth on Me, as the Scripture hath said, out of his belly
shall flow rivers of living water " (Jn. vii. 37 f.) ; and
hearing this, the officers sent by the Pharisees and Chief
Priests to arrest Him found themselves morally incapable of
carrying out their orders. Such was their awe that they
dared not lay hands upon this Nazarene teacher even at the
instance of " the Masters in Israel ". Questioned as to their
failure to bring Him, they replied simply and solely :
" Never man so spake " [A.V. " Never man spake like this
man "] (Jn. vii. 47). Their contact with Him had been
merely in the course of duty : a ' case ' to be dealt with in
temple police routine. Yet coming to Him wholly unbiased in His favour, they were irresistibly impressed by
some unique power, altogether beyond anything in their
whole life's experience, which left them convinced not merely
that no man ever had spoken as this One, but that One Who
so spoke must be, and was, more than Man.

To read the Gospels dispassionately, and to ponder them
merely as the story of a Palestinian Carpenter-Teacher of
two thousand years ago, must—if persevered in—lead to
precisely the same conviction that " Never man so spake ".
Honest, persistent, and prayerful study of the Gospels must
ultimately convince any and all who are open-minded that
this Man of Nazareth Whom they portray was also more
than Man. This something more than human in the
gloriously, comfortingly human Jesus of the Gospels is to be
found in :

(1) Their revelation of the interchange of function, in
relation to Man between Father, Son, and Holy Spirit.

(2) Their irresistible convincingness of the truth of Jesus' " I am the truth ", bearing within it His own witness to His Divinity.

(3) Their objective witness.

(4) Their subjective proofs.

The only way in which personality can ever be defined is in terms of function or effect. *Within the Godhead* the distinctive functions of each Person of the Blessed Trinity remain absolutely and eternally uninterchangeable : the Father alone begetting ; the Son alone begotten ; the Holy Spirit alone proceeding from Begetter and Begotten—the Begetting, Begottenness, and Procession, one entity single and indivisible : Uncreate Love. Without the Godhead, and in relation to Man, the distinctive functions of Creation, Redemption, and Sanctification, attach respectively to Father, Son, and Holy Spirit. But the Jesus of the Gospels is revealed, not only as the Lamb of God, Redeemer of the World, but also as Logos (" All things were made by Him ; and without Him was not anything made that was made " : Jn. i. 3), and Sanctifier (Jn. xvii. 19).

The Gospels likewise assign to Jesus the function of the Father and of the Holy Spirit to communicate to Man life inexhaustible and eternal. Function being but the outcome and expression of essential being and personality, this complete interchangeableness of function between Jesus, the Father, and the Holy Spirit, of necessity argues the absolute identity of Jesus' essential being and personality with that of the Divine Father and Holy Spirit. Such identity of Being and Personality between Jesus, the Father, and the Holy Spirit, means nothing less than that the sum total of Jesus' personality is not limited to that which is expressed in His Incarnate, Risen, and Ascended life ; His High Priesthood exercised " within the heavenly sanctuary " ; and in the Mystical Body and Communion of Saints ; but incorporates also that of the Father, and of the Holy Spirit, in Their entirety. So does Jesus embrace *in His Own Person* " the complete fulness " and infinity of the Godhead.

" Never man so spake " as spoke the Jesus of the Gospels. Such an one must either have been blasphemer, fanatic, madman, or else what He claimed to be—the Truth. No other alternative is open. On moral and intellectual grounds alone, it becomes utterly impossible, after honest study of the Gospels, to do other than reject *in toto* all idea of blasphemy, fanaticism, delusion, or insanity, in connection with One so essentially humble, so consistently sane, so heroically and creatively unselfish, as was Jesus of Nazareth.

His words by their supernatural beauty and wonder may cause us to stumble—" with men it is impossible "—and by their demandingness still more " offend " us. But beneath and beyond stumbling and offence, these same words ring irresistibly true to all who in any way genuinely ponder the internal evidence of the Gospels as to the character of Him Who uttered them. The more thoroughly, minutely, critically, the Gospels are investigated, the more incontestable the conviction they leave that Jesus in thought, word, deed, and Being, is Himself the Truth—so incontestable indeed, that plenary credence cannot but be given to *all* His sayings *simply because they are His.*

It is not to be expected that the sayings of Jesus recorded in the Gospels are His actual *ipsissima verba* ; but the same thorough, minute, and critical investigation of the Gospels leaves a likewise incontestable conviction that these sayings, equally—as scholars are more and more becoming agreed and certain—as they are recorded in the Johannine Gospel, as in the Synoptics, are the crystallisation of the true spirit of the *ipsissima verba* which they re-echo : and it is this ' spirit ' rather than the ' letter ' which evokes plenary credence. This applies without exception, even to sayings which if spoken by any other human being needs must be rejected as spurious ; and carries with it the evidential validity of those sayings in which Jesus testifies to, or virtually implies, His own Divinity : " If I bear witness of Myself, My witness is true " (Jn. v. 31).

The Fourth Gospel tells of Jesus as " knowing that the

Father had given all things into His hands, and that He was come from God, and went to God " (Jn. xiii. 3) : here is an evidently authentic echo of some disclosure made by our Lord Himself as to what was His own lifelong, basic interior disposition—conscious oneness with the Father. This oneness He, on another occasion, defined : " I and My Father are one " [Gk. neuter = lit. ' one thing ', i.e. one entity] (Jn. x. 30). As an assertion of His own Divinity nothing *could* be more explicit and categorical. The oneness is oneness of substance, nature, will, and mind : the substance, nature, will, and mind of Jesus one and identical with the Divine Substance, Nature, Will, and Mind of God the Father.

On still another occasion He declared : " Before Abraham was, I am " (Jn. viii. 58)—thereby deliberately and explicitly identifying Himself with God Self-revealed as the eternal I AM (Ex. iii. 14), and referring to that Divine Pre-existent Life of His which He later described in terms of " . . . the glory which I had with Thee " Father " before the world was " (Jn. xvii. 5). None can know the precise degree—let alone nature—of this incarnate recollection of a prior state as Pre-existent Son of God ; but that it must have been intense, if not recurrent, as well as articulate, is evidenced by the fact that in at least two other instances besides these He also made reference to it explicitly or by implication. " What then if ye should behold the Son of Man ascending where He was before ? " (Jn. vi. 62)—" Ye are from beneath ; I am from above : ye are of this world ; I am not of this world " (Jn. viii. 23). Nothing less than this underlying knowledge of His own Divinity could have enabled our Lord, with His infinite reverence for the Temple and all that it stood for—His Father's House which must at all costs be cleansed—to declare of Himself : " But I say unto you, that One greater than the temple is here " (Matt. xii. 6).

The Gospels likewise record a number of other sayings of His which self-knowledge of His own Divinity alone

could have brought to birth and substantiated, e.g. " I am
the resurrection, and the life ; he that believeth on Me,
though he die, yet shall he live . . ." (Jn. xi. 25) ; " Come
unto Me, all ye that labour and are heavy laden, and I will
give you rest " (Matt. xi. 28) ; " . . . he that hath seen Me
hath seen the Father " (Jn. xiv. 9).

The objective witness of the Gospels to the Divinity of our
Lord is particularly striking and forceful, coming, as it did,
from Jew and Gentile alike—both from His intimates
(Peter—Matt. xvi. 16 ; and Thomas—Jn. xx. 28) ; and from
foreigners who, far from being His friends, were merely
under orders to deal with Him as an offender (the temple
officers—Jn. vii. 46 ; and the Centurion—Mk. xv. 39).
Cumulatively this witness to our Lord's Divinity is peculiarly satisfying, since it is based upon its revelation in life,
in death, and in immortality. Men of utterly different
temperaments, beliefs, and traditions were brought either
by His daily life (that most acid of all tests of personality),
His teaching, His reaction to suffering and death, or by His
Resurrection, to the inescapable conviction that Jesus of
Nazareth could be, and was, none other than Son of God,
Himself God. In Peter's confession of faith in Him as Son
of the living God, our Lord not merely acquiesced, but
exulted : " Blessed art thou, Simon Bar-jona : for flesh and
blood hath not revealed it unto thee, but My Father which
is in heaven " (Matt. xvi. 17).

" No man can say that Jesus is the Lord, but by the Holy
Ghost " (1 Cor. xii. 3). This being so, it is probable that the
subjective proofs of the Gospels to the Divinity of our Lord
are as diverse as there are divers souls. Since the Holy
Spirit interprets and illuminates the Gospels to no two souls
in precisely the same way—and kindles in different souls by
altogether different lights the same burning conviction of
the Divinity of Jesus Christ—each soul will be convinced by,
and indeed see, only some fragment of the whole vast unity
of the Gospels' exhaustless subjective proof that He Whom
they portray is God not less than man. Therefore only the

barest suggestiveness in this connection is here possible,
even were it not that it passes within the region of dumb
worship.

"HE IS ALTOGETHER LOVELY" : this is the Gospels'
pæan of Jesus. All prayer-steeping in the Gospels progressively intensifies the soul's knowledge of *how* " altogether lovely " Jesus of Nazareth was at all points, and in
every single thought, word, and deed ; and deepens—till it
becomes a veritable rapture of wonder—her perception of
the range and degree of that ' altogether ', so wholly, so perfectly, so satisfyingly all-embracing. The Gospels reveal
the human Jesus of Nazareth, " full of grace ", as the inexhaustible abyss of all that is " altogether lovely " in
lovingness and lovableness indescribable ; in magnetic
holiness ; in compassion ; in understanding ; in serenity ;
in patience and long-suffering ; and in heroic selflessness.
They likewise reveal as an inexhaustible abyss of all that is
" altogether lovely " His prayer-life in relation both to God
and Man : a glorious abandonment of body, mind, and spirit
to the Beloved Father of all Creation, for His own sake, and
on behalf of His Creation.

The deeper, the closer, and the more comforting, becomes
the realisation of how altogether (unutterably, almost un-
thinkably) lovely was the human Jesus of the Gospels, the
deeper, the closer, and the more comforting, also becomes
the realisation—precisely through this Sacred, Sinless
Humanity of His—of His OTHERNESS. " Altogether lovely "
the words, life, death, and, above all, ceaseless prayer, of
Jesus of Nazareth : " Never man so spake", lived, died, or
prayed, " as this man " in one pure, quenchless, and un-
dimmed flame of love. A love-life, love-death, love-prayer,
of beauty so inexpressible, " the Spirit itself beareth witness
with our spirit " to be divine as He within us glorifies Jesus
as, and with, the Father's Self, Father and Son "one thing",
one entity of Love Uncreate.

The Gospels record the words, life, death, and prayer of the
historic Jesus in their localised Palestinian setting of two

thousand years ago. But His words and deeds alike, wholly transcend time and space. All He spoke, all He did, all He was, in Palestine, remain ever freshly creative for souls. Each word and episode of His historic life still remains as alive and potent now for us, as for those in whose midst they first'occurred. In His absolution of the Magdalen He makes countless souls, all down the ages and in all lands, to hear His absolution of themselves ; and in His Gethsemane " Arise, let us be going " to the disciples who had so failed Him, He as continuingly and widely draws His would-be lovers out of their failures to fresh opportunities of communion with Himself. Truly words and deeds so enduringly creative cannot but be those of the Divine Logos, one with the Father, by Whom all things are made, and in and with Whom alone is the source of all Life and Light.

The all-embracing love of the Jesus of the Gospels for each and every man, woman, and child with whom He was ever brought in contact, and His unfailing—and exhaustive —understanding of all, however different mentally, morally, spiritually, or temperamentally, unfolds itself such as could only be that of the Divine Creator Who had put something of Himself into each and every soul of His creating.

" He passed the whole night in the prayer of God " (Lk. vi. 12) is not merely a Lucan assertion of a single fact, but also the Gospel's cumulative revelation of the human and historic Jesus. The entire incarnate life of Jesus of Nazareth was a night between the Eternal Day of Preexistent Glory, and the Eternal Day of Risen and Ascended Glory, with the Father. This whole night—regardless alike of how the darkness deepened, or how the cost to self intensified—He passed in the prayer of God, *in the radiation of Love.* His humanity was deliberately, and consistently, kept within, and at the same time was itself to other souls, the radiation of Uncreate Love : which ineffable mystery could only be by the human self, being, mind, and will of Jesus truly " one thing ", one entity with the Divine Self, Being, Mind, and Will of the Father Who is Love Uncreate.

24

Life, both interiorly and externally, abundantly confirms for all who will allow themselves to be open to it, the Gospels' objective and subjective testimony to the Divinity of our Lord. Life is always ready to prove quite concretely, and time and time again—not least, but most, to those who pass through deepest waters, so be they keep open-eyed, and open-hearted—the all-sufficingness of the human Jesus in such a way as leaves no possibility of other than KNOWING that He is God of God, Light of Light, Very God of Very God, *because He has brought us to God the Father*, and lo They are One Spirit, the Alpha and Omega, the beginning and the end, The Triune One Who made, and will by His ceaseless drawing, eventually win, the soul for Himself alone, and in so doing make it to be one with all souls.

" If ye loved Me, ye would rejoice, because I said, I go unto the Father . . ." (Jn. xiv. 28), said Jesus to His disciples on the eve of His death ; and in these words He sounded a call to all souls, in time and for eternity, to rejoice with Him, and worship Him as He is in the Godhead.

The Incarnate Nature of Jesus, which needs must react in suffering to sin throughout time, has, together with His Divine Nature, been taken up into the Godhead at the Ascension, and taken up unaltered. Sin is a time-creation, which cannot outlast time which is non-existent in Eternity. Love alone can co-exist with Eternity, and so His Human Nature taken up into the Godhead in Eternity has nothing but Love to which to react ; and thus, although essentially unaltered by the Resurrection and Ascension, His Incarnate Nature has no longer any evil contact to call forth suffering reaction, and so the suffering has ceased *ipso facto*, and the love of the Incarnate Nature mingles with that of the Divine Nature in an eternal interaction of Love with Love in impenetrable Bliss.

In Eternity Jesus cannot suffer, and so we cannot now ' spare ' or ' share with Him ' present suffering. We can only try to avoid crucifying Him afresh in His Body the Church still on earth, and in the souls of our fellow-men, as well as in our own souls. Our 'reparation' can—and ought to—be offered to Him in so far as He is still suffering in the person of His Church, in the person of each and every soul for whom now as High Priest He is pleading His Atoning Sacrifice in the Presence of the Father. But since He Himself is now impassible in the Godhead, it means we cannot rest at " seeking to save Him suffering ", as though this were our completed love-offering—that is only part of the offering, and the more negative aim.

There must be the positive aim of trying to adore Him in Eternity, in Himself, in the Perfection of the Glory and Joy of the Blessed Trinity, apart altogether from any reaction to His Creation ; and of trying to add our mite of joy-offering to Him in the bottomless abyss of joy that is His in the Father and the Holy Spirit, and in the worship of the saints, and angels, and Jesus-lovers of all time. But for this— since of ourselves we cannot, and never shall be able to, pray—we must crave the Father to pour out His Spirit, now in our time, upon all flesh, that He within each and every soul may recognise, worship, and obey, Jesus as Lord and God, verily and indeed of one substance with the Father, Creator, and Redeemer of all in heaven and earth. So, and so only, shall " all the ends of the earth . . . see the salvation of our God " ; and be at peace as together " all nations shall come and worship ".

THANKS BE UNTO GOD FOR HIS UNSPEAKABLE GIFT : the gift of Himself in our Lord Jesus Christ, both God and Man.

APPENDIX OF SOME SAYINGS OF OUR LORD, QUOTED IN "CONCERNING HIMSELF"

Abba, Father, all things are possible unto Thee, remove this cup from Me : howbeit not what I will, but what Thou wilt (pp. 55, 114, 125).

All that ever came before Me are thieves and robbers : but the sheep did not hear them (p. 307).

All things are delivered unto Me of My Father . . . (pp. 69, 87).

And I, if I be lifted up from the earth, will draw all men unto Myself (pp. 71, 248, 269, 272).

And if thy right eye causeth thee to stumble, pluck it out and cast it from thee (pp. 95, 217).

And in praying use not vain repetitions (p. 117).

And when they lead you to judgment . . . be not anxious beforehand what ye shall speak (p. 59).

And when ye pray, ye shall not be as the hypocrites are (p. 195).

Are ye able to drink the cup that I drink ? or to be baptised with the baptism that I am baptised with ? (p. 124).

Arise, let us be going (pp. 235, 359).

As the Father hath sent Me, even so send I you (p. 294).

As the Father knoweth Me, even so know I the Father (p. 49).

Ask, and it shall be given you (p. 195).

Be not afraid of them which kill the body, but are not able to kill the soul (pp. 97, 114, 192).

Be not anxious for your life (pp. 97, 118).

Be ye therefore perfect, as your Father which is in heaven is perfect (p. 240).

Before Abraham was, I am (pp. 7, 27, 46, 88, 356).

Behold the birds of the heaven, that they sow not (p. 43).

Behold, thou art made whole : sin no more, lest a worse thing befall thee (p. 209).

Behold, we go up to Jerusalem (p. 36).

Behoved it not the Christ to suffer these things . . . ? (pp. 5, 36, 167).

Blessed are the merciful (p.195).

Blessed are the poor in spirit : for theirs is the Kingdom of Heaven (pp. 94, 194).

Blessed are the pure in heart : for they shall see God (p. 81).

Blessed are they that have been persecuted for righteousness' sake : for theirs is the Kingdom of Heaven (p. 165).

Blessed are they that hunger and thirst after righteousness (p. 195).

Blessed art thou, Simon Bar-jona : for flesh and blood hath not revealed it unto thee, but My Father which is in heaven (p. 357).

Blessed is he, whosoever shall find none occasion of stumbling in Me (p. 202).

But I say unto you, that One greater than the temple is here (p. 356).

But of that day and hour knoweth no one, not even the angels of heaven, neither the Son, but the Father only (pp. 126, 347).

Can the children of the bridechamber fast, while the bridegroom is with them ? . . . (p. 345).

Come unto Me, all ye that labour and are heavy laden, and I will give you rest (pp. 145, 357).

Consider the lilies of the field . . . (pp. 43, 81, 188, 193).

Cup (the) that I drink ye shall drink ; and with the baptism that I am baptised withal shall ye be baptised (p. 129).

Cup (the) which the Father hath given Me, shall I not drink it ? (p. 128).

Daughters of Jerusalem, weep not for Me, but weep for yourselves and for your children (p. 168).

Enter ye in by the narrow gate : for wide is the gate, and broad is the way, that leadeth to destruction (p. 96).

Even as the Father hath loved Me, I also have loved you (p. 160).

Even so it is not the Will of your Father . . . that one of these little ones should perish (pp. 69, 272, 314).

Even so let your light shine before men, that they may see your good works and glorify your Father which is in heaven (p. 52).

Every one that committeth sin is the bondservant of sin. And the bondservant abideth not in the house for ever : the son abideth for ever (pp. 155, 170).

Except ye believe that I am he, ye shall die in your sins (p. 170).

Except ye eat the flesh of the Son of Man, and drink His blood, ye have no life in you. Whoso eateth My flesh, and drinketh My blood, hath eternal life (pp. 149, 280).

Except ye see signs and wonders, ye will in no wise believe (p. 210).

Father (the) abiding in Me doeth His works (p. 48).

Father, forgive them (pp. 111, 146, 157).

Father, glorify Thy Name (pp. 32, 51, 53, 88, 146, 303).

Father (the) hath not left Me alone (p. 38).

Father, into Thy hands I commend My spirit (pp. 63, 159, 291).

Father, I thank Thee that Thou hast heard Me, And I knew that Thou hearest Me always (pp. 50, 60, 88, 112).

Father (the) loveth the Son, and sheweth Him all things that Him·self doeth (p. 87).

Father (the) that dwelleth in Me, He doeth the works (p. 269).

Father, that which Thou hast given Me, I will that, where I am, they also may be with Me ; that they may behold My glory, which Thou hast given Me (p. 296).

For as the Father hath life in Himself, even so gave He to the Son to have life in Himself (pp. 153, 301, 314).

For every one shall be salted with fire (pp. 59, 217).

For he that is not with Me is against Me (p. 115).

For I have not spoken of Myself ; but the Father which sent Me, He gave Me a commandment, what I should say, and what I should speak (p. 305).

For I say unto you, that this which is written must be fulfilled in Me (pp. 37, 248, 261).

For their sakes I sanctify Myself (pp. 32, 105, 111, 174, 226).

For verily the Son of Man came not to be ministered unto, but to minister, and to give His life a ransom for many (pp. 70, 153, 248).

Forbid him not ; for there is no man which shall do a miracle in My Name, that can lightly speak evil of Me (p. 322).

Foxes (the) have holes, and the birds of the heaven have nests, but the Son of Man hath not where to lay His head (p. 96).

Get thee behind Me, Satan : thou art a stumblingblock unto Me (pp. 16, 37, 185).

Give not that which is holy unto the dogs (pp. 61, 130).

Glory (the) which I had with Thee before the world was (pp. 46, 88, 356).

Go your way, and tell John what things ye have seen and heard (p. 207).

Good (the) man out of the treasure of his heart bringeth forth that which is good (p. 83).

Good (the) shepherd layeth down his life for the sheep . . . I am the good shepherd (p. 308).

Greater love hath no man than this, that a man lay down his life for his friends (p. 150).

Have faith in God (p. 60).

He is not the God of the dead, but of the living (pp. 112, 174).

He shall take of Mine, and shall declare it unto you (p. 200).

He that believeth on Me, the works that I do shall he do also ; and greater works than these shall he do ; because I go unto the Father (p. 71).

He that endureth to the end, the same shall be saved (p. 97).

He that hath seen Me hath seen the Father (pp. 54, 306, 357).

He that loveth his life loseth it (p. 53).

He that rejecteth Me, rejecteth Him that sent Me (p. 132).

Hear Me, all of you, and understand that there is nothing from without the man, that going into him can defile him : but the things which proceed out of the man are these that defile the man (pp. 170, 304).

Hereafter shall the Son of Man sit on the right hand of the power of God (p. 73).

Herein is My Father glorified, that ye bear much fruit (p. 52).

Hour (the) cometh, when neither in this mountain, nor in Jerusalem, shall ye worship the Father (pp. 40, 76).

Hour (the) is come that the Son of Man should be glorified (pp. 44, 52).

How is it that ye sought Me ? Wist ye not that I must be in My Father's house ? (pp. 50, 92, 227).

How often would I have gathered thee . . . but thou wouldest not (p. 25).

How sayest thou, Shew us the Father (p. 50).

Howbeit, when He, the Spirit of truth, is come, He shall guide you into all the truth (p. 153).

I am come down from heaven, not to do Mine own will, but the Will of Him that sent Me (p. 56).

I am come in My Father's Name (pp. 12, 47, 131).

I am come that they might have life (pp. 12, 153).

I am glad for your sakes that I was not there, to the intent ye may believe (p. 215).

I am in the midst of you as He that serveth (pp. 94, 101).

I am meek and lowly in heart (p. 94).

I am not alone, because the Father is with Me (p. 38).

I am not alone, but I and the Father that sent Me (p. 88).

I am the Bread of Life . . . yea, and the bread which I will give is My flesh for the life of the world (p. 198).

I am the door (p. 12).

I am the light of the world (p. 12).

I am the living bread which came down from heaven (pp. 27, 132).

I am the Resurrection and the Life (pp. 12, 357).

I am the Way, the Truth, and the Life (pp. 12, 150, 234).

I and $\left\{ \begin{array}{c} \text{My} \\ \text{the} \end{array} \right\}$ Father are one (pp. 27, 69, 160, 356).

I came not to judge the world, but to save the world (pp. 145, 348).

I can of Myself do nothing (pp. 47, 185, 266, 269).

I do always those things that are pleasing to Him (pp. 38, 55, 88).

I glorified Thee on the earth, having accomplished the work which Thou hast given Me to do (p. 51).

I go to prepare a place for you (pp. 174, 345).

I have finished the work which Thou hast given Me to do (p. 103).

I have given you an example (p. 232).

I have overcome the world (pp. 32, 176).

I have prayed for thee lest thy faith fail (p. 241).

I have yet many things to say unto you, but ye cannot bear them now (p. 247).

I judge no man (p. 348).

I kept them in Thy Name which Thou hast given Me, and I guarded them, and not one of them perished (p. 303).

I lay down My life for the sheep (p. 153).

I lay down My life . . . of Myself (pp. 38, 139, 300 f.).

I love the Father, and as the Father gave Me commandment, even so I do (p. 153).

I manifested Thy Name unto the men whom Thou gavest Me out of the world (p. 303).

I must be about My Father's business (pp. 5, 8, 50, 92).

I seek not Mine own will, but the Will of Him that sent Me (pp. 47, 54, 114).

I speak nothing of Myself (p. 103).

I speak the things which I have seen with My Father (p. 48).

I thirst (pp. 62, 159).

I was not sent but unto the lost sheep of the house of Israel (pp. 211, 311).

I will pray the Father, and He shall give you another Comforter, that He may abide with you for ever (p. 312).

I will see you again, and your heart shall rejoice, and your joy no man taketh from you. And in that day ye shall ask Me nothing (p. 349).

If any man cometh unto Me, and hateth not his own father, and mother, and wife and children . . . and his own life also, he cannot be My disciple (p. 98).

If any man thirst, let him come unto Me, and drink (pp. 70, 145, 353).

If any man would be first, he shall be the last of all and minister of all (p. 98).

If any man would come after Me, let him deny himself, and take up his cross daily (pp. 97, 185).

If I bear witness of Myself, My witness is true (p. 355).

If the world hateth you, ye know that it hath hated Me before it hated you (p. 131).

If ye keep My commandments, ye shall abide in My love (p. 91).

If ye loved Me, ye would rejoice, because I said, I go unto the Father (p. 360).

In My Father's house are many mansions (pp. 71, 174).

In your patience ye shall win your souls (p. 99).

Is it not for this cause that ye err, that ye know not the scriptures, nor the power of God ? (p. 65).

Is it not lawful for Me to do what I will with Mine own ? (p. 220).

It is finished (pp. 62, 159).

It is not for you to know times or seasons (pp. 219, 347).

Kingdom (the) of heaven is like unto a treasure hidden in the field (p. 84).

Lamp (the) of the body is the eye : if therefore thine eye be single, thy whole body shall be full of light (p. 60).

Lay not up for yourselves treasures upon the earth (pp. 83, 195).

Let the children first be filled : for it is not meet to take the children's bread and cast it to the dogs (p. 212).

Lo, I am with you alway, unto the end of the world (p. 238).

Love your enemies (pp. 114, 157).

Many be called, but few are chosen (p. 229).

Most (the) High . . . is kind toward the unthankful and evil (p. 140).

My Father worketh even until now, and I work (p. 277).

My God, My God, why hast Thou forsaken Me ? (pp. 62, 158, 266, 291).

My kingdom is not of this world (pp. 23, 72).

My meat is to do the Will of Him that sent Me (pp. 38, 54).

My teaching is not Mine, but His that sent Me (p. 48).

Neither do I condemn thee : go thy way ; from henceforth sin no more (pp. 111, 145, 171).

Neither do men light a lamp and put it under the bushel, but on the stand (p. 193).

No man hath seen God at any time, the only begotten Son which is in the bosom of the Father, He hath declared Him (pp. 54, 74).

No man having put his hand to the plough, and looking back, is fit for the kingdom of God (p. 96).

No one knoweth Who the Son is, save the Father, and Who the Father is, save the Son (p. 47).

No servant can serve two masters : for either he will hate the one and love the other ; or else he will hold to one, and despise the other (p. 98).

Not every one that saith unto Me, Lord, Lord, shall enter into the kingdom of heaven . . . (p. 228).

Not that any man hath seen the Father, save he which is from God, He hath seen the Father (p. 68).

Now is My soul troubled (p. 53).

Now is the judgment of this world (p. 348).

O faithless generation, how long shall I be with you : how long shall I bear with you ? (pp. 100, 260).

O Jerusalem, Jerusalem, which killeth the prophets . . . how often would I have gathered thy children together . . . and ye would not (pp. 111, 131).

Other sheep I have, which are not of this fold (pp. 12, 308, 311).

Peace, I leave with you ; My peace I give unto you : not as the world giveth, give I unto you (pp. 134, 283).

Prince (the) of this world cometh, and hath nothing in Me (pp. 15, 33, 147).

See My hands and My feet, that it is I Myself (pp. 234, 328).

See that ye despise not one of these little ones ; for I say unto you, that in heaven their angels do always behold the face of My Father, which is in heaven (pp. 79, 110).

She hath done what she could (p. 306).

Son (the) can do nothing of Himself, but what He seeth the Father doing (pp. 47, 65, 185).

Son (the) of Man came to seek and to save that which was lost (p. 145).

Son (the) of Man hath not where to lay His head (p. 309).

Son (the) of Man hath power on earth to forgive sins (p. 169).

Son (the) of Man shall send forth His angels, and they shall gather out of His kingdom all things that cause stumbling (p. 79).

Son, thy sins be forgiven thee (p. 209).

Sons (the) of the kingdom shall be cast forth into the outer darkness (p. 229).

Spirit (the) indeed is willing, but the flesh is weak (p. 119).

Strive to enter in by the narrow door: for many, I say unto you, shall seek to enter in and shall not be able (p. 228).

Suffer it to be so now : for thus it becometh us to fulfil all righteousness (p. 184).

Take, eat ; this is My Body (pp. 146, 327).

Take heed, and keep yourselves from all covetousness : for a man's life consisteth not in the abundance of the things which he possesseth (pp. 97, 193).

Take heed that ye do not your righteousness before men, to be seen of them (p. 96).

There are eunuchs, which made themselves eunuchs for the kingdom of heaven's sake (pp. 31, 98 f., 118).

Therefore every scribe who hath been made a disciple to the kingdom of heaven is like unto a man that is a householder (p. 84).

Think not that I came to destroy the law or the prophets : I came not to destroy, but to fulfil (pp. 6, 305).

Think not that I came to send peace on the earth : I came not to send peace, but a sword (p. 134).

Think ye that these Galilæans were sinners above all the Galilæans, because they have suffered these things ? I tell you, Nay . . . (p. 166).

This is My Blood of the New Testament, which is shed for you and for many for the remission of sins (p. 150).

This is My Body, which is given for you (p. 327).

This is My commandment, that ye love one another, even as I have loved you (p. 231).

This sickness is not unto death, but for that the Son of God may be glorified thereby (pp. 213 ff.).

Thou art Peter, and upon this rock I will build My church (p. 185).

Thou, Father, art in Me, and I in Thee (p. 32).

To this end was I born . . . . that I should bear witness unto the truth (pp. 12, 150).

Verily, I say unto thee, To-day shalt thou be with Me in Paradise (p. 157).

Verily, Verily, I say unto you, The hour is coming, and now is, when the dead shall hear the voice of the Son of God, and they that hear shall live (p. 112).

Watch and pray, that ye enter not into temptation (p. 33).

What I do thou knowest not now ; but thou shalt understand hereafter (pp. 220, 291).

What then if ye should behold the Son of Man ascending where He was before ? (p. 356).

What wilt thou that I should do unto thee ? (pp. 95, 274, 306).

When I sent you forth without purse, and wallet, and shoes, lacked ye anything ? (p. 260).

When thou doest alms, let not thy left hand know what thy right hand doeth (p. 117).

When thou prayest, enter into thy chamber, and having shut thy door, pray to thy Father which is in secret (pp. 83, 85).

Which of you convicteth Me of sin ? (pp. 15, 171).

Whosoever he be of you that renounceth not all that he hath, he cannot be My disciple (pp. 30, 185).

Whosoever shall not receive the kingdom of God as a little child, he shall in no wise enter therein (p. 47).

Whosoever shall seek to gain his life shall lose it : but whosoever shall lose his life shall preserve it (p. 98).

Whosoever shall speak a word against the Son of Man, it shall be forgiven him (p. 324).

Whosoever therefore shall break one of these least commandments . . . (p. 40).

Wind (the) bloweth where it listeth (pp. 6, 42).

Woman, behold thy Son ! . . . Behold, thy Mother ! (pp. 157 f.).

Would ye also go away ? (p. 282).

Ye are from beneath ; I am from above : ye are of this world ; I am not of this world (pp. 88, 356).

Ye are the salt of the earth (p. 194).

Ye are they which have continued with Me in My temptations (p. 15).

Ye leave the commandments of God, and hold fast the tradition of men (p. 199).

Ye shall know men by their fruits (p. 194).

Your Father which is in heaven . . . maketh His sun to rise on the evil and on the good (p. 43).

Your sorrow shall be turned into joy (p. 316).

INDEX

Abraham, 246
Angels, 72, 78 ff.
Atonement (the), 207 f., 268 ff.

Bride of Christ (the), 323, 342 ff.

Church (the), 320 ff.
Communion of Saints (the),
74 ff., 277 f., 296, 335 ff.

Departed (the), 112, 278 f.

Elijah, 74 ff.
Euthanasia, 253 ff.

Father (the), 46 ff., and *passim*
Father's Will (the), 54 ff.

Holy Spirit (the), *passim*

Jesus Christ :
  as Bridegroom, 342 ff.
  as Carpenter, 12, 188 f.
  as Countryman, 187
  as Good Shepherd, 307 ff., 343
  as Healer, 49, 202 ff.
  as High Priest, 13, 297 ff.
  as Judge, 313 f., 348
  as Lamb of God (Saviour ;
    Redeemer), 24 ff., 243 ff.
  Marriage of the Lamb, 342 ff.
  Wrath of the Lamb, 271 f.
  as Life, 153 f.
  as Lover of God and Man,
    222 ff.
  as Messiah, 302 f., 319
  as Perfect Man, 232 ff., 286
  as Suffering Servant, 247 f.,
    302, 338
  as Teacher, 182, 190 ff.
  as Word (Logos), 232 ff., 242,
    269, 308, 321, 335, 337,
    354, 359
  Blood of, 147 ff.

Jesus Christ (*contd.*) :
  Body of, 118 ff., 326 ff.
    Risen Body of, 233 f., 329 f.
    Sacrament of His Most
      Blessed Body (and Blood),
      121 f., 198 f., 277 ff.,
      285 f., 326 ff., 333
  Boyhood of, 3 ff.
  Changelessness of, 154 ff.
  Divinity of, 351 ff.
  Gospel Portrait of, 310 f., 338,
    353 ff.
    Johannine Christ, 66 ff.
    Synoptic Christ, 66 ff.
  Impassibility of (in the God-
    head), 360 f.
  Incarnation of, 179 ff., 337 f.
    Extension in His Mystical
      Body, 333 ff.
    " Fiat " for the Incarna-
      tion, 92 f., 161 f., 301
  Kingship of, 11 ff.
  Life Events :
    Ascension, 234 ff., 273 f.
    Attempts upon His Life,
      26 ff.
    Baptism, 19 f., 58, 87, 302
    Bereavement of John the
      Baptist, 29 f., 112
    Betrayal, 36 f., 102
    Cleansing of the Temple, 28,
      115
    Cross and Passion, 21, 30,
      37 f., 62 f., 102, 120 f.,
      127, 262 ff.
    Seven Last Words from
      the Cross, 157 ff.
    Gethsemane, 15, 31, 37, 55,
      57, 62, 125 ff., 138 f., 235,
      263 f.
    Harrowing of Hell, 112
    Hidden Years (the), 135,
      189, 222, 259